T0338572

Introduction to Engineering and Scientific Computing with Python

As more and more engineering departments and companies choose to use Python, this book provides an essential introduction to this open-source, free-to-use language. Expressly designed to support first-year engineering students, this book covers engineering and scientific calculations, Python basics, and structured programming.

Based on extensive teaching experience, the text uses practical problem solving as a vehicle to teach Python as a programming language. By learning computing fundamentals in an engaging and hands-on manner, it enables the reader to apply engineering and scientific methods with Python, focusing this general language to the needs of engineers and the problems they are required to solve on a daily basis. Rather than inundating students with complex terminology, this book is designed with a leveling approach in mind, enabling students at all levels to gain experience and understanding of Python. It covers such topics as structured programming, graphics, matrix operations, algebraic equations, differential equations, and applied statistics. A comprehensive chapter on working with data brings this book to a close.

This book is an essential guide to Python, which will be relevant to all engineers, particularly undergraduate students in their first year. It will also be of interest to professionals and graduate students looking to hone their programming skills, and apply Python to engineering and scientific contexts.

Introduction to Engineering and Scientific Computing with Python

David E. Clough
Steven C. Chapra

CRC Press
Taylor & Francis Group
Boca Raton London New York

CRC Press is an imprint of the
Taylor & Francis Group, an **informa** business

First edition published 2023
by CRC Press
6000 Broken Sound Parkway NW, Suite 300, Boca Raton, FL 33487-2742

and by CRC Press
4 Park Square, Milton Park, Abingdon, Oxon, OX14 4RN

CRC Press is an imprint of Taylor & Francis Group, LLC

© 2023 David E. Clough and Steven C. Chapra

Library of Congress Cataloging-in-Publication Data
Names: Clough, David E., author. | Chapra, Steven C., author.
Title: Introduction to engineering and scientific computing with Python / David E. Clough, Steven C. Chapra.
Description: First edition. | Boca Raton : CRC Press, 2023. |
Includes bibliographical references and index.
Identifiers: LCCN 2022012776 (print) | LCCN 2022012777 (ebook) |
ISBN 9781032188942 (hardback) | ISBN 9781032188973 (paperback) |
ISBN 9781003256861 (ebook)
Subjects: LCSH: Engineering mathematics—Data processing. |
Science—Mathematics—Data processing. | Python (Computer program language)
Classification: LCC TA345 .C584 2023 (print) | LCC TA345 (ebook) |
DDC 620.001/51—dc23/eng/20220706
LC record available at https://lccn.loc.gov/2022012776
LC ebook record available at https://lccn.loc.gov/2022012777

ISBN: 9781032188942 (hbk)
ISBN: 9781032188973 (pbk)
ISBN: 9781003256861 (ebk)

DOI: 10.1201/9781003256861

Typeset in Times
by codeMantra

This book is dedicated to the thousands of our former students at the University of Colorado, Tufts University, and Texas A&M University. Go Buffs, Go Jumbos, and Gig 'Em Aggies!

Contents

Contents

List of Examples

Preface

The primary purpose of this text is to provide background and experience in numerical problem solving by computing with the Python language. It is intended for first-year students in the engineering and science disciplines, but it may find utility for students at other levels such as advanced students at the pre-college level, students in pre-engineering programs in 2-year colleges, students transferring into engineering and science disciplines, and professionals seeking a review of numerical problem solving and wishing to learn the Python language for this purpose. We intend that this text provides the tools and knowledge that students can use in subsequent academic courses as the need for computer-based numerical problem solving arises.

This text is not designed to provide a broad, in-depth education in the Python programming language. Python has many capabilities that fall outside our focus on numerical problem solving. We do recommend, however, that students complement the learning from this text with further study of Python, if that suits their educational goals and interests. It is our intention that this book serve as an oft-utilized reference as students proceed through their academic careers and beyond.

For instructors considering this text for their students, we would like to address the question: Why this book? First, there is a growing audience that wants to use Python as their computing language, and few texts address this topic from an engineering and science perspective. Second, the authors have a decades long track record teaching introductory computing to thousands of students and have incorporated their experience in writing the text. Third, we have written the text keeping the students and their diverse backgrounds in mind. We believe the text is approachable by students. We have intently included basic explanations and examples along with elements that will challenge students.

The next question is Why Python? First, Python is a computing language that has gained a great deal of interest over the past few years. Second, from a practical stance, Python is available at no cost to the student, including down the road when access to institution-licensed software may not be available. Although Python is a broad-based, object-oriented computing language, there is a question whether it is well suited to the numerical problem solving commonly faced by engineers and scientists. By approaching Python with some care, and by not overwhelming the students with aspects of the language not needed in problem solving, we believe we have answered this concern in the affirmative. We chose the Spyder integrated development environment (IDE) because it is well suited to engineering computing and presents an interface similar to other dedicated software packages such as MATLAB®. Spyder's tools for developing and debugging Python scripts are excellent and of great aid to the student.

By illustrating how students can find information and answer questions about the use of Python, often via the Internet, we intend to equip students with the ability to extend their Python capabilities on their own. We illustrate this frequently in the text. We also encourage students to expand their general knowledge of Python, but outside the scope of the text and course they might be taking.

You might wonder what experience we the authors bring to the writing of this text. Together, in 1986 at the University of Colorado, we introduced the course, Introduction to Engineering Computing, and together, or subsequently on our own at different institutions, we taught the course over three decades. This course is still taught at the University of Colorado and Tufts. Of course, over the years, the computing tools used in the course have changed, but the general content and learning goals have not. For the first 15 years, the course was taught utilizing the Fortran and BASIC computer languages. Since then, the computing vehicles have included Excel, Excel VBA, Mathcad, MATLAB, and now Python. As a consequence of these years of experience, we have learned what works and is pertinent for students early in their academic careers (and what doesn't!). This background has brought us to the writing of this text.

For more than a decade, we taught as a team and learned from each other. Additionally, we have taught numerical methods to students later in their academic careers. Our collaboration has yielded a recent text in numerical methods with Python (Chapra & Clough, 2022), and teaching the implementation of numerical methods with Python has provided us with a comfort level of experience to be able to write this text for students earlier in their academic careers.

Our pedagogical approach tends to be more inductive rather than deductive. We like to present examples frequently and then generalize those to provide broader, extensible knowledge. This book uses what we call a "crawl-walk-run" approach. We illustrate methods using Python in the chapters and encourage students to replicate those on their own. Then we provide end-of-chapter problems to challenge the students and encourage independent work. It is our intention that students will be well equipped to handle numerical problem-solving scenarios they encounter after studying this text. Among the problems we include with each chapter are those which illustrate practical applications in the engineering disciplines, as well as from the sciences. The organization of the problems at the end of each chapter follows two strategies. First, the problems tend to follow the organization of the chapter chronologically. Second, the problems become more challenging toward the end.

As far as mathematical background required of the student, we do include content involving algebra, transcendental functions, and elementary calculus (derivatives and integrals). The text could still be used by instructors who have students with little to no background in calculus, if approached with some care. We do provide review material in the first chapter, and our use of examples should help those students with little or meager knowledge of calculus.

The arrangement of the material in the text is designed to provide a well-structured course curriculum. As depicted in Table P1, the first two chapters on numerical and computer-based calculations are general and not dependent on the use of computers or Python. The intent of these chapters is to level the playing field for a group of students with diverse backgrounds. Also, many students may have seen similar material in the past but will benefit from a review. It has been

TABLE P1

Organization of This Book

Numerical & Computer-Based Calculations	Introduction to Python	Vector/Matrix Calculations & Equation Solving	Rate Equations & Data
Chapter 1. Engineering and Scientific Calculations	Chapter 3. Python Basics	Chapter 6. Array and Matrix Operations	Chapter 9. Solving Differential Equations
Chapter 2. Computer-Based Calculations	Chapter 4. Structured Programming with Python	Chapter 7. Solving Single Algebraic Equations	Chapter 10. Working with Data
	Chapter 5. Graphics—Matplotlib	Chapter 8. Solving Sets of Algebraic Equations	

our experience that students often have gaps in their learning when it comes to the content of these two chapters.

Chapters 3–5 introduce the Python language. The first of these presents the rudiments of the language and the Spyder IDE. Instructors wishing to use another IDE would have to substitute their own orientation here. Chapter 4 deals with algorithm structure and completes the coverage of Python required for subsequent chapters. Chapter 5 focuses on plotting with the Matplotlib module. Plotting is common in problem-solving applications encountered in later chapters.

The remaining chapters are focused on applications with the Python tools put in place in Chapter 3–5. Chapter 6 introduces arrays and vector/matrix calculations. Chapter 7 is all about solving single, nonlinear, algebraic, and transcendental equations with common closed and open methods. Then, there is a natural transition to Chapter 8 where systems of linear and nonlinear algebraic equations are studied. Chapter 9, which deals with solving rate equations (i.e., differential equations), employs a simple approach using elementary methods of quadrature and integration.

The final Chapter 10 is devoted to the study of data and introduces concepts and methods of applied statistics in what could be described as a "statistics light" manner. This last chapter provides students with knowledge and skills that will be relevant to their laboratory courses, both early and later on in their academic careers. We also encourage, and strongly advocate, that all students should obtain more in-depth education in applied statistics via a course later in their academic career or otherwise.

In introducing concepts and methods in Chapters 6–10, we first illustrate with basic Python scripts and then invoke built-in capabilities from the NumPy and SciPy modules. Having students see the methods in their own code first helps understanding of the concepts and removes some of the mystery behind the built-in functions. Also, we illustrate that the methods can often be programmed with very few statements.

TABLE P2
Instructional Plans

Semester Plan		Quarter Plan		Python Module	
Week	Chapters	Week	Chapters	Week	Chapters
1	1 & 2	1	1 & 2	1	3, 4 & 5
2		2		2	
3	3, 4 & 5	3	3, 4 & 5	3	
4		4		4	6
5		5		5	7 or 10
6	6	6	6	6	
7	7	7	7		
8		8			
9	8	9	8, 9, or 10		
10		10			
11	9	11			
12		12	Review		
13	10				
14					
15	Review				

We have designed the text so that instructors might adapt it to different academic terms and course designs. Table P2 suggests plans for a 15-week semester, 12-week quarter, and a shorter 6-week Python module that might be part of a computing course that would have other element(s) such as a module on spreadsheets or one on MATLAB. Of course, there would be other schedule requirements, such as more intensive summer courses, and we believe the text can accommodate a variety of these structures.

As this text is employed in instruction and learning, we anticipate there will be valuable impressions, opinions, and recognitions of occasional errors. Although we hope the latter will be minimal, we know that they are inevitable. We encourage instructors, students, and other readers to provide feedback to us (see the email addresses below). We will respond and endeavor to improve the text in its second edition, and your criticisms and ideas will be valuable to us. We have thick skins and small egos, so bring it on!

Although our primary intent is to empower and inspire students, we have the ancillary objective of making this introduction exciting and pleasurable. We believe that motivated students who enjoy coding will ultimately make better professionals. If this book fosters enthusiasm and appreciation for these subjects, we will consider our efforts a success.

MATLAB® is a registered trademark of The MathWorks, Inc. For product information, please contact:

The MathWorks, Inc.
3 Apple Hill Drive
Natick, MA 01760-2098 USA
Tel: 508-647-7000
Fax: 508-647-7001
E-mail: info@mathworks.com
Web: www.mathworks.com

Acknowledgments

Both authors, David E. Clough and Steven C. Chapra, have lengthy careers and have benefited from many contributions and influences over the decades. David E. Clough had a high school math teacher, Miss Edith Benjamin, who introduced him to vectors, matrices and sets, and took him, along with two other students, down to Illinois Institute of Technology on Chicago's South Side, in the evenings, to learn how to program in Fortran. When he arrived at the then Case Institute of Technology in Cleveland, Ohio, in 1964, he was told that Fortran was passé and was taught the language of the future, Algol. Along the way, he learned other "languages of the future" like GE timesharing BASIC, Pascal, and APL. He learned machine and assembly language programming for use with real-time computer systems. Thirty years later, Fortran finally faded, and he learned C/C++, MATLAB®, Excel's VBA, and on to Python. It seems that the more computing tools change, the more that fundamentals stay the same. It is worth mentioning that, for Clough, none of this would have been possible without the guidance and facilitation of many individuals, beginning with Miss Benjamin at Arlington High School in Arlington Heights, Illinois.

Steve C. Chapra has never taken a formal course in computer programming. As a freshman at Manhattan College back in the Pleistocene (1966), such courses had yet to be taught. But the college did have a room-sized mainframe computer to manage its scheduling and accounting. He connected with some very bright and generous older physics majors who commandeered a classroom in the evening where they taught Steve and a few other younger students how to code in one of the early versions of IBM Fortran. They also urged him to volunteer to work at the computer center where he swept the floor, replaced vacuum tubes, and learned assembly language. But the coolest part was that he got a key to the computer center so that he and his mates could surreptitiously sneak in late at night to write numerically oriented programs on punch cards. From that point forward, his education and career have been dominated by computing as applied to his research area: environmental modeling. To paraphrase the *Saturday Night Live* character, Chico Escuela: "Computing has been berry, berry good to me!"

Both authors acknowledge the thousands of students they have taught at various institutions and in the professions. Students have kept us on our toes and have exposed any approaches to teaching/learning that are faulty. As we have aged, in many ways, they have and continue to keep our outlooks young.

We sincerely appreciate the willingness of CRC Press, Taylor & Francis Group, to take on this publishing project. Our collaboration with Editor Nicola Sharpe and Editorial Assistant Nishant Bhagat has been supportive and productive and has certainly contributed greatly to the quality of the publication.

Authors

David E. Clough is Professor Emeritus at the University of Colorado. He has experience in a wide array of programming languages and computing tools and has applied his expertise through his teaching, research, and industrial applications. Over his career, Clough has taught hundreds of short courses to practicing professionals on applied computing and problem solving.

Steven C. Chapra is the Emeritus Professor and Louis Berger Chair in Civil and Environmental Engineering at Tufts University. Before joining Tufts, he worked for the U.S. Environmental Protection Agency and the National Oceanic and Atmospheric Administration, and taught at Texas A&M University, the University of Colorado, and Imperial College London. He is a Fellow and Distinguished Member of the American Society of Civil Engineering (ASCE) and has received several awards for his scholarly and academic contributions, including the Rudolph Hering Medal (ASCE), and the Meriam-Wiley Distinguished Author Award (American Society for Engineering Education). As a strong proponent of continuing education, he has taught more than 90 workshops around the world for professionals on numerical methods, computer programming, and environmental modeling.

Authors' email addresses:
david.clough@colorado.edu
steven.chapra@tufts.edu

1 Engineering and Scientific Calculations

CHAPTER OBJECTIVES

- Review numerical calculations, including significant figures, positional and scientific notation.
- Understand the typical functions used in engineering and scientific computations, including absolute value, sign, logarithmic, exponential, trigonometric, and hyperbolic relations.
- Review operations with complex numbers, including rectangular and polar representation.
- Carry out conversions of units common to engineering and scientific calculations.
- Develop strategies for engineering and scientific problem solving.

Engineers and scientists carry out numerical calculations as a routine, day-to-day activity. Through years of experience, they have become accustomed to good practices that promote reliability in their results. The objective of this chapter is to review these practices and promote standards that will assist you in becoming functional members of STEM[1] professions. The rest of society plays fast and loose with numerical quantities and their interpretation. Engineers and scientists do not. Their work is examined closely and will be disregarded if it doesn't measure up. If numerical issues are not detected, they can sometimes lead to big problems in the products they create.

We will consider here numerical quantities, calculations involving them and the units associated with them. Also, approaches to problem solving will be considered.

Example 1.1 What is the Volume of the Earth?

Our Earth is known to be an *oblate spheroid,* a ball squashed a bit between the north and south poles. The radius from the center to the Equator is estimated to be 6,378 km. The common formula for the volume of a sphere is

$$V = \frac{4}{3}\pi r^3 \tag{1.1}$$

---

[1] Science, Technology, Engineering, and Mathematics

DOI: 10.1201/9781003256861-1

If we carry out this calculation using a calculator, or perhaps a computer program like a spreadsheet, we can obtain this result:

$$1.0867813 \times 10^{12} \, \text{km}^3$$

Since this number is so big, it is convenient to represent it in exponential or *scientific notation*. However, there are questions. By reporting the radius to be 6,378 km, we are assuming that it is not 6,377 or 6,379. In other words, our use of these four digits or figures carries with it the understanding of a level of *precision* in the measurement. If we were really unsure about the final digit, 8, it might be better to report the radius as 6,380, only claiming three digits of significance. The point here is that the number of digits reported carries with it the claim of precision to that extent.

This raises an important issue in carrying out and reporting the results of calculations. If we accept four digits of significance in the radius, why are we reporting eight digits in our volume result? The answer is simple—we shouldn't do so! Our answer should be reported to a similar number of *significant figures* as in

$$1.087 \times 10^{12} \, \text{km}^3$$

Now, we face another problem. The radius of the Earth at the poles is reported to be 6,357 km. The Earth is squashed by 42 km. Using this radius instead, we come up with a volume of

$$1.076 \times 10^{12} \, \text{km}^3$$

a difference of $1.070 \times 10^{10} \, \text{km}^3$. Do we think that discrepancy matters? Maybe yes, maybe no. It's a lot of volume!

We move on to find a better result. It is reasonable to conclude that the true volume is somewhere between our two results, but where? So, as an engineer or scientist, we look to refine our method and obtain a formula for an oblate spheroid,

$$V = \frac{4}{3}\pi ab^2 \tag{1.2}$$

where a is the major radius (or formally called semiaxis) at the Equator and b is the minor radius at the poles. Now, our result is, as expected, the intermediate value

$$1.080 \times 10^{12} \, \text{km}^3$$

As an engineer or scientist, we learn to be never quite satisfied with our results (and ever skeptical of them), always looking for ways to improve them and to evaluate the significance of improvement. Consequently, we might investigate variations in the radial distance because of changes in the surface of the Earth, for example Mount Everest (elevation about 8.48 km) to Dead Sea (elevation − 0.414 km). We won't do that here, but rather leave this example at this point.

1.1 NUMERICAL QUANTITIES

We all grow up using decimal, base-10 numbers. As you will see in Chapter 2, this is not the number system used internally in computers. In fact, we are so accustomed to decimal numbers that we forget about the basics of their structure. It is also important to review this structure because, when we move internally to computers, that number base is going to change from 10 to 2.

1.1.1 POSITIONAL AND SCIENTIFIC NOTATION

Positional notation is a good place to start. A number like

$$1234.56$$

uses the digits available in the decimal numbering system, 0 1 2 3 4 5 6 7 8 9. The positions of the digits indicate a contribution to the overall number by powers of the base of the number system, 10. If we index the positions according to Figure 1.1, then the contributions of the digits are represented as shown in Table 1.1.

Of course, the various contributions sum to the original number. This leads to the way of describing large and small decimal numbers that is common in engineering and science, positional notation, also commonly called *scientific notation*. Our example number 1234.56 expressed in typical positional notation is

$$1.23456 \times 10^3$$

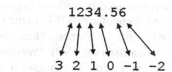

FIGURE 1.1 Positional notation.

TABLE 1.1
Contribution of Digits

Index	Digit	Contribution
3	1	$1 \times 10^3 = 1{,}000$
2	2	$2 \times 10^2 = 200$
1	3	$3 \times 10^1 = 30$
0	4	$4 \times 10^0 = 4$
−1	5	$5 \times 10^{-1} = 0.5$
−2	6	$6 \times 10^{-2} = 0.06$

The 1.23456 part is called the *significand* or *mantissa*,[2] and the power 3 is called the *characteristic* or *exponent*. It would have also been possible to express the number as

$$123456. \times 10^{-2}$$

but this is less common. In typical scientific notation, the number is *normalized* with only one digit to the left of the decimal point. Scientific notation gives us the ability to represent very large and small numbers conveniently. For example,

Avogadro's number: 6.022×10^{23}

Planck's constant: 6.626×10^{-34}

1.1.2 ACCURACY AND PRECISION

The arithmetical operations of addition, subtraction, multiplication, and division are the basis of all numerical calculations. We carry out these operations daily with or without the use of a calculator or computer, without much thought, and perhaps with the occasional error. It is not our purpose here to reteach you arithmetic; rather we would like to highlight a few features of these operations that raise issues in engineering and scientific calculations.

First, we need to introduce the concepts of *precision, significant figures* and *rounding*, since they govern how we report the results of these calculations. It is important to distinguish the terms precision and accuracy. *Accuracy* refers to measurements and their comparison with accepted standards. Ultimately, these standards are traceable to those maintained by national organizations, such as the National Institute of Standards and Technology (NIST) in the U.S. and Association Française de Normalisation (AFNOR) in France. These are members of the International Organization for Standardization (ISO). *Precision* has to do with the resolution with which a number is expressed. For example, if a measured temperature is 24°C, it is precise to 1°; whereas, 24.1°C is precise to 0.1°C. The second temperature is more precise than the first; yet, a common misconception is that it is more accurate than the first. When a measurement is written as 24°C ± 1°C, that usually implies the accuracy of the measurement, that is the true value of the temperature is somewhere between 23°C and 25°C; however, even this type of description must be understood clearly because in other contexts the ± interval may relate to the random error associated with making the measurement. Be careful with the terms accuracy and precision. In fact, precision is so misused to imply accuracy that it is preferable to use *resolution* instead of precision in scientific writing.

Compare the following:

65°F   18.3333°C

---

[2] The use of the term *mantissa* is common among computer scientists but has been discouraged by some because of confusion with the description of logarithms.

The second temperature is closely equivalent to the first, since it was converted using the formula[3]

$$°C = \frac{°F - 32}{1.8}$$

However, there is a significant difference in the way these two quantities are represented. By writing 65°F, we understand that the temperature is certainly in the 60s, and it is closer to 65°F than to 64 or 66. By writing 18.3333°C, we imply that the temperature is exact to 18.333 and closer to 18.3333 than to 18.3332 or 18.3334. Of course, it is impractical to make a temperature measurement to such precision, and the precision implied by the two quantities is entirely different. You can see that we should report the converted temperature as 18°C, implying a similar precision to that of 65°F. As described next, this leads us to the concept of *significant figures*.

1.1.3 SIGNIFICANT FIGURES

The *significant figures* are the digits in the number that are reliable and necessary to indicate the confidence or precision with which an engineer or scientist states a quantity. Operationally, the *significant figures* of a number are the digits from the first nonzero digit on the left to either

(*a*) the last digit on the right, zero or nonzero if there is a decimal point expressed, or
(*b*) the last nonzero digit of the number if there is no decimal point expressed.

Significant figures are almost always expressed as the "number" of significant figures; that is, the total number of digits that satisfy the definitions. Let's elaborate with several examples.

65°F	2 significant figures by rule (*b*)
18.3333°C	6 significant figures by rule (*a*)
0.00471	3 significant figures by rule (*a*)
43,500	3 significant figures by rule (*b*)
43,500.	5 significant figures by rule (*a*)

---

[3] The U.S. is one of the few countries in the world where the Fahrenheit temperature scale is still used widely, so Americans, stubborn to change, and visitors to the U.S. are often faced with conversions to and from the Celsius scale. As a shortcut assist, it is useful to learn the counts from 32 in steps of 18°F (−4, −14, 32, 50, 68, 86, 104, 122) because they are equivalent to steps of 10°C from 0 (−20, −10, 0, 10, 20, 30, 40, 50). Then, intermediate steps of 9°F are steps of 5°C, e.g., 59°F = 15°C. If you live in cold regions, it is "comforting" to know that −40 is the same in both scales. By the way, the only other countries where °F is used are Liberia and the Cayman Islands!

The last two examples raise an important point. What if the number is known exactly for the digits 4 3 5, and it is also known that the next 0 is closer than one digit above or below it? In other words, we have four significant digits, and the rules (*a*) and (*b*) don't cover that possibility. What to do? As a matter of fact, even the difference between 43,500 and 43,500. is easy to miss. The answer lies in using scientific notation. There is no ambiguity in the following three numbers:

4.35×10^4 3 significant figures
4.350×10^4 4 significant figures
4.3500×10^5 5 significant figures

and rule (*a*) applies to all of them. Consequently, we suggest using scientific notation whenever there could be ambiguity in the number of significant figures.

One additional point related to clarity: When expressing a decimal fraction in written work (hand-written or printed), it is important to include a leading zero before the decimal point. That is,

0.471   rather than .471

because the leading decimal point in the latter is so easily missed by the reader.

1.1.4 ROUNDING

The concept of significant figures carries over to numerical calculations and introduces the need to round numbers to a given digit position. With simple addition, forming the sum

```
 12.3
 14.36
 26.66
```

is easy. But note that the sum as expressed implies that the first number is known as 12.30. Since we don't know that number to such resolution (to the one-hundredths place), it would be better to round the second number to the precision of the first, 14.4, and carry out the sum as

```
 12.3
 14.4
 26.7
```

or at least round the former result, 26.66, to the 26.7 below. The same goes for subtraction.

The standard rules for rounding are:

When a number is to be rounded to the digit in the nth place,

a. add one to the digit in the nth place if the digit in the $(n-1)$th place is greater than 5, or
b. leave the digit in the nth place as is if the digit in the $(n-1)$th place is less than 5, or
c. if the digit in the $(n-1)$th place is equal to 5, and if there are following non-zero digits, apply Rule *a*; otherwise round either up or down to make the digit in the nth place even.

Rule (*c*) provides that the 5's will be rounded up about half the time and down about half the time. Study the examples in Table 1.2.

There may be a temptation in the fourth example to round first to 0.055 and then round again 0.06. Don't get caught in this trap—**round only once!**

There are specific rules that govern the management of significant figures in calculations:

a. For addition and subtraction:
The positions of the last significant figure of each number should be compared. Of these positions, the one farthest to the left is the position of the last permissible significant figure of the sum or difference.
b. For multiplication and division:
The number of significant figures retained in the result should equal the lowest number of significant figures of any of the multiplicands, divisors, or dividends.

TABLE 1.2
Rounding Examples

Original Number	Round to Place[a]	Result	Rule Applied
43,500	1,000	44,000	(*c*)
42,500	1,000	42,000	(*c*)
18.3333	0.1	18.3	(*b*)
0.05493	0.01	0.05	(*b*)
7.86×10^3	0.1	7.9×10^3	(*a*)

[a] Place in the significand, excluding the exponent.

When we carry out an addition or subtraction with numbers in scientific notation, it is necessary to change the positional notation of at least one of the numbers so that the exponents are the same. For example, to add

$$1.046 \times 10^{11}$$
$$7.64 \times 10^{10}$$

It should be converted to one of the following two forms

$$
\begin{array}{ll}
1.046 \times 10^{11} & 10.46 \times 10^{10} \\
\underline{0.764 \times 10^{11}} & \underline{7.64 \times 10^{10}} \\
1.810 \times 10^{11} & 18.10 \times 10^{10}
\end{array}
$$

The result of the second form can be normalized to give the same result as the first form.

When two numbers are multiplied, the number of digits required to represent the product can be as many as the sum of the number of digits in each quantity. For example,

```
    12.3×
    14.36
        .738
   3.69
   49.2
   123.
   176.628
```

There are six digits in the product, but there could be as many as seven or more. However, by applying the rule of significant figures for multiplication, the least number of significant figures is three (from 12.3); therefore, only three significant figures should be retained in the answer That is, the answer should be expressed as 177.

Rounding for long division deserves a closer look. Note that, if the divisor goes evenly into the dividend, the number of digits in the quotient can be no more than the difference between the number of digits in the dividend minus the number of digits in the divisor. Turning the above example around,

```
              14.36
      12.3 ) 176.628
            -123.
             53.628
            -49.2
              4.428
             -3.69
              0.738
             -0.738
              0.0
```

And, this quotient should be expressed as 14.4 to reflect the limiting number of significant figures in the divisor, 12.3. When the division does not come out even, it can be carried out as far as desired but will always have a remainder. The remainder is expressed as a fraction. Modifying the last example slightly,

$$
\begin{array}{r}
14.3 \\
12.3\ )\overline{176.6} \\
\underline{-123.} \\
53.6 \\
\underline{-49.2} \\
4.4 \\
\underline{-3.69} \\
0.71
\end{array}
$$

So the quotient for this case would be expressed as $14.3 + 0.71/12.3$.

As you can see from this example, it is best to carry out the division at least one place more than the eventual number of significant figures to make sure the correct rounding takes place.

When two numbers expressed in scientific notation are multiplied, the significands can be multiplied and the exponents added. It is convenient to normalize the resulting product, and it should be expressed with the correct number of significant figures, the least of the two multiplicands. For example,

$$
\begin{array}{r}
6.022 \times 10^{23} \\
\times\ 6.63 \times 10^{-34} \\
\hline
39.92586 \times 10^{-11} \quad \rightarrow \quad 3.99 \times 10^{-10}
\end{array}
$$

Not only is the product normalized on the right, it is expressed with the same limiting precision of the multiplicands.

In division, the divisor's significand can be divided into the dividend's significand, and the divisor's exponent subtracted from that of the dividend. Here is an example:

$$
7.65 \times 10^{10}\ )\overline{\begin{array}{c} 0.1369 \times 10^{1} \\ 1.046 \times 10^{11} \end{array}} \qquad \text{or} \qquad 1.37 \times 10^{0}
$$

Again, the quotient has been carried out an additional place and rounded down to the appropriate three significant figures.

1.2 MATHEMATICAL FUNCTIONS

In carrying out engineering and scientific calculations, it is frequently necessary to use a variety of mathematical functions, commonly including

- absolute value and sign functions,
- exponents and logarithms,

- trigonometric functions and
- hyperbolic functions.

In this section, we will review certain aspects of calculating these functions that are prone to cause errors in results. It is not our intention to repeat the exhaustive treatment that can be found in good books and videos on college algebra and pre-calculus mathematics. Such books and videos should be consulted if you need a more in-depth review.

1.2.1 ABSOLUTE VALUE AND SIGN FUNCTIONS

Calculating the absolute value of a number is easy. If the number is negative, change it to positive; otherwise, leave the number alone. The familiar symbol for the absolute value function is to surround the quantity with vertical bars, for example $|x|$. The absolute value function can be used in some creative ways though. For example, let's say that you wanted to have a method of squaring a quantity yet preserving the quantity's sign in the result. Applying this rule to -3 would yield -9, and applying it to 3 would yield 9. Consider the following formula, and you will see that it accomplishes this:

$$x\,|x|$$

Another related function is the sign (also called *signum*) function, abbreviated sgn. It can be expressed in terms of the absolute value function by the formula

$$\text{sgn}(x) = \frac{|x|}{x} \tag{1.3}$$

When x is positive, sgn(x)=1, and, when x is negative, sgn(x)=-1. This formula gets into trouble when $x=0$, yielding an indeterminate form 0/0; so, for that case, sgn(0) is just defined to be 0.

Note that the prior example, preserving the sign with the square, can be restated in terms of the sgn function,

$$x\,|x| = \text{sgn}(x)\,x^2 \tag{1.4}$$

1.2.2 EXPONENTS AND LOGARITHMS

Exponents and logarithms are dreaded by some students. That's too bad because they are an essential part of scientific and engineering formulas and calculations. The key relationship that defines the exponent and its inverse function, the logarithm, is

$$\log_x\left(x^y\right) = y \tag{1.5}$$

The term x^y means x raised to the power y, which you probably understand. For integer powers, raising to a power can be handled by repeated multiplication, and perhaps division, for example

$$1.5^4 = 1.5 \times 1.5 \times 1.5 \times 1.5 = 5.0625 \Rightarrow 5.1$$

$$1.5^{-3} = \frac{1}{1.5^3} = \frac{1}{1.5 \times 1.5 \times 1.5} = 0.296... \Rightarrow 0.30$$

$$(-1.5)^3 = (-1.5) \times (-1.5) \times (-1.5) = -3.375 \Rightarrow -3.4$$

Notice how the significant figures rule for multiplication/division is applied above. However, calculating x^y when y is a real number with a fractional part is not so straightforward. Consider the following examples:

$$1.5^{4.1} \qquad\qquad 1.5^{-0.41} \qquad\qquad (-1.5)^{1.4}$$

The scheme for computing when the power has a fractional part comes from the use of logarithms. Before doing that, it is useful to consider some specific types of logarithmic functions. The *common* (or base-10) *logarithm* is given by[4]

$$\log_{10}(10^y) = y$$

So, if $\log_{10}(2) = 0.301...$, that means that

$$10^{0.301...} = 2$$

To explain this in words, the common logarithm of a number is the power to which 10 is raised to give that number.

Likewise, the *natural* (or *Napierian*) *logarithm* has the base e, where e is defined by the infinite series

$$e = 1 + \frac{1}{1!} + \frac{1}{2!} + \frac{1}{3!} + \cdots \cong 2.718281828...$$

and

$$\log_e(e^y) = \ln(e^y) = y$$

---

[4] It is common in the print literature and on calculator buttons to use just **log** to represent **log10**, but we warn you that the **log** function in most computer programming languages is the natural or Napierian log (base-e), and there is a separate **log10** function built in.

Therefore, if $\ln(2)=0.693...$, then $e^{0.693...}=2$. The Napierian base arises frequently in calculus and differential equations, and the natural logarithm can be represented by another infinite series,

$$\ln(x) = 2 \cdot \left[\frac{x-1}{x+1} + \frac{1}{3} \left(\frac{x-1}{x+1} \right)^3 + \frac{1}{5} \left(\frac{x-1}{x+1} \right)^5 + \cdots \right] \quad \text{for } x > 0 \text{ only} \quad (1.6)$$

We can compute the natural logarithm to a given resolution by evaluating this series to the number of terms required to give convergence to that resolution. Notice that the logarithm is only defined for positive values of x.

Now, how do we use this ability to calculate the natural logarithm? Consider $\log_a(x)$ equal to some y. That means $a^y = x$. If we take the natural logarithm of both sides of this equation, $\ln(a^y) = \ln(x)$, or $y \cdot \ln(a) = \ln(x)$, the result is

$$\log_a(x) = y = \frac{\ln(x)}{\ln(a)} \quad (1.7)$$

This useful formula provides a way to and calculate the logarithm for any other base. For example

$$\log_{10}(100) = \frac{\ln(100)}{\ln(10)} = \frac{4.60517...}{2.30259...} = 2$$

Let's get back to that x^y where y is a real number with a fractional part. Represent the result of the calculation as z, so

$$z = x^y$$

and taking the natural logarithm of both sides of the equation, we get

$$\ln(z) = y \ln(x)$$

Taking e to the power of each side of this equation gives

$$e^{\ln(z)} = z = e^{y \ln(x)}$$

Thus, $x^y = e^{y \ln(x)}$. Since there is also an infinite series for e^x,

$$e^x = 1 + x + \frac{x^2}{2!} + \frac{x^3}{3!} + \cdots \quad (1.8)$$

We now can compute, from first principles, x^y, by calculating $\ln(x)$ approximately using the infinite series for the natural logarithm, then calculating $e^{y \ln(x)}$ from the infinite series given above. You should notice that this won't work for x less than or equal to zero. The one example cited above

$$(-1.5)^{1.4}$$

can't be done; in fact, it doesn't make any sense.

You will probably never calculate logarithms and exponents by hand using the series approximations – usually you'll just press the appropriate buttons on a calculator or use the corresponding built-in functions in a computer software, but it is useful to have some background on how these calculations are made and why certain limitations come into play. Reviewing our examples from above,

$$1.5^{4.1} = e^{4.1 \ln(1.5)} = e^{4.1 \cdot 0.405...} = e^{1.662...} \cong 5.3$$

$$1.5^{-0.41} = e^{-0.41 \ln(1.5)} = e^{-0.166...} \cong 0.85$$

$$(-1.5)^{1.4} \quad \text{Can't be done because} -1.5 \text{ is less than} 0$$

Appropriate significant figures are shown for each of these examples, although more precision is carried through in the intermediate calculations. Like we wrote above, calculating x^y, when y is a real number with a fractional part, is not that straightforward. This bears repeating.

Reviewing the key relationships from above,

$$\log_x\left(x^y\right) = y$$

$$\log_a\left(x^y\right) = y \log_a(x)$$

$$\log_a(x) = \frac{\ln(x)}{\ln(a)} \tag{1.9}$$

$$x^y = e^{y \ln(x)}$$

Other useful relationships involving exponents and logarithms are

$$\log_a\left(x\,y\right) = \log_a(x) + \log_a(y)$$

$$\log_a\left(\frac{x}{y}\right) = \log_a(x) - \log_a(y)$$

$$x^{y+z} = x^y\,x^z \tag{1.10}$$

$$a^{xy} = \left(a^x\right)^y$$

We provided you with specific rules regarding significant figures and the arithmetic operations of addition, subtraction, multiplication, and division. Matters aren't so easily defined when using logarithms, exponentials, and other nonlinear functions, such as trigonometric and hyperbolic functions. Let's illustrate this with a prior example:

$$1.5^{4.1}$$

There are evidently two significant figures in both quantities, 1.5 and 4.1. How many significant figures should be represented in the result? Let's take a numerical approach to this called *sensitivity analysis*. (This can also be approached with calculus and partial derivatives.) We will determine the effect on the result of changing each of the two numbers by one unit in their respective least significant digits. Table 1.3 gives us the answers to three significant digits.

Observe the dramatic effect of changing the 1.5 quantity by ±0.1! For a given exponent value, the answer changes by about ±1.5. The effect of changing the exponent 4.1 by ±0.1 is much milder, about ±0.2. So, if the resolution of the 1.5 value is as stated, we cannot really report the result to any more than one significant figure, that is, 5. This demonstrates that one must be very careful in reporting values that are results of calculations using nonlinear functions like exponentiation.

1.2.3 TRIGONOMETRIC FUNCTIONS

The various trigonometric functions occur all the time in scientific and engineering calculations. One problem that students encounter frequently in calculating formulas that include trigonometric functions is that most of these expect the angles to be in radians, not degrees. It seems that many students are accustomed to degrees from their previous math courses, especially those in high school. We will start by reviewing the basis of the three common "trig" functions and use this to understand the difference between degrees and radians.

The trigonometric functions relate the angles in a right triangle to its sides and hypotenuse. They are often conveniently represented on a two-dimensional graph using a unit circle, that is, a circle with a radius of 1. Compare the definitions in Equation 1.11 to the diagram in Figure 1.2.

TABLE 1.3
Sensitivity Analysis

	4.0	4.1	4.2
1.4	3.84	3.97	4.11
1.5	5.06	5.27	5.49
1.6	6.55	6.87	7.20

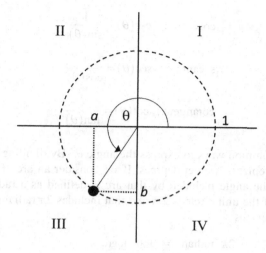

FIGURE 1.2 Trigonometric relationships on the unit circle.

$$\sin(\theta) = b$$

$$\cos(\theta) = a \qquad (1.11)$$

$$\tan(\theta) = \frac{b}{a}$$

The right triangle of reference has sides of length a and b and a hypotenuse of length 1, given by the radius of the unit circle. Note that the x-axis coordinate a is the length of the right triangle side adjacent to the angle θ, and the y-axis coordinate is the side opposite the angle θ. This gives rise to the right-triangle-based definitions:

$$\sin(\theta) = \frac{\text{opposite side}}{\text{hypotenuse}}$$

$$\cos(\theta) = \frac{\text{adjacent side}}{\text{hypotenuse}} \qquad (1.12)$$

$$\tan(\theta) = \frac{\text{opposite side}}{\text{adjacent side}}$$

and their reciprocal functions

$$\text{cosecant}: \quad \csc(\theta) = \frac{1}{\sin(\theta)}$$

$$\text{secant}: \quad \sec(\theta) = \frac{1}{\cos(\theta)} \qquad (1.13)$$

$$\text{cotangent}: \quad \cot(\theta) = \frac{1}{\tan(\theta)}$$

There are two common ways to express the angle θ.[5] By dividing the circle into 360 angular increments, we get degrees. If we consider an arc of length one on the unit circle, the angle included by that arc is defined as a radian. Since the circumference of the unit circle is 2π, and that includes 2π radians and $360°$, we have the equivalencies

$$2\pi \ \text{radians} = 360 \ \text{degrees}$$

$$1 \ \text{radian} = \frac{180}{\pi} \ \text{degrees} \cong 57.3°$$

$$\frac{\pi}{180} = 1 \ \text{degrees} \cong 0.0175 \ \text{radians}$$

As with the exponential function and natural logarithm, the trigonometric functions are defined in terms of infinite series, and these can be used to approximate numerical results. For example,

$$\sin(x) = x - \frac{x^3}{3!} + \frac{x^5}{5!} - \cdots \qquad (1.14)$$

This requires that x be expressed in radians, not degrees. Often you may use a calculator to compute trigonometric results, and you must be very aware whether the calculator expects the angles to be input in radians or degrees. Many calculators have a default setting for degrees and require a special action to switch them over to radians mode.

Here are some common trigonometric facts that many engineers and scientists have committed to memory:

---

[5] There is another, less frequently used unit for the angle called a *grad*. It is defined by dividing the right angle (90°) into 100 increments.

$$\sin(30°) = \sin\left(\frac{\pi}{6}\right) = 0.5 \qquad\qquad \cos(60°) = \cos\left(\frac{\pi}{3}\right) = 0.5$$

$$\cos(30°) = \cos\left(\frac{\pi}{6}\right) = \frac{\sqrt{3}}{2} = 0.866... \qquad \tan(45°) = \tan\left(\frac{\pi}{4}\right) = 1$$

$$\tan(60°) = \tan\left(\frac{\pi}{3}\right) = \sqrt{3} = 1.732... \qquad \tan(30°) = \tan\left(\frac{\pi}{6}\right) = \frac{\sqrt{3}}{3} = 0.577...$$

The *inverse* or "arc" *trigonometric functions* are used frequently in scientific formulas. Their mathematical definition is straightforward. For example,

$$y = \sin(x) \qquad \Rightarrow \qquad \sin^{-1}(y) = x$$

Instead of sin⁻¹(x), the terminology arcsin(x) is sometimes used. Notice that the result of the inverse sine formula is an angle, typically in radians. One way to think of the inverse sine formula above (this implies a method for obtaining it) is: "Given a value of y, what angle x will yield the sine of y?" To do that with a calculator, you might guess an x, compute the sine function, compare the result to y and guess new x's until your answer is close to y. Of course, many modern calculators have the inverse trigonometric functions built in, and, behind the scenes, they use a similar strategy.

There are some tricky aspects to the calculation of inverse trigonometric functions. You should appreciate this with the following example.

Consider the angle described on the unit-circle diagram in Figure 1.3.

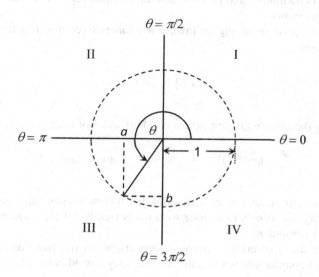

FIGURE 1.3   Unit circle diagram with quadrants.

The angle is clearly greater than π (180°) and less than $3\pi/2$ (270°). Notice that the coordinate values of a and b are both negative. By our definition,

$$\tan(\theta) = \frac{b}{a}$$

and, if we chose a value of θ and computed the tangent, the result would certainly be equal to the ratio of b to a. But consider the inverse tangent function for a moment. Say we knew b and a and wanted to compute θ (very common in engineering calculations). By definition again,

$$\theta = \tan^{-1}\left(\frac{b}{a}\right)$$

but when we carry out the calculation, taking the ratio of the negative values of b and a yields a positive result, and the inverse tangent result is an angle between 0 and $\pi/2$ (90°). You will notice that the quadrants of the unit circle are numbered with Roman numerals in Figure 1.3. By computing the ratio of b to a and losing the sense of their negative signs, we have failed to recognize that the answer should be an angle in quadrant III. To get the correct answer, we have to look at the values of a and b, recognize they are both negative and add π (180°) to the calculated result. There are similar considerations in distinguishing calculations in quadrants II and IV.

So, you can see that just punching the buttons of a calculator without understanding the nature of the functions you are using can get you into trouble. Computer software typically provides two inverse tangent functions, one returning angles in quadrants I and IV only, and another that returns the correct angles in all four quadrants.

A useful property involving the inverse trig functions comes from the common fact noted above,

$$\tan\left(\frac{\pi}{4}\right) = 1$$

By applying the inverse tangent function to both sides of the equation, we get

$$\frac{\pi}{4} = \tan^{-1}(1) \qquad \text{or} \qquad \pi = 4 \cdot \tan^{-1}(1)$$

If we have a convenient way of computing the inverse tangent, this last formula gives us a way of getting a value for π to as many significant digits carried by your calculator or computer.

There are many practical scenarios where trigonometric functions arise. One of these is in conjunction with quantities that vary periodically, like sine waves. Application areas include:

- electronic circuits
- electrical power distribution
- communications and signal processing
- mechanical and structural vibrations
- automation and control systems

Consider the sinusoidal signal shown in Figure 1.4, which is produced by graphing the function

$$1.47 \sin(0.89t + 0.32) \tag{1.15}$$

The *amplitude* of the sine wave is 1.47, and you can see in the graph that the peaks are ±1.47. The *frequency* of the sine wave is 0.89 radians/second, and, by comparing with the graph, you can confirm that the *period* of the sine wave is, as determined below,

$$\text{for } \omega = 0.89 \, \frac{\text{radians}}{\text{second}}$$

$$\text{and } f = \frac{\omega}{2\pi} \cong 0.14 \, \frac{\text{cycles}}{\text{second}} \text{ or Hertz (Hz)}$$

$$\text{then } P = \frac{1}{f} \cong 7.1 \text{ seconds}$$

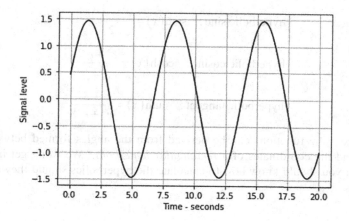

FIGURE 1.4   Example sinusoidal signal.

The *phase shift* of the sine wave is 0.32 radians (or 18°). A sine function without phase shift would have a value of zero at time$=0, \pm\pi/\omega, \pm 2\pi/\omega, \dots$ You can see from the graph that the wave starts early; in fact, at time$=-0.32/\pi$ the value is zero. The sine wave has been advanced in time by the phase shift. Of course, the phase shift could be negative, and the sine wave would be delayed.

By employing the "sum of angles" trigonometric identity,

$$\sin(\alpha+\beta) = \sin(\alpha)\cos(\beta) + \cos(\alpha)\sin(\beta) \tag{1.16}$$

our sine wave formula can be written in the equivalent form

$$1.47\sin(0.89t + 0.32) = 1.47\cos(0.32)\sin(0.89t) + 1.47\sin(0.32)\cos(0.89t)$$

$$\cong 1.40\sin(0.89t) + 0.462\cos(0.89t)$$

You can see then that a sine function with a phase shift (or cosine function with a phase shift) can be written as a sum of sine and cosine functions of the same frequency but differing amplitudes.

1.2.4 HYPERBOLIC FUNCTIONS

In deriving many engineering formulas, another family of functions arises: the *hyperbolic functions*. These are actually defined in terms of exponential functions; so, knowing how to calculate e^x gives us the capability to calculate the hyperbolics. Many calculators have e^x built in, but not the hyperbolic functions. A variety of software products used by engineers and scientists do have these functions available. Their definitions are

$$\text{hyperbolic sine}: \quad \sinh(x) = \frac{e^x - e^{-x}}{2}$$

$$\text{hyperbolic cosine}: \quad \cosh(x) = \frac{e^x + e^{-x}}{2}$$

$$\text{hyperbolic tangent}: \quad \tanh(x) = \frac{e^x - e^{-x}}{e^x + e^{-x}} \tag{1.17}$$

The hyperbolic functions can be derived from the angles formed between the origin and the coordinates of a *rectangular hyperbola*.[6] We won't get into that here, but you should know how to calculate the hyperbolics should they arise in formulas.

---

[6] A hyperbola for which the asymptotes are perpendicular. Hyperbola. https://en.wikipedia.org/wiki/Hyperbola. (Last edited date June 23, 2022.)

Example 1.2 Catenary Cable

A *catenary*[7] is the curve that a hanging chain or cable assumes under its own weight when supported only at its ends. Figure 1.5 depicts such a catenary cable suspended between two points, {–1, 3} and {3, 6}, with the lowest point at $x=0$.

The general equation describing the curve of the cable is

$$y = a \cosh\left(\frac{x}{a}\right) - b \tag{1.18}$$

where the parameters a and b can be determined with the relationships,

$$y_1 = a \cosh\left(\frac{x_1}{a}\right) - b \quad \text{and} \quad y_2 = a \cosh\left(\frac{x_2}{a}\right) - b$$

and the length of the cable is given by

$$L = a\left[\sinh\left(\frac{x_2}{a}\right) - \sinh\left(\frac{x_1}{a}\right)\right] \tag{1.19}$$

For the specific case in the graph,
$$a \cong 1.7418 \quad b \cong 0.9674 \qquad L \cong 5.775$$

This illustrates how hyperbolic functions are involved in an engineering calculation.

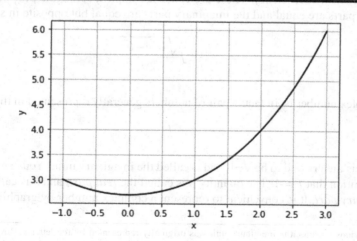

FIGURE 1.5   Suspended cable profile.

[7] The name derives from the Latin word for chain: "catenaria."

1.3   COMPLEX NUMBERS

Complex numbers arise in many engineering applications, perhaps most frequently in electrical engineering. You are undoubtedly familiar with them through the solution of the quadratic equation, $ax^2+bx+c=0$, by the quadratic formula

$$x = \frac{-b \pm \sqrt{b^2 - 4ac}}{2a}$$

(1.20)

In evaluating the quadratic formula, the term b^2-4ac is called the *discriminant* because, depending on its sign, very different solutions arise. When the discriminant is positive, two distinct real roots result. When it is zero, there are two equal real roots. When $b^2-4ac<0$, we are faced with the awkward situation of finding the square root of a negative number. This is handled by defining a symbol, j, to represent the square root of -1 as

$$j \triangleq \sqrt{-1}$$

then

$$\sqrt{b^2 - 4ac} = \sqrt{(-1)(4ac - b^2)} = j\sqrt{4ac - b^2}$$

which gives rise to two complex roots, each one having a real part and an imaginary part with coefficient j. These are called a complex, *conjugate pair* because the real parts are equal and the imaginary parts are equal but opposite in sign.

$$x = -\frac{b}{2a} \pm j\frac{\sqrt{4ac - b^2}}{2a}$$

(1.21)

A complex number is, in fact, a pair of numbers generally represented in the form

$$a + jb$$

where j is understood to be $\sqrt{-1}$, and is called the imaginary unit.[8] You can see by its definition that $j^2=-1$. The quantity a is called the *real part*, and b is called the *imaginary part*. It is convenient to represent a complex number by graphing it in

---

[8] For obvious reasons, the imaginary unit was originally represented by the letter i. However, in certain contexts, where the use of the letter i is problematic, the letter j is often used instead. For example, in electrical engineering, the imaginary unit is normally denoted by j instead of i, because i is commonly used to represent electric current. We will utilize j in this text, for a variety of reasons. For example, the symbols $\mathbf{i}$, $\mathbf{j}$, and $\mathbf{k}$ are employed for unit vectors in the directions of the x, y, and z axes, respectively. The use of j for distance along the y axis is more consistent with its sense in the real plane.

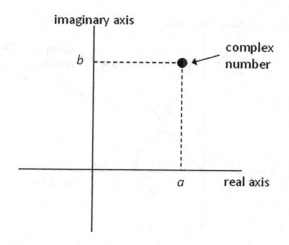

FIGURE 1.6 Number on the complex plane.

a plane with the horizontal axis used for the real part and the vertical axis for the imaginary part, as shown in Figure 1.6.

It is then possible to represent the number by polar coordinates instead of rectangular, Cartesian, coordinates (Figure 1.7) where $r = \sqrt{a^2 + b^2}$ and $\theta = \tan^{-1}(b/a)$.[9]

From trigonometry, we also have that

$$a = r\cos(\theta) \quad \text{and} \quad b = r\sin(\theta)$$

Therefore, the original representation of the complex number, $a + jb$, can also be written

$$a + jb = r\left(\cos(\theta) + j\sin(\theta)\right) \quad (1.22)$$

Euler proposed the following identity:

$$e^{j\theta} \equiv \cos(\theta) + j\sin(\theta) \quad (1.23)$$

which leads to

$$a + jb = re^{j\theta} \quad (1.24)$$

The expression on the right, $re^{j\theta}$, is called the polar form on the complex number. This also leads to the following identities for the trigonometric functions:

---

[9] Be aware of the four-quadrant arctangent.

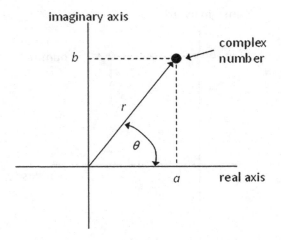

FIGURE 1.7   Number on the complex plane using polar coordinates.

$$\sin(\theta) \equiv \frac{e^{j\theta} - e^{-j\theta}}{2j} \qquad\qquad \cos(\theta) \equiv \frac{e^{j\theta} + e^{-j\theta}}{2} \qquad (1.25)$$

1.4   ENGINEERING UNITS[10]

One of the more confusing aspects of making engineering and scientific calculations is units of measurement. Table 1.4 illustrates that for common units of measurement for pressure as related to an SI standard unit, kPa:

Given this table, suppose you are faced with a pressure measurement in Hg (typical units used for barometric pressure in the U.S.), and you are asked to report the measurement in atmospheres. This shows how to make that conversion using the table:

TABLE 1.4

Common Units for Pressure (kPa)

Atmosphere	101.325	
in Hg	3.37685	kPa
in H_2O	0.24884	kPa
torr (mm Hg)	0.133322	kPa
psi	6.894757	kPa
bar	100	kPa
kg_f/cm^2	98.0665	kPa

---

[10] The units of measurement used by engineers are, of course, also used by scientists. So, it is a slight to scientists to call them engineering units, but that is the common terminology. Apology due to scientists.

TABLE 1.5
Basic Units of the SI System

Time	Second	s
Length	Meter	m
Mass	Kilogram	kg
Current	Ampere	A
Temperature	Kelvin	K
Amount	Mole	mol
Luminous intensity	Candela	cd

$$29.48 \text{ in Hg} \cdot \frac{3.37683 \text{ kPa}}{1 \text{ in Hg}} \cdot \frac{1 \text{ atm}}{101.325 \text{ kPa}} \cong 0.9825 \text{ atm}$$

Of course, you could look for a conversion factor from in Hg to atm directly; however, with so many pressure units in common use, just having the relationship with a standard SI unit, kPa, is a convenient way to create the conversion.

The international standard units of measurement are those defined by the *SI system* (*Système internationale d'unités*), which is a modern form of the metric system. The basic SI units of measurement are given in Table 1.5.

Commonly derived quantities encountered in engineering and scientific calculations are shown in Table 1.6.

For each of these quantities, you will encounter different units used. For example, civil engineers in the U.S. will encounter cubic feet per second (ft³/s or cfs) used for volumetric flow rate, and U.S. chemical engineers may encounter gallons per minute (gpm).

Scaled units are commonly used in describing quantities. For example, millimeters (mm) or micrometers (μm) may be used to measure dimensions of smaller particles. There are standard prefixes for scaling units, and these are presented in Table 1.7.

TABLE 1.6
Derived Quantities and SI Units

Area	m^2	
Volume	m^3	
Volumetric flow rate	m^3/s	
Density	kg/m^3	
Force	N	$kg \cdot m/s^2$
Pressure	Pa	N/m^2
Energy	J	$N \cdot m$
Power	W	J/s
Viscosity	Pa·s	$N \cdot s/m2$

TABLE 1.7

Scale Prefixes for Units

Scale Factor	Name	Abbreviation	Scale Factor	Name	Abbreviation
10	deca-	da	0.1	deci-	d
100	hecto-	h	0.01	centi-	c
1,000	kilo-	k	0.001	milli-	m
10^6	mega-	M	10^{-6}	micro-	μ
10^9	giga-	G	10^{-9}	nano-	n
10^{12}	tera-	T	10^{-12}	pico-	p
10^{15}	peta-	P	10^{-15}	femto-	f
10^{18}	exa-	E	10^{-18}	atto-	a

Specialized areas of science and engineering have specific units that are common. For example, in electrical engineering, Table 1.8 may be useful.

There are common constants used in calculations in chemistry, physics and engineering. One of these is the universal gas constant, R. This constant is employed to relate amount, temperature, pressure, and volume of a gas and appears in the ideal gas law as

$$PV = nRT \tag{1.26}$$

where P=pressure, V=volume of gas, n=number of moles of gas, and T is the temperature in absolute units. The units required for the gas law constant depend on the units used for these quantities. This is illustrated by solving the ideal gas law for R and incorporating the units at hand.

$$R = \frac{PV}{nT} \cong 8.3145 \frac{\text{Pa} \cdot \text{m}^3}{\text{mol} \cdot \text{K}}$$

TABLE 1.8

Common Units for Electrical Measurement.

Quantity	Unit	Abbreviation	Base Units
Electrical charge	Coulomb	C	s·A
Electrical potential	Volt	V	W/A
Capacitance	Farad	F	C/V
Resistance	Ohm	Ω	V/A
Magnetic flux	Weber	Wb	V·s
Inductance	Henry	H	Wb/A
Luminous flux	Lumen	lm	cd·sr

Note: For Luminous Flux, the Base Unit Abbreviation "sr" Stands for "Steradian."

TABLE 1.9

Common Units for the Gas Constant, R.

8.3144621...	Pa·m³/(mol·K)
8.3144621...	J/(mol·K)
0.08205746...	atm·L/(mol·K)
1.9858775...	cal/(mol·K)

Note: The unit "cal" is an abbreviation for calorie.

There are extensive tables available (e.g. on the Internet) of R in various units. In Table 1.9, we tabulate several of the most common used.

When working with mixed units in engineering and scientific calculations, we suggest the following steps:

- convert all input quantities to SI units,
- carry out the calculations, producing results in SI units,
- convert results to the units expected by your audience.

We strongly recommend that you do not bury unit conversions in formulas, rather keep them separate.

Example 1.3 Engineering Units in Calculations

The mass flow rate in a pipeline is related to the average velocity of the fluid by

$$w = \rho A v \qquad (1.27)$$

where w=mass flow rate, ρ=fluid density, A=cross-sectional area of the pipe, and v=average velocity of the fluid. The values provided for the calculation are

$$\rho = 55 \; \frac{\text{lb}_m}{\text{ft}^3} \qquad A = 50 \; \text{in}^2 \qquad v = 1 \; \frac{\text{m}}{\text{s}}$$

We need to calculate the mass flow rate in kg/min.
Step 1 Convert the input data to SI units

$$\rho = 55 \; \frac{\text{lb}_m}{\text{ft}^3} \cdot \frac{0.4536 \; \text{kg}}{\text{lb}_m} \cdot \frac{\text{ft}^3}{0.02832 \; \text{m}^3} \cong 881 \; \frac{\text{kg}}{\text{m}^3}$$

$$A = 50 \; \text{in}^2 \cdot \frac{6.452 \times 10^{-4} \; \text{m}^2}{\text{in}^2} = 0.03226 \; \text{m}^2$$

Step 2 Compute the result in SI units

$$w = \left(881 \frac{\text{kg}}{\text{m}^3}\right)(0.03226 \text{ m}^2)\left(1 \frac{\text{m}}{\text{s}}\right) \cong 28.42 \frac{\text{kg}}{\text{s}}$$

Step 3 Convert the result to the desired units

$$w = 28.42 \frac{\text{kg}}{\text{s}} \cdot \frac{60 \text{ s}}{\text{min}} \cong 1705 \frac{\text{kg}}{\text{min}}$$

We could have combined all the conversion factors and made the calculation with one formula:

$$w = 55 \cdot 50 \cdot 1 \cdot [0.6200] \cong 1705 \frac{\text{kg}}{\text{min}}$$

This is not a good approach. The conversion quantity, 0.6200, is sometimes called a *magic number* because, yes, it works, but there is little understanding where it came from, and, since it was computed separately without documentation, it is subject to errors that might never be discovered.

1.5   ORGANIZING AND PLANNING SOLUTIONS TO PROBLEMS

Your career as a scientist or engineer will be filled with problem-solving activities. You will be expected to be a proficient problem-solver, but you may not be that yet. How do you get from here to there?

One way, the long way, is through the "school of hard knocks." That is, by solving many, many problems, you will eventually get good at it. Of course, getting there will be painful. You should be interested in ways to become a better problem solver faster. The purpose of this section is to help you move along in that direction.

There are many good sources of information on problem solving. Many of these treat problem solving in a much more general setting, and others focus on the mathematical aspects of problems. We cannot equal the scope of books like these here, but we can point out some useful strategies that will pay off later in this text, in other courses in your curriculum, and in professional practice.

We start this section with a nice example to illustrate some features of problem solving. It is useful to deal with something concrete before considering general methods. Then, a general approach to problem solving is presented. As problems become more complicated, and especially when a team of people attacks a problem, a systematic, structured approach is of great value. Ways of categorizing typical problems are described. Much efficiency in problem solving comes from recognizing the pattern or type of a problem, leading directly to a solution strategy. Finally, several alternative examples are presented.

Example 1.4 Engineering and Scientific Problem Solving

Many of the problems you encounter as an engineering or science student will be relatively simple and straightforward. For example, consider the following problem statement:

A worker carried a 6 m ladder down a 2.3 m-wide hallway over her shoulder horizontally. The worker turned the corner into a 1.5 m-wide hallway running at a right angle to the previous hallway, and the ladder has become stuck against the walls of the two hallways and the corner between them. How much of the ladder is in the first hallway, and how much is in the second?

Some students, and many individuals in society, sense a mixture of fear and hate toward such problem statements. Engineers and scientists learn to solve them efficiently and even relish the challenge. But, just as when an author sits down to write a book, we need some way to start, to get pen to paper, to break the ice. The scientist or engineer falls back on a well-tested icebreaker: draw a diagram. Most problems can be represented with some type of diagram, anywhere from a realistic, to-scale drawing to an abstract sketch. Diagrams help crystallize your understanding of the problem at hand. A diagram of the problem is shown in Figure 1.8.

If the diagram is drawn to scale, it may be possible to solve the problem graphically to adequate precision without ever making a calculation! Just measure the lengths of the ladder in both hallways and use the scale of the drawing to convert these to meters. The diagram can even be constructed to simulate the problem. If matchsticks or toothpicks are used to construct the walls of the hallways and the ladder, you can move the ladder down the hallway and experience it getting stuck. This is called *physical modeling*. In any case, the

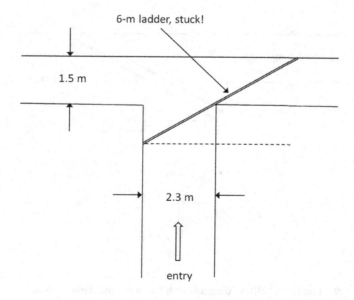

FIGURE 1.8 Ladder stuck in adjoining hallways.

diagram builds a useful picture of the problem at hand. It clarifies the information we have and the answers we must determine.

Studying the diagram gives us an idea how to obtain a more accurate solution to the problem. With the help of a couple dashed lines, we can see three
similar right triangles in the diagram. See below. We have added variable
names, x, y, and z, for three distances we don't know yet. See Figure 1.9.
Before we get too far, let's keep our objective in sight. If we know the value of
x in the diagram above, we can solve the problem. Next, given our three right
triangles, we can tabulate some relationships that we know must hold from
geometry:

$$\frac{6}{1.5+y}=\frac{x}{1.5}=\frac{6-x}{y} \quad \text{and} \quad \frac{6}{2.3+z}=\frac{x}{z}=\frac{6-x}{2.3}$$

Using the first equality above, we can easily solve for x, and, using the second
equality, we can solve for y.

$$x=\frac{9}{1.5+y} \quad \text{and} \quad y=\frac{9}{x}-1.5 \tag{1.28}$$

A little manipulation will show that these are equivalent. Using the second
equality, we can solve for x in terms of z.

$$x=\frac{6z}{2.3+z} \tag{1.29}$$

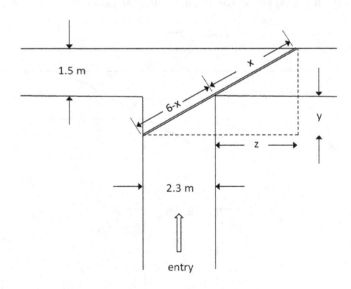

FIGURE 1.9 Ladder in hallway diagram with variables and dashed lines.

		Variable		
		x	y	z
Equation	1	+	+	
	2	+		+
	3	+		+

FIGURE 1.10 Occurrence matrix.

Now, we have two independent equations, but we have three unknowns. This means the problem is *underspecified*.[11] We need another independent relationship. This can be found using the *Pythagorean theorem*,

$$z^2 + 1.5^2 = x^2 \tag{1.30}$$

We now have three independent equations in three unknowns. They are

$$\textbf{1.} \quad x = \frac{9}{1.5 + y} \qquad \textbf{2.} \quad x = \frac{6z}{2.3 + z} \qquad \textbf{3.} \quad z^2 + 1.5^2 = x^2 \tag{1.31}$$

Although it may seem obvious to you how to solve these equations, that isn't always the case. The use of an *occurrence matrix* helps. With this matrix, illustrated in Figure 1.10, we map which variables appear in which equations.

If we rearrange the columns and rows of this matrix, we can get Figure 1.11. This suggests that we have a system of two equations in the two unknowns, x and z. Once we solve these for x and z, we can use the third equation in the last table, Equation 1.31(**3**), to solve for y. Let's start by solving the third equation for z,

$$z = \sqrt{x^2 - 2.25}$$

and then substituting this into Equation 1.2,

$$x = \frac{6\sqrt{x^2 - 2.25}}{2.3 + \sqrt{x^2 - 2.25}} \tag{1.32}$$

		Variable		
		x	z	y
Equation	2	+	+	
	3	+	+	
	1	+		+

FIGURE 1.11 Rearranged occurrence matrix.

---

[11] In the context of solving linear simultaneous equations, the terms *underdetermined* and *overdetermined* are commonly used to designate "too many unknowns" and "too many equations," respectively.

It looks like we have one equation in one unknown, but solving for x doesn't look that easy. However, this takes us to another phase of the problem. In fact, the form of Equation 1.32 suggests a way to solve it. First, we need an initial estimate for x. Back to our diagram! We'll start with an estimate of 4 for x. Evaluating the right-hand side of the above equation with this, we get

$$x = \frac{6\sqrt{4^2 - 2.25}}{2.3 + \sqrt{4^2 - 2.25}} \cong 3.703$$

Well, that doesn't give us the x we started with, so, we know we don't have the solution yet. What to do? One practical technique, which doesn't always work, is to use our new value for x again in the right-hand side of the equation. This is called the *successive substitution method* or also *fixed-point iteration*.

$$x = \frac{6\sqrt{3.703^2 - 2.25}}{2.3 + \sqrt{3.703^2 - 2.25}} \cong 3.573$$

Continuing this procedure, we get the result in Table 1.10.

After 20 iterations, the x value resulting from the calculations is the same, to seven significant figures, as the one entering the calculation. Practically, that means we have the solution for x. Now, what about the values for z and y? Before we solve for them, we should realize that we don't need their values! If we're curious, we can determine that

$$z = \sqrt{3.445122^2 - 2.25} \cong 3.101$$

and

$$y = \frac{9}{3.445122} - 1.5 \cong 1.112$$

TABLE 1.10
Substitution Results

Iteration	x	Iteration	x
1	4	11	3.445817
2	3.703101	12	3.445486
3	3.572858	13	3.445312
4	3.510253	14	3.445221
5	3.478818	15	3.445173
6	3.462683	16	3.445147
7	3.454309	17	3.445134
8	3.449937	18	3.445127
9	3.447648	19	3.445124
10	3.446447	20	3.445122

---

but we don't really need to. Since x is the length of the 6 m ladder in the second hallway, then the remaining length in the first hallway is

$$6 - 3.445122 = 2.55488$$

To summarize, with three significant figures,

3.45 m or 57.4% of the ladder is in the second hallway, and
2.55 m or 42.6% of the ladder is still in the first hallway.

We illustrate these results on our diagram in Figure 1.12.
Let's observe and summarize the steps followed in solving the Example 1.4.

1. Construct a diagram.
2. Introduce variable names for unknown quantities.
3. Derive as many independent relationships as there are variables.
4. Develop a solution scheme for solving the relationships.
5. Execute the solution and summarize the results.

This example has provided us with a taste of practical problem solving, but it is not general and certainly doesn't cover all the situations we might face. Consider the following re-worded problem statements:

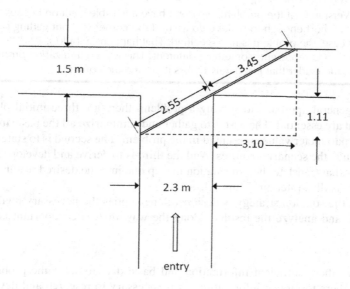

FIGURE 1.12 Solution of the ladder-hallway problem.

Version B

A worker carried a 6-m ladder down a 2.3 m-wide hallway over his shoulder horizontally. The worker turned the corner into a hallway running at a right angle to the previous hallway, and the ladder has become stuck against the walls of the two hallways and the corner between them. How much of the ladder is in the first hallway, and how much is in the second?

Version C

A worker carried a 5-m ladder down a 2.3 m-wide hallway over her shoulder horizontally. The worker turned the corner into a 1.5-m wide hallway running at a right angle to the previous hallway, and the ladder has become stuck against the walls of the two hallways and the corner between them. How much of the ladder is in the first hallway, and how much is in the second?

Version D

A worker is to carry a ladder down a 2.3-m wide hallway over his shoulder horizontally. The worker is to turn the corner into a 1.5-m wide hallway running at a right angle to the previous hallway. What is the longest ladder that the worker could negotiate through the hallways?

Before getting too far into the solution of Version B, we realize that we don't have enough specifications to solve the problem; in particular, we don't know the width of the second hallway. What to do? We could

- state that the problem cannot be solved,
- assume a reasonable value for the width of the second hallway and proceed, or
- go find the value, then solve the problem.

It is typical for problems to be underspecified like this. It is also possible for them to be *overspecified*.

In Version C of the problem, we don't have a feasible solution because the ladder is short enough to make it go around the corner without getting stuck! In this case, the problem is mis-specified. That happens a lot too.

Version D represents something different. This is an *optimization problem*, finding the ladder that just barely makes it around the corner.

In a general approach to solving a problem, there are three initial planning steps that are essential. The first is to gather and summarize all the basic information and parameter values presented in the problem. The second is to state clearly what results the scenario requires. And the third is to derive and develop the relationships that translate the information in step one into the desired results in step two. This is illustrated in Figure 1.13.

Once the solution strategy is designed, one applies the necessary methods to calculate and analyze the results. Along the way, there are important issues to address:

- Are there sufficient information and basic data to solve the problem? Is there too much information? Is it necessary to research and develop additional information?

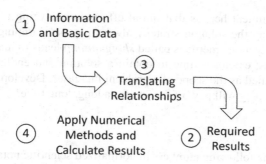

FIGURE 1.13 Problem-solving steps.

- Are the assumptions associated with the problem description valid? What factors might be missed?
- Does my strategy yield the requested results? It is a waste of time and effort to produce results that are not needed nor wanted.
- Are the methods employed to determine the solution valid? How do I validate the results?
- How are my results sensitive to changes in the input parameters? If the sensitivity is high, the results will be in doubt if the input parameter is uncertain.

We have addressed several of these issues with our simple ladder-hallway example. For example, we didn't need to solve for z and y, once we had a value for x. Solving for z and y would be wasted effort. Version B of the problem did not provide sufficient information. To validate our result, we might test it on our scale drawing. We could check the Pythagorean theorem for the big triangle in the diagram with sides $2.5 + z$ and $1.5 + y$ and the hypotenuse at 6 m. Of course, then we would have to solve for z and y.

As far as assumptions involved in the problem statement being valid, it is stated that the ladder is held horizontally. If you have ever tried to carry ladders in restricted spaces, you know that you would tilt the ladder to gain better access. If we change the problem description to allow this, we would need the height of the hallways and more dimensional information on the ladder (width and thickness). Also then, the problem would become more complicated. We analyzed the ladder as a line on our diagram. Ladders have a thickness dimension. Including this would affect our original problem description, even with horizontal alignment.

Judgment must be exercised in removing assumptions and consequently complicating problem descriptions and solutions. Even if our ladder is 10 cm thick, do we get a sufficiently good result ignoring that information? Such questions can be addressed based on experience, but, without that, it may be necessary to carry out a trial solution of a more complicated scenario and compare it with the simpler one.

Our final comment here is that initial efforts in analyzing the problem and carefully planning the solution strategy always pay off. Jumping right into the solution of a problem (sometimes called *shotgunning*) leads to many difficulties, erroneous results, extended time to obtain a solution and endless frustrations. All this is amplified as the scope of a problem increases. Develop the habits suggested here, and they will pay off for you for a long, long time.

PROBLEMS

1.1 Express the following numbers in normalized scientific notation.
(a) 0.0001005 (b) 3.14159 (c) 62459100 (d) 602.2×10^{21}

1.2 Carry out the following computations using a calculator or spreadsheet. Express the results to the appropriate number of significant figures.

(a) $\begin{array}{r} 6.001 \\ \times\ 0.15 \end{array}$ (b) $0.154\overline{)6.001}$ (c) $\begin{array}{r} 1.25 \times 10^{-2} \\ 7.61 \times 10^{-1} \\ +\ 3.06 \times 10^{-3} \end{array}$

(d) $1.017 \times 10^5 \div 3.64 \times 10^7$

1.3 Round the following to the place indicated.
(a) 1047560 to 1000
(b) 1.047 to 0.1
(c) 7450 to 100
(d) −15.43 to 1

1.4 Rework problem **1.2(b)** using long division.

1.5 For the components and sum shown below, calculate the percentage each component is of the total. Express your percentages with appropriate significant figures and ensure they sum to 100%.

$$\begin{array}{r} 375 \\ 44 \\ 145 \\ 14 \\ \underline{201} \\ 779 \end{array}$$

1.6 Compute the following functions using a calculator or spreadsheet.

(a) $\sin(1.84\pi)$ (b) $\tan\left(-\dfrac{\pi}{4}\right)$ (c) $\cos(47.9°)$ (d) $\tan^{-1}(25)$

1.7 Determine the roots of the following quadratic equations.

(a) $x^2 + 0.20 \cdot x + 0.70 = 0$ (b) $x^2 - 28.4 \cdot x + 201.64 = 0$

(c) $24 \cdot x^2 - 13 \cdot x = 0$ (d) $x^2 + 187 \cdot x - 24.0 = 0$

1.8 Write down an approximate equation for the waveform shown in Figure P1.8.

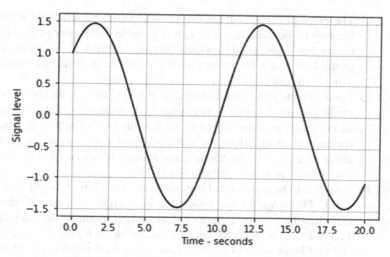

FIGURE P1.8 Waveform.

1.9 In the U.S., vehicle fuel economy is typically reported in miles per gallon (mpg). In Europe, the common measure is liters per 100 km (L/100 km). Americans would know a decent fuel economy to be 40 mpg. Help Europeans understand this by converting it to L/100 km.

1.10 Carry out the following unit conversions.
  (a) 150 kph = ?? mph (a moderate speed on the autobahn)
  (b) 7 ft–6 inches = ?? m (this is the altitude of Yao Ming – who is he?)
  (c) 45°C = ?? °F (typical summer temperature in the Middle East)
  (d) 12.4 psi = ?? Pa (typical atmospheric pressure at 1,800 m altitude)

1.11 In most countries, other than the U.S., a person's weight is reported in kilograms. Convert your weight (or a weight you would like to have) from pounds to kilograms (or vice versa). Also, in the U.K., weight is often cited in *stone*. Convert that weight to stone also.

1.12 A crude oil supertanker typically has a capacity of 100,000 dwt. The shipping unit dwt is called a deadweight ton and corresponds to a metric ton or 1,000 kg of capacity. Crude oil typically has a density of about 835 kg/m^3. Determine the amount of liquid fossil fuels consumed in the U.S. or a country of your choice on a monthly basis in terms of crude oil. Determine also what percentage of the crude oil is imported via ship. How many supertankers must unload at ports per month?

1.13 In most countries of the world, mountain heights are given in meters; whereas, in the U.S., feet are typically used. What are the altitudes, in both feet and meters, of the following well-known peaks in the world? Describe the location of each peak too. Mont Blanc, Denali, Mount Everest, Kilimanjaro, Aconcagua, Mount Fuji.

1.14 The price of regular, unleaded gasoline varies significantly from location to location. In the U.S., it is given in dollars per gallon. In most other countries, it is in their currency per liter. Pick a location in the U.S. and a European country. Compare current fuel prices using both bases.

1.15 For a triangle with sides of length a, b, and c, there is an inscribed circle of radius r and a circumscribed circle of radius R. The inscribed circle is the largest circle that fits inside the triangle and touches all three sides. The circumscribed circle is the smallest circle that contains the triangle and touches all three vertices. For $a=10$, $b=8$, and $c=5$, determine r and R.

1.16 A tank is to be constructed that will hold $500\,m^3$ of crude oil when filled. The shape of the tank is to be a right circular cylinder, including base, with a right conical section mounted on top (see Figure P1.16) with height equal to radius for each part. The material and labor costs to construct the cylindrical portion including the base are \$300 per m², and the costs for the conical section are \$400 per m². Find the cost of this tank.

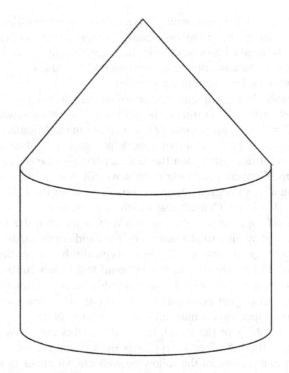

FIGURE P1.16 Cylindrical tank with conical top.

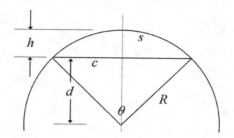

FIGURE P1.17   Sector and segment of a circle.

1.17 The sector and segment of a circle are related to various dimensions, shown in Figure P1.17.

Given values of θ and R,

$$s = R\theta$$

$$d = R\cos\left(\frac{\theta}{2}\right)$$

$$h = R - d$$

$$c = 2R\sin\left(\frac{\theta}{2}\right)$$

Formulas for area are

Sector: $A_{sect} = \frac{1}{2}Rs$ (sector is "pie slice")

Segment: $A_{seg} = \frac{1}{2}R^2[\theta - \sin(\theta)]$ (segment is between c and s curves)

If $R = 3.6$ and $s = 1.78$, determine the two areas.

2 Computer-Based Calculations

CHAPTER OBJECTIVES

- Understand how numerical quantities are stored and manipulated within computer architecture.
- Familiarize yourself with the different number bases and systems: decimal, binary, octal, and hexadecimal and how to convert numbers between the bases.
- Learn how integers are stored in computers including signed numbers and limits on range.
- Understand how real numbers with fractional parts and exponents are represented in computer architecture, including limits on precision and range.
- See how other types of information, such as text and True/False Boolean data, are stored and manipulated in computers.

What goes on inside a computer differs from what engineers and scientists do on paper, perhaps with the assistance of a calculator. Out in the real world, we deal with numbers using the *decimal system*, or *base 10*. Internal to computers, the basis for all operations is the *binary or base-2* system (0–1). The objective of this chapter is to build a bridge of understanding between these two worlds and understand any inherent limitations. With such an understanding, computer-literate engineers and scientists can observe computer actions and results without being baffled.

We will start with an example describing positional notation and conversion between decimal and binary numbers.

Example 2.1 What is the Radius of the Earth – Expressed in Binary?

As previously mentioned in Chapter 1, the radius from the center to the Equator is estimated to be 6,378 km. This is a decimal number and can be described by *positional notation*[1] as follows:

$$\left(6\times10^3\right)+\left(3\times10^2\right)+\left(7\times10^1\right)+\left(8\times10^0\right)$$

---

[1] The *Babylonian number system* employed base-60 numbers and was the first positional system to be developed. Its influence is still felt today in the way time and angles are enumerated; for example, 60 seconds in a minute and 360° in a circle.

DOI: 10.1201/9781003256861-2

You are well aware that the position of the digit in the number is "weighted" by a power of 10 corresponding to that position. This also applies to numbers with fractional quantities, such as an approximation of π, 3.1416:

$$\left(3\times10^{0}\right)+\left(1\times10^{-1}\right)+\left(4\times10^{-2}\right)+\left(1\times10^{-3}\right)+\left(6\times10^{-4}\right)$$

Positional notation works also for numbers in other bases, such as binary (2) or its commensurate relatives octal ($2^3 = 8$) and hexadecimal ($2^4 = 16$). Consider the binary number 101101_2:

$$\left(1\times2^{5}\right)+\left(0\times2^{4}\right)+\left(1\times2^{3}\right)+\left(1\times2^{2}\right)+\left(0\times2^{1}\right)+\left(1\times2^{0}\right)$$

A quick observation of the positional notation allows us to convert that number to decimal:

$$32+0+8+4+0+1=45_{10}$$

As shown here, we often append a subscript to indicate the number base, 10 or d for decimal, 2 for binary, 8 for octal, and 16 or h for hexadecimal. This is especially important when there could be any confusion as to the correct base.

Going the other way, converting from a decimal number to its binary equivalent, may not be so clear. There are two techniques that we can introduce using our simple example, 45_{10}. The first, called *successive approximation*, starts by determining the largest power of 2 that is less than or equal to our number. That would be 5, so we make a note of that and subtract $2^5 = 32$ from our number 45, yielding 13. With this remainder, we repeat the process, identifying $2^3 = 8$ and subtracting that to find 5 as a new remainder. Continuing the process, we identify $2^2 = 4$ with a new remainder of 1, and finally $2^0 = 1$, yielding a remainder of 0. Going back to our accounting, we have found

$$\left(1\times2^{5}\right)+\left(1\times2^{3}\right)+\left(1\times2^{2}\right)+\left(1\times2^{0}\right)=45_{10}$$

For the binary equivalent, we need to fill in with the zeros with the result 101101_2.

Another method is called *successive division*. A trivial example is converting 6,378 from decimal to decimal! Divide it by the number base, 10, and keep the remainder, 8. Divide the result again, keeping the remainder, 6. As you complete that process, your remainders will be 8, 7, 3, 6. Reversing that order, we have our original number. Not a surprise. Now, let's apply that to our simple decimal number, 45.

1. 45, divide by 2, 22, remainder 1
2. 22, divide by 2, 11, remainder 0
3. 11, divide by 2, 5, remainder 1
4. 5, divide by 2, 2, remainder 1
5. 2, divide by 2, 1, remainder 0
6. 1, divide by 2, 0, remainder 1

Reverse the order of the remainders, and we get 101101_2, the binary equivalent!

Finally, for our example, let's convert our approximate Earth radius to binary using successive approximation:

1. $6{,}378-2^{12} = 2{,}282$
2. $2{,}282-2^{11} = 234$
3. $234-2^7 = 106$
4. $106-2^6 = 42$
5. $26-2^4 = 10$
6. $10-2^3 = 2$
7. $2-2^1 = 0$

Noting the contributions with 1's and filling in with 0's, we get 1100011011010_2.

The *octal* and *hexadecimal* (often abbreviated as "hex") number bases are commensurate[2] with binary (8 and 16 are integer exponents of 2). These are exclusively used to communicate binary in a more compact fashion. Early on, there were computers with a 12-bit word length, and rather than write out (or print out) all these binary digits, octal representation was used so that four octal digits could represent one word.[3] As computer technology moved to 16-, 32-, and 64-bit word lengths, all divisible by 4 but not 3, hexadecimal representation became more common and is still used today. Table 2.1 shows the relationships between the three representations. You note immediately that, to represent base-16, six Roman letters are used. Thus, if you see a common "hex" notation like $FFFF_h$, it is equivalent to 1111111111111111_2, and is evidently a much more compact form for documentation.

2.1 NUMERICAL QUANTITIES AS STORED IN THE COMPUTER

Quantities internal to the computer are stored as binary digits and organized in groups. The fundamental grouping is called a *word*. In the early days of digital computers, words were groups of 8, 12, or 16 binary digits, or *bits*. A group of 8 bits is commonly called a *byte*.[4] As computer architectures became more sophisticated, word lengths of 32 and then 64 bits became common. Words in the computer typically represent either instructions or information, and they are of finite length.

2.1.1 INTEGER NUMBERS

Integers, "whole numbers" or numbers without fractional parts, are typically stored in one computer word, and possibly multiple words. Consider a simple

---

[2] Two non-zero real numbers a and b are said to be *commensurate* if their ratio a/b is a rational number (i.e. it is equivalent to the ratio of two integers).

[3] If you are unfamiliar with the concepts of word-length and bits, we discuss them in detail in the next section.

[4] Although it might seem like a "bit" of nerd humor, 4 bits have been dubbed a *nibble*. The term originated from the fact that 4 bits are "half a byte," as byte is a homophone for bite. To add insult to injury, some have adopted an alternative spelling, nybble, to be consistent with the spelling of byte. If, after reading this, you are laughing uncontrollably (as we still do), you could have a future in computing!

TABLE 2.1
Binary, Octal, and Hexadecimal Equivalents

Decimal	Binary	Octal	Hexadecimal
0	0000	0	0
1	0001	1	1
2	0010	2	2
3	0110	3	3
4	0100	4	4
5	0101	5	5
6	0110	6	6
7	0111	7	7
8	1000	10	8
9	1001	11	9
10	1010	12	A
11	1011	13	B
12	1100	14	C
13	1101	15	D
14	1110	16	E
15	1111	17	F
16	10000	20	10
17	10001	21	11

example, the 8-bit byte. We can represent all the possible binary numbers in a table from 00000000_2 to 11111111_2:

```
00000000
00000001
00000010
00000011
   •
   •
   •
11111101
11111110
11111111
```

Although it should be obvious to you, we will mention that there isn't any room for additional digits—we are restricted to 8. Now, we pose a question: What happens when we add 1 to the last number in the table? The result is 00000000_2. You might wonder about the 1 that was carried out of that addition, but there is no room for that. It has been said that it goes into the proverbial *bit bucket*. So, apparently, we added 1 to 11111111_2 and obtained 00000000_2. That means, taking signs into account, that 11111111_2 is equivalent to −1, and that opens the door to defining negative integers—that is, they have a 1 in the leading position.

Another convenient way of illustrating this is shown in Figure 2.1. Numbers on the left side of the circle are considered negative, and those on the right positive.

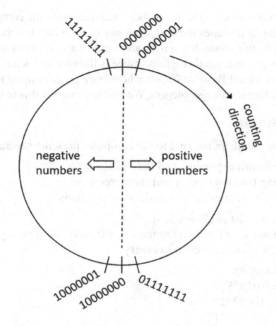

FIGURE 2.1 The number circle for a byte.

The only awkward consequence of this arrangement is at the bottom of the circle. Since we have an even number of binary arrangements, $2^8 = 256$, taking out 00000000_2, there is one left over, 10000000_2, which is self-negative (i.e. adding it to itself yields zero). By convention, since it has a leading 1, we consider it to be negative. Then, by converting to decimal, we see that our range of integers is from -128 to $+127$. This is called the *2's complement* representation of integers.

To generalize this concept, if the word length is n, here 8, then the integer range is -2^{n-1} to $+2^{n-1}-1$. This leads to Table 2.2, which shows the 2's complement integer range for different word lengths. For many computing software systems, the 32-bit and 64-bit word lengths, often called *short integer* (or simply *integer*) and *long integer*, respectively, are used and available to the programmer. In deciding between the two, the programmer needs to consider the range required for the application at hand.

TABLE 2.2
2's Complement Integer Range for Different Word Lengths

Word	Range		
Length	Low	High	
8	−128	127	
16	−32,768	32,767	"short integer"
32	−2,147,483,648	2,147,483,647	"long integer"

The long integer has a much wider range, but it requires twice the computer memory. Python is different. It allocates the computer words necessary to represent the integer at hand and, in this sense, has a *dynamic range* for integers of any magnitude. This removes the concern whether a finite range is limiting and is an advantage over languages such as Visual Basic or C/C++ where extra programming must be implemented when dealing with large integers. We will see more of this in Chapter 3.

2.1.2 REAL NUMBERS

Representing real numbers internal to the computer presents several challenges:

- how to deal with exponents and their range
- representing fractional parts and their precision
- lack of precise representation of decimal fractions

Let us deal with the last challenge first.

The conversion factor from feet to meters is 0.3048. To represent this fraction in the computer, we will convert it to binary:

$0.3048-2^{-2} = 0.0548$
$0.0548-2^{-5} = 0.02355$
$0.02355-2^{-6} = 0.007925$
$0.007925-2^{-7} = 0.0001125$
$0.0001125-2^{-14} = 0.00005146484375$

.
.

To this point, the binary fraction is 0.01001110000001..., but, apparently, the conversion would keep going. This illustrates an important point—*it is not possible to represent many (or in fact, most) decimal fractions with a binary fraction with finite digits*. Hence, the precision of the conversion will depend on the number of binary digits used. For example, the exact decimal number, 0.1, cannot be represented precisely in binary. That is, whereas 0.1 can be expressed exactly with a finite number of decimal digits, it cannot be represented exactly with a finite number of binary digits.

Considering scientific notation with decimal numbers, we have integer exponents of 10. We can then directly consider a range of binary equivalents. So, for example, if we allocate a byte for the exponent of a number, that will allow a range of 10^{-128} to 10^{127}, if the binary integers are represented in 2's complement format. For most engineering and scientific applications, that would be enough. Consequently, a decision must be made regarding how many binary digits to allocate for the exponent of a real number.

The last challenge relates to the precision of the stored number, which depends on the number of binary digits allocated. In the early days of digital computers, several different formats were used to store real numbers. Happily, over time, a common standard now called *IEEE 754 double-precision* is used by most computing systems, both in floating-point circuitry and software programs. A real number is stored in a 64-bit word (8 bytes) according to the layout illustrated in Figure 2.2.

The first bit is used to indicate the sign of the number, 0 for + and 1 for −. The exponent field of 11 bits is not laid out according to 2's complement but rather as shown in Table 2.3. This arrangement is called a *biased exponent*. In a way, it is like rotating the number circle in Figure 2.1. The range of exponents is then

$$2^{-1022} \cong 2.23 \times 10^{-308} \qquad \leftrightarrow \qquad 2^{1023} \cong 8.99 \times 10^{307}$$

or approximately 10^{-308} to 10^{307}. This is a more-than-ample range for most engineering and scientific calculations. Figure 2.3 illustrates how real numbers are represented on the real number line. Note the two gaps between the smallest positive and negative numbers and zero. In computer science, this is called the *hole at zero*.

The final part of the real number layout is the actual number or *mantissa*. In binary exponential notation, all numbers can be represented as

$$\pm \, mantissa \cdot 2^{exponent}$$

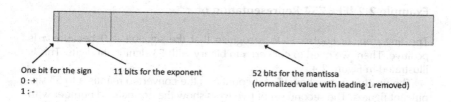

One bit for the sign
0 : +
1 : −

11 bits for the exponent

52 bits for the mantissa
(normalized value with leading 1 removed)

FIGURE 2.2 Layout of IEEE 754 standard for storage of real numbers.

TABLE 2.3
Biased Exponent Representation

Binary	Decimal Equivalent
11111111110	1,023
11111111101	1,022
•	•
10000000000	1
01111111111	0
01111111110	−1
•	•
00000000010	−1,021
00000000001	−1,022

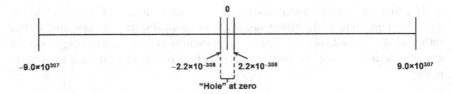

FIGURE 2.3   IEEE 754 representation of the real number line.

The mantissa can always be normalized with a leading 1 before the *binary point*. For example, to represent the number $(21.375)_{10}$, it would first be converted to binary $(10101.011)_2$, then it would be normalized to $(1.0101011 \times 2^4)_2$.

Because the mantissas of all numbers have 1 as their first digit (except 0 of course), the IEEE 754 format does not store that leading 1—it is just understood. The remaining 52 bits are used to represent the fraction to the right of the binary point. The number of unique binary numbers that can be represented is then $1.11\ldots11_2$ or $2^{54}-1$, which is approximately equal to 1.8×10^{16}. This implies that a real number can be stored with a precision of approximately one part in 10^{16} or to 16 significant digits. Again, this is more than adequate for most computations.

Example 2.2 IEEE 754 Representation of π

The first step, of course, is to recognize that the sign bit is 0 because π is positive. Then, we need to convert π to binary with 53 significant digits. This is illustrated in Figure 2.4.

The first two rows show the bit count and the converted mantissa to 53 significant figures. The second set of two rows show the normalized number with

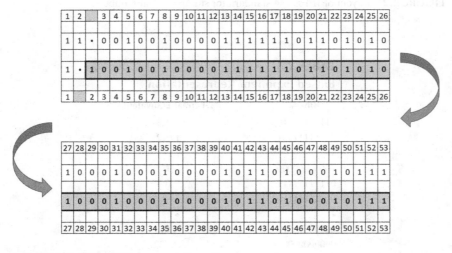

FIGURE 2.4   IEEE 754 representation of π.

the binary point shifted one position to the left and its bit count. The stored mantissa is boxed in. The exponent then is 2^1, so the biased exponent field would be 10000000000_2, taken from Table 2.3.

It is likely that you will never have to deal with the details of real number representation in the IEEE 745 format, but it is important that you understand the limitations in terms of range and precision.

2.2   HOW THE COMPUTER STORES TEXT

Internal storage of text or *string* information is very important since many computer applications deal with manipulation of such data (e.g. names or identification numbers that are not used in calculations). Although engineers and scientists may be more concerned with numerical data, it is important to know the basics of storing and manipulating strings. Happily, there has been a well-established standard for representing and storing text for decades. It is the ASCII code ("askey," American Standard Code for Information Interchange) and uses one byte to store each character. Tables 2.4 shows the ASCII codes for each text character.

For example, this is how the string "Yes" would be stored,

Y	e	s
59_h	65_h	73_h

It is important to note that the amount of memory required to store a text string is variable depending on its length. Also, the amount of memory can be substantial, as 8 bits are used to represent a single character.

2.3   BOOLEAN TRUE/FALSE INFORMATION

Boolean data are directly compatible with computer architecture, since only two states, True and False, need to be represented. The naive approach would be to do this with a single binary digit or bit. However, that does not fit well with computer architecture, which is organized in bytes and words. Consequently, it is common to use a wasteful scheme to represent a Boolean quantity, and that is to use an integer number 0 for False and 1 for True. If this is a "short" integer, requiring 32 bits, that means only the last digit is meaningful, and the other 31 are just set to zero.

Given this scheme, a Boolean quantity can be checked by testing whether it is equal to 1 or 0. However, it is typical for programming systems to have defined Boolean constants called True and False. In this way, there is no need to understand the equivalency between the words and the numbers.

TABLE 2.4
ASCII Codes for Standard Text Characters

Dec	Hex	Character	Description	Dec	Hex	Character	Dec	Hex	Character	Dec	Hex	Character
0	0	NUL	null	32	20	Space	64	40	@	96	60	`
1	1	SOH	start of heading	33	21	!	65	41	A	97	61	a
2	2	STX	start of text	34	22	"	66	42	B	98	62	b
3	3	ETX	end of text	35	23	#	67	43	C	99	63	c
4	4	EOT	end of transmission	36	24	$	68	44	D	100	64	d
5	5	ENQ	enquiry	37	25	%	69	45	E	101	65	e
6	6	ACK	acknowledge	38	26	&	70	46	F	102	66	f
7	7	BEL	bell	39	27	'	71	47	G	103	67	g
8	8	BS	backspace	40	28	(	72	48	H	104	68	h
9	9	TAB	horizontal tab	41	29	)	73	49	I	105	69	i
10	A	LF	NL: line feed, new line	42	2A	*	74	4A	J	106	6A	j
11	B	VT	vertical tab	43	2B	+	75	4B	K	107	6B	k
12	C	FF	NP: form feed, new page	44	2C	,	76	4C	L	108	6C	l
13	D	CR	carriage return	45	2D	-	77	4D	M	109	6D	m
14	E	SO	shift out	46	2E	.	78	4E	N	110	6E	n
15	F	SI	shift in	47	2F	/	79	4F	O	111	6F	o
16	10	DLE	data link escape	48	30	0	80	50	P	112	70	p
17	11	DC1	device control 1	49	31	1	81	51	Q	113	71	q
18	12	DC2	device control 2	50	32	2	82	52	R	114	72	r
19	13	DC3	device control 3	51	33	3	83	53	S	115	73	s
20	14	DC4	device control 4	52	34	4	84	54	T	116	74	t
21	15	NAK	negative acknowledge	53	35	5	85	55	U	117	75	u
22	16	SYN	synchronous idle	54	36	6	86	56	V	118	76	v
23	17	ETB	end of transmission block	55	37	7	87	57	W	119	77	w
24	18	CAN	cancel	56	38	8	88	58	X	120	78	x
25	19	EM	end of medium	57	39	9	89	59	Y	121	79	y
26	1A	SUB	substitute	58	3A	:	90	5A	Z	122	7A	z
27	1B	ESC	escape	59	3B	;	91	5B	[	123	7B	{
28	1C	FS	file separator	60	3C	<	92	5C	\	124	7C		
29	1D	GS	group separator	61	3D	=	93	5D	]	125	7D	}
30	1E	RS	record separator	62	3E	>	94	5E	^	126	7E	~
31	1F	US	unit separator	63	3F	?	95	5F	_	127	7F	DEL

2.4 COMPUTER STORAGE EVOLUTION AND TERMINOLOGY

Since the early days of digital computers, there has been an amazing evolution of storage technology. Early computer memories were based on the use of tiny magnetic cores, like donuts, through which four thin wires were strung. To store a 1, the core was magnetized, and to store a zero, it was demagnetized. A common size for a memory bank was 2^{12} or 4,096 12-bit words or 49,152 cores. In their era, the cost for such memory was about \$1/word or \$4,000 for one memory unit. Today, a two terabyte USB "thumb" drive can be purchased for \$40, and sizes continue to increase with costs decreasing.

To carry on this comparison, we need to understand some storage terminology. This is summarized in Table 2.5. The reduction in memory cost is phenomenal, amounting to a reduction by a factor of more than 10^{10}! Do note that the common terminology for computer storage is often (slightly) misunderstood. A megabyte (Mb) is not a million bytes, but about a million, and so forth.

There is more to it than just these numbers. In the early days, computer memory was so small and expensive that programming techniques often focused on using memory sparingly and carefully. In today's world, these techniques have largely disappeared since storage is so large and economical. The landscape of computer storage has changed dramatically.

TABLE 2.5
Computer Storage Terminology and Size

Term	Size
Bit	1 binary digit
Byte	8 bits
Kilobyte (kb)	$2^{10} = 1,024$ bytes
Megabyte (Mb)	$2^{20} = 1,048,576$ bytes
Gigabyte (Gb)	$2^{30} \cong 1.074 \times 10^9$ bytes
Terabyte (Tb)	$2^{40} \cong 1.1 \times 10^{12}$ bytes

PROBLEMS

2.1 Express the following base-10 numbers in binary.
(a) 18191 (b) 5389 (c) 66.3125

2.2 Convert the following binary numbers to decimal.
(a) 01001101 (b) 1110001101 (c) 1000.111

2.3 Express the following base-10 numbers in base-8, octal.
(a) 87 (b) 29 (c) 53

2.4 Conversions between binary, octal, and decimal systems.
(a) Convert the following binary numbers to octal.
011101000010 110101100001

(b) Convert the following binary numbers to hexadecimal.
1001110100001001 1111010110000100

(c) Convert the following hexadecimal numbers to binary.
ACDC F2D1

2.5 Express your age (or another age of your choice over 18) in **(a)** decimal, **(b)** binary, **(c)** octal, and **(d)** hexadecimal.

2.6 Using binary arithmetic, compute the following additions:
(a) $101 + 011$ **(b)** $0011 + 1001 + 0101$

2.7 Using binary subtraction, compute the following subtractions:
(a) $1010 - 0101$ **(b)** $11000 - 00111$

2.8 Repeat Prob. 2.7 but perform the subtractions by adding the 2's complement of the subtrahend. Use 8-bit integer representation.

2.9 Using binary arithmetic, compute the following product: 111011×1011

2.10 Using binary arithmetic, carry out the following long divisions:
(a) $101 \overline{)\, 101101}$ **(b)** $11 \overline{)\, 100100}$

2.11 Employ 2's-complement 8-bit integers to compute the negative of
(a) 01011010   **(b)** 11110000

2.12 Show the IEEE 745 binary layout for the following decimal quantities.
(a) 6.626196×10^{-27} (Planck's constant)
(b) 6.02252×10^{23} (Avogadro's number)

2.13 Compute the number of bytes and bits for the hard disk storage of your laptop computer.

2.14 Early in school, you undoubtedly learned about the primary colors: red, blue, and yellow and that there were three secondary colors, orange, green, and violet that are created by the addition of pairs of the primary colors (orange = red + yellow). Computers represent colors differently as they deal with the mixture of light. Thus, the three primary colors for computers, televisions, and electronics are red, green, and blue. This is called the *RGB color model,* standing for red, green, and blue. As depicted in Table P2.14, the secondary colors are yellow, magenta, and cyan. The RGB model is an additive model, meaning that colors are created through light waves that are added together in particular combinations in order to produce colors.

TABLE P2.14

The RGB Color Model Indicating the Mixtures of the Primary Colors that Yield the Secondary Colors

	R	G	B
R	Red	Yellow	Magenta
G		Green	Cyan
B			Blue

As with everything within the computer, colors are represented by a code. The color code for RGB uses a six-digit combination of hexadecimal numbers and letters preceded by a hash mark. Each pair of hexadecimal digits represents the mix of red, green, and blue (RGB) with the magnitude of each pair indicating the intensity of each color. For example, pure blue would be represented by #0000FF. Because we are "decimal" animals, the hexadecimal code is often expressed as a decimal RGB code for better human understanding and communication. Because FF_h corresponds to 255_{10}, the code for blue could be expressed in base-10 as

#0000FF ↔ RGB(0, 0, 255)

(a) Convert the code for pink (#FFC0CB) to the RGB code.

(b) To convince yourself of the usefulness of hexadecimal, convert the code for pink to the equivalent binary code.

Convert the following Hex codes to RGB codes and guess what colors they represent:

(c) #000000

(d) #FFFFFF

(e) #00FFFF

(f) #A020F0 (hint: Elvis and Prince loved this color)

If you would like to learn more about the fascinating topic of color mixing, check out https://en.wikipedia.org/wiki/Color_mixing. (Last edited date May 18, 2022.)

3 Python Basics

CHAPTER OBJECTIVES

- Gain familiarity with the features of the Spyder integrated development environment, including the IPython Console, the Spyder Editor, and the Explorer window.
- Learn how to implement algebraic expressions in Python, including those with logarithmic, exponential, trigonometric, and hyperbolic terms.
- Create variables and use them in Python computations. Track their properties and stored values in the Variable Explorer.
- Learn about objects, and their attributes and methods. Also, become familiar with data types, including integers, floating-point, Boolean and strings.
- Use the arithmetic, relational and logical operators, and understand their precedence in establishing the order of calculations.
- Learn about the various collections in Python with special attention given to lists, tuples and arrays.
- Create simple, well-presented plots in Python with the `pylab` module, including scatter and line plots with multiple data sets, legends and titles.
- Learn ways to input data and display results in Python, including the use of the IPython Console and external files.
- Practice using the various sources of help for the Spyder IDE, Python and its support modules, including NumPy and SciPy.

Python is a general-purpose programming language developed in the late 1990s by the Dutch programmer, *Guido van Rossum*. It emphasizes many desirable features including *code readability* which facilitates the creation of clear, logical programs. Because of such features as well as its comprehensiveness and sound design, it consistently ranks as one of the most popular programming languages for STEM[1] applications.

The current version of the Python language, Python 3, is widely available at no cost as an open-source software package. Python has broad capabilities as an object-oriented language and is supplemented by many modular packages that contain well-tested subprograms to assist with computing tasks without "reinventing the wheel." Python programs can be developed with a simple text editor and executed with elementary "command window" statements. Because that is a very "unfriendly" way to go about programming, several software products, called *integrated development environments* (*IDEs*), have been developed. We have selected one of these, IPython in the Spyder environment, for this text. It is a common choice for engineers and scientists for numerical problem solving

---

[1] Science, Technology, Engineering and Mathematics.

DOI: 10.1201/9781003256861-3

and has many features to facilitate program development, debugging, documentation and "help" access to important supplementary modules.

Python, its supporting modules, and the IDEs are subject to periodic revision and improvement. Consequently, with the passage of time, it is likely that you will have access to more recent versions. The changes that occur as new versions arise are generally incremental and backward compatible[2]; so, you should be able to adapt easily given the information and examples presented here.

Python has many features and capabilities that are not focused on engineering and scientific computations. It would be possible to expand this chapter and subsequent chapters significantly to encompass a broad coverage of Python. An outcome of such an expansion would be to drown you in details that, although perhaps interesting and necessary to paint a complete picture, are not essential to our purpose here. We do appreciate the interests of students to learn more about Python and suggest they seek out materials and courses in computer science or on the Internet that provide this. For now, let's get to the task at hand.

3.1   THE SPYDER/IPYTHON ENVIRONMENT[3]

To proceed, you first need to install the Spyder/IPython IDE on your computer. We suggest strongly that you do that before proceeding. This IDE is typically obtained by installing the *Anaconda software package*. Anaconda includes access to other open-source software packages and interfaces, such as RStudio and R for applied statistics. Information on acquiring Anaconda can be obtained via the Internet at the URL, https://www.anaconda.com/distribution/.

After installing and launching Anaconda, you will see an interface that provides an icon for Spyder. Versions are updated periodically, so it's likely that the version number you see will be higher than the one shown below.

Spyder

5.1.5
Scientific PYthon Development
EnviRonment. Powerful Python IDE with
advanced editing, interactive testing,
debugging and introspection features

Launch

---

[2] *Backward* (or *downward*) *compatibility* is a property of a computer language that allows programs written in an older version to be implemented without modification in a newer version.

[3] The best way to "read" this chapter is to "do" this chapter. That is, complete all the illustrations in the Spyder IDE as you work your way through this chapter.

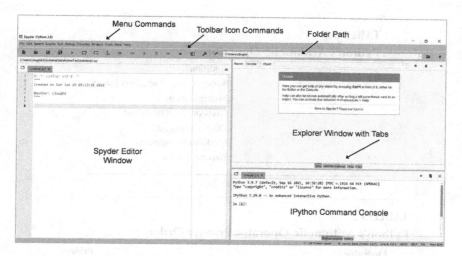

FIGURE 3.1 The Spyder interface.

Once Spyder has been launched the first time, it will be available for direct launch, bypassing the Anaconda interface, and a Spyder command icon can be added to your operating system:

The Spyder interface can be customized to different layouts, color schemes, etc., but the default presentation with a white background is shown in. Figure 3.1

For the purposes of this chapter, we will first be typing commands into the IPython Console window. Further orientation for the IDE can be obtained via the tutorial referenced in the Explorer window. In Section 3.7, we will enter code into the Editor window and run it from there.

The calculator mode for Python operates in a sequential fashion as you type in commands line by line. For each command, you get a result. Thus, you can think of it as a fancy calculator. For example, if you type in

```
In [1]: 55-16
```

the Console will display the result[4]

```
Out[1]: 39
```

Most calculations will involve *arithmetic operators*. These are included in *arithmetic expressions*. The arithmetic operators in Python are shown in Table 3.1.

---

[4] The IPython Console will automatically number the lines in sequence with the prompt `In[n]:` and produce the result with the matching `Out[n]:`. A blank line will be inserted after the result line. As needed, you can copy results from the Console and paste them into another document, e.g. Microsoft Word or PowerPoint.

TABLE 3.1

Python's Arithmetic Operators

+	Addition
−	Subtraction and negation (unary)
*	Multiplication
/	Division (floating point)
//	Division (integer)
%	Modulus (remainder)
**	Exponentiation

TABLE 3.2

Python's Arithmetic Operator Priority Order

Operator	Priority
**	Highest
− (unary minus)	.
*, /, //, %	.
+, − (subtraction)	Lowest

Note: The *unary minus operator* is used to indicate a negative number. For example: −53.76 means "negative fifty-three point seven six." The *binary subtraction operator* is used to indicate the subtraction of one number from another. For example: 55 − 16.

When these are combined in an expression to calculate a result, there is a priority order by which they are evaluated as summarized in Table 3.2.

Expressions are evaluated from left to right, except for repeated exponentiation which is from right to left. Parentheses are used to alter the order. The following examples are instructive.

```
0.5 ** 2 / 3 * 5 + 1.2
```

The calculation steps would be

```
0.5 ** 2 ⇨ 0.25
0.25 / 3 ⇨ 0.0833...
0.0833... * 5 ⇨ 0.4166...
0.4166... + 1.2 ⇨ 1.6166...
```

You might be tempted to think that the 5 is in the denominator, but following the left-to-right process, you can see that it is not. If we wanted the 5 to be in the denominator, there are two ways to accomplish that:

```
0.5 ** 2 / (3 * 5) + 1.2    or    0.5 ** 2 / 3 / 5 + 1.2
```

In the first case on the left, the denominator multiplication (3 * 5) is highest priority because of the parentheses. In the second case, because of left-to-right order, 0.25 is divided by 3 and then divided again by 5. Some programmers prefer the first case because it clearly sets off the denominator and relates well to the algebraic version,

$$\frac{0.5^2}{3\cdot5}+1.2$$

but either is valid.

The following example also brings the priorities into focus.

```
-3 ** 2 ⇨ -9
```

Here, since exponentiation (**) has the highest priority, that occurs first. Then, negation is carried out with the unary minus (–). This example is worth illustrating because you may find this priority switched in different software programs. For example, that is the case for the Excel spreadsheet where the unary minus has higher priority than exponentiation.

The third example illustrates the priority order of repeated exponentiation.

```
3 ** 2 ** 1.5 ⇨ ≅ 22.361...
```

The first operation is 2 ** 1.5 ⇨ ≅ 2.828... since repeated exponentiation is processed right to left. And then 3 ** 2.828... is carried out. If we consider the algebraic representation,

$$3^{2^{1.5}}$$

we might normally assume that $2^{1.5}$ would be computed first; so, Python follows this interpretation. However, you must be aware that this order is not common to other software programs. Of course, if you wanted the 3^2 to be calculated first, you could enforce that with parentheses, as in

```
(3 ** 2) ** 1.5
```

In any case, if you ever have questions or doubts about the priority of operations, you can determine that by trying a few test cases. Then, if you have further doubts, you can avoid these by using parentheses.

There are two arithmetic operators that may be less familiar to you. These are integer divide, //, and modulus, %. Here is an example of *integer division*:

```
12.435 // 2.9 ⇨ 4.0
```

Regular or *floating point division* would yield a value 4.28... Integer division carries out floating-point division and then truncates (or chops off) the fractional part of the result. It is a fine point right now but note the decimal point in the result, which indicates that the result is actually a floating-point number with a zero fractional part.

The *modulus* (also called the *modulo*) *operator* returns the remainder of the integer quotient divided into the dividend. That is, carrying out the division to obtain the quotient, then taking only the integer part of that value, multiplying it by the divisor and subtracting the result from the dividend to obtain the remainder. Following the above example,

```
12.435 % 2.9 ⇨ 0.835
```

Careful with the interpretation here. This is obviously not the remainder of floating-point division: 0.28... It is the result of 2.9*4 subtracted from 12.435, where 4 is the integer part of the quotient. The modulus operator is most often used with integer calculations where the interpretation is simpler. In this case, the result is just the remainder of integer division. For example, if we want to determine whether an integer is odd or even, we can employ modulus 2, and if the result is zero, the number is even—if it is one, the number is odd. For example,

```
1243 % 2 ⇨ 1 and 1244 % 2 ⇨ 0
```

You will note here that, since the two numbers are not entered with a decimal point, the results are integers with no decimal point.

One of the most common constants used in engineering and scientific calculations is pi (π). Some software packages provide pi directly for use. Python does not. To obtain a built-in value of pi, one must invoke a supporting module. There are two common modules that provide this value: Math and NumPy. We will introduce NumPy later in this chapter. For now, if you include the import math statement in your Console commands, pi will be available as follows:

```
import math
math.pi
3.141592653589793
```

With π available, here to 16 significant figures, a calculation using it, such as computing the volume of a sphere of radius 5, can be carried out.

```
4/3 * math.pi * 5**3 ⇨ 523.598...
```

As summarized in Table 3.3, other constants, such as the base of the Napierian logarithm *e* (also known as *Euler's number*), are available. Although most are not commonly used in mathematical expressions, they are sometimes displayed as the result of a calculation. For example, recalling our discussion of real numbers in Section 2.1.2, the maximum floating-point number for a 64-bit computer is on the order of $1 \cdot 10^{308}$. Therefore,

```
2*1e308 ⇨ inf
```

TABLE 3.3
Python's Built-in Constants

Name	Symbol	Definition	Value	Python
Pi	π	Ratio of circle's circumference to its diameter	3.14159265358979...	math.pi
Euler's number	e	Base of the natural logarithm	2.71828182845905...	math.e
Infinity	∞	Value that is boundless		math.inf
Not a number		Value that is not numeric		math.nan

3.2 MATHEMATICAL FUNCTIONS

In Chapter 1, we introduced the various math functions that appear regularly in engineering and scientific calculations. It is important for you to know how to invoke those functions in Python. First, there are a few available directly in Python. Two that we use frequently are absolute value, abs(•), and rounding, round (•).

The *absolute value function* operates on real numbers as we might suspect.

abs(-5) ⇨ 5 and abs(5) ⇨ 5

It also operates on a complex number and produces the magnitude, as in

$$|a + jb| = \sqrt{a^2 + b^2}$$

An example is

abs(-6+4j) ⇨ 7.211...

Notice how a complex quantity is represented in Python with the j symbol following the number for the imaginary part.

Here are examples of the round:

round(4.5) ⇨ 4 and round(3.5) ⇨ 4

Note that this function follows the convention, round 0.5 to even, that we discussed in Chapter 1.

There is an optional additional argument for rounding to *n* digits to the right of the decimal point that we illustrate here:

round(math.pi, 5) ⇨ 3.14159 and round(1250.33,-2) ⇨ 1300.0

Here, you will see that a positive rounding place applies to decimal fractions, a negative value to places to the left of the decimal point, and if *n* is zero, the

---

TABLE 3.4

Trigonometric and Hyperbolic Functions in the Math Module

Trigonometric		Hyperbolic	
sin(•)	asin(•)	sinh(•)	asinh(•)
cos(•)	acos(•)	cosh(•)	acosh(•)
tan(•)	atan(•)	tanh(•)	atanh(•)

---

number is rounded to the nearest integer. Also, in the second example, the round is not to even because the decimal fraction moves the value above 1,250 slightly.

As we move into exponential, logarithmic, trigonometric, and hyperbolic functions, again, we need to import these from a module. We will illustrate the *Math module* here.

```
math.exp(1)  ⇨ 2.718... and math.log(math.e)  ⇨ 1.0
```

The first example shows that exp (1) equals the Napierian *e*, and the second example illustrates that the log (•) function is the natural logarithm. Is there a base-10 logarithm?

```
math.log10(1000)  ⇨ 3.0
```

Yes, there is. The log(,•) function can also be used to determine the logarithm to an arbitrary base, here for base 2:

```
math.log(8192,2)  ⇨ 13.0
```

It is worth mentioning the math.sqrt(•) function as it is also used frequently.

Table 3.4 summarizes the trigonometric and hyperbolic functions available from the Math module.

The direct trigonometric functions, e.g. sin(•), require radians as the argument, and the inverse trig functions, e.g. asin(•), produce results in radians. Although it is fairly simple to convert back and forth between radians and degrees, the Math module does provide two functions for this.

```
math.degrees(1)  ⇨ 57.295... and math.radians(60)  ⇨ 1.047...
```

Example 3.1 Calculating the Great Circle Distance between Two Points on the Earth

An interesting navigational problem is to determine the shortest distance between two points on the Earth's surface. This shortest path can be determined using the mathematical concept of a *Great Circle*. This is a circle on

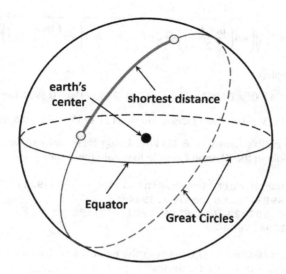

FIGURE 3.2 A Great Circle indicating the shortest distance between two points on the Earth's surface. Note that the equator is a Great Circle.

a sphere's surface that lies in a plane passing through the sphere's center (Figure 3.2). The path between two points lying along such a Great Circle (in geometry, called the *minimal arc distance*) represents the shortest distance between the two points. Consequently, following the *Great Circle distance* is the preferred route taken by a ship or aircraft.

As you are likely aware, locations on the Earth's surface are given by *latitude* (spherical angle on the polar axis measured from the equator) and *longitude* (spherical angle on the equator measured from the Prime Meridian at Greenwich, England). By convention, longitude angles west of the meridian are positive, and those east are negative. Latitude angles north of the equator are positive, and those south are negative.

In this example, we would like to calculate the distance between London, England, and Sydney, Australia. Only recently have airplanes made this trip without stops. First, we need to find the locations.

London, England – Heathrow Airport   51.4700°N, 0.4543°W
Sydney, Australia – Kingsford Smith Airport –33.9399°S, 151.1753°E

Notice that given our sign conventions, Heathrow's angles will be positive and Sydney's negative.

The formula used to compute the minimal arc distance is[5]

---

[5] It is interesting to study the derivation of this formula using spherical trigonometry. We do not take the time and space to do that here; however, there are many references available. One is Aviation Formulary V1.46 (edwilliams.org). There are also more complex formulas that account for the oblate (squashed) nature of the Earth, but there is little effect on the distance calculation with errors of about 0.05%.

$$d = 2\sin^{-1}\left(\sqrt{\left(\sin\left(\frac{lt_1 - lt_2}{2}\right)\right)^2 + \cos(lt_1)\cos(lt_2)\left(\sin\left(\frac{ln_1 - ln_2}{2}\right)\right)^2}\right) r \quad (3.1)$$

For our example,

$$lt_1 = 51.4700° \cong 0.8983 \text{ radians} \quad lt_2 = -33.9399° \cong -0.5924 \text{ radians}$$

$$ln_1 = 0.4543° \cong 0.007929 \text{ radians} \quad ln_2 = -151.1753° \cong -2.6385 \text{ radians}$$

and r = the earth's radius ($\cong$ 6,371 km). Using these values, we create this lengthy formula in the IPython Console to obtain the result.

```
2*math.asin(math.sqrt((math.sin((0.8983-(-0.5924))/2))**2 + \
math.cos(0.8983)*math.cos(-0.5924) * \
(math.sin((0.007929-(-2.6385))/2))**2))*6371
⇨ 17019.822798178586
```

The calculated distance is 17,020 km to the nearest km. This distance can be verified with various Internet websites.

You will note that there are two backslash (\) characters that allow the continuation of a long expression onto multiple lines, breaking it up to be more readable. The backslash is formally referred to as a *line continuation character*.

In making this calculation with the lengthy expression, it might have occurred to you that it would be more convenient and accurate to include the conversions to radians in our commands, and perhaps we would prefer to break up the calculations in parts to make them more manageable and easier to follow, debug, and verify. The next section addresses these needs.

3.3 VARIABLES AND ASSIGNMENT

When we write formulas and equations, we use symbols to represent the various involved quantities. The formula for the Great Circle distance (Equation 3.1) in the last section is an example of this. It is then natural for us to want to use symbols in our programming statements. This is accomplished using variable names. Values are associated with variable names through the process of assignment. Here is the simplest of examples:

```
a = 5
```

The variable name a represents a location in computer memory where, after the assignment statement executes, the value 5 will be stored. A convenient analog for this process is the mailbox shown in Figure 3.3.

The mailbox itself is the variable name (which corresponds to a memory location). The envelope is the value placed in the mailbox by assignment. If we follow the statement above with

```
a = -4
```

FIGURE 3.3 Mailbox analogy for assignment.

then the 5 envelope will be removed, discarded, and replaced with a -4 envelope.

Once a variable has been defined and assigned a value, it can be examined in the *Variable Explorer window* above the IPython Console. There, if you select the Variable Explorer tab, you will see

Name ▲	Type	Size	
a	int	1	-4

In addition to the variable name and the currently stored value, the type of the value stored, in this case an integer, is noted, and the size (number of items, here 1). As we will see later, it is possible to store collections of data under a variable name. Also, once defined, a variable can then be used in subsequent expressions. For example,

```
math.exp(a) ⇨ 0.01831...
```

What happens if we make the following assignment?

```
A = 12
```

and check the Variable Explorer:

Name ▲	Type	Size	
a	int	1	-4
A	int	1	12

You can see that A and a are distinct mailboxes (variables). Python distinguishes between upper- and lower-case letters. In formal terms, the Python language is *case sensitive.* It is also possible to have other characters than letters in variable names, but a variable name must start with a letter. Here are three examples:

```
b12      c_10       Temperature_Value
```

Most special characters will not work in names. If you are ever in doubt, try one, and you will find out. This is especially true for special characters that are operators, like +, −, *, /, and &. The use of the underscore (_) as shown above is good style for separating words that are part of a variable name.

It is a best practice to use variable names that have meaning to the problem you are solving. Sometimes, this relates to names on a schematic drawing, such as h and w for height and width. On other occasions, a longer, more meaningful name makes matters clearer; however, using many long names becomes intrusive.

You need to be especially careful not to use a name that is a *keyword* in Python. Spyder helps you with this because, either in the IPython Console or in the Editor window, as soon as you type a keyword, it is coded blue. A good example is the Greek letter name lambda, which you will see later is employed to define a user-defined function in shorthand fashion in Python.

Example 3.2 Using Variable Names with the Great Circle Formula

In Example 3.1, the Python expression we constructed from Equation 3.1 to compute the Great Circle distance was lengthy, and it included only numerical values. Most of these were computed separately and essentially copied into the formula. You may have wondered about this when you were entering the expression because it was subject to small errors, and it would be difficult to modify the expression for a different set of locations.

One feature of the IPython Console that is convenient is that you can recall a previously entered expression using the up-arrow key (↑). After the command is recalled, you can edit it, to modify it or to make a correction. Once the change is made, you can press the Enter key from any place in the expression, and it will be executed. And, by the way, if you want to recall a command from several lines prior, just repeat the arrow key until it shows up.

Let's try another distance calculation, but we will assign variables and break down our lengthy formula into "bite-size" pieces.

```
r = 6371
lt1d = 51.4700
lt1 = math.radians(lt1d)
ln1d = 0.4543
ln1 = math.radians(ln1d)
lt2d = -33.9399
lt2 = math.radians(lt2d)
ln2d = -151.1753
ln2 = math.radians(ln2d)
d1 = (math.sin(lt1-lt2)/2)**2
d2 = math.cos(lt1)*math.cos(lt2)*(math.sin((ln1-ln2)/2))**2
d = 2*math.asin(math.sqrt(d1 +d2))*r
```

The last command line assigns the distance result to the variable d. We can observe the value of d in the Variable Explorer, but we can also just enter d in the Console, and the value will be displayed there.

```
d
17019.601897936718
```

Now, suppose that we are interested in the distance between Tokyo and Cape Town.

Tokyo, Japan – Narita Airport   35.7653°N, 140.3856°E
Cape Town, S. Africa – Airport 33.9694°S, 18.5972°E

We can use the up arrow to retrieve the commands necessary to recompute the distance.

```
lt1d = 35.7653
lt1 = math.radians(lt1d)
ln1d = -140.3856
ln1 = math.radians(ln1d)
lt2d = -33.9694
lt2 = math.radians(lt2d)
ln2d = -18.5972
ln2 = math.radians(ln2d)
d1 = math.sin((lt1-lt2)/2)**2
d2 = math.cos(lt1)*math.cos(lt2)*(math.sin((ln1-ln2)/2))**2
d = 2*math.asin(math.sqrt(d1 + d2))*r
d
14780.78626470105
```

Observe that the main expressions computing the distance are unchanged. Oh, and it's still a long way between those locations, 14,780 km. The Variable Explorer is a good tool to observe all the values associated with our computation, as shown in Figure 3.4.

The type of all variables except r is "float" because these numbers have decimal fractional values. The r variable is integer because we made the assignment of 6,371 without a decimal point.

As we will see later, with such multi-step computations, it is more convenient to handle them in the Spyder Editor window.

3.4   OBJECTS, ATTRIBUTES, METHODS, AND DATA TYPES

Python is an object-oriented programming language. This takes some getting used to. All entities in Python are considered, generally, to be *objects*. This includes numbers and variables. In addition to the operations we carry out with variables and numerical

Name ▲	Type	Size	
d	float	1	14780.78626470105
d1	float	1	0.32681621249509624
d2	float	1	0.5137155357056657
ln1	float	1	-2.4501909423877515
ln1d	float	1	-140.3856
ln2	float	1	-0.32458237165188947
ln2d	float	1	-18.5972
lt1	float	1	0.624222242963528
lt1d	float	1	35.7653
lt2	float	1	-0.5928778749269618
lt2d	float	1	-33.9694
r	int	1	6371

FIGURE   3.4 Variable Explorer display.

quantities, we may refer to the object's *attributes* (also called *properties*), and we may invoke *methods* to act upon these objects. You will see many examples of this in this text. The syntax used in relating an object to its attributes or methods is

```
object_name.attribute       object_name.method()
```

The period (.) used above is not our typical decimal point—it separates the object name from what follows. The parentheses after the method name are commonly empty, but they may contain certain specifications or *arguments*. Here are two examples that are relevant to the next chapter:

```
(123456789).bit_length() ⇨ 27

a = 1234567890
a.bit_length() ⇨ 31
```

The bit _ length() *method* determines the number of binary digits (bits) that are required to store the given quantity. You will notice that, when a number (also called a *literal*) is the object, it is enclosed in parentheses. That is not required for a variable name.

Another example extracts the parts of a complex quantity using the `imag` and `real` attributes:

```
(24-0.3j).imag ⇨ -0.3
(24-0.3j).real ⇨ 24.0
```

Here, the parentheses associated with the attribute are not required. Often, we have alternatives between an object-oriented expression, as above, and the use of a built-in function, as shown here:

```
import numpy as np
np.real(24-0.3j) ⇨ 24.0
```

We import the NumPy numerical support module and give it a shortcut name np. You will find that this is a common operation and style for our Python programs. Then, we can use the built-in function `real(•)` to extract the real part of the complex quantity. You will need to become accustomed with both ways of accomplishing such tasks.

As we have moved along, we have seen two numerical data types: integer and float. We have also shown how these can be combined to form the complex number type. In Chapter 2, we discussed how these are stored internally in the computer memory. One interesting feature of Python is that it places no limit on the magnitude of integer quantities and will allocate the amount of memory required to represent those. You can see that above with our use of the `bit _ length()` method.

3.4.1 BOOLEAN TYPE

There are two other types of information that are frequently used in Python. These are the *logical* (or *Boolean*) type and the *character* (or *string*) type. Python has two literal values for the Boolean type, `True` and `False`. We can assign a variable as follows:

```
switch = True
```

Although you may not see it here, `True` is formatted in blue to indicate it is a keyword. If we look at the Variable Explorer,

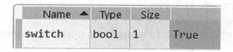

Name ▲	Type	Size	
switch	bool	1	True

you will see that the type of the variable is `bool` (Boolean), and its current value is `True`. Related to Boolean quantities, we can introduce the relational operators as in

TABLE 3.5
Python's Relational Operators

Example	Operator	Relationship
x == 0	==	Equal to
y != x	!=	Not equal to
a > 0	>	Greater than
s < t	<	Less than
3.9 >= a/3	>=	Greater than or equal to
r <= 0	<=	Less than or equal to

TABLE 3.6
Truth Table for Logical Operators

		Highest → Lowest		
x	y	not x	x and y	x or y
T	T	F	T	T
T	F	F	F	T
F	T	T	F	T
F	F	T	F	F

```
math.pi > 22/7 ⇨ False
```

Here, we are posing the True/False question: is π greater than its approximation as 22 sevenths? And, the answer is no, or `False`. The various *relational operators* are given in Table 3.5.

The last four may make immediate sense to you, but pay attention to the first two. We do not check equality (as a True/False test) with just one = sign, but rather two, ==.[6] And we test that the two quantities are not equal with !=. This latter operator varies from one programming language to the next.

In addition to the relational operators, there are *logical operators* that work with one or more Boolean quantity. For example,

```
switch = True
light = False
switch and light ⇨ False
```

A *truth table* showing the results of using these operators is displayed in Table 3.6.

---

[6] In the past, some computer languages (e.g. Superplan in 1951, the first versions of Fortran) used a single equal sign for both assignment and equality. Because this resulted in confusion for programming novices, most commonly-used languages such as Python employ different operators to distinguish between the two.

The not *operator* reverses the sense of its argument. The and *operator* provides a True result only when its two arguments are both True. And the or *operator*'s result is True when either or both of its arguments are True. Just as with the arithmetic operators, there is a precedence order when these operators are combined in an expression. This precedence is indicated Highest → Lowest at the top of the table.

It is common for the relational and logical operators to be combined in an expression. Here is an example

```
not 12 < 8 and -3 > -5
```

How does this work? First, the relational expressions are evaluated:

```
not False and True
```

Then, according to the table, the not operator is evaluated first,

```
True and True
```

and finally, the and operator is evaluated:

```
True
```

Just like arithmetic expressions, the order of these operations can be modified with parentheses. In later chapters, you will see that relational and logical expressions are essential to structured programming.

3.4.2 CHARACTER TYPE

Character (or *string*) data types store text. A string constant is denoted by enclosing it in either single or double quotation marks (' or "). Examples would be

```
'Isaac Newton' "Marie Curie" '123.5'
```

The open and closed marks must be the same – you can't mix them.

One can also assign a string constant to a variable name:

```
switch = 'on'
```

with the Variable Explorer showing

Name ▲	Type	Size	
switch	str	2	on

There are a variety of manipulations, operations, and functions that can be applied to strings. We don't deal with these in great detail here because our emphasis is

TABLE 3.7
String Functions

Len(s)	Number of characters in the string s
Str(x)	Convert the number x to a string
Int(s)	Convert the string s to integer number
Float(s)	Convert the string s to a floating-point number

numerical problem solving. However, there are a few features worth covering. First is *concatenation*, joining strings into longer strings. Here is an example:

```
'on' + 'off' ⇨ 'onoff'
```

A few useful string-related functions are shown in Table 3.7. What if you wanted to extract the first two characters of a string? Characters in a string can be referenced as follows:

```
string[start:stop:step]
```

To extract the first two characters, here is an example:

```
'onoff'[0:2] ⇨ 'on'
```

Note that the index of the first character is zero, and the selection is up to but not including the stop index, 2. For the last three characters, we can use

```
'onoff'[-3:] ⇨ 'off'
```

Indices are also used to select one or more characters in the middle of a string. For example,

```
'onoff'[1:3] ⇨ 'no'
```

That's enough on string data types for now.

3.5 COLLECTIONS OF DATA

In engineering and scientific problem solving, we are often interested in more than one data item, whether it is a number, Boolean or string. It is natural that we would want to associate a variable name with the entire collection. There are several questions that we need to address as we explore this topic:

- Does our collection contain different data types?
- Do we need to be able to manipulate the elements in our collection, add elements, remove them and rearrange them?

TABLE 3.8
Python Representations of Collections of Data

Type	Description	Example
List	A collection of various data types; e.g. using brackets	`[2, False, 'oats', 0.618034]`
Tuple	An immutable list (cannot be extended, shrunk, have elements removed or reassigned); e.g. using parentheses	`(2, False, 'oats', 0.618034)`
Set	An unordered collection of unique objects; e.g. using braces	`{2, False, 'oats', 0.618034}`
Dictionary	A collection of objects, each identified by a key, not a numerical index or subscript; e.g. value pairs within braces	`Fourteeners={'Elbert':4401.2, 'Massive':4398., 'Harvard':4395.6}`
Array	A collection of a single data type indexed by integer subscripts for use in numerical methods and statistical calculations, provided by the NumPy module	See examples below

- If our collection contains just numbers, do we need to be able to manipulate the entire collection mathematically, e.g. multiply all members by a number?

Python provides several alternatives for representing collections of data (Table 3.8). At first, this is confusing, but, for engineering and scientific calculations, we use mainly one of these. Two others come up occasionally, and two do not.

The simplest type of collection is the *list*. It can contain different data types, and its contents have a distinct order (first element, second element, etc.). In defining a list, as shown in the example, brackets are used. Here is an example where the list in the example is assigned to a variable name:

```
mylist = [2, False, 'oats', 0.618034]
```

We can refer to specific members or elements of the list as follows:

```
mylist[0] ⇨ 2
mylist[3] ⇨ 0.618034
```

There are two important observations here. First, brackets, not parentheses, are used following the variable name to refer to a specific element in the list. Second, the first element in the list is indexed zero, not one. This index is often called a *subscript* since it relates to subscripts in typical mathematical notation. Some confusion arises because it is customary in math notation that the first element is indexed as one, not zero. You will have to deal with this over and over in your Python programming.[7] We will introduce more features of subscripting in dealing with arrays.

A *tuple* is a list that is *immutable* (unchangeable). You will note that it is set off with parentheses, not brackets. Once created its elements cannot be changed. Often in Python, a tuple is produced by a function, and, as a result, it wouldn't naturally be changed, but it is typical to extract elements of a tuple, as shown here:

```
mytuple = (2, False, 'oats', 0.618034)
mytuple[2] ⇨ 'oats'
```

We won't spend time on the *set* and *dictionary* collections here. You may find them useful for general Python applications but less so in engineering and scientific problem solving.

The *array* is the central collection type you will see in this book. This is provided by the NumPy module in what is called a *class* named *ndarray*. The array must contain only elements of the same type. It can be created from a list or a tuple using the array function or constructor from NumPy. See these two examples:

```
import numpy as np
x = np.array([2.3, -4, 23.45, 5.6, -14.77])
y = np.array((1, 2, 3, 4, 5))
```

and how the x and y variables are denoted in the Variable Explorer:

Name ▲	Type	Size	
x	Array of float64	(5,)	[2.3 -4. 23.45 5.6 -14.77]
y	Array of int32	(5,)	[1 2 3 4 5]

You will notice how we use a convenient abbreviation of numpy to np with the import statement. The statement creating the x array converts a list into an array. The second item in the list shows as an integer, but it is converted (or elevated) into a floating-point number in the x array, and thus shows as -4. in the Variable Explorer. The type of the array is float64 where the 64 refers to the number of *binary digits* (*bits*) used to store each number (recall Section 2.1.2). Notice that the size is now given as (5,). The reason for the comma (,) is that an array can have two dimensions, often interpreted in matrix terminology as rows and columns. The statement that creates the y array converts a tuple into an array. The type is int32, meaning integer with each number stored with 32 bits. It is an integer array because all elements in the tuple are integers.

---

[7] This is also the case for the C/C++ programming language, but not for the MATLAB® software. When it comes to the VBA programming language associated with Microsoft Excel, zero-based indexing is the default, but it is possible to shift that to one-based with a simple declaration statement.

Just as with lists and tuples, we can refer to individual elements in an array with subscripts, as in

```
x[2]  ⇨ 23.45
```

Again, we note the zero-based indexing.

At this point, it is timely to introduce another feature about subscripts. This is the use of the colon (:). It is employed to specify a range of subscripts. A first example is

```
y[1:3]  ⇨ array([2, 3])
```

Notice that the result appears to be the second and third element of the y array. Also, in the Console, the result is displayed as an array. We could understand the second element, since the first index is 1 (zero-based indexing again!). But what about this third element? Based on our use of 1:3, we might expect the second through the fourth element. Not so. When we use an index range, i:j, it extracts the ith element (again, remember, zero-based) and up to *but not including* the jth element. You may think that this makes no sense. Welcome to another idiosyncrasy of Python!

The use of the colon can be extended by leaving out one of the indices:

```
x[1:]  ⇨ array([ -4., 23.45, 5.6, -14.77])
y[:3]  ⇨ array([1, 2, 3])
```

In the first example, leaving out the second index means "through the end of the array," so we get the second through the fifth element. In the second example, leaving out the first index indicates "from the beginning of the array," and we get elements 0, 1, and 2. Remember, it is up to but not including the index 3 element. This indexing takes some getting used to. Be patient as understanding comes with practice.

The final feature that will be illustrated with arrays (i.e. for now—there will be more in subsequent chapters) has to do with numerical calculations. Check these examples out.

```
2.3*y  ⇨ array([ 2.3, 4.6, 6.9, 9.2, 11.5])
x*y  ⇨ array([ 2.3, -8., 70.35, 22.4, -73.85])
```

First, you can see that we can multiply arrays by a constant. Of course, we could also divide by a constant. Second, arrays can be multiplied by each other if they contain the same number of elements. This multiplication is called an *array operation* because the multiplications take place item by item. In Chapter 5, we will introduce vector-matrix operations like dot and cross products. Those follow different rules but are just as important.

Operations like this *cannot* be performed with lists or tuples. This pair of examples is also instructive:

```
math.sqrt(x)
TypeError: only size-1 arrays can be converted to Python
scalars
np.sqrt(y) ⇨ array([1., 1.41421356, 1.73205081, 2.,
2.23606798])
```

In the first example, we attempt to use the sqrt function from the Math module to extract the square roots. We get an error because the functions in the Math module cannot be applied to an array, only to a single, or scalar value. For the second example, we use instead the sqrt function from the NumPy module, and it extracts the square roots into a corresponding array. We might expect this because the *ndarray* class is defined within NumPy. Because the functions in the Math module are also available in NumPy, you will find that we use the NumPy functions more frequently in later chapters.

The final feature to be illustrated at this point is the creation of a two-dimensional array from a two-dimensional list. See this example:

```
X = np.array([ [ 1., 2., 3. ], [4., 5., 6.], [7., 8., 9.] ])
X ⇨ array([[1., 2., 3.],
           [4., 5., 6.],
           [7., 8., 9.]])
```

We used an upper-case X here to indicate a matrix. This is not required, just a typical convention. We can interpret the array in terms of rows and columns, here 3×3. To extract an element from the array, we need two indices, both zero-based,

```
X[1,1]  ⇨  5.0
```

Two-dimensional arrays still support mathematical operations, such as

```
np.log10(X)
with the result
array([[0.         , 0.30103   , 0.47712125],
       [0.60205999, 0.69897   , 0.77815125],
       [0.84509804, 0.90308999, 0.95424251]])
```

We will feature two-dimensional arrays frequently later in the text.

3.6   CREATING PLOTS

Python provides the pylab module that allows plots to be created quickly and conveniently. The "parent" module for graphics in Python is *Matplotlib*. We will introduce more features of Matplotlib and its pyplot submodule in later chapters. Many plots created in engineering and scientific problem solving are relatively simple, and pylab serves well to create these. We can include the capabilities of pylab in typical fashion with the statement

```
import pylab as py
```

Here we are defining the abbreviation `py` to use instead of typing `pylab` each time we use its commands.

Engineering and scientific plots are typically created from data or calculated with analytical functions. When there are measured data points, but not an overwhelming number, it is typical to plot these with symbols, formally called *markers*. Occasionally, we will connect these markers with straight lines to aid in pattern recognition. When there are hundreds of data, it is typical to suppress the markers to eliminate clutter and just connect the data points with straight lines. If we are plotting an analytical function, we use many points, often hundreds, and connect these with straight lines to give the appearance of smooth curves. We recommend against using markers in the plotting of analytical functions.

If more than one series is plotted, we are faced with the decision of how to distinguish the series on the plot. For data, different marker styles are available. For lines, we can use different line styles. It is possible to use colors to distinguish markers or lines, but we must be assured that these colors will be replicated in any documents or presentations where the plot appears. If there are more than one series on the plot, it is usually a requirement to include a legend to distinguish them.

We will start with a simple scatter plot of a few data. This begins with creating arrays for our x-axis and y-axis variables.

```
import numpy as np
x = np.array([1.5, 2.6, 4.3, 6.7, 9.9])
y = np.array([25.7, 12.9, 17.6, -3.4, 7.7])
```

This is the command to create the plot:

```
py.scatter(x, y)
```

The plot is visible in the Explorer window above the Console by selecting the Plots tab. This is shown in Figure 3.5.

On the right, eventually there will be a stack of previous plots that you can return to display. The plot in this window can be copied to the clipboard by right-clicking it and then clicking the Copy Image icon or by using the shortcut Ctrl-C. From there, it can be pasted elsewhere in a document or presentation.

We notice some features of the plot above that we would like to modify and others that we would like to add. Here is a list:

- The markers are blue by default. We would prefer black.
- Engineers and scientists usually like gridlines to be able to align the data points with the scales.
- How about axis titles? And a title for the plot too?

There are many, many options that can be specified for plots. We can address the points above with these changes:

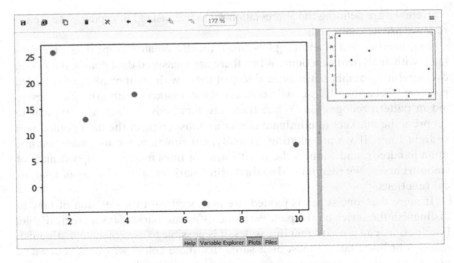

FIGURE 3.5   Display in Explorer window with the Plots tab selected.

```
py.grid()
py.xlabel('x')
py.ylabel('y')
py.title('my first plot')
```

But first, there is a problem. We cannot enter these commands one-by-one in the IPython Console. That will not work. (Try it!) We must enter all the statements required in the *Spyder Editor* window as a Python script. It should then appear as shown in Figure 3.6.

In the future, we will use the Editor to develop our Python scripts. The Console will be reserved for exploring and testing commands and one-time calculations. The Spyder Editor operates like a simple text processor, like Notepad in the Windows operating system. Although colors are not displayed in Figure 3.6, you will note in the Editor window that it automatically color codes keywords (blue), data in lists (red), and strings (green).

```
1   import numpy as np
2   import pylab as py
3   x = np.array([1.5, 2.6, 4.3, 6.7, 9.9])
4   y = np.array([25.7, 12.9, 17.6, -3.4, 7.7])
5   py.scatter(x,y,color='k')
6   py.grid()
7   py.xlabel('x')
8   py.ylabel('y')
9   py.title('my first plot')
10
```

FIGURE 3.6   Spyder Editor window with Python script.

We'll deal with more details of the Spyder Editor in the next section of this chapter, but, for now, it is good practice to save the script as a .py file before you run it. There are three ways to do that. First, from the File menu, you can select Save. You will note there that you can also save the file with a shortcut, Ctrl-S.

Also, on the toolbar below the menu bar, there is a Save File icon, 🖫 . Here, we have saved the file in a convenient folder with the name `firstplot.py`. Once the file is saved, you should see the Save icon grayed out. Then, to run the script, there are choices too.

First, you can select Run from the Run menu, and you will see an F5 key short-cut there. You can also click the Run button, ▶ . In the Explorer Plots window, you should see the display in Figure 3.7.

From Figure 3.6, you can see that the color code for black is `'k'`. Table 3.9 lists the various color choices.

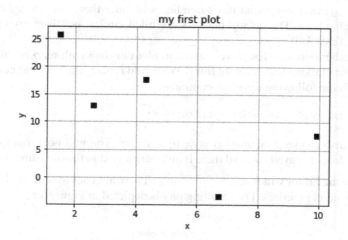

FIGURE 3.7 Plot display in Explorer window.

TABLE 3.9
Color Codes

Character	Color
k	Black
b	Blue
g	Green
r	Red
c	Cyan
m	Magenta
y	Yellow
w	White

TABLE 3.10
Marker Codes

Character	Symbol	Description
.	●	Point
o	○	Circle
+	+	Plus sign
x	×	
D	◊	Diamond
v	∇	Del
^	Δ	Triangle
s	□	Square

The `py.grid()` command has parentheses because there are options that we are not using here. The default markers are filled circles, but there are options, shown in Table 3.10.

As another option, what if we wanted to plot our data with markers and also connect the markers with straight lines? We would replace the `py.scatter` command with the following `py.plot` command:

```
py.plot(x, y, color='k', marker='s')
```

We have also changed the marker style to a square. You will note that the Save icon is no longer grayed out, and there is an asterisk next to the file name in the tab just above the Editor window, firstplot.py* ✕ . These are cues to re-Save the script (a good general practice). The resulting plot is depicted in Figure 3.8.

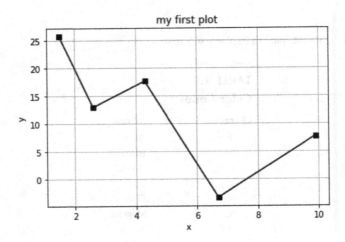

FIGURE 3.8 Plot with markers and lines.

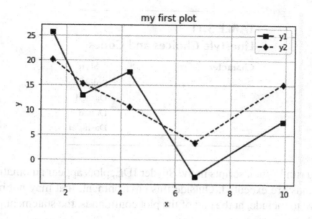

FIGURE 3.9 Plot with two series and a legend.

Next, the script is modified to add another data series with its own marker and line styles and provide a legend to distinguish the curves. The result is in Figure 3.9.

```
import numpy as np
import pylab as py
x = np.array([1.5, 2.6, 4.3, 6.7, 9.9])
y1 = np.array([25.7, 12.9, 17.6, -3.4, 7.7])
y2 = np.array([20.2, 15.3, 10.6, 3.4, 15.2])
py.plot(x, y1,color='k', marker='s', label='y1')
py.plot(x, y2,color='k', linestyle='--', marker='d',
label='y2')
py.grid()
py.xlabel('x')
py.ylabel('y')
py.title('my first plot')
py.legend()
```

There are a couple of new elements here. First, there is a second `py.plot` command for the second `y2` series. The `label` argument provides text for the `py.legend()` command. We specify diamond markers and a dashed linestyle. The linestyle choices are shown in Table 3.11.

As we create more plots like this, we will find it convenient to use certain abbreviations for the arguments in the `py.scatter` and `py.plot` commands. The two most common are:

color	c
linestyle	ls

There are many more specifications that can be made on `pylab` plots; however, what has been presented here is sufficient for you to create many functional, attractive engineering and scientific plots. In Chapter 5, we will introduce the Matplotlib `pyplot` module that is more comprehensive than `pylab`; but, on the other hand, it's more complicated to use.

TABLE 3.11
Linestyle Choices and Codes

Character	Style
-	Solid
--	Dashed
:	Dotted
-.	Dash-dot

When you run Python scripts in the Spyder IDE, plots appear automatically when their commands are executed. Outside this environment, that may not be the case. You may have to include, at the end of the plot commands, the statement py.show().

3.7 THE SPYDER EDITOR

In the last section, we introduced the use of the Spyder Editor and mentioned that it operates like a text editor. That is certainly true, but the Editor provides many more features that help your Python program development. The two that are most prominent are *error diagnostics* and *debug tracing*. We will explore these in this section.

Starting with the firstplot.py script from the last section,

```
import numpy as np
import pylab as py
x = np.array([1.5, 2.6, 4.3, 6.7, 9.9])
y1 = np.array([25.7, 12.9, 17.6, -3.4, 7.7])
y2 = np.array([20.2, 15.3, 10.6, 3.4, 15.2])
py.plot(x, y1,color='k', marker='s', label='y1')
py.plot(x, y2,color='k', linestyle='--', marker='d',
label='y2')
py.grid()
py.xlabel('x')
py.ylabel('y')
py.title('my first plot')
py.legend()
```

We will remove a right bracket (]) from the x = statement and notice how the Editor reacts.

```
❌  3   x = np.array([1.5, 2.6, 4.3, 6.7, 9.9)
```

Immediately a red ❌ error warning appears. If we hover the mouse pointer on the ❌, a tooltip also appears:

```
❌  3   x = np.array([1.5, 2.6, 4.3, 6.7, 9.9)
        Code analysis
  5
  6     ❌ Closing parenthesis ')' does not match opening parenthesis '[' (pyflakes E)
```

It alerts us to a *syntax error*,[8] and we need to check the statement carefully, and add the right bracket to balance the earlier left bracket. One of the common syntax errors in coding is parentheses or brackets that are out of balance.

There is a second type of notification that the Spyder Editor will provide. Suppose that we type:

```
7  py.plot(z,y2,color='k',linestyle='--',mr='d',label='y2')
```

Here, we have made a typographical error and entered z instead of x as the first argument of the py.plot command. The Editor immediately flags that with the tooltip

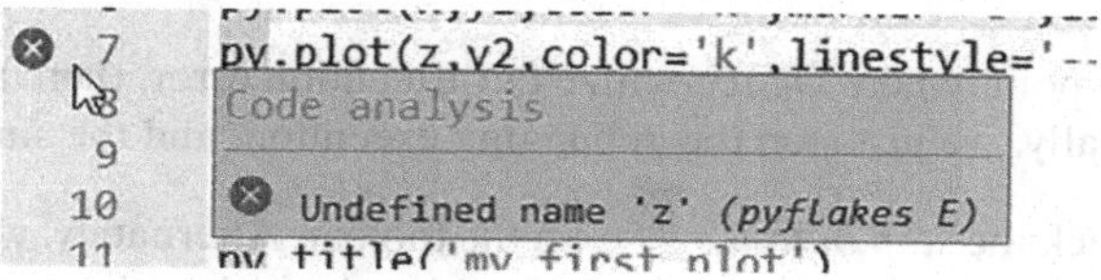

py.plot(z,y2,color='k',linestyle='--
Code analysis
Undefined name 'z' (pyflakes E)

The statement uses a variable name, z, that has not been defined yet. That should help us recognize the typo.

Another error-trapping feature of the Editor is that it recognized (what it thinks are …) extraneous statements in the code. For example, if we add the statement

```
3  import math
```

we see a warning triangle, ⚠, with the corresponding tooltip

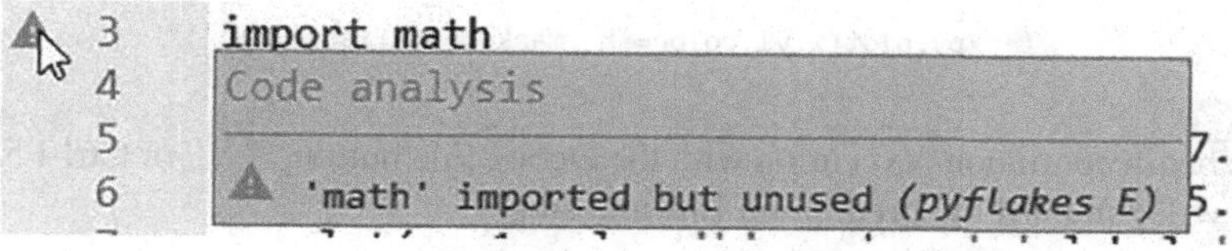

import math
Code analysis
'math' imported but unused (pyflakes E)

As soon as we would add a statement utilizing a function from the Math module, this warning would disappear. Some warnings are a bit of a nuisance, but it is still good to keep a watchful eye on them.

Even if our code contains no Editor warnings, there still may be errors that only show up when the script is run. The Spyder Editor provides a good debugging tool to help in discovering the source of such *execution* (or *runtime*) *errors*. The strategy is to *single step* through the code and keep an eye on the values of the variables in the Variable Explorer window. With our current script, choose Debug from the Debug menu of the Editor. Notice the shortcut Ctrl-F5. You can also click the Debug icon on the tool bar. Upon initiating debugging, an

[8] Syntax errors are mistakes in the source code, such as spelling and punctuation errors and incorrect labels that cause an error message to be generated when the code is compiled.

arrow appears adjacent the statement about to be executed, and the execution is stalled there.

```
1➡  import numpy as np
```

We single step the code by pressing the Ctrl-F10 combination or clicking the icon on the tool bar. After we pass the x = statement, the x variable appears in the Explorer window as

Name	Type	Size	
x	Array of float64	(5,)	[1.5 2.6 4.3 6.7 9.9]

If we pass the point where we recognize our execution error, there are two alternatives. Typically, we just stop the debugging execution, and the simplest way to do this is to click the *stop button*, ▪ , on the toolbar. Alternately, we might want to let the program execute without single stepping through to the end of the script. To do that, click the *continue execution button*, ▶▶ .

When the Python script is longer, it often would take too many single steps to reach the point of interest in the code. A technique we can use in such cases is to place a *breakpoint* in the code, execute continuously to that point, and then begin single stepping. For example, we might like to stop at the first py.plot command. If you move the mouse point up and down slowly just to the right of the line number in the Spyder Editor, you will see red dots appear. Stop at the line where the breakpoint will be set and click the red dot. That places the breakpoint there.

```
7●  py.plot(x,y1,color='k',marker='s',label='y1')
```

If we begin continuous execution with the Debug File button, ▶❚ , or Ctrl-F5, the code will run until the breakpoint line and stop.

```
7➡  py.plot(x,y1,color='k',marker='s',label='y1')
```

There we can examine variables and continue execution, either continuously, ▶▶ , or single stepping, ↷ . When there is no more need for the breakpoint, it can be removed by clicking the red dot. More than one breakpoint can be set, and a breakpoint can also be set or removed by selecting the line of code and pressing the F12 key. There is an option on the Debug menu to clear all breakpoints. With practice, you will find these debugging operations natural and very convenient, especially for large scripts.

It is common to be working with more than one Editor window at a time. A new window can be created from the File menu, New File command, using the Ctrl-N shortcut, or clicking the New File icon ▤ on the left end of the toolbar.

The new window will appear with a suggested heading that we can either edit, remove, or possibly replace. One feature that you observe in this heading is text between triple quotations, """. In Python, this is called a *docustring* and is used to provide information about the Python script, possibly including a description of its purpose, author, and date of development. With simple scripts where we are just exploring Python, we typically remove this *header information*. Later, we will use them regularly.

An important feature of Python programming is to include explanatory *comments* within the code. These non-executable labels are essential for making your code readily understandable by others and even for you if you have been away from the script for some time. Comments are preceded by the character # and can be inserted on their own line or added to the end of lines of code. Here are two examples:

```
x = np.array([1.5, 2.6, 4.3, 6.7, 9.9])   # assign x values
y1 = np.array([25.7, 12.9, 17.6, -3.4, 7.7])
y2 = np.array([20.2, 15.3, 10.6, 3.4, 15.2])
# create plot
py.plot(x,y1,color='k',marker='s',label='y1')
```

The Spyder Editor shows the comments in a light gray italic font.

When the Python script file is no longer needed, you can remove it from the Spyder Editor window by clicking the ⨯ on the tab. If the latest version of the file has not been saved, the Editor will remind you to save it before removing it.

Example 3.3 Creating a Script for the Great Circle Calculation

In Example 3.2, the use of variables and multiple commands to complete the Great Circle calculation was illustrated using the IPython Console. This type of calculation is not well suited to the Console and would be better coded as a script in the Spyder Editor. That script is shown in Figure 3.10.

This script closely replicates the commands from the previous example; however, a leading docustring has been added along with numerous comments for clarification. Also, a final print statement displays the result of the calculation in the Console. When the script is run, here is the Console output:

```
Distance = 13112.648691661389 km
```

By default, Python's print statement displays the calculated distance to full precision. These are far more digits than we would like to see. In the next section, we will deal with formatting such output.

If there were an error in the script, most likely in the three-part distance formula, we could examine it, perhaps debug it and compare against a test calculation or on-line value and make a correction without having to recreate the formula.

Another convenient Editor feature is *parentheses matching*. If we place the cursor just past the first parenthesis in the d1 = statement, we see

```
"""
Script to calculate the Great Circle distance
between two points on the Earth
Formula from www.edwilliams.org
29 Nov 2020
"""
import math
r = 6371  # km
# specify latitude and longitude of two locations
# London Heathrow airport
lt1d = 51.4700  # degrees
lt1 = math.radians(lt1d)
ln1d = 0.4543  # degrees
ln1 = math.radians(ln1d)
# Sydney Kingston Smith airport
lt2d = -33.9399  # degrees
lt2 = math.radians(lt2d)
ln2d = -151.1753  # degrees
ln2 = math.radians(ln2d)
# compute Great Circle distance
d1 = math.sin((lt1-lt2)/2)**2
d2 = math.cos(lt1)*math.cos(lt2)*(math.sin((ln1-ln2)/2))**2
d = 2*math.asin(math.sqrt(d1+d2))*r
# display result in the Console
print('Distance =',d,' km')
```

FIGURE 3.10   Python script for the Great Circle distance calculation.

the two matching parentheses highlighted (in green in the Editor window). We can move the cursor, best with the arrow keys, back and forth through the expression and check that the parentheses match and are in the correct locations. This is a very helpful way to catch common errors.

To change to a different set of locations, as was done in Example 3.2,

Tokyo, Japan – Narita Airport   35.7720°N, 149.3929°E
Cape Town, S. Africa – Airport 33.9175°S, 18.6021°E

we just edit the appropriate lines in the script:

```
# Tokyo Narita airport
lt1d = 35.7653 # degrees
lt1 = math.radians(lt1d)
ln1d = -140.3856 # degrees
ln1 = math.radians(ln1d)
# Cape Town airport
lt2d = -33.9694 # degrees
lt2 = math.radians(lt2d)
ln2d = -18.5972 # degrees
ln2 = math.radians(ln2d)
```

Before executing the script, since we have made changes and might not want to lose our original version, we can select Save As from the File menu and save the script under a new name, like GreatCircle1.py. Then, upon running the script, the Console shows

```
Distance = 14780.78626470105 km
```

There are other features to be added to make the Great Circle script more "friendly," and we will consider those in the next section.

We should add here that, when developing a Python script, it is good practice to save it frequently. This is accomplished easily by clicking the Save File icon, , or the Ctrl-S key combination. Additionally, as scripts are modified and expanded, it is good practice to save evolving scripts under different file names, e.g. MyFile1.py, MyFile2.py, etc. To do this, you need to choose Save As from the File menu or use the shortcut Ctrl-Shift-S. In this way, if you try out a change or expansion of a script that is not productive, it is easy to return to a previous version.

There are several additional Spyder features that are worth mentioning. When using the Variable Explorer in conjunction with Editor debugging, as you run the script over and over, variables displayed in the Explorer are not removed—some are just updated. This means that the Explorer window can become cluttered with previous variables that are no longer of interest. A way to handle this is to clear the window, and this is done by clicking the icon in the toolbar at the upper left of the Variable Explorer window.

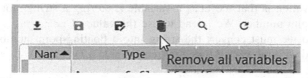

There is a similar icon in the top right corner of the Console that performs the same action.

While we are in the business of *clearing*, if the IPython Console has a long history of commands that are no longer of interest, you can type clear as a command, and that history will be removed. You will start over with a blank window.

Spyder provides a *Preferences window* on the Tools menu or by clicking the wrench icon, . Although we won't go into that in detail here, this provides many options for customizing Spyder including the overall appearance and layout of the windows, background colors (some prefer a black background with light fonts). It also allows for setting preferences having to do with functional features of Spyder, such as run execution, the Editor, the Variable Explorer, and keyboard shortcuts.

3.8   INPUT AND OUTPUT

There are numerous ways to get information into a Python script and getting results out. As far as input goes, the two common methods are (1) input directly from the user during the execution of a script and (2) input of large amounts of data from an external file. Output methods are displaying results in the Console and outputting results to an external file. Along with the output methods comes the issue of formatting of results.

3.8.1   Console Input and Output

User input is commonly employed for scripts to allow user interaction. Here is a simple example:

```
tempF = input('enter a temperature in degrees F: ')
```

When this statement is executed, the string within parentheses of the input statement appears as a prompt in the Console, where you can type in a value followed by the Enter key.

```
enter a temperature in degrees F: 72
```

After executing this statement, checking the Variable Explorer, we see

Name	Type	Size	
tempF	str	1	72

A key observation is that the tempF variable is storing a string, not an integer or floating-point number. We intend to use the value of tempF as a number in a formula, so we must convert the string into a floating-point number. This is accomplished with the float function (recall Table 3.7),

```
tempF = float(input('enter a temperature in degrees F: '))
```

and, after execution, the Variable Explorer now shows

Name	Type	Size	
tempF	float	1	72.0

which indicates that tempF is now type float and ready for calculations. A statement can then be added to convert the temperature to Celsius.

```
tempC = (tempF-32)/1.8
```

When the script is run, the Variable Explorer now shows

Name	Type	Size	
tempC	float	1	22.22222222222222
tempF	float	1	72.0

Although we can see the converted value, it would be more convenient to display that value in the Console right after the input query. To do that, we add the statement

```
print('temperature in degree C is', tempC)
```

and the combined display in the Console shows as

```
enter a temperature in degree F: 72
temperature in degree C is 22.22222222222222
```

Of course, the display of so many fractional digits is not satisfying, and we will get back to that later.

3.8.2 FILE INPUT AND OUTPUT

An alternate type of input is to read data in from an external file. These are most often *text files*, either .txt or .csv type. The .csv file may be produced by saving data on an Excel spreadsheet and indicates that, if there are multiple data on a line (or record), these are separated by commas (*comma delimited*). Information in a text file may be numerical or strings or a combination. Table 3.12 presents an example set of data counting the number of Atlantic hurricanes per year from 1851 to 2020.[9]

These data have been stored from a spreadsheet in a text file, AtlanticHurricaneHistory.csv, with each year and number on a line separated by a comma. We would like to import the data into a Python script and create a plot of number of hurricanes versus calendar year. You can see that it would not be practical to enter these values into our script one by one. To read these data into our script, we use the loadtxt function from the NumPy module:

```
import numpy as np
year, hurr = np.loadtxt('AtlanticHurricaneHistory.csv' \
        , unpack=True, delimiter=', ')
```

When this is executed, the Variable Explorer shows

Name	Type	Size	Value
hurr	Array of float64	(170,)	[3. 5. 4. ... 8. 6. 13.]
year	Array of float64	(170,)	[1851. 1852. 1853. ... 2018. 2019. 2020.]

Notice that, even though the numbers appear as integers in the data file, they are imported as floating-point. The unpack=True specification asks the loadtxt function to separate the items on each record into distinct array variables. The delimiter specification is because we have a .csv file. Now, we can add the

---

[9] http://tropical.atmos.colostate.edu/Realtime/index.php?arch&loc=northatlantic.

TABLE 3.12

Number of Atlantic Hurricanes Per Year from 1851 to 2020

Year	#	Year	#	Year	#	Year	#	Year	#	Year	#	Year	#	Year	#	Year	#
1851	3	1871	6	1891	7	1911	3	1931	3	1951	8	1971	6	1991	4	2011	7
1852	5	1872	4	1892	5	1912	4	1932	6	1952	6	1972	3	1992	4	2012	10
1853	4	1873	3	1893	10	1913	4	1933	11	1953	6	1973	4	1993	4	2013	2
1854	3	1874	4	1894	5	1914	0	1934	7	1954	8	1974	4	1994	3	2014	6
1855	4	1875	5	1895	2	1915	5	1935	5	1955	9	1975	6	1995	11	2015	4
1856	4	1876	4	1896	6	1916	10	1936	7	1956	4	1976	6	1996	9	2016	7
1857	3	1877	3	1897	3	1917	2	1937	4	1957	3	1977	5	1997	3	2017	10
1858	6	1878	10	1898	5	1918	4	1938	4	1958	7	1978	5	1998	10	2018	8
1859	7	1879	6	1899	5	1919	2	1939	3	1959	7	1979	5	1999	8	2019	6
1860	6	1880	9	1900	3	1920	4	1940	6	1960	4	1980	9	2000	8	2020	13
1861	6	1881	4	1901	6	1921	5	1941	4	1961	8	1981	7	2001	9		
1862	3	1882	4	1902	3	1922	3	1942	4	1962	3	1982	2	2002	4		
1863	5	1883	3	1903	7	1923	4	1943	5	1963	7	1983	3	2003	7		
1864	3	1884	4	1904	4	1924	5	1944	8	1964	6	1984	5	2004	9		
1865	3	1885	6	1905	1	1925	1	1945	5	1965	4	1985	7	2005	15		
1866	6	1886	10	1906	6	1926	8	1946	3	1966	7	1986	4	2006	5		
1867	7	1887	11	1907	0	1927	4	1947	5	1967	6	1987	3	2007	6		
1868	3	1888	6	1908	6	1928	4	1948	6	1968	4	1988	5	2008	8		
1869	7	1889	6	1909	6	1929	3	1949	7	1969	12	1989	7	2009	3		
1870	10	1890	2	1910	3	1930	2	1950	11	1970	5	1990	8	2010	12		

Source: http://tropical.atmos.colostate.edu/Realtime/index.php?arch&loc=northatlantic

code to produce a plot of the data. Since there are quite a few, we won't use markers, just straight lines connecting the data points.

```
import numpy as np
import pylab as py
year, hurr = np.loadtxt('AtlanticHurricaneHistory.csv', \
            unpack=True, delimiter=', ')
py.plot(year, hurr, c='k')
py.grid()
py.xlabel('Year')
py.ylabel('Number of Hurricanes')
py.title('Atlantic Hurricane History')
```

The plot produced is shown in Figure 3.11

There is a companion NumPy function called savetxt that allows you to save a data set to a text file. From there, it might be imported by other software, such as an Excel spreadsheet. Another need that may arise is saving data for future access in another Python script. Although that could be managed using savetxt and loadtxt functions, NumPy provides save and load functions to export an array in a binary format for subsequent importing into a Python script.

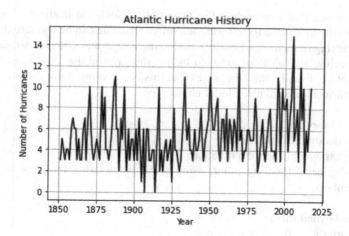

FIGURE 3.11   Plot of Atlantic hurricane data.

3.8.3 FORMATTING OUTPUT

We have used the print function earlier in this chapter to display results in the IPython Console. An issue that we pointed out was that the numbers displayed were to full precision with too many digits. The way to manage this is to include format information in the print statement. Here is an earlier example:

```
tempF = float(input('enter a temperature in degrees F: '))
tempC = (tempF-32)/1.8
print('temperature in degrees C is', tempC)
```

with the Console display

```
enter a temperature in degrees F: 88
temperature in degrees C is 31.11111111111111
```

Perhaps we would like to display the converted temperature only to the tenths place. A modification to the print statement accomplishes this.

```
print('temperature in degrees C is {0:5.1f}'.format(tempC))
```

with the resulting output

```
temperature in degrees C is 31.1
```

What did we do here? There are two changes. First, we included a format specification in the string, {0:5.1f}. This governs the display of the tempC value. It is fairly cryptic, so it deserves some explanation.

First, notice that it is enclosed in braces, {●}. Next, the leading 0 indicates that this is the first value to be formatted (more than one can be formatted—zero-based indexing rears its head again!). Following a separator colon (:), we see 5.1f. The 5 specifies the width of the field for the display and the .1 indicates to one decimal place. Finally, the f indicates that this is a floating-point display.

There are other formatting letter characters:

- b – binary
- d – decimal (for integers)
- e – exponent (scientific notation)
- g – general (floating point, using scientific notation for large or tiny numbers)

and more beyond these.

Here are three illustrative examples:

```
numdays = 44165
print('number of days since Jan 1, 1900: {0:6d}'.format(numdays))
number of days since Jan 1, 1900: 44165
------------------------------------------------------------------
Planck = 6.62607015e-34 # J*s
print("Planck's constant is {0:15.8e}".format(Planck))

Planck's constant is 6.62607015e-34
------------------------------------------------------------------
mu = 0.000001 # m
print('one micron is {0:3.1g} meters'.format(mu))
mm = 0.001 # m
print('one millimeter is {0:3.1g} meters'.format(mm))
one micron is 1e-06 meters

one millimeter is 0.001 meters
```

Things to notice: The number of days is an integer, so the d format is appropriate. Planck's constant requires scientific notation with the e format.[10] The g format chooses to display the micron equivalent in scientific notation, but the millimeter equivalent in floating-point format. It turns out that 0.001 is the dividing point for that decision. The upper dividing point depends on the number of decimal places requested and is 10 raised to that number.

You will see many examples of print formatting used in this text. We have found that a good practice is to display results first with a simple print statement and then add formatting later to make the output look better. It is worth mentioning that formatting is a more general topic. There are many alternatives, and we have chosen one here to limit the complexity.

---

[10] A fine point: Since we want to use the possessive Planck's in the text string, we delimit that string with a double quotation mark ", not a single quotation mark '.

Information on `print` formatting and functions like `loadtxt` and `savetxt` is available from Python and NumPy documentation. That introduces the next section where we discuss how to find help on Python, its modules like NumPy, and the Spyder IDE.

3.9 OBTAINING HELP

It is a common and very frequent need when programming Python scripts to look for assistance. This occurs at several levels:

- recalling the arguments or specifications that accompany a built-in function, e.g. `loadtxt` from NumPy,
- finding information on a feature or function that you think exists or should exist, e.g. a four-quadrant arctangent function in NumPy or elsewhere, and
- asking a general question, "How do I . . . in Python?"

There is far more detail associated with Python and its various support modules that we can present in this text. You may wish to supplement your library with one or more general texts on Python programming. Good examples are Deitel and Deitel (2020) and Gaddis (2018). In addition, there are a plethora of videos on Python that you can access on the Internet.

The Spyder Editor provides timely assistance as you enter a Python function. An example is shown in Figure 3.12 for the `print` function used in the previous section.

The floating tooltip shows the arguments or parameters of the function and provides additional information below. This may not occur with all keywords and functions but is commonly provided. One can also hover the mouse pointer on a

```
print()

    print(*values: object, sep: Optional[Text]=..., end:
        Optional[Text]=..., file: Optional[_Writer]=...,
        flush: bool=...) -> None

    print(value, ..., sep=' ', end='\n', file=sys.stdout,
    flush=False)

    Prints the values to a stream, or to sys.stdout by default.
    Optional keyword arguments: file: a file-like object
    (stream); defaults to the current sys.stdout.
    sep: string inserted between values, default a space.
    end: string appended after the last value, default a
    newline.
    flush: whether to forcibly flush the stream.
```

FIGURE 3.12   Example Spyder Editor tooltip for the `print` function.

keyword or function and press Ctrl-I. For example, on the print function, this provides help information in the Explorer Window.

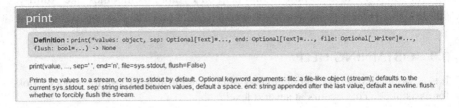

The next level of assistance is provided via the *Spyder Help menu*.

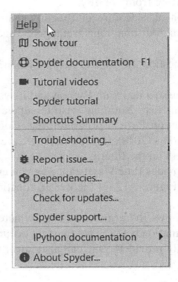

There are several, general resources here of interest, including Spyder documentation, tutorial videos, and Spyder tutorial. As for specific help on Python, NumPy, and another frequently used module, SciPy, this is found via the Internet. For the version of Python (3.9) shown here: https://docs.python.org/3.9/.

You will find numerous choices there as shown in Figure 3.13.

There is also a Quick search field where we could type abs, and it would take us to

abs(x)

> Return the absolute value of a number. The argument may be an integer, a floating point number, or an object implementing __abs__(). If the argument is a complex number, its magnitude is returned.

Often, we are searching for information on features of the NumPy or SciPy modules. A good place to start at is https://docs.scipy.org/doc/.

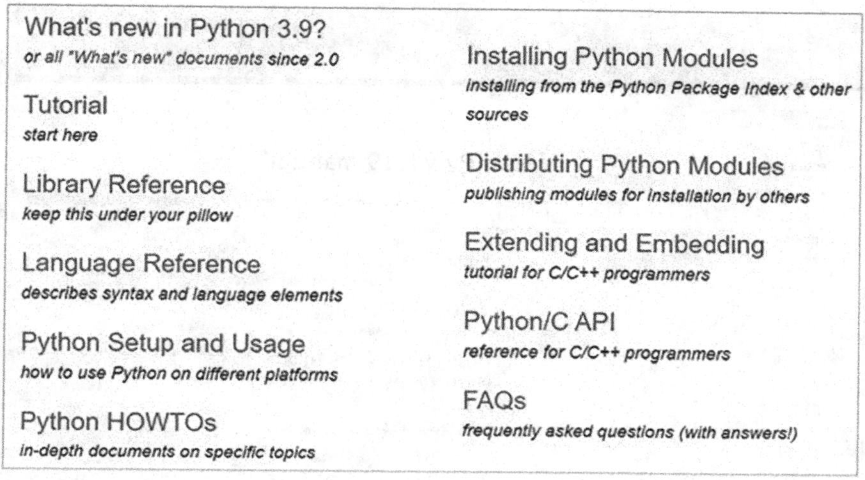

What's new in Python 3.9?
or all "What's new" documents since 2.0

Tutorial
start here

Library Reference
keep this under your pillow

Language Reference
describes syntax and language elements

Python Setup and Usage
how to use Python on different platforms

Python HOWTOs
in-depth documents on specific topics

Installing Python Modules
installing from the Python Package Index & other sources

Distributing Python Modules
publishing modules for installation by others

Extending and Embedding
tutorial for C/C++ programmers

Python/C API
reference for C/C++ programmers

FAQs
frequently asked questions (with answers!)

FIGURE 3.13   Python Help selections.

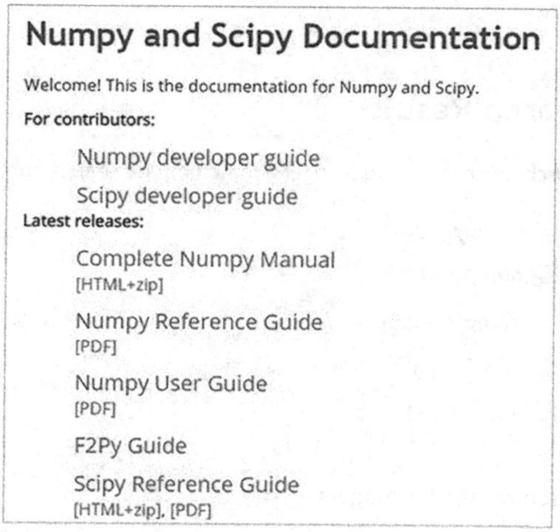

Numpy and Scipy Documentation

Welcome! This is the documentation for Numpy and Scipy.

For contributors:

Numpy developer guide

Scipy developer guide

Latest releases:

Complete Numpy Manual
[HTML+zip]

Numpy Reference Guide
[PDF]

Numpy User Guide
[PDF]

F2Py Guide

Scipy Reference Guide
[HTML+zip], [PDF]

FIGURE 3.14   NumPy and SciPy Help selections.

You will see there the display in Figure 3.14.

Our typical choices here will be Complete Numpy Manual or SciPy Reference Guide. As an example, choosing the former provides the display in Figure 3.15.

We can type `tangent` in the Quick search field and click Search (or press Enter), and the result is shown in Figure 3.16..

The `arctan2` entry looks interesting as far as a four-quadrant arctangent, so, selecting that, we get the detail depicted in Figure 3.17.

Below this, it provides details on all the parameters or arguments to the function.

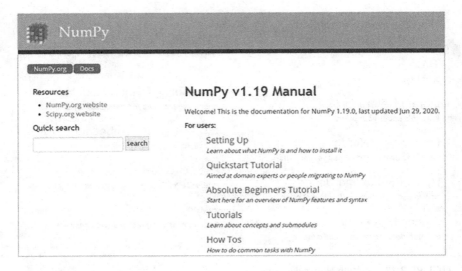

FIGURE 3.15   NumPy Help selections.

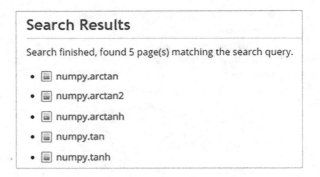

FIGURE 3.16   Search results for tangent.

numpy.arctan2

numpy.**arctan2**(*x1, x2, /, out=None, *, where=True, casting='same_kind', order='K', dtype=None, subok=True[, signature, extobj]*) = <ufunc 'arctan2'>

Element-wise arc tangent of x1/x2 choosing the quadrant correctly.

The quadrant (i.e., branch) is chosen so that arctan2(x1, x2) is the signed angle in radians between the ray ending at the origin and passing through the point (1,0), and the ray ending at the origin and passing through the point (x2, x1). (Note the role reversal: the "*y*-coordinate" is the first function parameter, the "*x*-coordinate" is the second.) By IEEE convention, this function is defined for x2 = +/-0 and for either or both of x1 and x2 = +/-inf (see Notes for specific values).

This function is not defined for complex-valued arguments; for the so-called argument of complex values, use angle.

FIGURE 3.17   Detail information on the arctan2 function.

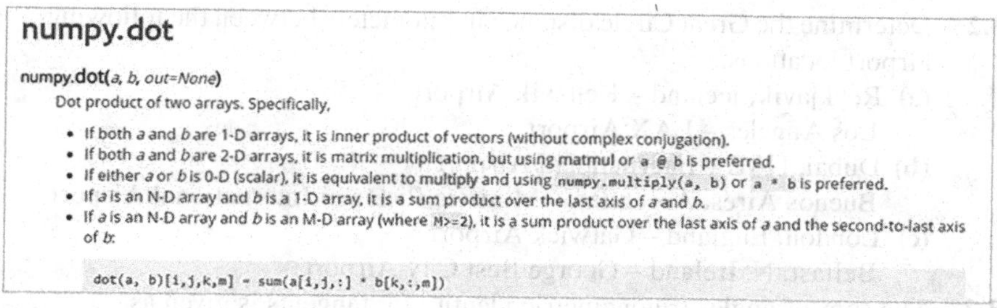

---

numpy.dot

numpy.dot(a, b, out=None**)**

Dot product of two arrays. Specifically,

- If both a and b are 1-D arrays, it is inner product of vectors (without complex conjugation).
- If both a and b are 2-D arrays, it is matrix multiplication, but using matmul or a @ b is preferred.
- If either a or b is 0-D (scalar), it is equivalent to multiply and using numpy.multiply(a, b) or a * b is preferred.
- If a is an N-D array and b is a 1-D array, it is a sum product over the last axis of a and b.
- If a is an N-D array and b is an M-D array (where M>=2), it is a sum product over the last axis of a and the second-to-last axis of b:

```
dot(a, b)[i,j,k,m] - sum(a[i,j,:] * b[k,:,m])
```

FIGURE 3.18   Internet search results for the dot product.

Finally, we come to the most general "How do I ...?" inquiry about Python. The open nature of Python stimulates a lot of information available on the Internet. An example that relates to Chapter 5 in this text might be

> How do I compute a dot product in Python?

There are many results. One is displayed in Figure 3.18.

As you make your way through programming in Python to solve engineering and scientific problems, you will encounter many questions and perhaps frustrations. Although we sympathize, this is the way it goes. And, in fact, it is the nature of problem solving in general. After looking for help online, via the Spyder IDE or the Internet, you should keep in mind consulting with others: instructors, teaching assistants, fellow students, etc. Some worry that, by seeking assistance, they are exposing their lack of knowledge. Don't fall into that trap.

Also, avoid spending too much time with a "try this, try that" approach, sometimes called *shotgun programming*, hoping for success without really understanding what you're doing. It's better to look for help and examples that will shortcut the time to success in solving your problems.

PROBLEMS

3.1   Implement the following arithmetic expressions in the IPython Console and report the numerical results.

(a) $\dfrac{12-\dfrac{5}{2}}{\left|\dfrac{22}{7}-\pi\right|}$

(b) $\pi \cdot 11^2 \left(\dfrac{3 \cdot 15 - 11}{3} \right)$

(c) $\dfrac{1}{\dfrac{1}{20}+\dfrac{3}{11}-\dfrac{0.6}{0.2}}$

3.2 Determine the Great Circle distance in kilometers between the following airport locations.
  (a) Reykjavik, Iceland – Keflavik Airport
      Los Angeles – LAX Airport
  (b) Dubai, UAE – International Airport
      Buenos Aires, Argentina – Ministro Pistarini International Airport
  (c) London, England – Gatwick Airport
      Belfast, N. Ireland – George Best City Airport

3.3 The sum-of-angles trigonometric identity for tangents is given as

$$\tan(\alpha + \beta) = \frac{\tan(\alpha) + \tan\beta}{1 - \tan(\alpha)\tan(\beta)}$$

Verify this identity with computations in the IPython Console for $\alpha = 37°$ and $\beta = 107°$.

3.4 As shown in Figure P3.4, a *lune* is a three-dimension, pie-like slice of a sphere. The volume of a lune is given by $2r^2\theta$ where r is the radius of the sphere, and θ is the included angle. Using Python, compute the volume of a lune of the Earth in cubic kilometers from the longitude of Istanbul, Turkey, to that of Madrid, Spain.

3.5 Find the worldwide annual production of methanol in million metric tons. Obtain the density of methanol at room temperature and compute the corresponding volume of methanol in cubic meters. Determine the volume of a typical tanker truck used for transporting liquid chemicals. Compute the number of tanker trucks required to contain this annual production. Estimate the length of the tanker truck including its tractor. If the computed number of tanker trucks were lined up one after another,

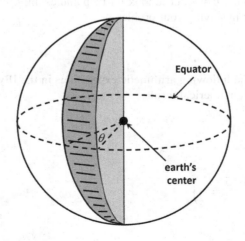

FIGURE P3.4 Depiction of a lune.

how long would the line be? How does that compare to the circumference of the Earth at the Equator?

3.6 The Colorado River Aqueduct carries about 1.1 million acre-feet of water per year from the Colorado River at the Arizona-California border to the Los Angeles basin. The average daily consumption of water in Los Angeles County is 85 gallons. How many people could be supplied water by the Colorado River Aqueduct?

3.7 Using Python, complete the following expressions and explain the results.

(a) `round(np.pi,8)` and `round(np.pi,7)`

(b) `2**3**4` and `(2**3)**4`

(c) `np.arctan(1.5)` and `np.arctan2(-3.,-2.)`

(d) `4+-3`

3.8 The following data represent the density of water, ρ (kg/m³), at sea-level atmospheric pressure for temperatures, T, from 0°C to 100°C. Use Python's `pylab` module to create a neatly labeled plot of the data and comment on any characteristics you observe.

T (°C)	ρ (kg/m³)	T (°C)	ρ (kg/m³)	T (°C)	ρ (kg/m³)	T (°C)	ρ (kg/m³)
0	999.87	20	998.23	50	988.07	80	971.83
2	999.97	25	997.08	55	985.73	85	968.65
4	1,000	30	995.68	60	983.24	90	965.34
6	999.97	35	994.06	65	980.59	95	961.92
10	999.73	40	992.25	70	977.81	100	958.38
15	999.13	45	990.25	75	974.89		

3.9 Download, as a .csv file, the history of global average temperature deviation from the 20th Century average from NOAA's National Centers for Environmental Information (NCEI)- Climate at a Glance website. Write a Python script to import these data and create a neatly labeled plot.

3.10 Download, as a .txt file, the history of atmospheric global CO_2 concentration from https://gml.noaa.gov/ccgg/trends/data.html. Write a Python script to import these data and create a neatly labeled plot. If you also solved Problem 3.9, plot the two datasets on the same graph with a legend. To do this, you will have to "trim" the temperature dataset so the years match those of the CO_2 history. Also, scale down the CO_2 data by a factor of 1,000.

3.11 Write a Python script that computes the volume of liquid in a horizontal, cylindrical tank. See Figure P3.11. Specify a tank diameter of 2 m and length of 4 m. Allow the user to input the liquid depth at the centerline of

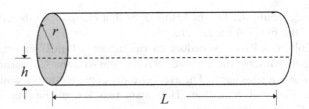

FIGURE P3.11   Horizontal, cylindrical tank containing a liquid.

the tank. Produce output in the Console displaying the liquid volume in liters. The formula to be used is

$$V = \left(r^2 \cos^{-1}\left(\frac{r-h}{r}\right) - (r-h)\sqrt{2rh-h^2} \right) L$$

where V = volume of liquid, r = tank radius = diameter/2, L = length of the tank, h = liquid depth. All dimensions used in the formula must be consistent.

3.12 Newton's Universal Law of Gravitation is given by

$$F = \frac{G m_1 m_2}{d^2}$$

where F = gravitational force (N), m_1 and m_2 = the two involved masses (kg), d = distance between the centers of the two masses (m) and G = the universal gravitation constant (6.673×10^{-11} N·m²/kg²). Determine the gravitational force for the following two cases:

(a) A person with mass 80 kg standing on the surface of the Earth. The radius of the Earth is 6,371 km, and its mass is estimated as 5.98×10^{24} kg.

(b) The mass of the planet Jupiter is estimated as 1.898×10^{27} kg. The mass of Jupiter's moon Europa is 4.8×10^{22} kg. The orbital radius of Europa is 670,900 km.

3.13 When counting hours on a twelve-hour clock, you count up to 12 and then wrap back to 1. For example, say you want to determine what time it would be 10 hours after 9:00 a.m. On a twelve-hour clock, you cannot simply add 10 to 9 because you would get 19. Complete the last two statements of the following code fragment to compute the time for a 24-hour clock (t24) and use the modulus operator to compute the 12-hour clock time (t12):

```
tinit = 9
deltat=10
t24 =
t12 =
```

4 Structured Programming with Python

CHAPTER OBJECTIVES

- Understand the need for modifications to the sequential structure of Python programs.
- Learn about selection structures and be able to implement the various `if` statement types to accomplish the required decisions.
- Know how to use the `for` loop structure to implement count-controlled iteration.
- Be able to program the `while` loop structure to accomplish pre-test, mid-test, and post-test loops, and combinations of those.
- Create user-defined functions to "package" calculations.
- Know how to break down programs into manageable modules, often with user-defined functions.
- Understand the concept of variable scope as it relates to subprograms.
- Learn how to store functions as separate Python program files and import those files into Python scripts.

The Python scripts introduced in Chapter 3 consisted of a set of statements that were executed in sequence. That arrangement works well for simple calculations but runs into problems when faced with the following scenarios:

- different calculations are required depending on one or more True/False conditions that are evaluated,
- code needs to be repeated many times,
- a calculation needs to be "packaged" so that it may be invoked several times, perhaps from different locations in a script, or
- a Python script grows to be hundreds (or thousands!) of statements and needs to be broken down into "bite-size" modules to become more manageable.

Of course, these challenges have confronted programmers from the beginning of digital computer technology in the mid-20th century, and all programming languages have provided features to handle these scenarios. The purpose of this chapter is to introduce these features as provided by Python.

DOI: 10.1201/9781003256861-4

4.1   AN OVERVIEW OF PROGRAM STRUCTURE

A big picture view of a programming task is illustrated in Figure 4.1. The primary concept presented here is that of a linear sequence. The oversimplified flowchart on the left is expanded on the right to illustrate the typical first and final steps with a main segment of computations in between.

As we delve into the program computations, situations arise that require deviation from the sequential, step-by-step scheme. The first of these scenarios is when a condition needs to be satisfied before one or more statements are executed. These are *decision structures*, also called *selection*, and are illustrated in the flowcharts in Figure 4.2.

For the *One-way If*, a logical condition is checked, and, if True, a set of program statements is executed. If False, that set is skipped. In either case, the subsequent program segment continues from the same position. The *Two-way If* structure provides a separate set of computations when the logical condition tests False. It is worth mentioning that, within the computations blocks in the figure, there can and will be imbedded structures, including If structures. In the next section, we will see how to implement these structures in Python.

The second scenario is when computations need to be repeated. This is called a *loop structure*, also *repetition*, and there are two implementations. The first of these, called the *general loop*, is presented in Figure 4.3. The second implementation includes the *list-controlled* and *count-controlled loops*. These are illustrated in Figure 4.4. The distinction between the two implementations is that, for the general loop, the number of repetitions cannot be determined before the loop is entered; whereas, for the list-controlled and count-controlled loops, the number of repetitions can be calculated prior to loop entry.

Referring to Figure 4.3 for the general loop, the diagram shows a circle, or "bubble," as the entry point to the loop. In terms of programming, there must be a statement that provides this function.

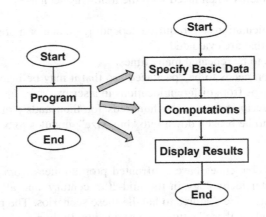

FIGURE 4.1   Overall program structure.

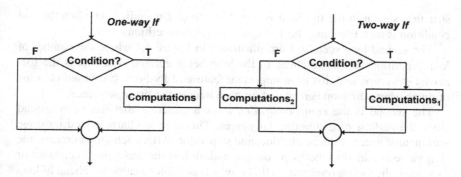

FIGURE 4.2 Decision structure: One-way and Two-way If.

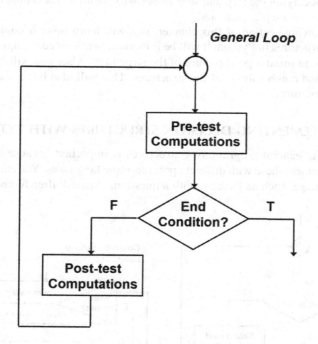

FIGURE 4.3 Repetition structure: the general loop.

Also, although there is no bubble shown, there must be a way of signaling the end of the loop at the bottom of the figure. Within the loop, there always has to be a way to exit; otherwise, there would be a so-called *infinite loop*. This is denoted as a single decision block, although there may be more than one. There will be computations either before the loop exit decision or after or in both locations, depending on what the repetition task requires. If the exit decision is just after the loop entry, this is called a *pre-test loop*. Alternately, if the decision as at the bottom, with no post-test computations, it is called a *post-test loop*. For the full structure shown in the figure, it is a *mid-test loop*. Depending on when the end condition is met, there may be 1, 10, 100, or 1,000 repetitions.

The second loop scenarios are illustrated in Figure 4.4 where the number of loop repetitions is known ahead of the loop being entered. The first is the *list-driven structure*, and this is an important feature of Python[1]. It is based on a list of items where the loop is repeated for each item in the list in sequence.

The second is the *count-controlled loop*, a structure that has been around since the earliest programming languages. This loop is characterized by three parameters: a start value, end value, and step value. After each loop iteration, the step value is added to the loop counter, and, unless the end value is equaled or exceeded, the loop is repeated. In this way, it is possible to calculate ahead of loop entry how many times the loop will be repeated. In fact, once the loop is being executed, modifying the step and stop values will not affect the number of repetitions, since they are precalculated.

In a following section of this chapter, you will learn how to implement the repetition structures in Python. It will be important to reference the figures shown here to keep in mind a good picture of the structures. Also, you will learn some variations and combinations of the structures. This will also be the case for the selection structures.

4.2 IMPLEMENTING DECISION STRUCTURES WITH PYTHON

Learning the general programming structures is important because it prepares you to implement these with different programming languages. You can approach a new language, such as Python, with a question, "Since I already know what a

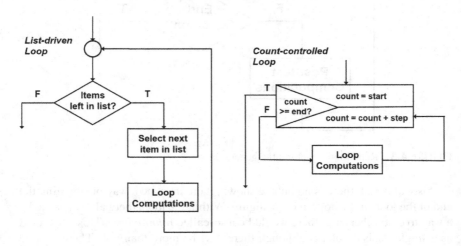

FIGURE 4.4 List-driven and count-controlled loop structures.

---

[1] We note that the list-driven loop is not common to other programming systems, such as MATLAB®, Excel VBA, and Fortran.

Two-way If is, how do I implement a Two-way If in Python?" In other words, once you learn a procedural programming language like Python, you are never starting from scratch.

The first, simplest decision structure is the *One-way If*, as shown in Figure 4.2. The general syntax for this in Python is quite simple:

```
if condition:
    statements
```

Notice the use of the colon (:) and the indentation (four spaces) for the program code that executes if the condition is True. An example might be to square a quantity but preserve the sign of the quantity:

```
Sgnx2 = x**2
if x < 0:
    Sgnx2 = - Sgnx2
```

After the `if` statement and statement that executes if True, the code would continue, but not indented. There is no formal statement to terminate the `if` structure—it is denoted by returning to the indentation of the `if` statement.

When the statements executed if True are brief, typically one statement, a compact version of the One-way If is available:

```
Sgnx2 = x**2
if x < 0: Sgnx2 = - Sgnx2
```

This style is often called a *One-line If*. It is possible to add statements to the `if` line delimited by semicolons (;), but this is usually not done in favor of the previous style where the indented statements follow the `if` line.

The *Two-way If*'s syntax is that of the One-way If with an "`else`" clause added:

```
if condition:
    statements1
else:
    statements2
```

Again, the structure is terminated when the following statements return to the indentation of the `if` and `else` statements. In this example, the square of the quantity is included in the Two-way If structure:

```
if x < 0:
    Sgnx2 = - x**2
else:
    Sgnx2 = x**2
```

Python and many other programming languages include an expanded version called the *Multi-alternative If* structure. This allows for multiple decisions to be

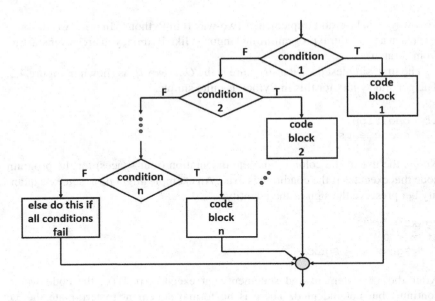

FIGURE 4.5   The Multi-alternative If structure.

cascaded if the prior decision is False. This is illustrated in Figure 4.5. The general syntax for this structure is

```
if condition1:
    statements1
elif condition2:
    statements2
.
.
elif condition_n:
    statements_n
else:
    else statements
```

The `else` clause is optional. A somewhat trivial example of the Multi-alternative If is:

```
if temperature < 0:
    print('Brrr!')
elif temperature < 10:
    print('Chilly')
elif temperature < 20:
    print('Comfortable')
elif temperature < 30:
    print('Warm')
elif temperature < 40:
    print('Whew! Hot!')
```

```
else:
    print('Ssssss! Gimme a break!')
```

It is important to note the `elif` clauses have to follow a particular order. The condition test `temperature<30` implies that the temperature is >= 20 because of the previous test. For this example, the order is obvious, but, in other cases, you must pay close attention to the order of the `elif` clauses.

It is worth mentioning here that some other programming languages, e.g. MATLAB, Excel/VBA, C/C++, have an additional multi-alternative structure that doesn't require the condition tests to be ordered in the sequence of evaluation; however, generally, the tests have to be mutually exclusive. (Only one test can evaluate True at a time.) These structures may be called *switch* or *select-case* and are typically used for menu selections. Python doesn't have such a structure, but that doesn't limit numerical computations to any great extent.

Finally, it is important to consider that one decision structure can be imbedded in another. As an example, for consider adding another Two-way If in place of code block 1 in the figure. The general syntax would then be

```
if condition1:
    if condition1a:
        statements1a
    else:
        statements1b
elif condition2:
    statements2
•
•
elif condition_n:
    statements_n
else:
    else statements
```

After either `statements1a` or `statements1b` are executed, the overall Multi-alternative If structure is terminated and program flow continues below it.

Notice how indentation emphasizes the imbedding of the `condition1a` Two-way If structure into the `condition1` True branch. And the indentation is mandatory! But beyond being required, indentation makes the resulting code more easily readable and its underlying structure more transparent. We consider this a positive attribute of Python.

Example 4.1 Converting Thermocouple Millivolt Readings to Temperature

The most common industrial instrument used to measure temperature is the *thermocouple*. It is based on a thermoelectric phenomenon called the *Seebeck effect*. The diagram in Figure 4.6 presents a simplified thermocouple circuit.

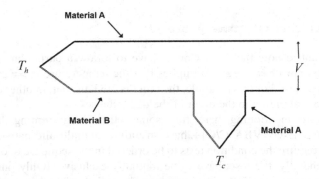

FIGURE 4.6   Thermocouple circuit.

The difference in the mobility of electrons across the junctions at T_h and T_c causes a small electromotive force (emf) or voltage, typically in the millivolt range, and this emf is dependent on temperature. So, assuming that the temperatures at the two junctions are different, a small voltage, V, can be measured and is proportional to $\Delta T = T_h{-}T_c$ temperature difference, but not quite linearly so. If T_c is known (or controlled), then T_h can be computed as $T_c + \Delta T$.

There are many types of thermocouples depending on the metals or alloys used for Materials A and B. One of the most common of these, designated Type J, is a combination of iron and an alloy called constantan (55% copper, 45% nickel). NIST[2] provides polynomial formulas to compute dT from V that apply to different ranges of temperature. These are presented in simplified form as Equations 4.1–4.3. Note that the values for V are in millivolts (mV).

For $-8.10 \le V \le 0.0\ mV$:

$$dT = 19.53V - 1.229V^2 - 1.075V^3 - 0.5909V^4$$

$$-0.1726V^5 - 0.02813V^6 - 2.396\times10^{-3}V^7 \tag{4.1}$$

$$-8.382\times10^{-5}V^8$$

For $0.0 \le V \le 42.92\ mV$:

$$dT = 19.78V - 0.2001V^2 + 0.01037V^3 - 2.550\times10^{-4}V^4$$

$$+3.585\times10^{-6}V^5 - 5.344\times10^{-8}V^6 + 5.100\times10^{-10}V^7 \tag{4.2}$$

For $42.92 \le V \le 69.55\ mV$:

$$dT = -3114.0 + 300.5V - 9.948V^2 + 0.1703V^3 - 1.430\times10^{-3}V^4$$

$$+4.739\times10^{-6}V^5 \tag{4.3}$$

---

[2] NIST = National Institute of Standards and Technology for the U.S.

We desire a Python code segment that will compute the temperature, T_h, given the measured voltage, V, and the cold junction temperature, T_c. This will require a Multi-alternative If structure. If we assume the given voltage, V, will be greater than the minimum −8.10 mV and less than the maximum 69.55 mV, the Python code would be

```python
V = float(input('Enter voltage in mV: '))
Tc = float(input('Enter cold junction temperature in degC: '))
if V <= 0.:
    dT = 19.53*V - 1.229*V**2 - 1.075*V**3 \
    - 0.5909*V**4 - 0.1726*V**5 - 0.02813*V**6 \
    - 2.396e-3*V**7 - 8.382e-5*V**8
elif V <= 42.919:
    dT = 19.78*V - 0.2001*V**2 + 0.01037*V**3 \
    - 2.550e-4*V**4 + 3.585e-6*V**5 - 5.344e-8*V**6 \
    + 5.100e-10*V**7
else:
    dT = -3114.0 + 300.5*V - 9.948*V**2 \
    + 0.1703*V**3 - 1.430e-3*V**4 + 4.739e-6*V**5

Th = Tc + dT
print('\nHot junction temperature = {0:7.2f} degC'.format(Th))
```

We can try several example values of V to test the validity of the code:

```
Enter voltage in mV: 5
Enter cold junction temperature in degC: 22
Hot junction temperature = 117.04 degC
-------------------
Enter voltage in mV: 35
Enter cold junction temperature in degC: 50
Hot junction temperature = 682.00 degC
-------------------
Enter voltage in mV: -6
Enter cold junction temperature in degC: 0
Hot junction temperature = -135.38 degC
```

Now, we return to the issue of "out of bounds" input values. One technique is to "bracket" the code with a *validity test* and not let the calculation proceed if the V value is beyond the limits.

```python
if V >= -8.1 and V <= 69.55:
    if V <= 0.:
        dT = 19.53*V - 1.229*V**2 - 1.075*V**3 \
        - 0.5909*V**4 - 0.1726*V**5 - 0.02813*V**6 \
        - 2.396e-3*V**7 - 8.382e-5*V**8
    elif V <= 42.919:
        dT = 19.78*V - 0.2001*V**2 + 0.01037*V**3 \
        - 2.550e-4*V**4 + 3.585e-6*V**5 - 5.344e-8*V**6 \
        + 5.100e-10*V**7
    else:
        dT = -3114.0 + 300.5*V - 9.948*V**2 \
        + 0.1703*V**3 - 1.430e-3*V**4 + 4.739e-6*V**5
    Th = Tc + dT
    print('\nHot junction temperature={0:7.2f} degC'.format(Th))
```

```
else:
    print('\nVoltage is out of acceptable range')
```

This is what happens when an out-of-range voltage is entered:

```
Enter voltage in mV: 70
Enter cold junction temperature in degC: 22
Voltage is out of acceptable range
```

We will return to this issue in Section 4.4 when we consider user-defined functions and consider another technique called input validation.

4.3   IMPLEMENTING REPETITION STRUCTURES WITH PYTHON

We will consider the three loop structures, illustrated in Figures 4.3 and 4.4 separately, since the implementations in Python are different.

4.3.1   THE GENERAL LOOP STRUCTURE

Python provides us with a while statement that allows implementation of the general loop structure. To do this, we don't use the statement quite like it was intended. The general syntax for the while statement is

```
while condition:
    loop statements
```

If the logical condition tests True, the loop statements (indented) are executed, and the loop is repeated. If False, the loop is exited.

Referring to Figure 4.3, the while code is similar to the pre-test version of the general loop, but the exit test is inverted, staying in the loop on True, and exiting on False. We need to modify the while code to provide the pre-, mid-, and post-test alternatives. This is accomplished with the following general syntax:

```
while True:
    pre-test statements
    if condition: break
    post-test statements
```

First, since the while condition is always True, the loop will never exit there. Instead, we provide the opportunity for exit with the One-line If statement. When its condition is True, the break command exits the while loop. In this way, we have the flexibility needed to leave out the pre-test code and have a pre-test loop or leave out the post-test code and have a post-test loop. Also, this allows for the inclusion of more than one if statements in the loop for multiple exit opportunities.

Example 4.2 Using the `while` Structure for Input Validation

Continuing Example 4.1, we can consider a different way to protect against invalid input data. This is called *input validation* and involves using the `while` loop. Here is the general syntax:

```
while True:
    acquire input value
    if input value is valid: break
    print error/corrective message
```

If we apply this to the thermocouple code, here is the code:

```
while True:
    V = float(input('Enter voltage in mV: '))
    if V >= -8.10 and V <= 69.55: break
    print('Voltage out of range, please re-enter')

Tc = float(input('Enter cold junction temperature in degC: '))

if V <= 0.:
    dT = 19.53*V - 1.229*V**2 - 1.075*V**3 \
       - 0.5909*V**4 - 0.1726*V**5 - 0.02813*V**6 \
       - 2.396e-3*V**7 - 8.382e-5*V**8
elif V <= 42.919:
    dT = 19.78*V - 0.2001*V**2 + 0.01037*V**3 \
       - 2.550e-4*V**4 + 3.585e-6*V**5 - 5.344e-8*V**6 \
       + 5.100e-10*V**7
else:
    dT = -3114.0 + 300.5*V - 9.948*V**2 \
       + 0.1703*V**3 - 1.430e-3*V**4 + 4.739e-6*V**5

Th = Tc + dT
print('\nHot junction temperature = {0:7.2f} degC'.format(Th))
```

As you can see, the loop will never exit on the `while` statement because of the True specification – it will only do so when the `if` statement tests True, meaning the input voltage is acceptable. Otherwise, an error prompt is displayed with the `print` statement and the loop is repeated. Again, here is a test run:

```
Enter voltage in mV: 70
Voltage out of range, please re-enter
Enter voltage in mV: 69
Enter cold junction temperature in degC: 25
Hot junction temperature = 1226.12 degC
```

A disadvantage of this input validation structure is that, if the user can't figure out what a valid input is, the loop will never exit. As a result, the user will usually just have to bail out of the program execution. A way to manage this is to provide a limit on the number of tries (as you have probably experienced in general situations such as struggles to provide log-in information). We could modify the code to accomplish this, but it would require the addition of a count-controlled loop. Stay tuned!

4.3.2   THE LIST-DRIVEN AND COUNT-CONTROLLED LOOP STRUCTURES

The need for the *list-driven loop* doesn't occur that often in engineering and scientific applications, but it is worth learning, and it provides the context for the count-controlled loop. Python provides this capability with the `for` command. Here is the general syntax:

```
for variable in [list]:
    loop statements
```

Notice the use of the word `in` between the variable and the list. The operation of the `for` loop is simple—it is repeated for each item in the list. Here is a trivial example:

```
import numpy as np

for x in [30, 45, 75, 125]:
    print('{0:5.2f}'.format(np.cos(np.radians(x))))
```

The value of the cosine is displayed for several angles (in degrees) specified in the list. Here are the results:

```
 0.87
 0.71
 0.26
-0.57
```

We encounter scenarios frequently in our computations where the `for` loop list would include a sequence of values, often integers, with a start value, step interval, and end value. This list might be very long, possibly containing hundreds of values. For this we need a modification of the list-driven `for` structure, and that is provided by the `range` type. It is used to provide a list of integers for the `for` loop. Here are several examples accompanied by explanations:

> `range(10)` provides a list of integers from 0 to 9 in steps of 1
> `range(n)` assuming n is an integer variable, provides a list from 0 to n–1
> `range(1,11)` provides a list of integers from 1 to 10
> `range(0,11,3)` provides a list of integer values, 0, 3, 6, 9

The general syntax is

```
range(start, end, step)
```

If `start` and `step` are left out, `start` is 0 and `step` is 1. If a `step` different than 1 is needed, a `start` value must be included. We generally don't see the result of the `range` type directly because it is used in the `for` statement, but it can be viewed using the `list` function:

```
x = range(0,12,3)
print(list(x))

[0, 3, 6, 9]
```

If you are having trouble with a `range` type, you can check it this way.

There are several common scenarios for use of the count-controlled loop:

- providing a limit on the number of loop iterations,
- varying the subscript of an array or matrix, and
- carrying out a set of calculations for a sequence of floating-point values.

We will illustrate all these with examples.

Example 4.3 Using a `for` Loop to Limit Iterations

Let's return to the input validation `while` loop illustrated in Example 4.2:

```
while True:
    V = float(input('Enter voltage in mV: '))
    if V >= -8.10 and V <= 69.55: break
    print('Voltage out of range, please re-enter')
```

We will modify this code, replacing the `while` loop with a `for` loop.

```
for i in range(5):
    V = float(input('Enter value for voltage in mV: '))
    if V >= -8.10 and V <= 69.55: break
    print('Voltage out of range, please re-enter')
```

In this case, the `for` loop will be exited either when a valid voltage value is input or when the loop limit is reached. The dilemma is how to determine which exit was taken. A way to do this is to check the value of `i` when the loop is exited. If it is equal to 4 (recall that `range(5)` provides values of 0 through 4), the exit occurred at the loop limit. The following code could then be added after the loop,

```
import sys
if i == 4: sys.exit('too many bad inputs')
```

This makes use of the `exit` function that is part of the `sys` module. When tested with five out-of-bounds inputs, the results are

```
Enter voltage in mV: -20
Voltage out of range, please re-enter

Enter voltage in mV: -18
Voltage out of range, please re-enter

Enter voltage in mV: -16
Voltage out of range, please re-enter

Enter voltage in mV: -14
Voltage out of range, please re-enter

Enter voltage in mV: -12
Voltage out of range, please re-enter
```

```
An exception has occurred, use %tb to see the full traceback.
```

```
SystemExit: too many bad inputs
```

In later chapters, we will use `for` loops to limit iterations as we consider numerical methods for solving equations.

Example 4.4 Using a `for` Loop to Vary Subscripts of an Array

In engineering and scientific numerical computations, the most common application of the `for` loop is in managing subscripts of arrays. The loop variable or index is used as a subscript. Let's consider two applications to illustrate this.

First, here is the code to compute the sum of only the positive elements of an array, x.

```
import numpy as np

x = np.array([2.3, -6.8, -0.7, 1.5, 8.4, -43.])

n = len(x)
sumpos = 0.
for i in range(n):
    if x[i] > 0:
        sumpos = sumpos + x[i]

print('sum of positive elements = ',sumpos)
```

After assigning a list of numbers as an array to x, the number of items in the array is computed using the Python built-in `len` function and assigned to n. A variable for the sum of the positive numbers, `sumpos`, is assigned zero (not necessary here, but good programming practice in general). The `for` loop is set up with an index variable i and a `range` type to establish the values 0, 1, 2, ..., n–1 (n values). The `if` statement tests the ith value of the x array by specifying the array subscript and, if positive, adds it to the `sumpos` variable, which accumulates the sum of the positive numbers. After the `for` loop, the `print` statement displays the result,

```
sum of positive elements = 12.2
```

Notice that the `range` type sets up a list of integers that match the array subscript requirements starting at zero.

A second example involves a two-dimensional array. Here, we would like to compute the square root of the sum of squares of the elements of the array. Example code would be

```
import numpy as np

X = np.matrix(' 3. 1.,2. ; -4., 11., 0. ; -1., 6., 14.')

sumsq = 0.
for i in range(3):
    for j in range(3):
        sumsq = sumsq + X[i,j]**2
```

```
sumsqrt = np.sqrt(sumsq)
print('square root of sum of squares = ',sumsqrt)
```

In this case, we use the matrix type to create the X array. Again, a sum variable, sumsq, is initialized to zero. A difference here is that two for loops are used, the one with index variable j is imbedded in the for loop with index variable i, both with the range(3) type specification (values 0, 1, 2). As the outer for loop iterates from 0 to 2, for each i value, the inner loop iterates j from 0 to 2. This generates pairs of subscript values that reference all the elements of X. The squares are accumulated in sumsq, and, when the loops are exited, the square root of that sum is computed and displayed as

```
square root of sum of squares = 19.595917942265423
```

You will see many examples of for loops used to manage array subscripts in this text, and there will be ample opportunity to practice by solving problems.

Example 4.5 Carrying Out a Set of Calculations
Based on a Sequence of Values

As you now know, count-controlled for loops use integers for their index variables, and they provide a sequence of integers for use within the loop. But what if we are faced with a need for a sequence of floating-point values instead. For example, for our Type J thermocouple scenario from Example 4.1, we might prefer to have a sequence of voltage values from −8 to 62 mV in steps of 2 mV. This would correspond to 36 values, including the limits. There are various ways to work with this sequence, but here we illustrate the use of a for loop.

```
import numpy as np
import pylab

Tc = 20.

Vplot = np.array([])
Tplot = np.array([])

for i in range(36):
    V = -8. + 2.*i
    if V <= 0.:
        dT = 19.53*V - 1.229*V**2 - 1.075*V**3 \
            - 0.5909*V**4 - 0.1726*V**5 - 0.02813*V**6 \
            - 2.396e-3*V**7 - 8.382e-5*V**8
    elif V <= 42.919:
        dT = 19.78*V - 0.2001*V**2 + 0.01037*V**3 \
            - 2.550e-4*V**4 + 3.585e-6*V**5 - 5.344e-8*V**6 \
            + 5.100e-10*V**7
    else:
        dT = -3114.0 + 300.5*V - 9.948*V**2 \
            + 0.1703*V**3 - 1.430e-3*V**4 + 4.739e-6*V**5
    Th = Tc + dT
```

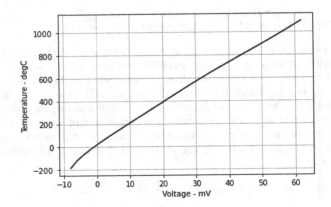

FIGURE 4.7   Use of a `for` loop to create a thermocouple plot.

```
    Vplot = np.append(Vplot,V)
    Tplot = np.append(Tplot,Th)

pylab.plot(Vplot,Tplot,c='k')
pylab.grid()
pylab.xlabel('Voltage - mV')
pylab.ylabel('Temperature - degC')
```

In the Python script above, the value of the cold junction temperature, Tc, is set to 20°C, and two empty arrays, Vplot and Tplot, are created for voltage and temperature values to come. The for loop is set up with 36 values of i from 0 to 35. In the first statement, a value of voltage, V, is calculated based on the ith current value. The dT and Th values are then computed with the code developed in previous examples. The last two statements in the for loop append the V and Th values to the Vplot and Tplot arrays, respectively. After the loop, the pylab module is used to generate the plot shown in Figure 4.7.

4.3.3   THE break AND Continue STATEMENTS WITH THE for LOOP

It is worth mentioning two features of the while and for structures that are useful on occasion. In Section 4.3.1, we employed the break statement to exit a while loop prematurely. The same break statement can be used to exit a for loop. Here is a simple example:

```
import numpy as np

testdata = np.array([])
for i in range(10):
    datain=float(input('enter data item or -9999 to stop: '))
    if datain == -9999: break
    testdata = np.append(testdata,datain)

print(testdata)
```

and an example run:

```
enter data item or -9999 to stop: -12
enter data item or -9999 to stop: 14
enter data item or -9999 to stop: 9
enter data item or -9999 to stop: 3
enter data item or -9999 to stop: -4
enter data item or -9999 to stop: -9999
[-12.   14.    9.    3.   -4.]
```

This script allows the user to enter a dataset of up to ten values and signal an early end of the entry with an unusual value, here −9999. When that occurs, the for loop exits on the break statement. The −9999 used to terminate the input sequence is called a *sentinel value*.

A question that arises is how the break command behaves when there are nested for loops. As with many Python features, an effective way of answering questions is to investigate by developing a test script. Here is such a script that is designed to answer the question:

```
for i in range(3):
    for j in range(3):
        if j > 0: break
    print('outerloop',i,j)
print('after loops',i,j)
```

Here, there is a break from the inner loop. Does that just exit to the outer loop? Or does the break exit both loops? Here is the script's output:

```
outerloop 0 1
outerloop 1 1
outerloop 2 1
after loops 2 1
```

It is clear that the break statement only exits the inner loop and not the outer loop. Well, that raises another question: What if we wanted both loops to be exited? An answer to that is to put the break test in both loops, as in

```
for i in range(3):
    for j in range(3):
        if j > 0: break
    if j > 0: break
    print('outerloop',i,j)
print('after loops',i,j)
```

with the result

```
after loops 0 1
```

In conclusion, the use of the `break` statement with `for` loops is not as common as it is with the `while` loop, but it happens from time to time.

There are occasions where we want part or all of the `for` (or `while`, for that matter) loop code to be skipped, but we want the loop to continue repeating. With Python, this involves the use of the `continue` statement. Here is an example:

```
import random
import pylab

testdata = []
for i in range(1000):
    rannum = random.normalvariate(0.,1.)
    if rannum < 0.: continue
    testdata.append(rannum)

pylab.hist(testdata,bins=20)
```

The `for` loop generates 1,000 random numbers, emulating the standard normal distribution (mean = 0, standard deviation = 1)[3]. The `random` module provides a family of functions related to random numbers. A common use of the module is to generate a sequence of random numbers that appear to have been drawn from a particular distribution. One common distribution is the *uniform distribution* where the probability of drawing numbers between two limits is constant. If the limits are 0 and 1, the probability of drawing a number between 0 and 0.1 is the same as that between 0.7 and 0.8.

The other common distribution is the *normal* or *Gaussian distribution* which is modeled by the classical bell curve. It is more probable to generate values near the center of the distribution, the mean, and that probability drops off as the distance from the mean increases. We use the `random` module frequently to generate a series of random numbers. They do not follow the specified distribution exactly and so are often referred to as pseudorandom numbers. You can find out more about the `random` module from https://docs.python.org/3/library/random.html.

The `if` statement skips the following `append` statement if the current random number is negative. If the number is positive, it is appended to the `testdata` array. After the `for` loop, a histogram of the `testdata` array is generated and illustrated in Figure 4.8 with a histogram plot. There were 495 data used to form this plot, about one-half of the `for` loop iterations, as expected.

4.4   USER-DEFINED FUNCTIONS IN PYTHON

We have seen the use of many built-in functions in Python and its supporting modules, like NumPy and SciPy. An important and essential feature of Python is the ability to create your own function. The concept of such a *user-defined function* is illustrated in Figure 4.9.

Functions are useful on several counts. First, they allow you to "package" a calculation so it can be invoked at several different locations in a script. Second, by carefully validating a function, the reliability of the calculation is enhanced. Third, functions are portable in that they can be made available to different scripts and programmers.

---

[3] We discuss distributions, including the normal and standard normal distributions, in Chapter 10.

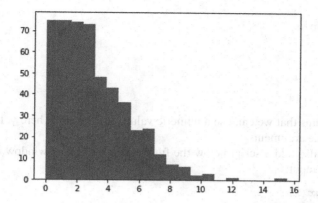

FIGURE 4.8 Histogram of positive values generated from the standard normal distribution.

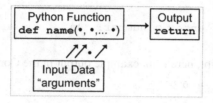

FIGURE 4.9 Illustration of the Python user-defined function.

The general syntax for a Python function is

```
def function_name(argument list):
    statements
    return results
```

Using our example from Section 4.2, squaring a value but preserving its sign, we can construct

```
def sgnsqr(x):
    sgnx2 = x**2
    if x < 0: sgnx2 = -sgnx2
    return sgnx2
```

Here, the function name is sgnsqr, and there is one argument, x. The code to attach the sign of x to the result variable, sgnx2, is like what we have seen before. The result is provided with the return statement. To use this function, either in a script or in the IPython Command window, the script must be executed or run first. If that is done, then here are examples of using the function in the Command window:

```
sgnsqr(-2)
Out[8]: -4

sgnsqr(2)
Out[9]: 4
```

```
sgnsqr(0)
Out[10]: 0

y = -12

sgnsqr(y)
Out[12]: -144
```

This illustrates that we can use a numeric value, or a variable, here y, that stores a value as the argument.

We can also add a script below the function in the Editor window to prompt the user for input:

```
def sgnsqr(x):
    sgnx2 = x**2
    if x < 0: sgnx2 = -sgnx2
    return sgnx2

y = float(input('enter a number: '))
print(sgnsqr(y))
```

When we run the script, here is an example output in the Command window:

```
enter a number: -400
-160000.0
```

Because of the requirement to run the function code before invoking the function, you will see that we place one or more functions at the beginning of longer scripts before the ensuing script code. To enhance portability, it is also possible to save a Python code file of just the function code and then import the function into another script. If the function is saved as sgnsqr_function.py, we can import it as follows:

```
from sgnsqr_function import sgnsqr

y = float(input('enter a number: '))
print(sgnsqr(y))
```

and the script will execute properly. A requirement here is that the path in the file system must be such that the file can be found by the `from` command. In a sense, the .py file is our own, user-defined module, and it might contain a family of useful functions.

4.4.1 `lambda` Functions

Python provides a convenient, one-line style for creating simple functions. These are called `lambda`[4] *or anonymous functions*. For example, we can create an abbreviated function definition like

```
def gety(x,a,b):
    return a*x**b
```

---

[4] Note that `lambda` is a reserved word in Python. Don't try to use it otherwise, such as a variable name.

that implements a formula $a \cdot x^b$. This can also be written more concisely as

```
gety = lambda x,a,b: a*x**b
```

Alternately, we can define the function without the parameters a and b,

```
gety = lambda x: a*x**b
```

but then those parameters must be defined in the main script. Here is example code with accompanying execution:

```
a = 4
b = -0.32

gety = lambda x: a*x**b

y = []
for x in [0.1,0.5,0.9]:
    y.append(gety(x))

print(y)
```

```
[8.357184523416159, 4.9933221956064475, 4.137160678619936]
```

You see that the variables a and b are first assigned values. Then, they are available to the gety lambda function. A list-driven for loop is used to fill out a list y with three evaluations of the gety function, and the results being displayed in the Console.

4.4.2 Function Arguments

The list of arguments in a function definition can take various forms. First, it is possible that arguments are not required, so the list is empty. Following an example in the previous section, we might want to have a function that provides a random value from the positive half of the standard normal distribution. That function definition, along with a test, would then be

```
import random

def halfrand():
    while True:
        rannum = random.normalvariate(0.,1.)
        if rannum > 0.: break
    return rannum

print(halfrand())
```

An example result is

```
0.28609469258613235
```

Next, we can have a similar function but with multiple arguments. Here, the function requires specification of the mean and standard deviation of the normal distribution.

```
def halfrand(mu,sig):
    while True:
        rannum = random.normalvariate(mu,sig)
        if rannum > mu: break
    return rannum

print(halfrand(100.,20.))
```

with the result

```
95.48642189840088
```

As a third variation on this theme, we might want to allow for specification of the mean and standard deviation, and, if not supplied, assume the values for the standard normal distribution, 0. and 1., respectively. This is accomplished by using *keyword arguments*.

```
def halfrand(mu=0.,sig=1.):
    while True:
        rannum = random.normalvariate(mu,sig)
        if rannum > mu: break
    return rannum
```

In this case, one or both arguments can be supplied. If only the second argument is supplied, it must be accompanied with the associated keyword.

```
print(halfrand(sig=0.1))
```

```
0.18326947282604794
```

If both arguments are provided in the correct order, keyword identifiers are not required, and, if both arguments are left out, the function will use the default values. Here are two example statements with explanations:

`halfrand(20.,5.)` Here, mu = 20 and sig = 5.
`halfrand()` Since no arguments are specified, the default values are used.

In many instances, we would like to have function arguments that are arrays. It would be typical that the arrays supplied to the function would have different numbers of elements, so, within the function, the number of elements would have to be determined. As an example, we might like to create our own function to determine the *percentile value* of an ordered array. Here is a Python function that accomplishes this.

```
def pctile(x,pct):
    n = len(x)
    mp = pct/100*(n-1)
```

```
mp1 = int(mp)
xp = (mp-mp1)*x[mp1]+(1-(mp-mp1))*x[mp1+1]
return xp
```

The two arguments are an array (or list or tuple) of numerical values sorted in ascending order, and the percentile value desired (in %). The function first determines the number of elements in x. Then the fractional percentile location, mp, is calculated, where n-1 is used because of the zero-based indexing of x. The integer part of the percentile location is determined using the built-in int function. Then, the percentile value is computed proportionately between the mp location x value and the mp+1 location x value. This value is returned. Here is an example of the use of the pctile function:

```
x = [0.1, 0.5, 0.8, 1.2, 1.7, 2.3, 3.1, 4.7, 5.1, 6.7]
print(pctile(x,25.))
```

```
1.0999999999999999
```

We can consider enhancements to the pctile function to make it more versatile. The requirement that the input array be sorted is restrictive. Therefore, we can add code to the function to sort the x array into another y array, and then determine the percentile using y. There are many ways to do this. To keep it simple here, we take advantage of the sort function from the NumPy module.

```
import numpy as np

def pctile(x,pct):
    y = np.sort(x)
    n = len(y)
    mp = pct/100*(n-1)
    mp1 = int(mp)
    xp = (mp-mp1)*y[mp1]+(1-(mp-mp1))*y[mp1+1]
    return xp

x = [0.1, 0.5, 0.8, 1.2, 6.7, 2.3, 3.1, 4.7, 5.1, 1.7]
print(pctile(x,25))
```

which produces the same result, but now the x array does not have to be presorted in ascending order.

You can see in this last example that we invoked a function, sort, within another function, pctile. We can certainly do this with our user-defined functions too. Consider we would like to compute the *interquartile range* (iqr), which is the difference between the 75th and 25th percentile values—containing the centrally located 50th percentile value of our data. Given our pctile function, this becomes easy.

```
def iqr(x):
    pct25 = pctile(x,25)
    pct75 = pctile(x,75)
    return pct75 - pct25
```

And testing it with our x array yields

```
x = [0.1, 0.5, 0.8, 1.2, 6.7, 2.3, 3.1, 4.7, 5.1, 1.7]
print('iqr = {0:5.2f}'.format(iqr(x)))
```

```
iqr =  2.40
```

An important feature of function arguments is that, apart from variables, they can be the names of other functions. These have been called *function functions*. Let's illustrate this with a simple example, a function to compute the average of a set of values computed from a formula supplied by a second function.

```
import numpy as np

def funavg(func,x):
    n = len(x)
    y = np.zeros(n)
    for i in range(n):
        y[i] = func(x[i])
    return np.mean(y)
```

The first argument of the funavg function is the name of a function, func, not a variable. The second argument, x, is an array variable to contain a set of values. In the function code, an array y is created the same size as x, and, with a for loop, the y array is filled with the values of the func function evaluated with the values in the x array. Finally, the average of the y array values is returned using the mean function from the NumPy module.

The funavg function can be tested as follows:

```
f = lambda x: x**3 - 0.28*x**2 + 0.43*x - 17.4

x = np.linspace(-10,10)
favg = funavg(f,x)
print(favg)
```

with the result

```
-27.11428571428567
```

Notice here that we use the alternate lambda form for the function definition. The function f used here could be changed to another function and generate a corresponding different result. You can then see the flexibility of this arrangement. The concept of having a function name as an argument to another function is implemented easily and directly in Python. That is not the case in other programming languages and software packages where the implementation is more complicated or perhaps not even feasible.

This brings us to the last topic regarding function arguments. In our example above, rather than having the function f defined as shown there, we might want more flexibility by adding variables to define the coefficients of the polynomial expression, as in

```
f = lambda x,a,b,c,d: a*x**3 + b*x**2 + c*x +d
```

Our `funavg` function must now "pass" the values of a, b, c, and d on through to the `func` call. But we can't do that explicitly because then `funavg` would lose its generic character. This is accomplished by using a generic argument `*args` as shown below.

```
def funavg(func,x,*args):
    n = len(x)
    y = np.zeros(n)
    for i in range(n):
        y[i] = func(x[i],*args)
    return np.mean(y)
```

Then, the script can be modified and tested with the same polynomial as follows:

```
f = lambda x,a,b,c,d: a*x**3 + b*x**2 + c*x +d

x = np.linspace(-10,10)
a = 1. ; b = -0.28 ; c = 0.43 ; d = - 17.4
favg = funavg(f,x,a,b,c,d)
print(favg)
```

The same result is produced.

As a variation on this method, we consider the situation where one or more of the arguments to our function `f` are keyword arguments, typically representing default values. We can illustrate this with a modification of the script computing a set of values from the positive half of the normal distribution, but now using a function `genrand`.

```
import random
import pylab

def genrand(mu=0.,sig=1.):
    testdata = []
    for i in range(1000):
        rannum = random.normalvariate(mu,sig)
        if rannum < 0.: continue
        testdata.append(rannum)
    return testdata

testdata = genrand(sig=4.)

pylab.hist(testdata,bins=20)
```

You will note that when the `genrand` function is invoked (or "called"), only the `sig` variable is specified. This means that the default value of the `mu` variable will be used. The resulting histogram plot is shown in Figure 4.10.

Now, let's suggest that we modify our `funavg` function to accommodate a simpler `genrand` function that produces a single, positive value from the normal distribution, and we do so preserving the use of keyword arguments. Here is the code that results

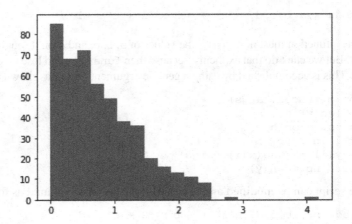

FIGURE 4.10   Histogram of data generated with the genrand function for a `sig` value of 4.0.

```
import random
import numpy as np

def funavg(func,x,**kwargs):
    n = len(x)
    y = np.zeros(n)
    for i in range(n):
        y[i] = func(x[i],**kwargs)
    return np.mean(y)

def genrand(x,mu=0.,sig=1.):
    while True:
        rannum = random.normalvariate(mu,sig)
        if rannum > 0.: break
    return rannum

n = 1000
x = np.arange(1,n+1)

normavg = funavg(genrand,x,sig=4.)
print(normavg)
```

First, notice that we have replaced the *args generic keyword argument with
**kwargs (two asterisks!). Since the random.normalvariate function doesn't
really have an "x" argument, a "dummy" x array of numbers from 1 to 1,000 is set
up using the np.arange function. With the funavg call, the genrand function
name is supplied, the dummy x array and only one of the keyword arguments.
(The other, mu, will employ the default value of 0.) The use of the while loop in
the genrand function repeats the random number generation until a positive value
is produced. The genrand function only returns a single value. The result is

```
3.0213502792531117
```

Generally, the order of argument values supplied to a function has to agree with those in the function definition. If there are extra `*args` or `**kwargs`, these must follow the other arguments. Any `*args` must agree in order with their function definition and be supplied completely. Keyword arguments can be supplied partially or in different order, but they must follow other arguments, and it is common practice for them to follow required `*args` arguments. This may seem a bit confusing, but, in time, you will get used to it. Also, you will see many examples in later chapters.

4.4.3 Variable Scope

A simple way of defining variable scope is that it describes where a variable and its value(s) can be "seen" from different locations in a script. A good way to understand scope is to explore it with a few simple examples and then generalize our observations. Here is a first example:

```
def func(x):
    a = 4.
    b = -0.32
    return a*x**b

print(func(12.3))
print(a,b)
```

When this code it entered in the Spyder Editor, an error is immediately noted beside the last `print` statement. This is because the values of a and b are not available in the main script – they are "local" to the function definition. If we modify the code to

```
def func(x):
    a = 4.
    b = -0.32
    print(a,b)
    return a*x**b

print(func(12.3))
```

there are no errors noted, and the code executes to produce

```
4.0 -0.32
1.7918033972156524
```

As we would expect, there is no problem with the `print` command inside the function because the a and b values are available there.

Now let's turn the tables on this example.

```
def func(x):
    print(a,b)
    return a*x**b
```

```
a = 4.
b = -0.32

print(func(12.3))
```

This code produces the same results as above. It is evident that the variables (and their values) a and b are available in the function definition even though they are defined in the main script.

So, our first and important observation is that variables defined within functions cannot be seen outside the function; whereas, variables outside functions in the main script can be seen inside functions. The former are said to have local scope and the latter global scope. This observation excludes function arguments which reference variables outside the function and return results.

This observation raises a question: Is there any way to force a variable inside a function to be seen everywhere else in the script? The answer is yes, and this script illustrates how:

```
def func(x):
    global a
    a = 4.
    b = -0.32
    return a*x**b

print(a)
print(func(12.3))
```

with the output display

```
1.7918033972156524
4.0
```

The use of the global declaration expands the scope of a variable so that it can be seen everywhere – it then has global scope.

PROBLEMS

4.1   Write a Python script for the flowchart depicted in Figure P4.1.

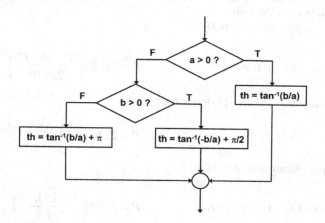

FIGURE P4.1   Flowchart.

4.2   Consider a vertical, cylindrical bin with conical base partially filled with grain. Refer to Figure P4.2. Develop and test a Python function named binvol that has arguments of the bin cylindrical radius, r, the heights of the cylindrical, hcyl, and conical, hcon, sections, and the overall depth of the grain in the bin, h. The function should return the volume of grain, gvol. It should also check that the grain depth is feasible—not greater than the sum of the conical and cylindrical heights.

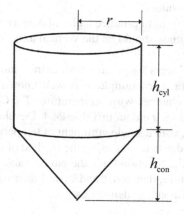

FIGURE P4.2   Grain bin.

4.3   Approximate models for the variation of temperature and pressure versus altitude in the Earth's atmosphere are available.[5] They provide formulas for three atmospheric layers: the troposphere, lower stratosphere, and upper stratosphere.

troposphere ($h < 11{,}000$):

$$T = 15.04 - 0.00649h \qquad P = 101.29\left(\frac{T + 273.15}{288.08}\right)^{5.256}$$

lower stratosphere ($11{,}000 < h < 25{,}000$):

$$T = -56.46 \qquad P = 22.65\,e^{1.73 - 0.000157\,h}$$

upper stratosphere ($25{,}000 < h$):

$$T = -131.21 + 0.00299h \qquad P = 2.488\left(\frac{T + 273.15}{216.6}\right)^{-11.388}$$

In the formulas above, the specific units required are
h: meters (m) T: °C P: kilopascals (kPa)
and the density of air is related to temperature and pressure by

$$\rho = \frac{P}{0.2869(T + 273.15)} \qquad \rho : \text{kg/m}^3$$

(a) Develop a Python function, atm, that has a single argument, h, and returns the temperature, T, pressure, P, and density, rho. Test this function for different h values.

(b) Use your function from to produce a plot of density versus altitude from 0 to 25,000 m. Altitude should be the vertical axis.

4.4   Scientists and engineers frequently must extract numerical information from tables of data. For example, it is well known that the density of water, ρ (kg/m³), changes with temperature, T (°C). This relationship can be represented by the data in Table P4.4. Develop and test a Python function, H2Oden, with a single argument of temperature, T, that returns an estimate of the density, rho, using the method of *linear interpolation*. For this method, the function finds the pair of table entries that bracket the input temperature, denoted 1 and 2, and then uses a straight line to estimate the corresponding density, as in

$$\rho = \frac{T - T_1}{T_2 - T_1}(\rho_2 - \rho_1) + \rho_1$$

---

[5] https://www.grc.nasa.gov/www/k-12/airplane/atmosmet.html.

TABLE P4.4
Density of Water versus Temperature

T (°C)	ρ (kg/m³)	T (°C)	ρ (kg/m³)	T (°C)	ρ (kg/m³)	T (°C)	ρ (kg/m³)
0	999.87	20	998.23	50	988.07	80	971.83
2	999.97	25	997.08	55	985.73	85	968.65
4	1,000.00	30	995.68	60	983.24	90	965.34
6	999.97	35	994.06	65	980.59	95	961.92
10	999.73	40	992.25	70	977.81	100	958.38
15	999.13	45	990.25	75	974.89		

4.5 What is wrong with the following Python code segment? Propose a corrected version.

```
if x <= 0.:
    fval = -x
else:
    if x < 1:
        fval = x**2
    else:
        fval = 1
```

4.6 The graph shown in Figure P4.6 describes a functional relationship between an input variable, x, and an output variable, y. Electrical engineers might call this a linear function with saturation. Develop and test a Python function, sat, which accepts an input argument, x, and returns the y value.

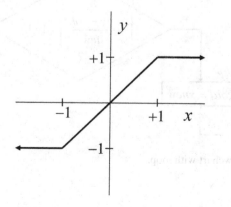

FIGURE P4.6 Saturation function.

4.7   An environmental scientist is developing a computer program to determine whether it is safe to introduce a weed herbicide into a lake. According to scientific studies, the chemical should only be applied when the water temperature is less than 30°C, the dissolved oxygen concentration is above 6 mg/L, and the pH is between 6.8 and 8. Develop a Python function, weedtest, with arguments temperature, T, dissolved oxygen concentration, DO, and pH, and returns a string, either 'safe' or 'unsafe'. Test your function for various input values.

4.8   Write and test a Python function, findrx, that has one argument, x, and returns rx. The value of x is required to be positive or zero, so the function should check for this and return an error message is x is negative. If the value of x is zero, the function simply returns a value of zero. For positive x values, the function implements the flowchart shown in Figure P4.8. Test your function with various values of x. What calculation does your function perform?

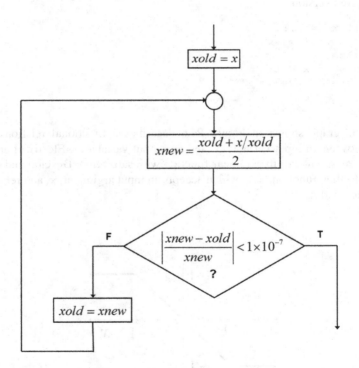

FIGURE P4.8   Flowchart with loop.

4.9   The famous *Fibonacci series* starts with the sequence 0 and 1. Each subsequent number in the series is the sum of the two previous numbers. Applying that to the first two numbers, the series evolves with the numbers 0, 1, 1, 2, 3, 5, ... Develop a Python function, fibo, that has an integer input argument, n. The function computes n terms of the Fibonacci series (n must be greater than 2) and returns the ratio of the second last term to the last term. Experiment with the function to see whether the ratio converges for larger values of n. Compare the ratio to the *Golden Ratio*, given by

$$\frac{\sqrt{5}-1}{2}$$

As a supplement, do some reading on the Fibonacci series, its evidence in nature and its relationship to the Golden Ratio.

4.10 Develop a Python function, sumn, that has an integer input argument, n, and returns the sum of the integers from 1 to n. Test your function and compare the result to the shortcut formula

$$\frac{n(n+1)}{2}$$

4.11 The American Association of State Highway and Transportation Officials provides the criteria in Table P4.11 for classifying soils in accordance with their suitability for use in highway subgrades and embankment construction. Develop a Python function, soilclass, that has average grain size, gsize, as an input argument and returns the classification.

TABLE P4.11
Soil Classification

Grain Size mm	Classification
Size > 75	Boulders
2 < size ≤ 75	Gravel
0.05 < size ≤ 2	Sand
0.002 < size ≤ 0.05	Silt
Size ≤ 0.002	Clay

4.12 Write a Python code segment to implement the flowchart shown in Figure P4.12.

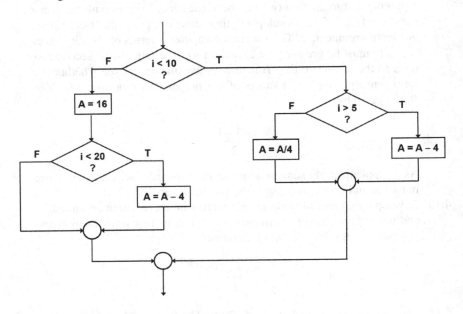

FIGURE P4.12 Flowchart with embedded structure.

4.13 The ideal gas law is widely used to predict the pressure, temperature, or volume of a gas at conditions that are not extreme, especially not inordinately high pressure. It can be expressed as

$$P\hat{V} = RT$$

where P: pressure, $\hat{V}$: specific volume, R: the gas law constant and T: the absolute temperature. For typical SI units, P [=] kPa, $\hat{V}$ [=] m³/kmol, T [=] K, and the value of R is approximately 8.3145 kPa·m³/[kmol·K]

Develop a user-defined Python function called idealgas that has input arguments of P, $\hat{V}$ and T. Use keyword arguments. When invoked, only two of the three arguments are provided, and the function returns the third. Test your function for various scenarios.

4.14 As temperature increases, solid materials expand. This expansion can be quantified by a coefficient with the formula

$$\Delta L = \alpha \, \Delta T \, L$$

where ΔL is the change in length, α is the linear expansion coefficient, ΔT is the change in temperature and L is the length of the material at the base temperature, T.

The table below lists the expansion coefficients for several common materials.

Material	Expansion Coefficient $\times 10^6$ m/[m·°C]
Copper	16
Aluminium	22.5
Glass	5.9
Steel	11.5
Polyethylene	125

Create a Python function called `linexp` that has input arguments of material type (text string), temperature change, and base length. The function should return the expanded length. Test your function with various examples.

4.15 In the U.S., vehicle fuel economy is typically reported in units of miles per gallon (mpg); whereas, in Europe, the quantity used is L/100 km traveled (L/100 km). Create a `lambda` function that converts mpg to L/100 km. If a good value for fuel economy in the U.S. is 40 mpg, use your function to compute the value in L/100 km.

4.16 At some point, you may have the adventure of purchasing a new or used vehicle (perhaps you have experienced this treat already). It is usually necessary to finance part of the purchase with a loan. Key parameters associated with the loan are its amount or principal, P, the interest rate, i, the term of length of the loan (n = number of monthly payments), and the constant monthly payment, A. These are related by the formula

$$A = P\frac{i(1+i)^n}{(1+i)^n - 1}$$

If the interest rate is given in annual terms, and the payments are monthly, the interest rate divided by 12 must be used in the formula.

Develop a Python function called `loanpmt` with the arguments of loan amount, annual interest rate, and number of years of the loan period. The function should return the monthly payment.

Imagine that you can afford a monthly payment of $400, and you can obtain a loan term of 6 years at 4.8% annual interest rate. If a 20% down payment is required to qualify for the loan, experiment with your function to determine the maximum purchase price you can afford.

4.17 Ohm's Law describes the relationship of electrical current, I, and voltage, V, for a resistance, R. Standard units are amperes (A), volts (V) and ohms (Ω), and the Ohm's Law formula is

$$V = I \cdot R$$

Develop a Python function called ohmslaw with three keyword arguments, I, V, and R. When the function is invoked, two of these three are supplied and the function computes and returns the third. Test your function with several examples.

5 Graphics—Matplotlib

CHAPTER OBJECTIVES

- Learn about the Matplotlib module and its `pyplot` submodule.
- Be able to create scatter and line plots using `pyplot`.
- Customize plot axes including the addition of a right-side axis.
- Learn how to create subplots for multiple plots in a figure object.
- Create and customize bar graphs with more flexibility than with `pylab`.
- Explore creating other plots, such as polar plots, stem plots, and pie charts.
- Learn how to create plots with logarithmic axis scales.
- Be able to create contour and surface plots to depict two-dimensional data and functions.

In Chapter 3, you learned how to use the `pylab` module to create various plots. That module provides a convenient interface for many graphics applications but lacks the flexibility and capabilities provided by the more comprehensive Matplotlib module. The purpose of this chapter is to expand your ability to create plots that are common and useful in engineering and science.

5.1 INTRODUCTION TO MATPLOTLIB

The *Matplotlib module* provides extensive graphics capabilities for use with Python. A comprehensive coverage of Matplotlib is not feasible in this chapter. The Matplotlib User's Guide will help you expand your knowledge.[1] Here, we focus on Matplotlib's `pyplot` submodule and its features most useful for engineering and science.

The typical command line we use to access `pyplot` is

```
import matplotlib.pyplot as plt
```

using the `plt` abbreviation to save keystrokes later in the script. This is just like using `np` for the NumPy module. Many of the simpler plots are generated in a similar fashion to `pylab`. We will illustrate this with some examples.

Plotting an analytical function is a common task. Consider generating a plot of the curve of the function

$$f(x) = \cos(x)\cosh(x) - 1 \qquad 0 \le x \le 5 \qquad (5.1)$$

---

[1] https://matplotlib.org/stable/users/index.html

DOI: 10.1201/9781003256861-5

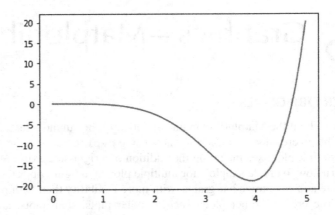

FIGURE 5.1   A simple line plot of an analytical function.

Here is the Python code to produce the plot shown in Figure 5.1.

```
import numpy as np
import matplotlib.pyplot as plt

x = np.linspace(0,5)
f = lambda x: np.cos(x)*np.cosh(x)-1
plt.plot(x, f(x))
plt.show()
```

The code for Figure 5.1 makes use of the `plot` function in `pyplot`. Also, the NumPy module is included to utilize the `linspace`, `cos`, and `cosh` functions. Since our function is simple, we use a `lambda` definition. Although not visible to you, the curve on the figure is blue. The `linspace` function provides 50 points by default, and these are enough to depict most continuous curves well. We already see opportunities to improve the plot and will get to them later.

Next, we see how to create simple plots of discrete data sets. Individual data are typically plotted as markers, unless there are a large number which would clutter the plot unnecessarily. In the latter case, the data are often connected with straight lines and without markers. We will illustrate both cases here.

Example 5.1 Freezing Point of Aqueous Ethylene Glycol Solutions

Ethylene Glycol (CH_2OHCH_2OH) is commonly mixed with water to provide antifreeze solutions for cooling systems in vehicle engines. As glycol is added to water, the freezing point of the solution drops rapidly. However, as pure glycol is approached, the freezing point rises quickly. Table 5.1 presents data on freezing point versus per cent glycol.

Typical antifreeze solutions are 50% glycol providing protection down to −36.8°C (−34.2°F); although, because of slush formation, protection is usually cited not quite that low. Here is Python code, using the `pyplot` module, to create the plot displayed in Figure 5.2.

TABLE 5.1

Freezing Point Data for Glycol-Water Solutions

Glycol (% by volume)	0	10	20	30	40	50	60	80	90	100
Freezing point (°C)	0	−3.4	−7.9	−13.7	−23.5	−36.8	−52.8	−46	−30	−12.8

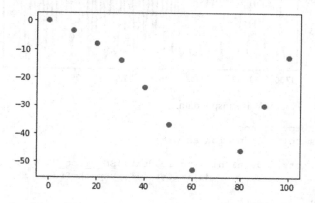

FIGURE 5.2 Simple scatter plot.

```
import matplotlib.pyplot as plt

PG = [0.,10.,20.,30.,40.,50.,60.,80.,90.,100.]
FP = [0.,-3.4,-7.9,-13.7,-23.5,-36.8,-52.8,-46.,-30.,-12.8]

plt.scatter(PG, FP)
plt.show()
```

The difference you will note is that we have used the `scatter` function instead of the `plot` function. The markers are solid circles and colored blue by default. We will want to add features and will see how to do that later in this chapter.

Example 5.2 Sunspot Observations

In 1848, *Johann Rudolph Wolf* devised a method for quantifying solar activity by counting the number of individual dark spots or groups of spots on the sun's surface. He computed a quantity, now called the *Wolf sunspot number*,[2] by adding ten times the number of groups plus the total count of individual spots in a year.

The data set for annual counts extends back to 1700! These data are available in .csv format for download from http://www.sidc.be/silso/datafiles, as filename SN_y_tot_V2.0.csv. The Python code below used the `loadtxt` function to acquire the data from this file and creates a plot shown in Figure 5.3.

---

[2] You may also see these referred to by the German possessive form, *Wölfer Sunspot Numbers*.

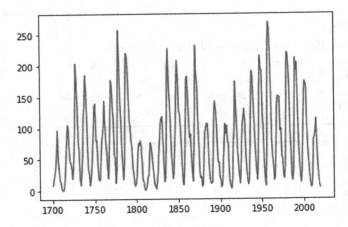

FIGURE 5.3 Plot of Wolf sunspot data.

```
import numpy as np
import matplotlib.pyplot as plt

year, nspots, sd, n1,n1 = np.loadtxt('SN_y_tot_V2.0.csv', \
                          delimiter=';', unpack=True)

plt.plot(year, nspots)
```

There are 320 data points for this plot. It's easy to see that this would become cluttered if we used the scatter function. We also add the observation that the data reveal an up-down periodic nature. We'll explore that in a later chapter. The plot connects straight line segments between each pair of data, and the lines are blue.

To this point, we have generated three typical plots with the Matplotlib's pyplot module. There are many combinations and enhancements that now must be considered. The next section addresses these needs.

5.2 CUSTOMIZING LINE AND SCATTER PLOTS

There are numerous features we would like to add to simple plots to improve their appearance, readability, and complexity. Here is list:

- adding gridlines, axis titles, and a plot title,
- customizing the properties of lines and markers, including colors,
- combining markers and lines in plotting a data set,
- plotting more than one series and adding a legend,
- adjusting axis limits, and
- adding an axis on the right of a plot with an appropriate legend.

Later we will consider creating multiple plots on a single figure object and other types of plots used by engineers and scientists.

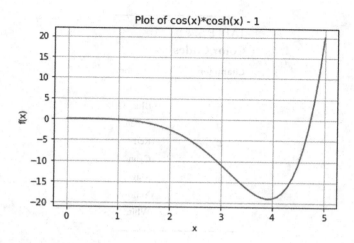

FIGURE 5.4 Line plot with grid and titles.

Let's return to the simple plot illustrated in Figure 5.1 and add code to provide grid lines, and axis and plot titles. The result is shown in Figure 5.4.

```
import numpy as np
import matplotlib.pyplot as plt

x = np.linspace(0,5)
f = lambda x: np.cos(x)*np.cosh(x)-1
plt.plot(x, f(x))
plt.grid()
plt.xlabel('x')
plt.ylabel('f(x)')
plt.title('Plot of cos(x)*cosh(x) -1')
plt.show()
```

These additions are identical to the statements we used in Chapter 3 with the simpler `pylab` module. Most engineers and scientists like to have grids on their plots because they help reading the plot and avoiding *parallax errors*. Of course, good axis titles and a plot title help provide an accurate description of the plot.

Employing color and different styles of lines are useful for making your plots more attractive and readable. For plots that will be rendered in black-and-white documents, we might change the color of the line from the default blue to black. This involves specifying a color choice as part of the plot command. The color choices, shown here in Table 5.2, are the same as those presented in Chapter 3 as Table 3.7.

```
plt.plot(x, f(x), color='k')
```

Note: You can use the shorthand notation c for `color`. We do not show the result here as it is the same as Figure 5.4, just with the line color now black.

TABLE 5.2
Color Codes

Character	Color
k	Black
b	Blue
g	Green
r	Red
c	Cyan
m	Magenta
y	Yellow
w	White

In certain situations, we may want to employ a different style of line, such as a dashed line. This occurs most often used to distinguish one plotted curve from another. We can achieve this by adding a linestyle specification to the plot command. Table 5.3 presents the choices for linestyle.

For example, we can change the solid line to a dashed line with

```
plt.plot(x, f(x), color='k', linestyle='--')
```

Figure 5.5 shows this version of the plot. *Note*: You can use the shorthand notation ls for linestyle.

Before we move on to customizing markers, we can consider how to change the width or "weight" of the line. We do this by adding the linewidth (or lw) specification to the plot command. For example,

```
plt.plot(x, f(x), color='k', linestyle='--', linewidth=2.5)
```

and you will get used to a shortened version of this statement:

```
plt.plot(x, f(x), c='k', ls='--', lw=2.5)
```

The default linewidth is 1.5, and you can experiment with different values to find the one that works for your plot.

TABLE 5.3
Linestyle Choices and Codes

Character	Style
-	Solid
--	Dashed
:	Dotted
-.	Dash-dot

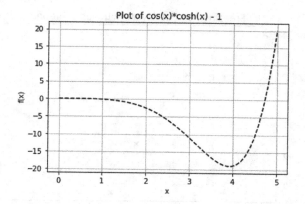

FIGURE 5.5   Plot with black curve and dashed line.

Now, on to marker options. We can specify *marker color* in the same way we did for lines, using the color (or c) specification in the scatter command. We may be interested in changing the marker style, and these are presented in Table 5.4.

In our glycol freezing point plot (), we might want to change the markers to black x's. Along the way, we can also add a grid and titles. Here is the modified Python code to implement these modifications. The resulting plot is shown in Figure 5.6.

```
import matplotlib.pyplot as plt

PG = [0., 10., 20., 30., 40., 50., 60., 80., 90., 100.]
FP = [0., -3.4, -7.9, -13.7, -23.5, -36.8, -52.8, -46.,
-30., -12.8]

plt.scatter(PG, FP, marker='x', c='k')
plt.grid()
plt.xlabel('Glycol - % by volume')
plt.ylabel('Freezing Point - degC')
plt.title('Freezing Point of Glycol Aqueous Solutions')
plt.show()
```

TABLE 5.4
Marker Codes

Character	Symbol	Description
.	●	Point
o	○	Circle
+	+	Plus sign
x	×	
D	◊	Diamond
v	∇	Del
^	Δ	Triangle
s	□	Square

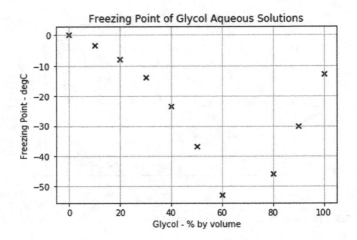

FIGURE 5.6   Freezing point plot with black "×" markers, grid, and titles.

For the marker styles that have edges, e.g. circle, diamond, square, it is possible to customize the edges and the interior of the marker. This is accomplished by using the `edgecolors` specification and the `color` specification for the interior. Here is an example:

```
plt.scatter(PG, FP, marker='s', c='w', edgecolors='k')
```

Figure 5.7 shows the result.

The last enhancement we will consider for a scatter plot is to connect adjacent markers with lines. This is accomplished by adding marker specification(s) to the `plot` command, not by using the `scatter` command. We add lines to Figure 5.7 by replacing the `scatter` command with

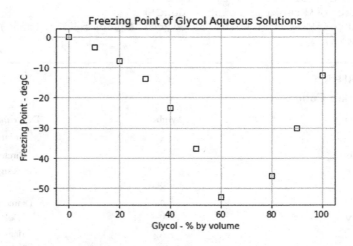

FIGURE 5.7   Freezing point plot with square markers, black edges, and white interiors.

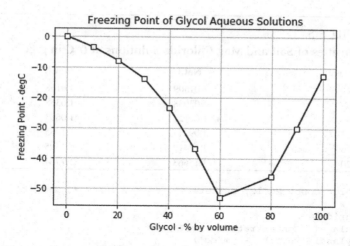

FIGURE 5.8   Freezing point plot with lines connecting markers.

```
plt.plot(PG, FP, c='k', marker='s', markeredgecolor='k' \
, markerfacecolor='w')
```

with the result shown in Figure 5.8. Notice that we used the markeredgecolor (or mec) and markerfacecolor (or mfc) here to distinguish them from the color (or c) specification for the line.

We often use lines connecting markers to reveal patterns in the data. This only becomes limiting when we have hundreds of data points, and the markers clutter the plot too much. Next, we move to depicting more than one data series on the same plot.

Beyond what we've shown so far, there are many, many other specifications available for the plot command. It is useful to reference these in the *Matplotlib documentation* available from https://matplotlib.org/stable/users/index.html.

Example 5.3 Plotting the Densities of Salt and Mag Chloride Solutions

The use of salt (NaCl) solutions to de-ice road surfaces has been replaced in recent decades by magnesium chloride ("mag" chloride or $MgCl_2$) to reduce corrosion on steel in vehicles and other structures (although mag chloride does have an adverse corrosive effect on aluminum). The properties of these solutions are of interest, and Table 5.5 presents the densities of these solutions at 0°C.

A plot using markers with connected lines for both data sets is created with the following Python code:

```
import matplotlib.pyplot as plt

Conc = [2, 4, 8, 12, 16, 20]
NaCl = [1.01509, 1.03038, 1.06121, 1.09244, 1.12419, 1.15663]
MgCl2 = [1.0168, 1.0338, 1.0683, 1.1035, 1.1395, 1.1764]
plt.plot(Conc, NaCl, marker='o', c='k', mec='k', mfc='w')
```

TABLE 5.5
Densities of Salt and Mag Chloride Solutions at 0°C in g/cc

Per cent	NaCl	MgCl$_2$
2	1.01509	1.0168
4	1.03038	1.0338
8	1.06121	1.0683
12	1.09244	1.1035
16	1.12419	1.1395
20	1.15663	1.1764

```
plt.plot(Conc, MgC12, marker='s', c='k', ls='--', mec='k',
mfc='w')
plt.grid()
plt.xlabel('Concentration - wt%')
plt.ylabel('Density - gm/cc')
plt.title('Density of Salt and Mag Chloride Solutions')
plt.show()
```

The resulting plot is shown in Figure 5.9. You can see that we use a separate plot command for each series.

An immediate deficiency is that it is not apparent which of the two curves is for NaCl and which is for MgCl$_2$. We need a *legend*. This is accomplished by adding the legend command and label specifications in the plot commands. Here are the modified plot commands and the legend command. The plot with the legend is shown in Figure 5.10.

```
plt.plot(Conc, NaCl, marker='o', c='k', \
          mec='k', mfc='w', label='NaCL')
plt.plot(Conc, MgC12, marker='s', c='k', ls='-- ', \
          mec='k', mfc='w', label='MgC12')

plt.legend()
```

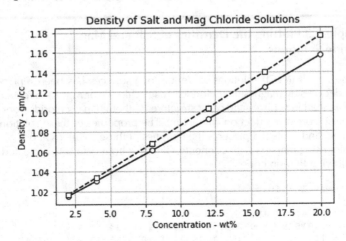

FIGURE 5.9 Densities of NaCl and MgCl$_2$ Solutions at 0°C.

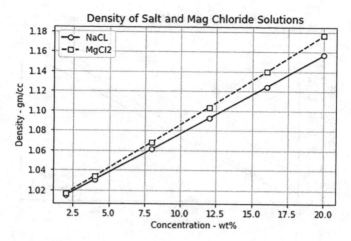

FIGURE 5.10 Densities of NaCl and MgCl$_2$ Solutions at 0°C with legend.

Now, it is clear which line is which. The `legend` command automatically positions the legend so as to minimize conflict with the plotted data. It is possible to force the location of the legend by adding a `loc` specification to the `legend` command. This is shown here.

```
plt.legend(loc='lower right')
```

As the command indicates, the legend will now be placed in the lower right of the plot. It is noted that perhaps it isn't necessary here to use different linestyles because the markers differentiate the series—as far as the legend is concerned.

There are times when we are not satisfied with the axis scales adopted automatically by `pyplot`. It is possible to enforce axis limits and tick intervals of our own choosing. For example, in Figure 5.10, we might prefer that the x-axis have limits of 0 and 22 with tick intervals of two units, and the y-axis with limits 1.0–1.2 with tick intervals of 0.02. Here is the code that accomplishes the rescaling.

```
import numpy as np
import matplotlib.pyplot as plt

Conc = [2, 4, 8, 12, 16, 20]
NaCl = [1.01509, 1.03038, 1.06121, 1.09244, 1.12419, 1.15663]
MgCl2 = [1.0168, 1.0338, 1.0683, 1.1035, 1.1395, 1.1764]

plt.plot(Conc, NaCl, marker='o', c='k', mec='k', mfc='w',
label='NaCL')
plt.plot(Conc, MgCl2, marker='s', c='k', ls='-- \ ', mec='k',
mfc='w', label='MgCl2')
plt.grid()
plt.xlim(0., 22.)
plt.ylim(1., 1.2)
plt.xticks(np.arange(0,24,2))
plt.yticks(np.arange(1,1.22,0.02))
plt.xlabel('Concentration - wt%')
plt.ylabel('Density - gm/cc')
```

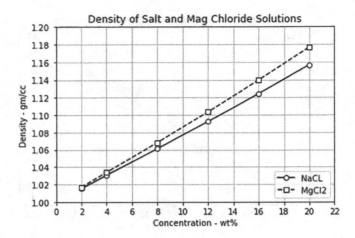

FIGURE 5.11   Densities of NaCl and MgCl₂ solutions with adjusted axes scales.

```
plt.title('Density of Salt and Mag Chloride Solutions')
plt.legend(loc='lower right')
plt.show()
```

The xlim and ylim functions set the axis limits, and, if specific tick intervals are desired, the xticks and yticks functions can be used. Note how the arange function uses a limit one step beyond that desired. Alternately, one can provide a list of values. Figure 5.11 shows the result.

    There are occasions when a plot of more than one series doesn't appear well because the series have different magnitudes. One resolution to this problem is to provide another vertical axis on the right side of the plot. The next example illustrates how to accomplish this with Matplotlib.

Example 5.4 Plotting Weather Data—Temperature and Relative Humidity

We have collected a week of weather data (late October to early November) at 15-minute intervals from the author's weather station. This represents over 2,000 data points. The data selected are temperature (°C) and relative humidity (%). These are available in a comma-delimited file, ClimateData.csv.

    When we create a plot with the following Python script, the result is shown in Figure 5.12.

```
import numpy as np
import matplotlib.pyplot as plt

i, T, H = np.loadtxt('ClimateData.csv', delimiter=', ',
unpack=True)

plt.plot(i, T, c='k', label='T')
plt.plot(i, H, c='k', ls='--', label='RH')
plt.grid()
plt.xlabel('Sample Number')
```

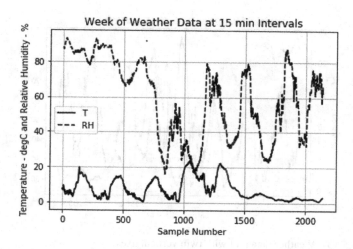

FIGURE 5.12   Weather data plot with a single vertical axis.

```
plt.ylabel('Temperature - degC and Relative Humidity - %')
plt.title('Week of Weather Data at 15 min Intervals')
plt.legend(loc='center left')
```

With the legend and the linestyles, we can differentiate the two curves. However, humidity varies well across the vertical axis range; whereas, temperature is compressed at the bottom. We can modify the code to place an axis on the right side of the plot and use that for one of the series using the twinx function. Here is a first version of that script.

```
import numpy as np
import matplotlib.pyplot as plt

i, T, H = np.loadtxt('ClimateData.csv', delimiter=', ',
unpack=True)

plt.plot(i, T, c='k', lw=1.0,label='T')
plt.grid()
plt.xlabel('Sample Number')
plt.ylabel('Temperature - degC')
plt.title('Week of Weather Data at 15 min Intervals')
plt.twinx()
plt.plot(i, H, c='k', ls='--', lw=1.0,label='RH')
plt.ylabel('Relative Humidity - %')
```

The resulting plot is shown in Figure 5.13. The two curves cover more of the vertical range now. A missing item here is the legend. As illustrated next, it turns out that it is not that simple in Python and pyplot to add the legend.

The following Python code can be used to include a legend on the plot with twin axes. It follows that presented by Hill (2016). The result of the plot function is assigned to an object, curve1 or curve2. These objects are combined in the object curve. Then, the legend labels for each curve are appended into a labels object, which is used in the legend command. The resulting plot is shown in Figure 5.14.

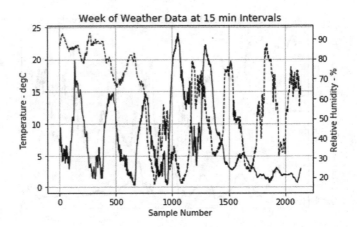

FIGURE 5.13 Weather data plot with twin vertical axes.

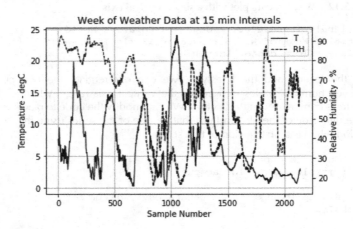

FIGURE 5.14 Weather data with twin axes and a legend.

```
import numpy as np
import matplotlib.pyplot as plt

i, T, H = np.loadtxt('ClimateData.csv', delimiter=', ',
unpack=True)

curve1 = plt.plot(i, T, c='k', lw=1.0,label='T')
plt.grid()
plt.xlabel('Sample Number')
plt.ylabel('Temperature - degC')
plt.title('Week of Weather Data at 15 min Intervals')
plt.twinx()
curve2 = plt.plot(i, H, c='k', ls='--', lw=1.0,label='RH')
plt.ylabel('Relative Humidity - %')
curves = curve1 + curve2
labels = []
for curve in curves:
```

```
labels.append(curve.get_label())
plt.legend(curves, labels)
```

The plotted weather data presented in Figure 5.14 may not be satisfactory to some viewers because of the overlay of the two curves. This might be addressed by using different colors for the curves if color is acceptable as a feature. Another approach is to use separate plots stacked vertically. We will consider that in the next section.

5.3   USING FIGURE WINDOW OBJECTS

The use of figure objects provides additional flexibility in the creation of plots using Matplotlib and pyplot. We can create multiple plot objects within a script, and we can include multiple plots in a single figure.

One scenario where multiple plots are desired is where we want a plot of two functions versus an independent variable, and then we also need a *phase plot* where the two function values are plotted against each other with the independent variable as a running parameter. This is accomplished with the repeated use of figure command, as shown in the script below.

```
import numpy as np
import matplotlib.pyplot as plt

x = np.linspace(0,np.pi, 100)
fun1 = lambda x: np.sin(x)
fun2 = lambda x: np.cos(x)

plt.figure()
plt.plot(x, fun1(x), c='k', label='sin(x)')
plt.plot(x, fun2(x), c='k', ls='--', label='cos(x)')
plt.grid()
plt.xlabel('x')
plt.ylabel('sin(x) and cos(x)')
plt.title('trig functions')
plt.legend()
plt.show()

plt.figure()
plt.plot(fun1(x), fun2(x), c='k')
plt.grid()
plt.xlabel('sin(x)')
plt.ylabel('cos(x)')
plt.title('cos(x) vs sin(x) for x = 0 to pi')
```

The two figures created are shown side-by-side in Figure 5.15. These are independent plot figures and can be arranged in documentation as preferred. You can see that creating multiple plots is simple—just use the figure command prior to each.

If we would like to create an array of plots within a single figure, this requires the use of axes objects and the specification of the array—how many plots in each row and how many rows. Let's first apply this method to the previous two trigonometric function plots. In the script below, we create a figure object, fig, and then

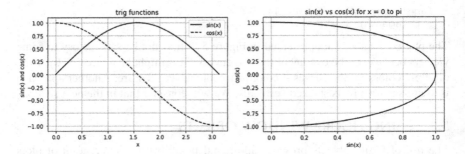

FIGURE 5.15   Two figures to plot sin(*x*) and cos(*x*).

add axes objects, `ax1` and `ax2`, using the `add _ subplot` method. The specified arrangement, `121` or `122`, is 1 row and 2 columns with the last digit indicating which subplot in the figure, counting across rows. Then, instead of using `plt` for the plot and other commands, we use the axes objects. Also, note that previous commands, like `xlabel`, are now `set _ xlabel`. The plot arrangement is shown in Figure 5.16.

```
import numpy as np
import matplotlib.pyplot as plt

x = np.linspace(0,np.pi, 100)
fun1 = lambda x: np.sin(x)
fun2 = lambda x: np.cos(x)

fig = plt.figure()
ax1 = fig.add_subplot(121)
ax1.plot(x, fun1(x), c='k', label='sin(x)')
ax1.plot(x, fun2(x), c='k', ls='--', label='cos(x)')
ax1.grid()
ax1.set_xlabel('x')
ax1.set_ylabel('sin(x) and cos(x)')
ax1.set_title('trig functions')
```

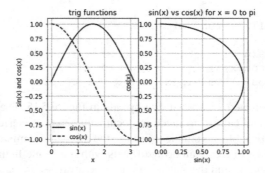

FIGURE 5.16   Side-by-side plots of trigonometric functions in a single figure.

```
ax1.legend()

ax2 = fig.add_subplot(122)
ax2.plot(fun1(x), fun2(x), c='k')
ax2.grid()
ax2.set_xlabel('sin(x)')
ax2.set_ylabel('cos(x)')
ax2.set_title('cos(x) vs sin(x) for x = 0 to pi')

plt.show()
```

A "cosmetic" problem is immediately apparent in Figure 5.16. The two plots crowd and overlap each other. There are two remedies available for this common phenomenon. The first is to add space between the plots with the wspace specification. The neater arrangement is shown in Figure 5.17.

```
fig.subplots_adjust(wspace=0.5)
plt.show()
```

Perhaps, we don't like that the two plots in Figure 5.17 are compressed somewhat horizontally. This can be addressed by changing the aspect ratio (width, height) of the figure window by modifying the figure statement as

```
fig = plt.figure(figsize=(8,3))
```

The result is more pleasing and is shown in Figure 5.18. The same wspace specification is used here. *Note*: To adjust spacing between rows of plots, you can use the hspace specification.

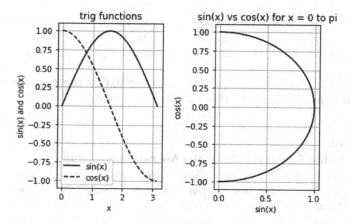

FIGURE 5.17   Side-by-side plots with space added between.

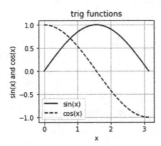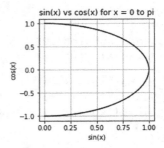

FIGURE 5.18   Side-by-side plots with aspect ratio changed.

5.4   CREATING BAR PLOTS INCLUDING HISTOGRAMS

Engineers and scientists encounter the need to display information in bar charts frequently. Matplotlib `pyplot` provides a flexible capability to produce these, more so that its `pylab` submodule. One of the common applications is the histogram, so we will consider that first, then generalize to other uses.

Histogram charts are used to describe the variability in measurements of the same quantity. For example, we could consider repeated dimensional measurements on many samples of the same manufactured part. Table 5.6 presents inside diameter measurements for engine piston rings (Montgomery, 2013).

The basis of the histogram is to devise a set of measurement intervals and count the number of measurements in each interval. For the 40 measurements in the table, four-to-six intervals would be recommended. Here are some sample statistics for the data:

Number	40
Average	74.002
Minimum	73.982
Maximum	74.035

We propose intervals based on approximately one-sixth of the range (maximum – minimum). Here are the "edges" of the intervals chosen.

TABLE 5.6

Engine Piston Ring Inside Diameter Measurements, mm

74.030	73.995	73.988	74.002	73.992	74.009	73.995	73.985	74.008	73.998
73.994	74.004	73.983	74.006	73.984	74.000	73.994	74.006	73.984	74.000
73.982	74.004	74.010	74.015	73.982	74.012	73.995	73.987	74.008	74.003
73.994	74.008	74.001	74.015	74.030	74.001	74.015	74.035	74.017	74.010

73.980
73.990
74.000
74.010
74.020
74.030
74.040

The NumPy module has a `histogram` function that provides the count data. The Python script below illustrates this.

```
import numpy as np

diam = np.loadtxt('PistonData.txt')
hist, bin_edges = np.histogram(diam,
bins=6, range=[73.98, 74.04])
print(bin_edges)
print(hist)
```

with the results displayed in the Console as[3]

```
[73.98 73.99 74. 74.01 74.02 74.03 74.04]
[ 8 8 14 7 0 3]
```

Next, we add the code to create a bar chart using the count data computed by `hist`. The chart is presented in Figure 5.19. The first set of statements creates an array of the center points of the bars to be displayed. In the `bar` command, the

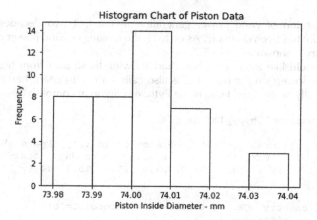

FIGURE 5.19 Histogram chart of piston data.

---

[3] There is a question with histograms as to how to count a value that falls on an edge value. Here, the histogram function counts such a value in the next interval, or as seen in the chart, in the bar to the right. Another technique in creating histograms is to use edge values that cannot coincide with a data item.

hist values provide the heights of the bars, and there are additional specifications for the width of the bars (equal to the bin widths, so the bars are touching), the interior color, and edge color of the bars.

```
bin_width = bin_edges[1]-bin_edges[0]
n = len(hist)
bin_centers = np.zeros((n))
for i in range(n):
    bin_centers[i] = (bin_edges[i]+bin_edges[i+1])/2

import matplotlib.pyplot as plt
plt.bar(bin_centers, hist, width=bin_width, color='w', \
    edgecolor='k')
plt.xlabel('Piston Inside Diameter - mm')
plt.ylabel('Frequency')
plt.title('Histogram Chart of Piston Data')
```

The chart shows the most frequent measurements in the interval 74.00–74.01. The rest of the measurements are not distributed symmetrically about that interval, and there appear to be just two parts with unusually high measurements.

We can customize the plot by changing the color scheme. We could narrow the bars by replacing width=bin_width with width=0.7*bin_width. There are other options to be found in the Matplotlib manual on the Spyder help menu.

A more general bar plot is the *categorical chart*. Here is an example to illustrate this chart.

Example 5.5 Worldwide Wind Power Generation

The expansion of wind power generation in the first two decades of the millennium has been dramatic. As of 2021, the ranking of wind power capacity by country is shown in Table 5.7.

We would like to create a bar chart showing these data from highest on the left to lowest on the right (this is also called a *Pareto chart*.[4]) and labeled categorically by country. Here is the Python script to accomplish this.

```
import matplotlib.pyplot as plt

country = ['China', 'USA', 'Germany', 'India', 'Spain' \
         , 'UK', 'France', 'Brazil', 'Canada', 'Italy']
GW= [221.0, 96.4, 59.3, 35.0, 23.0, 21.7, 15.3, 14.5, 12.8,
10.0]

plt.bar(country, GW, edgecolor='k', facecolor='c')
plt.xticks(rotation=-90)
plt.grid(axis='y')
plt.title('Wind Power Capacity by Country in 2021')
```

---

[4] The chart is named for Vilfredo Pareto (1848–1923), a noted Italian civil engineer, economist, and philosopher. The chart is a visual expression of the *Pareto principle*, which states that for many outcomes, roughly 80% of consequences come from 20% of causes (which Pareto called the "vital few." Hence, the principle is often referred to as the *80/20 rule*.

TABLE 5.7
Wind Capacity in GW by Country in 2021

	Capacity (GW)
China	221.0
U.S.	96.4
Germany	59.3
India	35.0
Spain	23.0
UK	21.7
France	15.3
Brazil	14.5
Canada	12.8
Italy	10.0

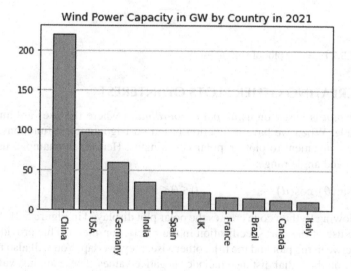

FIGURE 5.20 Wind capacity in GW by country in 2021.

Instead of using numerical values for the location of the bars, we use the country names. Also, since the country names overlap when displayed horizontally, the xticks command is used with the rotation parameter to create vertical names. The grid command produces only horizontal gridlines. The resulting plot is shown in Figure 5.20.

There are several variations possible for bar charts. One of the more common changes is to have horizontal bars instead of vertical. That is possible with the barh command. Cosmetically, it is possible to fill the bars with patterns, not solid colors, using the hatch specification. You will find a lot of information on customization of Python bar charts on the Internet.

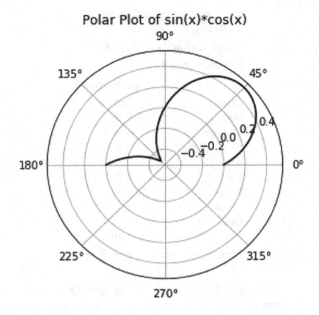

FIGURE 5.21   Polar plot of sin(*x*)·cos(*x*).

5.5 CREATING OTHER PLOTS OF INTEREST

A *polar plot* is based on using *polar coordinates* where the axes are angle and magnitude. When we have a function based on trigonometric functions, it may be more convenient to plot on polar coordinates. Here is an example, using the function and angle range:

$$f(\theta) = \sin(\theta) \cdot \cos(\theta) \qquad\qquad 0 \le \theta \le \pi \qquad\qquad (5.2)$$

The following Python code creates the polar plot displayed in Figure 5.21. You will note the use of the pad specification in the title command. This provides more space between the plot and the title; otherwise, they overlap. You will also note that the scale on the radial distance includes negative values. These are just values that the function produces when the sign of the cosine function is negative between $\pi/2$ and π. You can see in the plot that the values are negative in this range.

```
import numpy as np
import matplotlib.pyplot as plt

theta = np.linspace(0., np.pi, 100)

f = lambda th: np.sin(th)*np.cos(th)
plt.polar(theta, f(theta), c='k')
plt.title('Polar Plot of sin(x)*cos(x)', pad=15)
plt.show()
```

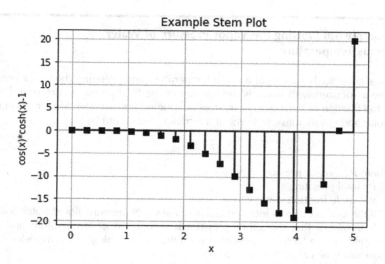

FIGURE 5.22   Stem plot of $\cos(x)\cdot\cosh(x) - 1$.

A style of plot that some prefer to use in certain situations is the *stem plot*. It uses markers and connects a vertical line or "stem" from the abscissa to each marker. Here is an example based on a function we used at the beginning of this chapter, Equation 5.1. The plot is shown in Figure 5.22.

```
import numpy as np
import matplotlib.pyplot as plt

x = np.linspace(0,5,20)
f = lambda x: np.cos(x)*np.cosh(x)-1
plt.stem(x, f(x), linefmt='k-', markerfmt='ks', basefmt='k-' \
, use_line_collection=True)

plt.grid()
plt.xlabel('x')
plt.ylabel('cos(x)*cosh(x)-1')
plt.title('Example Stem Plot')
plt.show()
```

In the stem command, the specifications are vertical lines as solid black (k-) and the markers as black squares (ks). The baseline is also solid black. To follow the latest version of Matplotlib, we set the use _ line _ collection specification to True.

There are occasions where we want to use logarithmic axes, either x or y or both. This usually arises when the range of values covers several decades of magnitude, and the behavior of the plot in each decade is of interest.

Example 5.6 Plotting the Vapor Pressure of Water versus Temperature

If we consider humid air at a given temperature and pressure, the *vapor pressure* associated with water is the fraction of the total pressure corresponding to the fraction of the air-water mixture accounted for by water. That fraction is molar and not by mass. In terms of a formula, that would be

$$P_w^V = P\, y_w \qquad (5.3)$$

where P_w^V: vapor pressure of water
  P: total pressure
  y_w: mole fraction water vapor
  If the total pressure is reduced to that of the vapor pressure, liquid water boils.
  It turns out that the vapor pressure is a function of temperature and is reported in data tables, commonly called the *steam tables*, and is modeled by a formula type called the *Antoine equation*:

$$P^V = 10^{A - \frac{B}{T+C}} \qquad (5.4)$$

where A, B, and C are model parameters.
  Values of vapor pressure from the steam tables are shown in Table 5.8. The temperatures here have been converted from Fahrenheit (0–210 in steps of 10 plus 212). The Antoine equation parameters for water, for temperature in °C and pressure in kPa, are

$$A = 7.2325 \quad B = 1750.3 \quad C = 235$$

We want to develop a plot of vapor pressure versus temperature including both the data and the Antoine equation curve.
  First, we create a Python script based on the plot command.

TABLE 5.8
Vapor Pressure of Water versus Temperature

T (°C)	P^V (kPa)	T (°C)	P^V (kPa)
−17.8	0.1275	48.9	11.6712
−12.2	0.2128	54.4	15.3276
−6.7	0.3479	60.0	19.9210
−1.1	0.5078	65.6	25.6384
4.4	0.8386	71.1	32.6920
10.0	1.2270	76.7	41.3190
15.6	1.7659	82.2	51.7883
21.1	2.5023	87.8	64.3993
26.7	3.4946	93.3	79.4718
32.2	4.8136	98.9	97.3781
37.8	6.5016	100.0	101.3289
43.3	8.7911		

```
import numpy as np
import matplotlib.pyplot as plt

TF = np.arange(0., 220., 10.)
TF = np.append(TF, 212.)

TC = (TF-32.)/1.8

PV = np.array([0.1275, 0.2128, 0.3479, 0.5078, 0.8386
              , 1.227, 1.7659, 2.5023, 3.4946, 4.8136
              , 6.5016, 8.7911, 11.6712, 15.3276, 19.921
              , 25.6384, 32.692, 41.319, 51.7883, 64.3993
              , 79.4718, 97.3781, 101.3289])

A = 7.2325; B = 1750.3; C = 235.
PA = 10**(A-B/(TC+C))


plt.plot(TC, PV, c='w', marker='s', mec='k', mfc='w', \
         label='Steam Tables')
plt.plot(TC, PA, c='k', lw=1.0,label='Antoine Equation')
plt.grid()
plt.xlabel('Temperature - degC')
plt.ylabel('Vapor Pressure - kPa')
plt.title('Vapor Pressure of Water Versus Temperature')
plt.legend()
```

The first `plot` command places markers without lines (the lines have white color). The second `plot` command adds black lines connecting the Antoine equation results for each temperature. It is evident that the model fits the data well. The plot is shown in Figure 5.23.

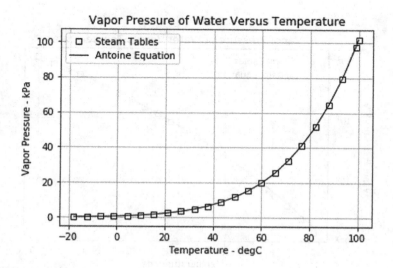

FIGURE 5.23 Plot of vapor pressure of water versus temperature—steam tables data and Antoine equation.

A disadvantage of the plot is that it compresses the variations in vapor pressures at low temperatures. One method to present this better is to use a logarithmic scale for vapor pressure. This is accomplished by replacing the `plot` commands with `semilogy` commands.

```
plt.semilogy(TC, PV, c='w', marker='s', mec='k', mfc='w'\,
label='Steam Tables')
plt.semilogy(TC, PA, c='k', lw=1.0,label='Antoine Equation')
```

The resulting plot is shown in Figure 5.24. You can see how the comparison of the data and the model equation at low temperatures is more apparent, and there is some deviation there.

Note: The latter plot actually corresponds to expressing the Antoine equation as

$$\log_{10} P^V = A - \frac{B}{T+C} \tag{5.5}$$

which often is how the Antoine equation is expressed.

If the situation calls for it, a logarithmic scale can be employed for the x axis using the `semilogx` command, and, on other occasions, log scales are needed for both axes and you will use the `loglog` command.

Another type of plot that is used frequently in presentations is the pie chart. Matplotlib `pyplot` provides a `pie` function to create *pie charts*. We illustrate that here with an example.

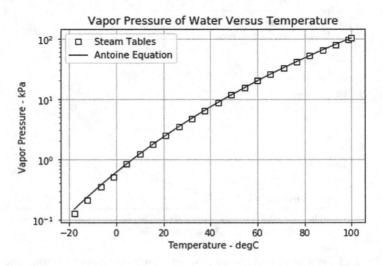

FIGURE 5.24 Semilog plot of vapor pressure of water versus temperature—steam tables data and Antoine equation.

Example 5.7 Creating a Pie Chart for World Energy Production by Source

The demand and production of energy from different sources is an important topic, and this information can be depicted effectively using a pie chart. Table 5.9 provides data for 1973 and 2019.

The following Python script produces side-by-side pie charts from these data.

```python
import matplotlib.pyplot as plt

source = ['oil', 'coal', 'natural gas' \   , 'biofuels',
'nuclear', 'hydro']
en2019 = [187,162,141,57,30,15]
en1973 = [117,63,41,26,2,5]

fig=plt.figure(figsize=(8,3))
ax1 = fig.add_subplot(121)
ax1.pie(en1973,labels=source, labeldistance=1.2)
ax1.set_title('Energy Production -1973\n254 EJ')

ax2 = fig.add_subplot(122)
ax2.pie(en2019,labels=source, labeldistance=1.2)
ax2.set_title('Energy Production -2019\n606 EJ')
```

The data from the table are entered as lists and assigned to variables. Two axes objects, ax1 and ax2, are added to a figure object, fig. The pie function creates the two pie charts with labels. The distance from the chart to the labels is increased slightly using the labeldistance specification. There are other adjustable specifications that can be found in the Matplotlib manual. The resulting plots are presented in Figure 5.25. The "pie slices" are in different colors, although that is not visible in the figure as shown.

One can compare the two pie charts and conclude the trends in terms of proportions of energy sources, e.g. the increase in natural gas, but what's missing from the charts is in the title, a 240% increase in overall production.

TABLE 5.9
World Energy Production by Source for 1973 and 2019
(EJ = exajoule = 10^{18} J)

Source	1973	2019
Oil	117	187
Coal	63	162
Gas	41	141
Biofuels	26	57
Nuclear	2	30
Hydro	5	15
Other	0	13
Total	254	606

Source: https://www.iea.org/reports/key-world-energy-statistics-2021/supply.

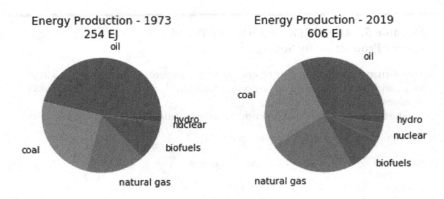

FIGURE 5.25   Pie charts of world energy production in 1973 and 2019.

5.6   CONTOUR AND SURFACE PLOTS

We are all familiar with looking at and reading maps. Essentially, we extract information that is superimposed on two dimensions. Less frequently, continuous information is present on a map. The best example is the *topographic map*, an example shown in Figure 5.26. The contours on the map, called *isobars* for constant pressure curves, represent elevations. Hikers know well how to interpret these maps in terms of slopes and directions.

In science and engineering, we encounter situations where there is a quantity we need to study that is described in terms of more than one variable. When it is two variables, a *contour plot* is a possibility. We can also consider a three-dimensional representation that is created on a two-dimensional surface. There are two types of these contour and surface plots that are of interest. The first is based on an array of discrete data, often measurements, and the second is taken from a mathematical function. We will use the latter here to illustrate how to create contour and surface plots with Python and Matplotlib.

Consider the following function of two independent variables, x and y,

$$f(x, y) = 89 + 0.04x - 0.16y - 8.09x^2 - 5.78y^2 - 5.89xy \qquad (5.6)$$

over the domain $-2 \le x \le 2$, $-2 \le y \le 2$. The following Python script creates the contour plot illustrated in Figure 5.27.

```python
import numpy as np
import matplotlib.pyplot as plt

def f(x, y):
    return 89.+0.04*x-0.16*y-8.09*x**2-5.78*y**2-5.89*x*y

x = np.linspace(-2., 2.)
y = np.linspace(-2., 2.)
X, Y = np.meshgrid(x, y)
Z = f(X, Y)
```

FIGURE 5.26 Example topographic map. (With permission from https://blog-assets.thedyrt.com/uploads/2019/06/shutterstock_75803032-1.jpg.)

```
plt.figure()
contplt = plt.contour(X, Y, Z, [80., 85., 88., 92., 95.],
colors='k')
plt.grid()
plt.clabel(contplt)
plt.xlabel('x')
plt.ylabel('y')
```

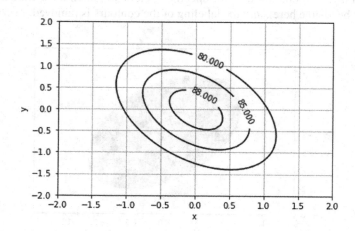

FIGURE 5.27 Simple contour plot.

The first feature to notice in the code is the use of the `meshgrid` function. This function takes two arrays of x and y values respectively and creates two-dimensional arrays, X and Y, that are essentially a map of locations; that is, coordinates of the grid. The figure below illustrates this with a 4-by-4 array. The first digit in each pair represents the X array and the second the Y array.

1,4	2,4	3,4	4,4
1,3	2,3	3,3	4,3
1,2	2,2	3,2	4,2
1,1	2,1	3,1	4,1

y (label on left), x (label on bottom)

A two-dimensional z array is computed using the f function with the X and Y arrays as arguments. This is an *array operation* where the function is applied to each pair of x and y values. The `contour` function from Matplotlib is used, assigning the result to the `contplt` object variable. This is done so that the contour label function, `clabel`, can be applied to that object.

The plot in Figure 5.26 is useful because values of the function can be interpolated and read given the labeled contours. Another way to use a contour plot is with colored, filled contours which provide a "feel" for the function but do not allow reading of values easily. The following modified portion of the script accomplishes this, and the contour plot is shown in Figure 5.28. The `contourf` function fills the contours with the specified colors (although the different colors may not be visible here), and the labeling of the contours is removed.

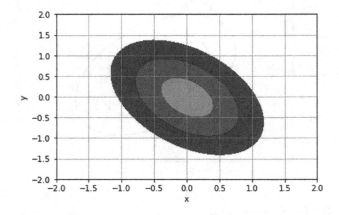

FIGURE 5.28   Filled contour plot.

```
plt.figure()
plt.contourf(X, Y, Z, [80., 85., 88., 92., 95.] \
             , colors=['b', 'g', 'c', 'm'])
plt.grid()
plt.xlabel('x')
plt.ylabel('y')
```

Example 5.8 Contour Plot from Data of Salt Solution Density

Alternately, we may be provided with an array of data instead of an analytical function. In this case, to create contours, the plotting function must interpolate in the array. Consider the density of salt solutions at different concentrations and temperatures, as shown in Table 5.10. Here is Python code that provides a contour plot using these data.

```
import numpy as np
import matplotlib.pyplot as plt

wtpct = np.array([1., 2., 4., 8., 12., 16., 20., 24., 26.])
temp = np.array([0., 10., 25., 40., 60., 80., 100.])
W, T = np.meshgrid(wtpct, temp)
D = np.loadtxt('SaltDensity.csv', delimiter=',', unpack=True)

plt.figure()
contplt = plt.contour(W, T, D, colors='k')
plt.grid()
plt.clabel(contplt)
plt.xlabel('Concentration - wt%')
plt.ylabel('Temperature - degC')
plt.title('Density of Salt Solutions in gm/cc')
```

TABLE 5.10
Density of Salt (NaCl) Solutions in g/cc at Different Concentrations (wt%) and Temperatures (°C)

		Temperature - °C						
		0	10	25	40	60	80	100
Salt Con	1	1.00747	1.00707	1.00409	0.99908	0.9900	0.9785	0.9651
centration	2	1.01509	1.01442	1.01112	1.00593	0.9967	0.9852	0.9719
- wt%	4	1.03038	1.02920	1.02530	1.01977	1.0103	0.9988	0.9855
	8	1.06121	1.05907	1.05412	1.04798	1.0381	1.0264	1.0134
	12	1.09244	1.08946	1.08365	1.07699	1.0667	1.0549	1.0420
	16	1.12419	1.12056	1.11401	1.10688	1.0962	1.0842	1.0713
	20	1.15663	1.15254	1.14533	1.13774	1.1268	1.1146	1.1017
	24	1.18999	1.18557	1.17776	1.16971	1.1584	1.1463	1.1331
	26	1.20709	1.20254	1.19443	1.18614	1.1747	1.1626	1.1492

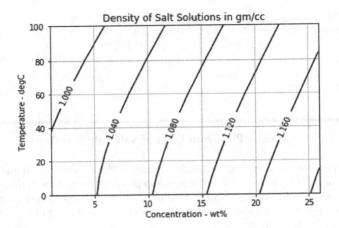

FIGURE 5.29   Contour plot from data of salt solution density.

Given the number of density data, we prefer to load these from a comma-delimited text file (created with Excel). The contour intervals are provided automatically by the contour function, and the contours are based on interpolations of the data table. We could have specified the contours so that more would be displayed. The resulting plot is shown in Figure 5.29.

The relationship of a quantity to two independent variables can also be depicted by rendering a three-dimensional surface on a two-dimensional space. Just as with a filled-color contour plot, a surface plot provides a feel for the dependency of the quantity on the input variables. There are two styles of surface plots provided by Matplotlib: mesh plots and solid, shaded surface plots. We will illustrate these with the analytical function used with contour plots earlier.

The Python script below is used to produce the *mesh plot* shown in Figure 5.30. First, you will notice that we have imported the Axes3D module. You may notice that

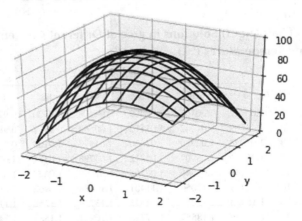

FIGURE 5.30   Mesh plot of an analytical function, $f(x, y)$.

the Spyder Editor provides a warning that this module is imported but not utilized. This warning is incorrect, so you can ignore it. Next, you see that we have created the plot as a subplot of an axes object, ax1, in a figure object, fig. The plot _ wireframe function is used to generate the plot, and the "stride" specifications define the number of mesh contours. Following that and the grid statement, the tick intervals on the three axes are set, and plot labels are provided.

```python
import numpy as np
import matplotlib.pyplot as plt
from mpl_toolkits.mplot3d import Axes3D

def f(x, y):
return 89.+0.04*x-0.16*y-8.09*x**2-5.78*y**2-5.89*x*y

x = np.linspace(-2., 2.)
y = np.linspace(-2., 2.)
X, Y = np.meshgrid(x, y)
Z = f(X, Y)

fig = plt.figure()
ax1 = fig.add_subplot(111,projection='3d')
ax1.plot_wireframe(X, Y, Z, color='k', rstride=5,cstride=5)
ax1.grid()
ax1.set_xticks([-2., -1., 0., 1., 2.])
ax1.set_yticks([-2., -1., 0., 1., 2.])
ax1.set_zlim(0., 100.)
ax1.set_zticks(np.arange(0., 120., 20.))
plt.xlabel('x')
plt.ylabel('y')
plt.zlabel('f(x, y)')
```

There are additional commands that allow rotation of the viewpoint of the surface. For example,

```python
ax1.view_init(35)
```

rotates the viewpoint upward by 35°. More information is available from the Matplotlib User's Guide (https://matplotlib.org/stable/users/index.html).

An alternate presentation is to use a shaded surface instead of a mesh. The modifications to the Python script are to add the import of the cm module from Matplotlib and replace the plot _ wireframe command with plot _ surface as shown below.

```python
from matplotlib import cm
ax1.plot_surface(X, Y, Z, cmap=cm.gray)
```

Figure 5.31 shows the shaded surface plot. Of course, it is possible to use colors for the surface if that suits the mode of presentation of the plot.

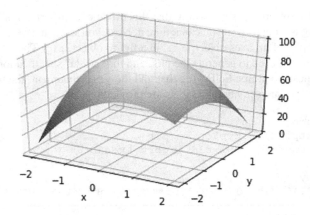

FIGURE 5.31   Surface plot of an analytical function, $f(x, y)$.

We have barely opened the door when it comes to surface and mesh plots provided by Matplotlib. There are many examples available in the Matplotlib manual. We encourage you to experiment with these to develop the most effective presentations of multidimensional functions and data.

One question that arises is what to do when there are more than two independent variables that describe a quantity of interest. A typical approach is to pick a pair of independent variables and study them for specific values of the others. This is akin to providing pictures of "slices" of the multidimensional space to get a picture of paired relationships.

In this chapter, we have provided you with many examples of the typical plots that engineers and scientists use frequently in their Python programming and work. These are meant to give you a good start and basis for moving forward with your work. The problems that follow provide you with the opportunity to practice using most of these plot types.

PROBLEMS

5.1   Develop a Python script using the Matplotlib `pyplot` module to produce a well-labeled line plot of the function

$$f(x) = x^2 |\sin(x)| - 4$$

over the domain $0 \le x \le 4$.

5.2   Table P5.2 presents greenhouse gas emissions by the U.S. over the years 1990–2019. Write Python scripts using Matplotlib `pyplot` to generate the following well-labeled plots:

   (a) a scatter plot of total emissions versus year, and

   (b) a line plot of carbon dioxide, methane and nitrous oxide emissions by year using twin axes. Employ different linestyles and a legend.

   https://cfpub.epa.gov/ghgdata/inventoryexplorer/#allsectors/allsectors/allgas/gas/all

TABLE P5.2

Greenhouse Gas Emissions by the U.S. from 1990 to 2019 (MMT CO$_2$ Equivalent)

	1990	1991	1992	1993	1994	1995	1996	1997	1998	1999
Carbon dioxide	5113.5	5057.9	5167.5	5267.3	5358.8	5421.5	5610.6	5686.5	5731.0	5804.7
Methane	776.9	781.8	780.5	770.7	777.0	767.7	760.8	746.8	731.7	713.4
Nitrous oxide	452.7	443.2	443.1	471.3	457.0	468.8	480.8	466.8	467.7	457.5
Fluorinated gases	99.7	90.7	95.3	95.0	99.0	117.9	129.0	136.4	152.9	149.9
Total	6442.7	6373.6	6486.3	6604.3	6691.8	6775.9	6981.2	7036.5	7083.3	7125.4

	2000	2001	2002	2003	2004	2005	2006	2007	2008	2009
Carbon dioxide	6010.5	5904.9	5946.8	6011.8	6114.0	6134.5	6051.7	6131.0	5914.1	5478.2
Methane	707.6	699.8	692.8	692.7	687.0	686.1	690.8	693.9	700.8	689.7
Nitrous oxide	444.7	460.4	458.8	459.8	469.9	455.8	452.5	463.5	446.9	445.6
Fluorinated gases	150.9	137.9	145.9	137.0	144.6	146.6	149.5	161.2	162.8	158.5
Total	7313.6	7203.0	7244.3	7301.4	7415.5	7423.0	7344.5	7449.6	7224.6	6772.0

	2010	2011	2012	2013	2014	2015	2016	2017	2018	2019
Carbon dioxide	5675.8	5540.2	5338.7	5474.3	5522.8	5371.8	5248.0	5207.8	5375.5	5255.8
Methane	692.1	666.2	658.2	654.4	651.0	651.5	642.4	648.4	655.9	659.7
Nitrous oxide	455.0	445.6	416.8	463.9	474.0	468.2	450.8	446.3	459.2	457.1
Fluorinated gases	168.2	175.5	172.3	172.1	177.1	179.6	179.1	180.9	180.8	185.7
Total	6991.1	6827.4	6585.9	6764.7	6825.0	6671.1	6520.3	6483.3	6671.4	6558.3

5.3 In the production of sugar (sucrose, $C_{12}H_{22}O_{11}$), the concentration of sucrose solutions is typically measured by refractive index (using an instrument called a *refractometer*). The data in Table P5.3 present relevant measurements. A relationship between refractive index, n, and sucrose concentration, *pctS*, has been proposed as

$$n = 1.32495 + 1.99515 \times 10^{-3} pctS$$

Create a Python script using the Matplotlib `pyplot` module that produces a plot of the sucrose concentration data using only markers and adds the model to the plot using lines. Label the plot and add a legend.

TABLE P5.3
Refractive Index of Sucrose Solutions

Per cent Sucrose	Refractive Index	Per cent Sucrose	Refractive Index	Per cent Sucrose	Refractive Index
0	1.3330	30	1.3811	60	1.4418
5	1.3403	35	1.3902·	65	1.4532
10	1.3479	40	1.3997	70	1.4651
15	1.3557	45	1.4096	75	1.4774
20	1.3639	50	1.4200	80	1.4901
25	1.3723	55	1.4307	85	1.5033

5.4 Create a two-by-two array of line plots in a `pyplot` `figure` window for the following hyperbolic functions over the domain $-1 \leq x \leq 1$.

$\sinh(x)$ vs. x	$\cosh(x)$ vs. x
$\tanh(x)$ vs. x	$\text{sech}(x)$ vs. x

5.5 Table P5.5 below presents the escape velocities from planets in the solar system. Employ the Matplotlib `pyplot` module in a Python script to create an ordered (Pareto style) horizontal bar chart to display these data.

TABLE P5.5
Escape Velocity (km/h) for Planets in the Solar System

	Escape Velocity (km/h)
Mercury	1.302E+04
Venus	3.747E+04
Earth	4.027E+04
Mars	1.831E+04
Jupiter	2.145E+05
Saturn	1.278E+05
Uranus	7.666E+04
Neptune	8.525E+04

5.6 Example 5.5 presents data and illustrates a bar chart for wind power capacity by country. Create a similar plot based on data of solar capacity by country.

5.7 An analytical function that we used in this chapter for examples of line and stem plots is

$$f(x) = \sin(x)\cosh(x) - 1 \quad 0 \leq x \leq 4$$

Create a polar plot of this function over the given domain (radians) using a Python script and the Matplotlib `pyplot` module. Label the plot.

5.8 The data in Table P5.8 were collected from a set of experiments involving a chemical reaction at different temperatures and catalyst concentrations. Using the `stem` function from Matplotlib `pyplot`, create a three-dimensional `stem` plot of these data. Access the Matplotlib Users Guide, if necessary.

TABLE P5.8

Product Yield at Different Temperatures and Catalyst Concentrations

Catalyst Concentration (g/L)	Temperature (°C)	Product Yield (%)
0.54	110	83
0.63	117	87
0.71	113	84
0.48	107	82
0.57	118	92
0.63	117	89
0.59	102	78
0.60	118	91

5.9 A rectangular wave is depicted in Figure P5.9. This waveform can be broken down into an infinite series of sinusoidal components called a *Fourier series*.

$$f(x) = \frac{4}{\pi}\cos(x) - \frac{4}{3\pi}\cos(3x) + \frac{4}{5\pi}\cos(5x) - \frac{4}{7\pi}\cos(7x) + \cdots$$

Write a Python script that produces a line plot for $-\pi \le x \le \pi$ including curves of the first term above, the first two terms, the first three terms, and so on to the first five terms. Use colored curves and provide a legend on the plot.

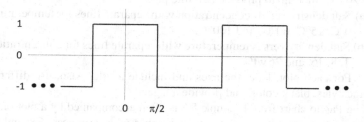

FIGURE P5.9 Rectangular wave.

5.10 A study has been conducted on the effect of water temperature and time in solution on the amount of dye absorbed by a type of fabric yarn. A standard amount of dye (200 mg) was added to a fixed amount of water. The three temperatures used in the experiments were 105°C, 120°C, and 135°C. The fabric was left in the water 15, 30, or 60 minutes. For each of these temperature-time combinations, the amount of dye absorbed by the yarn was measured. The experiments yielded the results shown in Table P5.10.

TABLE P5.10
Dye Absorption for Different Solution Times and Temperatures

Dye in Yarn (mg)	Time in Solution (min)	Temperature (°C)
120.4	15	105
143.0	30	105
190.6	60	105
111.2	15	120
134.8	30	120
182.6	60	120
98.4	15	135
123.9	30	135
173.2	60	135

Create a meshplot of the dye absorbed versus time in solution and temperature.

5.11 Develop mesh and surface plots for the following model developed from experimental data of a response, y, for different values of two independent variables, x_1 and x_2.

$$y = 60.64 - 3.672x_1 + 11.661x_2 - 3.514x_1^2 - 0.924x_2^2 + 2.220x_1x_2$$

Determine a meaningful range for each of the independent variables to illustrate the function near its minimum and display this case as your final plot.

5.12 For the salt density data presented in Table 5.9, use the Matplotlib pyplot module to produce two line plots:

(a) Salt density versus concentration with separate lines for temperatures 0°C, 25°C, 60°C, and 100°C.

(b) Salt density versus temperature with separate lines for concentrations 1, 8, 16, and 26 wt%.

For each plot, label the axes and include a title. Also, use different linestyles, black color, and provide a legend.

5.13 The Pareto chart from Example 5.5 is often accompanied by a plot of the cumulative percentages of the total number of occurrences. Expand the Python code from Example 5.5 to compute the cumulative % of total wind power capacity and develop a line plot of cumulative capacity versus country.

6 Array and Matrix Operations

CHAPTER OBJECTIVES

- Be able to create arrays from numerical lists and tuples using the ndarray class with the NumPy module.
- Learn how to create arrays of more than one dimension to represent matrices.
- Be able to create special arrays, such as those filled with zeros, and combine and split arrays.
- Learn how to implement subscripts as array indices, including the use of the colon (:) to reference ranges of indices.
- Understand vectorization and learn how calculations can be vectorized using NumPy arrays.
- Be able to write Python code to carry out matrix math operations, including addition, subtraction, scalar and matrix multiplication, and transpose.
- Understand the meaning of the inverse of a square matrix and how this matrix can be used to solve a set of linear algebraic equations.
- Become familiar with the NumPy linalg module and its inv function.

Computations made by engineers and scientists often involve individual numerical quantities and their variables. These have been the focus of previous chapters. Now, we consider collections of numbers. Although we can use the Python's lists and tuples for storing such collections, we find that these are not useful structures when it comes to numerical calculations. This is where arrays created within the ndarray class of the NumPy module come into play. These arrays are the focus of this chapter.

What are typical computational tasks that involve arrays? Here are several examples:

- storing and accessing tables of data, such as those that describe physical or chemical properties of substances, alloys, composites, or mixtures,
- collections of measurements from experiments, manufacturing processes, or environmental phenomena,
- discrete approximations of continuous quantities, such as temperatures throughout a solid object like a cooling fin,
- case studies where input parameters are varied over a range of interest, and output results are computed and displayed in plots, and

DOI: 10.1201/9781003256861-6

- physical or chemical variables that occur in staged processes, such as those used to separate desired products from waste or materials to be recycled.

To proceed, we need to know how to create arrays, either in one or two dimensions. Next, we must know how to include arrays in numerical calculations, often called array operations. Then, we move on to vector/matrix calculations including multiplication and transpose. Finally, we introduce the linalg module which contains many useful functions for array and matrix calculations.

A caution to the student. This chapter introduces many concepts and methods that are likely to be new to you. To make the presentation complete, we introduce alternate methods to accomplish certain computations. You will have the opportunity to select methods with which you are most comfortable, and your instructor may have preferences. Also, after the introduction provided in this chapter, you will see the methods repeated in subsequent chapters, and, in that way, you will be able to become better oriented to them. We have two suggestions as you study this chapter. First, work through everything carefully, replicating all the example code, and trying variations. Second, be patient and do not get too discouraged if you encounter difficulties.

6.1   CREATING ARRAYS IN PYTHON

Python provides the list and tuple collection types for storing multiple items. The items can include numbers and text. It turns out that lists and tuples have limitations when it comes to numerical calculations that engineers and scientists frequently carry out. To meet these needs, the NumPy module provides the ndarray class that allows us to create numerical arrays.

First, let's illustrate why the array collection is needed. What happens if we create a numeric list in Python and multiply that list by a constant value? Here is an example:

```
list1 = [1.5, 3.2, -6.4, 0.9]
list2 = 2*list1
print(list2)

[1.5, 3.2, -6.4, 0.9, 1.5, 3.2, -6.4, 0.9]
```

You can see that multiplying the list by two just extended it by duplication. In numerical calculations, we would expect rather that each element of the list would be doubled, and the length of the list would be preserved.

If we try

```
list3 = [0., 1., 4., -2.]
list4 = list1*list3
```

the result in the Console is

```
TypeError: can't multiply sequence by non-int of type 'list'
```

In other words, you cannot do that. We might have expected the corresponding items in the two lists to be multiplied to yield a list of the same length. Not so.

So, the short answer to this dilemma is to convert the lists into arrays. This requires the NumPy module, and the code might look like

```
a = np.array(list1)
b = 2*a
print(b)

c = np.array(list3)
d = a*c
print(d)
```

with the resulting output:

```
[  3.     6.4 -12.8    1.8]
[  0.     3.2 -25.6   -1.8]
```

We see that the operations take place as we hoped. Multiplying the array a by two gives an array b with the values in a doubled. Multiplying the arrays a and c carries out item-by-item multiplication. These are called *array operations*.

The Variable Explorer provides information about the types of variables and their values (Figure 6.1). You will notice that arrays are created for floating-point numbers, and their size is displayed with a comma. The arrays created are one-dimensional, sometimes called *vectors* or *vector arrays*.

It is also common to have multidimensional arrays, usually two-dimensional, sometimes called *matrices*. Here is example code to create a two-dimensional array:

```
import numpy as np

A = np.array([[2., -3.], [6., 1.]])
print(A)
```

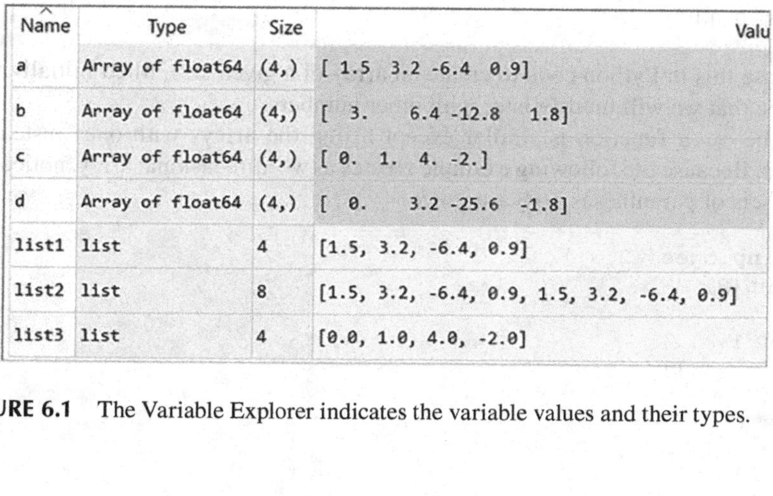

Name	Type	Size	Valu
a	Array of float64	(4,)	[1.5 3.2 -6.4 0.9]
b	Array of float64	(4,)	[3. 6.4 -12.8 1.8]
c	Array of float64	(4,)	[0. 1. 4. -2.]
d	Array of float64	(4,)	[0. 3.2 -25.6 -1.8]
list1	list	4	[1.5, 3.2, -6.4, 0.9]
list2	list	8	[1.5, 3.2, -6.4, 0.9, 1.5, 3.2, -6.4, 0.9]
list3	list	4	[0.0, 1.0, 4.0, -2.0]

FIGURE 6.1   The Variable Explorer indicates the variable values and their types.

```
[[ 2.  -3.]
 [ 6.   1.]]
```

The resulting matrix has two rows and two columns. The rows are contained in the extra sets of brackets, [•]. Notice how each one-dimensional array is presented as a single row. If, instead, we use

```
b = np.array([[1], [2], [3], [4]])
print(b)

[[1]
 [2]
 [3]
 [4]]
```

The array b is displayed as a *column vector.*

We will mention here that Python and NumPy allow a special type of array, defined as a matrix. This type allows the creation of vectors and matrices with a style similar to the MATLAB® software. We do not emphasize that in this text because we can accomplish the calculations using just the array type.

6.1.1 CREATING SPECIAL ARRAYS

Python and NumPy provide functions to create special arrays and to combine or split up arrays. Here are examples of three functions that we use frequently.

The zeros function is the most common. It allows us to create a one- or two-dimensional array, filled will zeros. For example,

```
A = np.zeros((3,2))
print(A)

[[0.  0.]
 [0.  0.]
 [0.  0.]]
```

We use this in Python code to create an array of a given size, filled initially with zeros, that we will modify later with other numbers.

The ones function is similar except filling the arrays with ones instead of zeros. Because the following example creates a two-dimensional array, notice that two sets of parentheses, ((•)) are used

```
B = np.ones((2,3))
print(B)

[[1.  1.  1.]
 [1.  1.  1.]]
```

If we create a one-dimensional array of zeros or ones, only one set of parentheses is required, as in

```
d = np.zeros(5)
print(d)
```

```
[0. 0. 0. 0. 0.]
```

The eye function creates a square *identity* or "I" array. The single specification gives the number of rows and columns, both equal. For example,

```
C = np.eye(4)
print(C)
```

```
[[1. 0. 0. 0.]
 [0. 1. 0. 0.]
 [0. 0. 1. 0.]
 [0. 0. 0. 1.]]
```

6.1.2 COMBINING, STACKING, AND SPLITTING ARRAYS

There are times that we want to combine arrays, either side-by-side or by stacking them, or split arrays into subarrays. Here are illustrations of the functions that accomplish this.

First, we define two 2×2 arrays.

```
import numpy as np

A = np.array([[3.6, 2.1], [-1.4, 0.7]])
B = np.array([[-12., 7.7], [2.1, -1.9]])
```

Next, we create a new 4×2 array by stacking A on top of B using the vstack function.

```
C = np.vstack((A, B))
print(C)
```

```
[[ 3.6 2.1]
 [ -1.4 0.7]
 [-12. 7.7]
 [ 2.1-1.9]]
```

Alternately, B can be placed to the right of A using the hstack function.

```
D = np.hstack((A, B))
print(D)
```

```
[[ 3.6 2.1-12. 7.7]
 [ -1.4 0.7 2.1-1.9]]
```

Going in the opposite direction, we can split an array into subarrays. Here are examples. First, the `vsplit` function with the argument 2 splits C vertically into two equal-size arrays.

```
A1,B1 = np.vsplit(C, 2)
print(A1)
print('\n', B1)

[[ 3.6   2.1]
 [-1.4   0.7]]

 [[-12.     7.7]
 [  2.1   -1.9]]
```

By using the `hsplit` function, we can separate the D array into two equal-size arrays.

```
A3,B3 = np.hsplit(D, 2)
print(A3)
print('\n', B3)

[[ 3.6   2.1]
 [-1.4   0.7]]

 [[-12.     7.7]
 [  2.1   -1.9]]
```

6.1.3 RESHAPING ARRAYS

Although it doesn't arise frequently in engineering calculations, it is possible to reshape arrays into different row/column formats. One of the simplest methods is to *flatten* a multidimensional array into one dimension.[1] For example, we can flatten our A array from above with the command

```
a = A.flatten()
print(a)
[ 3.6   2.1-1.4   0.7]
```

You will note that the method flattens the array by rows. This method doesn't change the dimensions of A, but recasts A into a one-dimensional array that is assigned to a.

Although it may be a bit confusing to you at this point, there is an alternate method, `ravel`, that provides another *view* of the same array, and any modifications of the array affect both the new view and the original array. This is illustrated by

---

[1] Python programmers often refer to the dimensions of arrays as axes. By flattening a two-dimensional array into one dimension, they describe it as flattening it onto a single axis.

```
print('\n')
b = A.ravel()
print(b)
b[2] = 99.
print(b)
print(A)

[ 3.6  2.1 -1.4  0.7]
[ 3.6  2.1 99.   0.7]
[[ 3.6  2.1]
 [99.   0.7]]
```

You see here that, first, the `ravel` method flattens A into b. Then, the third element of b is modified to 99 as in the second display of a. And finally, by displaying A again, we see that the corresponding element was changed to 99 there too. So, b and A reference the same memory locations but do so with a different view.

Alternately, we can reshape an array into a different arrangement of rows and columns. Here is an example.

```
B = np.array([[1., 3., 5.], [2., 4., 6.]])
D = B.reshape(3,2)
print D

[[1. 3.]
 [5. 2.]
 [4. 6.]]
```

The original B array is two rows by three columns. The array is then reshaped into three rows and two columns. There is an alternate `resize` method that, like the `ravel` method, provides a different view of an array, but does not change the array's structure.

Arrays can also be created using the NumPy `loadtxt` function, retrieving data from external text files. You have seen example of this in earlier chapters.

6.2 INDEXING: ARRAY SUBSCRIPTS

It is very common to refer to individual elements or sets of elements in arrays. This is accomplished through *indexing*, also called *subscripting*. This raises an important point and source of confusion when relating mathematical descriptions and Python arrays. This is illustrated in Figure 6.2. The observation we make is that typical mathematical subscripting has an origin of 1, and Python's subscripting has an origin of 0.[2]

---

[2] As you use different software packages, it will be important to take note of this. MATLAB utilizes origin 1 subscripting aligned with mathematical descriptions. Excel's VBA uses 0-based subscripting, but it is possible to switch that with the Option Base 1 declaration. The C/C++ languages use origin 0, and the Fortran language uses base 1.

$$\begin{bmatrix} x_{11} & x_{12} & x_{13} & x_{14} \\ x_{21} & x_{22} & x_{23} & x_{24} \\ x_{31} & x_{32} & x_{33} & x_{34} \end{bmatrix} \quad \begin{bmatrix} x_{[0,0]} & x_{[0,1]} & x_{[0,2]} & x_{[0,3]} \\ x_{[1,0]} & x_{[1,1]} & x_{[1,2]} & x_{[1,3]} \\ x_{[2,0]} & x_{[2,1]} & x_{[2,2]} & x_{[2,3]} \end{bmatrix}$$

FIGURE 6.2 Mathematical and Python array indexing.

First, let's consider a simple, one-dimensional array,

```
import numpy as np

a = np.array([1.2, 3.5, 7.9, 8.4, 9.9])
print(a[2])
```

```
7.9
```

You can see that we use the index 2, and that selects the third element of the array.

Next, we illustrate this further with a two-dimensional array. Notice that brackets, [•], are employed for subscripts.

```
B = np.array([[1., 3., 5.], [2., 4., 6.]])
print(B[1,2])
```

```
6.0
```

The [1,2] indices select the element of B in the second row and third column. This may take some getting used to, but be patient. With practice, it will become second nature.

Next, we introduce the use of the colon, :, in indexing. When used alone, the colon indicates "all." Here is an example using the B array from above.

```
print(B[:, 1])
```

```
[3. 4.]
```

The second column (index 1, all rows) is extracted and displayed in the Console.

We can also use the colon to select ranges of subscripts. When we do this, there is a further point of confusion possible. This example illustrates it.

```
print(a[1:3])
```

```
[3.5 7.9]
```

The second and third element of the a array are selected. With zero-based indexing, we might have expected the second through the fourth element, but that didn't happen. Just like the arange function and the range type, specifying [1:3] provides elements up to but not including the final index, 3. Extending this technique, suppose we want to select the second and third rows and columns of the following array:

$$
\begin{bmatrix}
3 & -2 & 7 & 1 \\
4 & -1 & 6 & 5 \\
9 & -8 & 4 & 2 \\
-5 & 8 & -7 & -3
\end{bmatrix}
$$

That would then be

```
import numpy as np

Z = np.array([[ 3, -2,  7,  1],
              [ 4, -1,  6,  5],
              [ 9, -8,  4,  2],
              [-5,  8, -7, -3]])
print(Z[1:3,1:3])

[[-1  6]
 [-8  4]]
```

Commonly, subscripts are used as indices in for loops. For example, this script sums the squares of the elements of a.

```
sumsqa = 0
for i in range(5):
    sumsqa = sumsqa + a[i]**2
print(sumsqa)

244.67000000000002
```

You will recall from Chapter 4 that the range type generates a sequence from 0 to 4, and these align well with the zero-based indexing of the a array. The squares of the five elements are accumulated in the sumsqa variable and then displayed. It is of note here, with Python, that the sumsqa variable must be initialized first by assigning zero to it; otherwise, there will be an error in the statement that uses sumsqa on the right of the equal sign. This is not necessarily the case with other programming systems where the variable is created automatically with a zero value.

Similarly, we can accumulate the square roots of the B array with nested `for` loops as follows.

```
sumsqrtB = 0
for i in range(2):
    for j in range(3):
        sumsqrtB = sumsqrtB + np.sqrt(B[i,j])
print(sumsqrtB)
```

```
10.83182209022494
```

Here, the `i` index is for rows 0 and 1, and the `j` index is for columns 0, 1, and 2.

When working with arrays and subscripting, you always must keep in mind the zero-based subscripting and the way the colon is used with ranges of subscripts. At times, it's best to make sketches by hand to make sure you have it right, and then, of course, check results carefully.

6.3   ARRAY OPERATIONS

There are two types of mathematical operations that are applied to arrays. One is item-by-item or array operations, and the other is vector/matrix operations. For certain operations, the calculations are the same, such as addition, subtraction, and multiplication/division by a constant. However, in other cases, such as multiplication and division, there are differences. In the example below, we illustrate division of an array a by a constant, 3. The result is as we would expect, each element of a is divided by 3 giving a new array of the same dimension or shape as a. This is called an array operation and has the characteristic item-by-item.

```
a = np.array([1.2, 3.5, 7.9, 8.4, 9.9])
b = a/3
print(b)
```

```
[0.4        1.16666667 2.63333333 2.8        3.3       ]
```

When addition and subtraction are carried out, a restriction comes into play. The arrays must have the same shape (or dimensions). We illustrate that here with two examples, one that is successful and another that is erroneous.

```
import numpy as np

a = np.array([1.,3.,5.])
b = np.array([2.,4.,6.])

print(a+b)

d = np.array([7.,9.])
print(a+d)
```

```
[ 3.   7.  11.]
```

```
ValueError: operands could not be broadcast together with
shapes (3,) (2,)
```

We see that the a and b arrays have the same number of elements, and their addition produces the expected item-by-item sum. However, when an addition of a and d is attempted, there is an error because they do not have the same shape.

Now, we move on to multiplication and division. In the last example, what happens if we attempt to multiply a times b?

```
print(a*b)
```

```
[ 2.  12.  30.]
```

Like addition and subtraction, we see that the multiplication takes place item-by-item. The same would be true for division. As we will see in the next section, there are differences when we wish to carry out an operation like a vector dot product.

The basics of array operations extend to more complicated expressions. We can evaluate a polynomial as shown in the code below. This provides an array of three results with the calculation carried out item-by-item.

```
import numpy as np

x = np.array([0.1,0.2,0.3])
print(x**3-2*x**2 + 0.4*x + 3)
```

```
[3.021 3.008 2.967]
```

An important distinction arises when we consider using built-in functions. For example, if we want to evaluate the sine of the x array, we might try the following.

```
import math
import numpy as np

x = np.array([0.1, 0.2, 0.3])

print(math.sin(x))
```

```
TypeError: only size-1 arrays can be converted to Python
scalars
```

Evidently, we are unable to use the sin function from the math module for array operations. On the other hand, see the code below.

```
print(np.sin(x))
```

```
[0.09983342 0.19866933 0.29552021]
```

```
import numpy as np
x = np.linspace(0,10,25)
n = len(x)
```

item-by-item ⬇   ⬇ vectorized

```
y = np.zeros(n)
for i in range(n):
    y[i] = np.cosh(x[i])
```
```
y = np.cosh(x)
```

FIGURE 6.3   Contrast of item-by-item and vectorized computational strategies.

So, we see that using the similar `sin` function from the NumPy module does support array operations.

Figure 6.3 illustrates the contrast between item-by-item and *vectorized* calculations. For item-by-item calculation, a `for` loop is used to cycle through all the items in an array making individual calculations of the hyperbolic cosine (`cosh`) function. The vectorized calculation simplifies this significantly by placing the entire x array as an argument to the `np.cosh` function and a corresponding y array is created. Also, notice that, with the item-by-item approach, we need to create the y array first before populating its values in the `for` loop. Alternately, we could have created an empty y array and populated it using the `append` method.

Example 6.1 Using Arrays in a Case Study

For this example, we allow one or more parameters in a calculation to vary over a range and observe the changes in the results. To do this, we employ arrays and array operations.

Figure 6.4 describes an open, rectangular channel with water flowing at a volumetric rate, Q (m^3/s). The width of the channel is B (m), and the depth of the water is d (m). The channel surface is described by a roughness factor, n, and the slope of the channel is S (m/m).

Civil engineers use *Manning's equation* to quantify the relationship between the channel characteristics, water depth and volumetric flow rate:

$$Q = \frac{1}{n} \frac{(dB)^{\frac{5}{3}}}{(B+2d)^{\frac{2}{3}}} \sqrt{S} \tag{6.1}$$

For the following parameter values, $B=4$ m, $n=0.017$, $S=0.0015$ m/m, we wish to create a Python script to conduct a case study of the dependence of flow rate on depth ranging from 0.2 to 2 m. The results would be best seen in a plot. Figure 6.5 presents the Python script for the case study. A function Manning

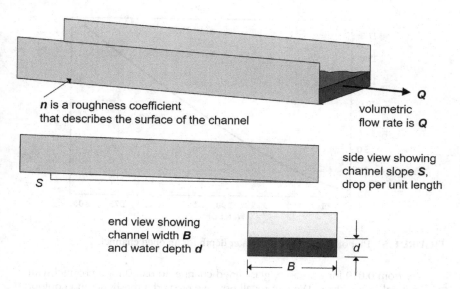

FIGURE 6.4 Water flowing down an open channel.

```
import numpy as np
import matplotlib.pyplot as plt

B = 4  # m
n = 0.017
S = 0.0015  # m/m

def Manning(d,B,n,S):
    Q = 1/n * (d*B)**(5/3) / (B + 2*d)**(2/3) * np.sqrt(S)
    return Q

d = np.linspace(0.2,2.)
Q = Manning(d,B,n,S)

plt.plot(d,Q,c='k')
plt.grid()
plt.xlabel('Water Depth- m')
plt.ylabel('Flow Rate- m3/s')
```

FIGURE 6.5 Python script for case study of open-channel flow.

computes the formula given the four arguments, d, B, n, and S. The Manning function is invoked for an array of *d* values and single parameter values for *B*, *n*, and *S*. The result is an array of *Q* values, and a plot is created of *Q* versus *d*. That plot is presented in Figure 6.6.

We observe from the plot that the flow rate varies from about 0.5 to 18 m³/s. Also, the relationship is not linear for the lower depths but becomes more linear at the higher depths.

Now, we might like to extend our case study to include variations in another parameter, such as the roughness coefficient, *n*. This coefficient is known to

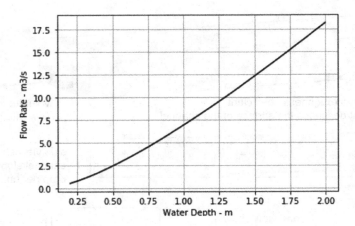

FIGURE 6.6   Plot of flow rate versus water depth for an open channel.

vary from 0.010 for a smooth, glass-lined channel to 0.030 for a channel with a natural, soil surface. We can recall how we created a meshgrid and contour plot in Chapter 5 involving two factors. See the Python script in Figure 6.7. The contour plot produced is illustrated in Figure 6.8.

The Python script illustrates how two-dimensional arrays, here D and N created by the meshgrid function, are passed to the Manning function, and a two-dimensional result, flow rates in the variable Q, is returned. Then, the contour function from the Matplotlib pyplot module is used to create the plot. The contours are lines of equal flow rate, and we can observe how they change with the two study parameters.

```python
import numpy as np
import matplotlib.pyplot as plt

B = 4   # m
S = 0.0015  # m/m

def Manning(d,B,n,S):
    Q = 1/n * (d*B)**(5/3) / (B + 2*d)**(2/3) * np.sqrt(S)
    return Q

d = np.linspace(0.2,2.)
n = np.linspace(0.010,0.030)
D,N = np.meshgrid(d,n)
Q = Manning(D,B,N,S)

cplot = plt.contour(D,N,Q,colors='k')
plt.grid()
plt.xlabel('Water Depth - m')
plt.ylabel('Roughness coefficient')
plt.clabel(cplot)
plt.title('Flow Rate - m3/s')
```

FIGURE 6.7   Python script for a case study with two parameters: water depth and roughness coefficient.

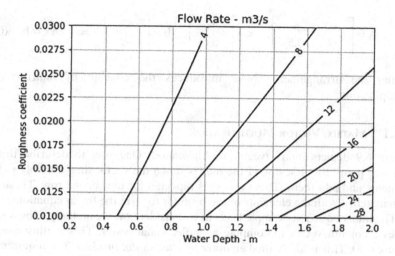

FIGURE 6.8 Contour plot of fluid flow rate versus water depth and roughness coefficient.

As you write Python code and construct expressions, you need to consider whether it is important to support arrays and array operations. If so, care is needed in implementing nonlinear functions, both built-in functions from the NumPy module and user-defined functions.

6.4 VECTOR/MATRIX OPERATIONS

Multidimensional computations occur frequently in engineering and science. Representing quantities as vectors and matrices often represents a compact, efficient way to accomplish computational tasks. Take, for example, a set of linear algebraic equations.

$$-2x_1 + 5x_2 = 43$$
$$7x_1 + 0.5x_2 = -9 \tag{6.2}$$

We find it convenient to represent these in vector/matrix form:

$$\begin{bmatrix} -2 & 5 \\ 7 & 0.5 \end{bmatrix} \cdot \begin{bmatrix} x_1 \\ x_2 \end{bmatrix} = \begin{bmatrix} 43 \\ -9 \end{bmatrix} \tag{6.3}$$

and with the definitions shown below, we can describe the equations in a compact, general form.

$$\mathbf{A} = \begin{bmatrix} -2 & 5 \\ 7 & 0.5 \end{bmatrix}, \quad \mathbf{x} = \begin{bmatrix} x_1 \\ x_2 \end{bmatrix}, \quad \mathbf{b} = \begin{bmatrix} 43 \\ -9 \end{bmatrix} \quad \Rightarrow \quad \mathbf{Ax} = \mathbf{b} \quad (6.4)$$

Seeing the arrangement above introduces the concept of matrix/vector multiplication.

6.4.1 MATRIX/VECTOR MULTIPLICATION

Figure 6.9 depicts matrix/vector multiplication. One way to describe this is that we "pour" the first row of the matrix down the vector then multiply paired elements and add them. This process is repeated for the second row. These are then matched with the elements of the **b** vector to form the linear equations.

The linear equation example leads us to consider how we multiply a row vector times a column vector to compute a single, scalar result. This is illustrated in Figure 6.10. This is also called an *inner product* or *dot product*. The requirement that is evident is that the number of elements of each array must be the same.

How do we accomplish an inner or dot product of two arrays in Python? The code below illustrates this using the dot method.

```
import numpy as np

a = np.array([0.5, 1.7, -6.2, 4.3])
b = np.array([-0.7, 3.3, 5.1, -7.2])
```

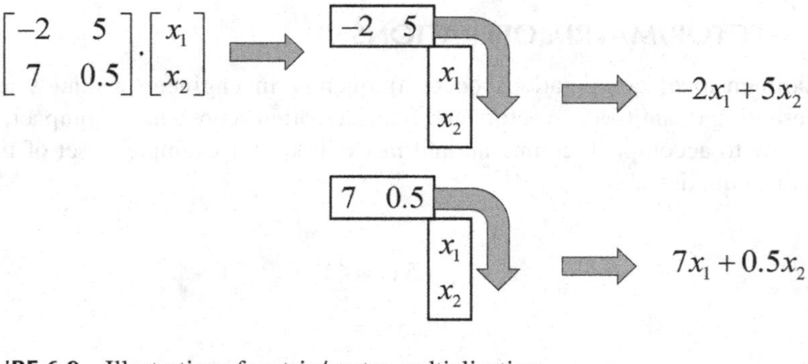

FIGURE 6.9   Illustration of matrix/vector multiplication.

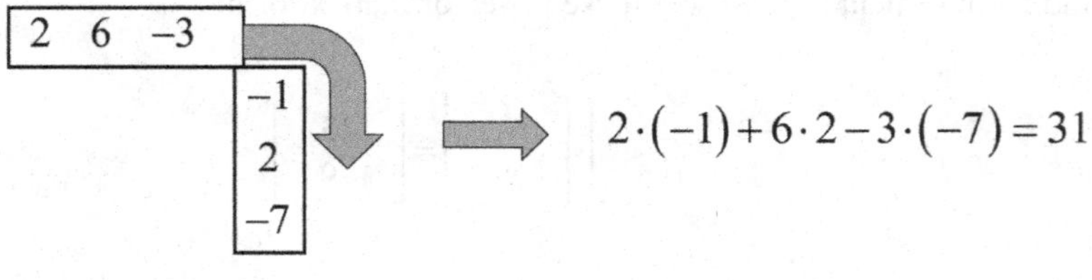

FIGURE 6.10   Row vector×column vector to obtain scalar result.

```
c = a.dot(b)
print(c)

-57.32
```

Next, we consider how to carry out *matrix multiplication*. Figure 6.11 illustrates this process.

You will notice that each row of the first matrix and each column of the second matrix perform a dot product. The third row of the first matrix and the second column of the second matrix produce the corresponding result in the product matrix. Here, we see that a 3×2 matrix multiplies a 2×3 matrix to yield a 3×3 matrix. The general scheme and requirement for matrix multiplication for the product $C = A \cdot B$ is shown in Figure 6.12 which illustrates in detail the dot product that produces element c_{ij}. The figure also illustrates that the inner dimensions of the matrices A and B, n, must match (it illustrates them "canceling out" and leaving the outer dimensions), and the outer dimensions, m and p, form the dimensions of the product matrix C.

Given this scheme, we can construct a Python function to implement matrix multiplication; however, we must account for zero-based indexing.

```
import numpy as np

def matmult(A,B):
    (m,nA) = A.shape
    (nB,p) = B.shape
    if nA != nB:
        return "matrix inner dimensions are not equal"
    n = nA
    C = np.zeros((m,p))
    for i in range(m):
```

$$\begin{bmatrix} -2 & 5 \\ 7 & 0.5 \\ -4 & 3.4 \end{bmatrix} \cdot \begin{bmatrix} 0.2 & -0.4 & 1.2 \\ 4.2 & 12 & -6 \end{bmatrix} \implies \begin{bmatrix} 20.6 & 60.8 & -32.4 \\ 3.5 & 3.2 & 5.4 \\ 13.48 & 42.4 & -25.2 \end{bmatrix}$$

$\begin{bmatrix} -2 & 5 \end{bmatrix}$ $\begin{bmatrix} 0.2 \\ 4.2 \end{bmatrix} \implies -2 \cdot 0.2 + 5 \cdot 4.2 = 20.6$ $\begin{bmatrix} -2 & 5 \end{bmatrix}$ $\begin{bmatrix} -0.4 \\ 12 \end{bmatrix} \implies 60.8$ $\begin{bmatrix} -2 & 5 \end{bmatrix}$ $\begin{bmatrix} 1.2 \\ -6 \end{bmatrix} \implies -32.4$

$\begin{bmatrix} 7 & 0.5 \end{bmatrix}$ $\begin{bmatrix} 0.2 \\ 4.2 \end{bmatrix} \implies 3.5$ $\begin{bmatrix} 7 & 0.5 \end{bmatrix}$ $\begin{bmatrix} -0.4 \\ 12 \end{bmatrix} \implies 3.2$ $\begin{bmatrix} 7 & 0.5 \end{bmatrix}$ $\begin{bmatrix} 1.2 \\ -6 \end{bmatrix} \implies 5.4$

$\begin{bmatrix} -4 & 3.4 \end{bmatrix}$ $\begin{bmatrix} 0.2 \\ 4.2 \end{bmatrix} \implies 13.48$ $\begin{bmatrix} -4 & 3.4 \end{bmatrix}$ $\begin{bmatrix} -0.4 \\ 12 \end{bmatrix} \implies 42.4$ $\begin{bmatrix} -4 & 3.4 \end{bmatrix}$ $\begin{bmatrix} 1.2 \\ -6 \end{bmatrix} \implies -25.2$

FIGURE 6.11 Example illustration of matrix multiplication.

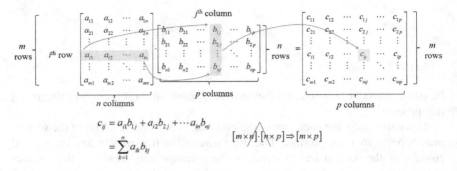

FIGURE 6.12 General illustration of matrix multiplication and the dimensional requirements.

```
        for j in range(p):
            C[i,j] = 0
            for k in range(n):
                C[i,j] = C[i,j] + A[i,k]*B[k,j]
    return C
```

In the `matmult` function, the numbers of rows and columns of the A and B arguments are determined using the `shape` attribute for each. Then, the inner dimensions are checked for equality with an error message returned if they are not. A product array C is created, filled with zeros. The matrix multiplication is accomplished with three nested `for` loops. The outer `for` loop iterates the i index from 0 to n-1 for the number of rows in the product. The next inner `for` loop iterates the j index from 0 to m-1 for the number of columns in C. The innermost loop computes the dot product of row i of A with column j of B to yield the i, j element of C. Here is a test of the `matmult` function corresponding to the example in Figure 6.11.

```
A = np.array([[-2, 5],[7, 0.5],[-4, 3.4]])
B = np.array([[0.2, -0.4, 1.2],[4.2, 12, -6]])
C = matmult(A,B)
print(C)

[[ 20.6    60.8   -32.4 ]
 [  3.5     3.2     5.4 ]
 [ 13.48   42.4   -25.2 ]]
```

Alternately, we can attempt to use the `dot` method for the matrix multiplication.

```
D = A.dot(B)
print(D)

[[ 20.6    60.8   -32.4 ]
 [  3.5     3.2     5.4 ]
 [ 13.48   42.4   -25.2 ]]
```

It is evident that the `dot` method accomplishes this in a more concise fashion, and our longer, home-grown `matmult` function is not required. However, the `matmult` function does illustrate how this operation takes place.

6.4.2 TRANSPOSE

Another common vector/matrix operation is the *transpose*. When an array is transposed, its rows become columns and vice versa as illustrated below,

$$
\begin{bmatrix} -2 & 5 \\ 7 & 0.5 \\ -4 & 3.4 \end{bmatrix}^{T} = \begin{bmatrix} -2 & 7 & -4 \\ 5 & 0.5 & 3.4 \end{bmatrix} \tag{6.5}
$$

where the transpose operation is denoted with a superscript T. Python has a `transpose` method to implement the operation. Here is an example of its use.

```
import numpy as np

A = np.array([[-2, 5],[7, 0.5],[-4, 3.4]])
B = A.transpose()
print(A)
print(B)

[[-2.   5. ]
 [ 7.   0.5]
 [-4.   3.4]]
[[-2.   7.  -4. ]
 [ 5.   0.5  3.4]]
```

6.4.3 MATRIX INVERSION

The final matrix operation we consider in this chapter is the *matrix inverse*. It is applied to square matrices (same number of rows as columns). We are all familiar with the concept of the inverse in scalar calculations. Here are examples.

$$
a \cdot \frac{1}{a} = 1 \qquad \sin(\theta) \cdot \sin^{-1}(\theta) = 1 \qquad \ln\big(\exp(b)\big) = 1
$$

The result of applying the inverse to a quantity, whether via division or a function, is unity, 1. When we consider the inverse of a matrix, multiplication by the inverse cannot yield unity but rather results in a matrix of 1's on the diagonal, also known as an *identity matrix*.

$$
\mathbf{A} \cdot \mathbf{A}^{-1} = \mathbf{I} \tag{6.6}
$$

An example of this would be

$$\begin{bmatrix} -2 & 5 \\ 7 & 0.5 \end{bmatrix} \cdot \begin{bmatrix} ai_{11} & ai_{12} \\ ai_{21} & ai_{22} \end{bmatrix} = \begin{bmatrix} 1 & 0 \\ 0 & 1 \end{bmatrix} \tag{6.7}$$

where the values of ai_{ij} represent the elements of the inverse matrix. These can be found here by multiplying out to yield four linear equations which can be solved in pairs with the results shown.

$$\begin{aligned} -2ai_{11} + 5ai_{21} &= 1 \\ -2ai_{12} + 5ai_{22} &= 0 \\ 7a_{11} + 0.5ai_{21} &= 0 \\ 7ai_{12} + 0.5ai_{22} &= 1 \end{aligned} \qquad \begin{bmatrix} -2 & 5 \\ 7 & 0.5 \end{bmatrix}^{-1} = \begin{bmatrix} -\dfrac{1}{72} & \dfrac{5}{36} \\ \dfrac{7}{36} & \dfrac{1}{18} \end{bmatrix} \tag{6.8}$$

We can test our inverse matrix using matrix multiplication in a Python script.

```
import numpy as np

A = np.array([[-2, 5], [7, 0.5]])
AI = np.array([[-1/72, 5/36], [7/36, 1/18]])

print(A.dot(AI))

[[1.00000000e+00 0.00000000e+00]
 [1.38777878e-17 1.00000000e+00]]
```

The result is an identity matrix with a tiny roundoff error in the lower left element.

Although this example and method are illustrative, this is not the way that the inverse is computed with numerical methods. We consider that in Chapter 8. In the meantime, we can illustrate how to obtain the inverse using the `inv` function from NumPy's `linalg` submodule.

```
from numpy import linalg

Ainv = linalg.inv(A)
print(Ainv)
print(Ainv.dot(A))

[[-0.01388889  0.13888889]
 [ 0.19444444  0.05555556]]

[[1.00000000e+00 1.38777878e-17]
 [0.00000000e+00 1.00000000e+00]]
```

The inverse matrix, `Ainv`, is displayed followed by the matrix product `Ainv·A` to confirm that it is a valid inverse. You will also note, from our two last examples, that $\mathbf{A^{-1} \cdot A}$ gives the same result as $\mathbf{A \cdot A^{-1}}$. In other words, the order of multiplication of a matrix and its inverse is *commutative*. That is not generally the case for matrix multiplication which is not commutative; that is, $\mathbf{A \cdot B} \neq \mathbf{B \cdot A}$. Except for square matrices, one of these products is not feasible because of the requirements for matrix multiplication.

Although we have illustrated the vector dot product and matrix multiplication of arrays with the `dot` method, it is worthwhile to point out that the NumPy `linalg` module also has functions that accomplish these and many other linear algebra operations. For example, there are `matmul` and `vdot` functions available. More information is available in the NumPy manual (https://numpy.org/doc/stable/).[3]

Example 6.2 Solving a Set of Linear Equations with Vector/Matrix Operations

Here is the example from the beginning of this section,

$$-2x_1 + 5x_2 = 43$$

$$7x_1 + 0.5x_2 = -9$$

This system of equations can also be expressed in vectors/matrix notation as

$$\begin{bmatrix} -2 & 5 \\ 7 & 0.5 \end{bmatrix} \cdot \begin{bmatrix} x_1 \\ x_2 \end{bmatrix} = \begin{bmatrix} 43 \\ -9 \end{bmatrix}$$

or concisely as

$$\mathbf{Ax = b} \tag{6.9}$$

where

$$\mathbf{A} = \begin{bmatrix} -2 & 5 \\ 7 & 0.5 \end{bmatrix}, \quad \mathbf{x} = \begin{bmatrix} x_1 \\ x_2 \end{bmatrix}, \quad \mathbf{b} = \begin{bmatrix} 43 \\ -9 \end{bmatrix}$$

So, a general set of linear equations can be described in this last form, $\mathbf{Ax = b}$. Consider what happens when we multiply both sides of this vector/matrix equation by the inverse of the $\mathbf{A}$ matrix.

---

[3] We referred to the matrix subclass of arrays in Section 6.1. With these arrays, one can use the * operator to perform matrix multiplication.

$$\mathbf{A}^{-1} \cdot \mathbf{A} \cdot \mathbf{x} = \mathbf{A}^{-1} \cdot \mathbf{b} \qquad (6.10)$$

The first product, $\mathbf{A}^{-1} \cdot \mathbf{A}$ is equal to the identity matrix, $\mathbf{I}$, and $\mathbf{I} \cdot \mathbf{x}$ is the same as $\mathbf{x}$, so the solution to the equations can be expressed as

$$\mathbf{x} = \mathbf{A}^{-1} \cdot \mathbf{b} \qquad (6.11)$$

and the operations we have learned in this chapter can be used to solve the equations. Here is a Python script to solve the example.

```
import numpy as np

A = np.array([[-2, 5],[7, 0.5]])
b = np.array([43, -9])

Ainv = np.linalg.inv(A)
x = Ainv.dot(b)
print(x)

[-1.84722222  7.86111111]
```

Although this is a simple approach to solving linear algebraic equations, we will find in Chapter 8 that it is not the most efficient. Here, we note that the `linalg` module has another function, `solve`, that implements a better method or algorithm.

PROBLEMS

6.1 Write a Python script to create the two-dimensional array shown below, and then add statements to extract the subset array indicated. Hint: Use the colon in array indexing. Use `print` statements to document your results.

```
1  2  3  4  5
2  3 |4  5| 6
3  4 |5  6| 7
4  5 |6  7| 8
```

6.2 Write a Python script using a `for` loop to create a one-dimensional array with odd numbers from 1 to 9. Use `print` statements to document your results.

6.3 Employ the stack commands to add the following to the array in Problem 6.1.

(a) Add this row to the bottom of the array: $\quad -1 \quad -2 \quad -3 \quad -4 \quad -5$

(b) Add this column to the right side of the array:
$$\begin{matrix} 6 \\ 7 \\ 8 \\ 9 \end{matrix}$$

Provide your Python code and document your results.

6.4 Write Python code to create an array of one hundred x values from 0 to 5, and then use this array to create a well-formatted plot of the following function:

$$e^{-x/4}(2-x)-1$$

6.5 Write a compact set of Python statements to create a 7×7 array filled with sevens. Use a `print` statement to display the array.

6.6 Develop Python code that changes this row array

$$\begin{matrix} -1 & -2 & -3 & -4 & -5 \end{matrix}$$

into a column array. Do so with both the `reshape` function and the `transpose` method and compare the results.

6.7 Create a Python function called `fnorm` that computes the square root of the sum of squares of an array. The function should perform with one- or two-dimensional arrays. Test it for both. Compare your result to that from using the `norm` function from the NumPy `linalg` module. This is called the *Frobenius norm*.

6.8 The *vector product*, $\mathbf{x}^T \mathbf{x}$, is equivalent to the dot product of $\mathbf{x}$ with itself. A more general form is the *quadratic form*,

$$\mathbf{x}^T \cdot \mathbf{Q} \cdot \mathbf{x}$$

where $\mathbf{Q}$ is a symmetric, square matrix. The form of the $\mathbf{Q}$ matrix is such that its transpose is the same matrix. The elements on opposite sides of the diagonal are equal.

$$\begin{bmatrix} q_{11} & q_{21} & \cdots & q_{n1} \\ q_{21} & q_{22} & \cdots & q_{n2} \\ \vdots & \vdots & \ddots & \vdots \\ q_{n1} & q_{n2} & \cdots & q_{nn} \end{bmatrix}$$

Develop a Python function, called `quadform`, that takes arguments of x and Q and computes the quadratic product as shown above. The function should check that the dimension of x matches the number of rows and columns of Q. It should also check that Q is a square matrix and a symmetric matrix. Test and document your results.

6.9 Write a Python script to determine the inverse of the following matrix.

$$
\begin{bmatrix}
1.13 & 3.83 & 1.16 & 3.40 \\
0.53 & 1.79 & 2.53 & 1.54 \\
3.41 & 4.93 & 8.76 & 1.31 \\
1.24 & 4.99 & 10.67 & 0.02
\end{bmatrix}
$$

Include in your script a test of the inverse by multiplying it by the original matrix with the result of an approximate identity matrix.

6.10 Solve the following set of linear equations via a Python script using the `inv` function from the NumPy `linalg` module and the `dot` method. Test your solution using the equations.

$$8x_1 + 2x_2 + 3x_3 = 30$$

$$x_1 - 9x_2 + 2x_3 = 1$$

$$2x_1 + 3x_2 + 6x_3 = 31$$

6.11 Develop and test a Python function, called `trace`, which has a square array as an argument and returns the sum of the diagonal elements of the array. The function should check that the input argument is a square matrix.

6.12 Develop and test a Python function, called `absnorm`, which is an alternate to the Frobenius norm. This norm sums the absolute values of the array elements.

7 Solving Single Algebraic Equations

CHAPTER OBJECTIVES

- Learn bracketing methods for solving single equations, both bisection and false position.
- Implement the bracketing methods by developing Python functions.
- Understand the background behind open methods for solving single equations, including the Newton-Raphson method and the secant method.
- Develop Python functions to implement the open methods.
- Learn about a hybrid, bracketing/open method, Brent's method, and how to use the built-in `brentq` function from the SciPy `optimize` module.
- See how some equations occur naturally in a successive substitution or circular format, $x = g(x)$, and understand the characteristics that govern convergence of fixed-point iteration.
- Program Python to apply fixed-point iteration to the solution of circular, $x = g(x)$, equations.
- Learn the Wegstein method as an enhancement of fixed-point iteration and how it can be implemented with a Python function.

In solving numerical problems, engineers and scientists frequently must compute a series of formulas implemented as Python expressions in assignment statements. There are many occasions, however, when sequential calculations are not the complete story. Numerical solution of equations is a routine activity for engineers and scientists, and they need to be well equipped to solve such equations with Python.

There are several, well-recognized categories of equations needing solution. In this chapter, we consider single, nonlinear algebraic, and transcendental equations. An *algebraic equation* consists of constants, variables, and the basic algebraic operations of addition, subtraction, multiplication, division, and raising to a power. Examples include simple polynomials such as

$$f(x) = 6x^5 - 3x^3 + 5x + 7 \tag{7.1}$$

A *transcendental equation* is one which "transcends" algebra by including terms such as the exponential and trigonometric functions. For example,

$$f(x) = e^{-0.5x} \sin(3x - 1) \tag{7.2}$$

DOI: 10.1201/9781003256861-7

In subsequent chapters, you will learn how to use Python to solve systems of linear and nonlinear algebraic equations and equations that describe rates of change—differential equations. This and the following two chapters open the door to the study of numerical methods. You may well take one or more courses in numerical methods later in your academic career, but here our purpose is to introduce you to methods that you can apply to advantage now and in your upcoming studies.

7.1   THE NATURE OF SINGLE, NONLINEAR EQUATIONS IN ONE UNKNOWN

In a typical application, we will have an equation that has terms on both sides of the equal sign. Here is an example:

$$\sin(x+2)\cosh(x) = -2 \tag{7.3}$$

To solve the equation, we need to find a value of x so that the left-hand side of the equation evaluates to -2. By convention, when we are solving equations like this, we move all terms to one side of the equation. Here, that would then be

$$\sin(x+2)\cosh(x) + 2 = 0 \tag{7.4}$$

Thus, the *root* is the value of x that makes the function on the left-hand side equal to zero. More generally, the root satisfies

$$f(x) = 0 \tag{7.5}$$

As in Figure 7.1, an effective way to visualize the scenario is the plot the left-hand side, $f(x)$, versus x for a range of x values and examine the behavior. By reading the graph, we can see that $f(x) = 0$ at about $x = 1.8$. Although this is a good first approximation, we may need a more precise answer for the solution or root of the equation, and we return to that.

Next, instead of plotting the curve for x from 0 to 3, Figure 7.2 displays the curve from -3 to 3.

Imagine we plot a different function and produce Figure 7.3. Examining this plot, we reach the conclusion that this function has no roots; or more accurately, no real roots. The equation plotted here is

$$x^2 - 6x + 13 = 0 \tag{7.6}$$

and its roots, by the quadratic formula, are a complex conjugate pair, $3 \pm 2j$. The message to be drawn from these plots is that it is worthwhile to study graphically the behavior of the equation you are going to solve so that you understand better the situation you are facing.

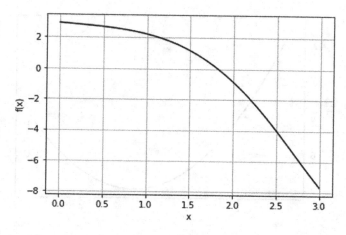

FIGURE 7.1 Example plot of $f(x)$.

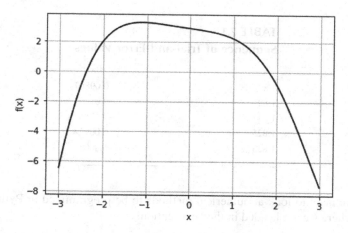

FIGURE 7.2 Plot of Equation 7.1 with an expanded x range.

Now, going back to Equation 7.1 and Figure 7.1, one way to determine a more precise root is by trial-and-error. Table 7.1 shows a sequence of values for x and corresponding $f(x)$ results where we are trying to home in on a solution.

With the four additional estimates from the initial $x = 1.8$ from our plot, we have a good estimate of the solution, $x = 1.823$, to four significant figures.

If we only had to solve an equation once and be on our way, the plot and trial-and-error method may be all we need. It is a simple approach, and it is not necessary to involve more complicated techniques for a one time solution. However, maybe we need to solve this equation thousands of times as part of a bigger computational scheme, or perhaps we need a very, very precise solution.

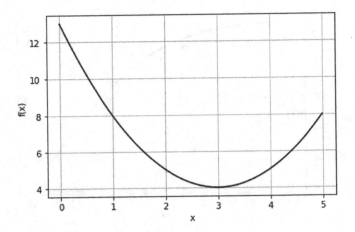

FIGURE 7.3   Plot of a function with no real roots.

TABLE 7.1
Sequence of Trial-and-Error Values

x	$f(x)$
1.8	0.09867
1.82	0.01257
1.84	−0.07539
1.825	−0.00924
1.823	−0.00050

Then, we need to look at numerical methods to be programmed in Python, and that is where we are headed in the next section.

7.2   BRACKETING METHODS—BISECTION

The numerical methods that use a bracketing technique require two initial estimates, x_1 and x_2 (sometimes called guesses, but usually "educated guesses") for the root that are on either side of the true root; that is, which "bracket" the root. Referencing Figure 7.1, we could choose as our initial estimates 0 and 3 or, more narrowly 1.5 and 2.

How do we tell whether our initial estimates do bracket a root? Typically, the signs of $f(x_1)$ and $f(x_2)$ are opposite, but we must be careful. Referring to Figure 7.2, if we chose −3 and 3 as initial estimates, both would produce negative signs for $f(x)$, and you can see that this is because we have two roots between those estimates. So, when we apply bracketing methods, we need to check that there is only

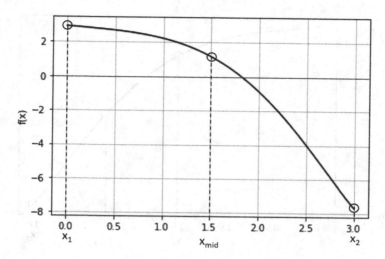

FIGURE 7.4   Illustration of the first iteration of bisection.

one root in our bracket and that $f(x)$ is a smooth function over that range with no weird characteristics like discontinuities. Most of the real problems that engineers and scientists solve will be like this, but there are exceptions.

We introduce the simplest of the bracketing methods with the illustration in Figure 7.4. By choosing the initial estimates $x=0$. and 3., we note on the figure that $f(x_1)>0$ and $f(x_2)<0$, which establishes that the product $f(x_1) \cdot f(x_2)<0$.

The *bisection method*, as its name implies, chooses the midpoint between x_1 and x_2, called x_{mid} on the diagram, as the next estimate for the solution. The next step of the method is to determine which half of the bisected interval contains the solution. That's easy to tell from the plot, but how do we do so analytically? Since we are still looking for a sign change in $f(x)$, we can compare the signs of $f(x_1)$ and $f(x_2)$ with that of $f(x_{mid})$. Where there is a match, x_{mid} replaces either x_1 or x_2 as the bracket for the next round of the method. In our case above, x_{mid} replaces x_1 and the next round or iteration looks like the updated plot in Figure 7.5.

We can see that the next midpoint is at $x=2.25$, and the root is located between x_1 and x_{mid}. Consequently, x_{mid} will become x_2 for the third iteration of the method.

Notice that the original interval has width 3; the second's interval is 1.5, and the third interval will be 0.75. The interval containing the solution is cut in half each iteration. If the method is conducted for n iterations, the final interval of uncertainty containing the solution will be given by

$$\frac{\text{orginal interval}}{2^n}$$

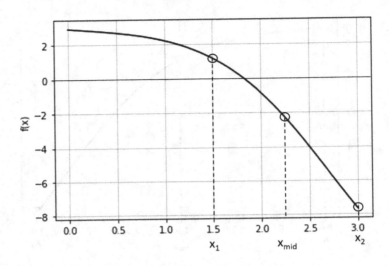

FIGURE 7.5   Second iteration of the bisection method.

Two examples: For ten iterations, the final interval will be the original divided by 1,024. For 20 iterations, it will be divided by $2^{20} = 1,048,576$ or about a million. Practically, knowing the solution to one part in a million of the original interval is generally good enough, and the best part is that it is guaranteed!

The next step is to code the bisection method as a function in Python. That code is presented in Figure 7.6.

The bisect function is designed to be general purpose. Its first argument is the name of the Python function that provides the value of $f(x)$ given a value of x.

```
def bisect(func,x1,x2,maxit=20):
    """
    Uses the bisection method to estimate a root of func(x).
    The method is iterated maxit (default = 20) times.
    Input:
        func = name of the function
        x1 = lower guess
        x2 = upper guess
    Output:
        xmid = root estimate
        or
        error message if initial guesses do not bracket solution
    """
    if func(x1)*func(x2)>0:
        return 'initial estimates do not bracket solution'
    for i in range(maxit): # carry out maxit iterations
        xmid = (x1+x2)/2  # calculate midpoint
        if func(xmid)*func(x1)>0:  # check if f(xmid) same sign as f(x1)
            x1 = xmid    # if so, replace x1 with xmid
        else:
            x2 = xmid   # if not, replace x2 with xmid
    return xmid  # return the latest value of xmid as the solution
```

FIGURE 7.6   Python bisection function.

The second and third arguments are the bracket values of x, and the final keyword argument, maxit, is the maximum number of iterations with a default value of 20 if it is not specified. The bisect code first checks to make sure that the signs of $f(x_1)$ and $f(x_2)$ are opposite. If not, an error message is returned. Following that, the function uses a for loop to iterate the bisection method maxit times. For each iteration, the function computes the f(xmid) value and checks if it is the same sign as f(x1). Note that this is accomplished by taking the product of the two and testing to see if that is positive. If it is, xmid becomes the next x1. If not, xmid becomes the next x2. Finally, the last value of xmid is returned as the solution estimate.

Notice that the bisect function only has nine executable statements. It is compact and easy to understand. Simplicity and brevity are good features of Python code. We can apply this bisect function to solve for the root of the equation from the previous section with the Python script:

```
import numpy as np

def f(x):
    return np.sin(x+2)*np.cosh(x)+2.

x1 = 0. ; x2 = 3.
xsoln = bisect(f,x1,x2)
print('solution is {0:6.4f}'.format(xsoln))
```

and the display in the Console is

```
solution is 1.8229
```

You can see that this is close to our trial-and-error solution of 1.823, but it is precise to one part in a million of the original interval, 3., or a precision of $3/2^{20} \cong 3 \times 10^{-6}$.

Example 7.1 Finding the Depth of Liquid in a Spherical Tank Given the Volume

Industrial liquids are frequently stored in spherical tanks, either above or below ground. Figure 7.7 shows the key required variables relating the interior radius of the tank, R, the depth of the liquid at the center of the tank, h, and the liquid volume, V. The formula relating these quantities is

$$V = \pi h^2 \left(\frac{3R - h}{3} \right) \qquad (7.7)$$

A tank with internal radius of 5 meters has a total volume given by

$$V_{\text{total}} = \frac{4}{3}\pi R^3 \cong 523.6\,\text{m}^3 \qquad (7.8)$$

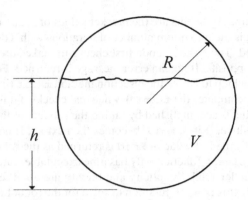

FIGURE 7.7   Spherical tank with liquid.

What depths correspond to liquid volumes 100, 200, 300, 400, and 500 cubic meters?

This task calls for solving the tank liquid formula as an equation in *h* five times for the respective liquid volumes. Each time, we can use our bisect function. The formula can be rearranged as follows:

$$f(h) = h^3 - 3Rh^2 + \frac{3V}{\pi} = 0 \qquad (7.9)$$

Since this is a cubic polynomial in *h*, there are potentially three real roots. In choosing our initial estimates, we should be assured they bracket only one realistic root for *h*. An effective way to investigate this is a Python script to find the roots of *f(h)* for one of our volume cases, 200 m³.

```
import numpy as np
V = 200   # m3
R = 5   # m
coef = np.array([1., -3.*R, 0., 3.*V/np.pi])
r = np.roots(coef)
print(r)
```

The displayed roots are

```
[14.02970369  4.20648373 -3.23618742]
```

We see that the first root is greater than 10 m, that is, above the tank, and the third root is clearly below the tank, as it is negative. Consequently, if we choose initial estimates of empty tank ($h_1 = 0$) and full tank ($h_2 = 2R$), we can be assured that only one, valid depth will be found.

Below, we construct a Python script with a for loop to solve the five cases for the corresponding liquid depths.

```
import numpy as np

def f(h):
```

```
    return h**3 - 3*R*h**2 + 3*V/np.pi

R = 5.   # m
h1 = 0.   # m
h2 = 2.*R   # m

Vtest = [100., 200., 300., 400., 500.]   # m3

for V in Vtest:
    hsoln = bisect(f,h1,h2)
    print('V = {0:4.0f} m3, h = {1:5.3f} m'.format(V,hsoln))
```

and here are the results as displayed in the Console:

```
V = 100 m3, h = 2.797 m
V = 200 m3, h = 4.206 m
V = 300 m3, h = 5.488 m
V = 400 m3, h = 6.843 m
V = 500 m3, h = 8.718 m
```

There are certain features to note in the script code:

- The function, f(h), references R and V, which are not defined in the function, but, since they are assigned values in the general script, their scope makes them available within the function.
- The Vtest values are defined as a simple list. This allows the for statement to cycle through the elements of the list.
- Notice the two format specifications in the print statement. The first is coded with 0: and the second with 1:.

A practical note, smaller tanks, especially those that are underground, often have their liquid depths measured with a dipstick. These include tanks at fueling stations, although these are typically cylindrical with hemispherical or dished ends. The operator notes the depth and goes to a chart to read the volume. By expanding the calculations above to many more even increments of volume, it would give us what we need to produce a dipstick calibrated directly in volume.[1] You can explore this application in a problem at the end of this chapter.

7.3   BRACKETING METHODS—FALSE POSITION

As elementary numerical methods, like bisection, are introduced, it is worthwhile to consider modified or enhanced versions; that is, taking one step beyond the base method. That will be a theme in this chapter (as well as numerical methods in general), and we start with an enhancement of the bisection method called *false position*. This method is illustrated in the diagram in Figure 7.8.

---

[1] We could also fit a polynomial to the {V, h} data and use that to calibrate a dipstick. Fitting polynomials to data is considered in Chapter 10.

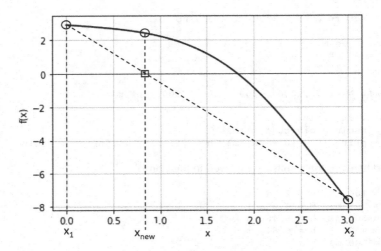

FIGURE 7.8 False position method.

Instead of using the midpoint between the initial estimates, the false position (also called *regula falsi*[2] in some references) method projects a straight line between the estimates and obtains the next estimate, x_{new}, where the line crosses $f(x)=0$. With the x_{new} value in hand, the same logic used in bisection applies in determining whether x_{new} becomes the new x_1 or x_2 for the next iteration of the method. In the illustration in the diagram, evidently x_{new} will become the next x_1.

What we need then is a formula that allows us to calculate x_{new}. We can obtain this by equating the ratios of sides of two similar triangles as follows:

$$\frac{f(x_1)-f(x_2)}{x_2-x_1} = \frac{f(x_1)-0}{x_{new}-x_1} \tag{7.10}$$

and then solve this analytically for x_{new}:

$$x_{new} = \frac{x_1 f(x_2)-x_2 f(x_1)}{f(x_2)-f(x_1)} \tag{7.11}$$

You will note in the diagram above that the first x_{new} value is farther away from the solution than the first x_{mid}. This will not always be the case. You can imagine if the $f(x)$ curve were more linear (that is, less curved), the false position method would get very close to the solution in the first iteration.

Modifying our `bisect` function to accommodate the false position method is easy. See the result in the `falpos` function in Figure 7.9. The midpoint formula

---

[2] The use of Latin might tip you off the false position is a very old method. In fact, simplified expressions of it can be found in cuneiform tablets from ancient Babylon, and in papyri from ancient Egypt.

```
def falpos(func,x1,x2,maxit=20):
    """
    Uses the false position method to estimate a root of func(x).
    The method is iterated maxit (default = 20) times.
    Input:
        func = name of the function
        x1 = lower guess
        x2 = upper guess
    Output:
        xnew = root estimate
        or
        error message if initial guesses do not bracket solution
    """
    if func(x1)*func(x2)>0:
        return 'initial estimates do not bracket solution'
    for i in range(maxit): # carry out maxit iterations
        xnew = (x1*func(x2)-x2*func(x1))/(func(x2)-func(x1)) #calculate new x
        if func(xnew)*func(x1)>0:   # check if f(xnew) same sign as f(x1)
            x1 = xnew    # if so, replace x1 with xnew
        else:
            x2 = xnew  # if not, replace x2 with xnew
    return xnew  # return the latest value of xnew as the solution
```

FIGURE 7.9 Python false position function.

from `bisect` has been replaced by the false position formula (Equation 7.5) and all the `xmid` notations have been changed to xnew to be consistent with our terminology. We can evaluate the `falpos` function by solving Equation 7.1,

$$\sin(x + 2)\cosh(x) + 2 = 0 \qquad (7.12)$$

with initial estimates $x_1 = 0$ and $x_2 = 3$. Here is the script and the results:

```
import numpy as np

def f(x):
    return  np.sin(x+2)*np.cosh(x)+2.

x1 = 0.
x2 = 3.

xsoln = falpos(f,x1,x2)
print('x = {0:6.4f}'.format(xsoln))

x = 1.8229
```

Although the false position method appears to find the root just as well as the bisection method, there is a lingering doubt. One of the advantages of bisection is that, knowing the number of iterations taken (20 as default), the precision of the solution is guaranteed (one part in 2^{20} of the original interval). That is not the case with false position. This raises the possibility of determining precision, or at least convergence, in another way. This is accomplished by examining the current x_{new} value in comparison with its value from the previous iteration. When there is negligible change in these two successive values, we can conclude that the method has converged to a sufficient extent to provide a solution. In comparing these two values, we usually want to measure the change as a fraction or percentage of the values themselves. This leads to a definition of percent relative error as follows:

$$\varepsilon_a = \left| \frac{\text{current } x_{new} - \text{previous } x_{new}}{\text{current } x_{new}} \right| \times 100\% \qquad (7.13)$$

When the percent relative error, ε_a, falls below a specific tolerance, ε_s, the method is considered converged, the solution is terminated, and the current root estimate is returned. Note that the subscript "a" designates that ε_a is an "approximate" error whereas the subscript "s" designates that ε_s is a "stopping" error.

Using an error tolerance/convergence scheme raises another issue. We usually want this convergence to occur within a maximum number of iterations. If the maximum is reached, the method should signal that the maximum has been reached along with returning the current estimate. Here, we introduce two different algorithm structures that accomplish this. The first uses a for loop that will execute the maximum number of iterations. Within the loop, it tests for convergence and exits (or returns) if the tolerance is met. The second uses a while loop with two exits, one if convergence is achieved, and another if the maximum iterations is met.

For the first algorithm structure, we modify the falpos function to falpos1 as shown in Figure 7.10. You will notice that the fractional (not percentage here)

```
def falpos1(func,x1,x2,Ea=1.e-7,maxit=30):
    """
    Uses the false position method to estimate a root of func(x).
    The method is iterated a maximum of maxit (default = 30) times.
    The method converges when the fraction relative error falls below
    Ea (default value 1.e-7)
    Input:
        func = name of the function
        x1 = lower guess
        x2 = upper guess
    Output:
        xnew = root estimate
         = number of iterations required
        or
        error message if initial guesses do not bracket solution
    """
    if func(x1)*func(x2)>0:
        return 'initial estimates do not bracket solution',0
    xnewprev = (x1+x2)/2  # initial xnew = midpoint between x1 & x2
    for i in range(maxit): # carry out maxit iterations
        xnew = (x1*func(x2)-x2*func(x1))/(func(x2)-func(x1)) #calculate new x
        if abs((xnew-xnewprev)/xnew) < Ea:  # check if converged
            iter = i+1
            return xnew,iter  # if converged, return xnew and iterations
        if func(xnew)*func(x1)>0:  # check if f(xnew) same sign as f(x1)
            x1 = xnew  # if so, replace x1 with xnew
        else:
            x2 = xnew # if not, replace x2 with xnew
        xnewprev = xnew
    iter = i+1
    return xnew,iter  # here if maxit reached
```

FIGURE 7.10 Python false position function falspos1 with relative error convergence using a for loop structure.

error tolerance, Ea, has been added to the function arguments with a default value of 1×10^{-7}, and the maximum iterations, maxit, now has a default value of 30. Of course, we hope that the method converges before the maximum iterations is reached. Next, the function returns two values, usually the solution estimate and number of iterations taken (since i starts at zero, the number of iterations taken is i+1). If the initial estimates do not bracket a solution ($f(x_1)$ and $f(x_2)$ are not the same sign), an error message and zero iterations are returned.

To get the calculation of relative error off the ground, an initial value of xnew is required, called xnewprev and set equal to the midpoint between x1 and x2. What's new in the for loop is that the relative error is calculated, and, if it is less than the error tolerance, there is a return with the solution estimate and the number of iterations taken—a good return! Otherwise, the same logic is used as before in determining whether xnew becomes the new x1 or x2. What is added after that is that the xnew value is saved in xnewprev for the next iteration. If the for loop is completed, having reached the maximum iteration limit, the current value of xnew and the number of iterations is returned. By checking the iterations returned against the maximum, it can be determined whether the iteration limit has been reached.

If we apply this new false position function, falpos1, to the solution of the previous equation, here is a script and the results.

```
import numpy as np

def f(x):
    return  np.sin(x+2)*np.cosh(x)+2.

x1 = 0.
x2 = 3.

xsoln,iter = falpos1(f,x1,x2)
print('x = {0:6.4f}'.format(xsoln))
print('number of iterations taken = {0:3d}'.format(iter))

x = 1.8229
number of iterations taken =  17
```

We obtain the same solution to five significant figures and note that 17 iterations were required.

To implement the second algorithm structure, we modify the falspos1 function to a new falspos2 function, replacing the for loop with a while loop. This is shown in Figure 7.11. To save space, we have omitted the initial docstring comments. You will note that there is a while True: statement that creates a general iterative loop. As we discussed in Chapter 4, this loop will not exit on the while statement, but rather depends on exit or termination based on if tests within the loop. There are two such if tests, one for convergence and another for exceeding the iteration limit. Rather than exiting the while loop with a break statement, we use a return statement to terminate the function.

```
def falpos2(func,x1,x2,Ea=1.e-7,maxit=30):
    if func(x1)*func(x2)>0:
        return 'initial estimates do not bracket solution',0
    xnewprev = (x1+x2)/2   # initial xnew = midpoint between x1 & x2
    iter = 0
    while True: # carry out maxit iterations
        iter = iter + 1
        xnew = (x1*func(x2)-x2*func(x1))/(func(x2)-func(x1)) #calculate new x
        if abs((xnew-xnewprev)/xnew) < Ea:  # check if converged
            return xnew,iter   # if converged, return xnew and iterations
        if iter > maxit:  # check if maximum iterations exceeded
            return 'maximum iterations exceeded',iter
        if func(xnew)*func(x1)>0:  # check if f(xnew) same sign as f(x1)
            x1 = xnew   # if so, replace x1 with xnew
        else:
            x2 = xnew   # if not, replace x2 with xnew
        xnewprev = xnew
```

FIGURE 7.11 Python false position function `falspos2` with relative error convergence using a `while` loop structure.

If we test the `falspos2` function, it produces the same solution as the `falspos1` function. Also, we can evaluate it with a lower limit on iterations that will be met.

```
xsoln, iter = falpos2(f, x1,x2,maxit=10)
print(xsoln)
print(iter)
```

with the results

```
maximum iterations reached
11
```

As we encounter iterative methods that test for convergence and have an iteration limit, you can implement these with either the `for` or `while` loop structures. We will illustrate both in later chapters.

Two bracketing methods, bisection and false position, have been introduced, which raises the question, which is the best to use? That is not that easy to answer. If we are solving a nonlinear, algebraic equation only once, bisection can get us the answer to a desired precision, even though the method might require more iterations than false position. We do encounter applications where solving the equation is embedded in a larger calculation which may require the equation to be solved thousands of times. If that is the case, the efficiency of the method becomes relevant. This will be discussed in the next section.

7.4 OPEN METHODS—NEWTON-RAPHSON

The bracketing methods introduced in the previous two sections have an advantage and possibly a disadvantage. If the initial estimates encompass a single root of the equation, generally the methods, bisection or false position, will find the root. That's good. However, with the way that the methods proceed, they typically plod along and would not be considered efficient. With some analysis, we can demonstrate that the bracketing methods reduce the relative error each iteration in a linear fashion. Consequently, there is interest in finding and using methods which converge more quickly. Also, the bracketing methods require two initial estimates. In order that they always encompass the root of the equation, we may have to set their interval wide. That also slows the process down when we are repeating the solution many times.

Open methods provide an alternative. These methods also involve systematic trial-and-error iterations but require only a single starting value or two starting values that do not necessarily bracket the root. As such, they sometimes diverge

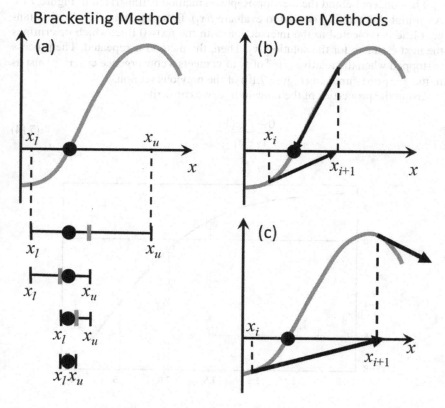

FIGURE 7.12 Graphical depiction of the fundamental difference between (a) bracketing and (b) and (c) open methods for root location (modified from Chapra & Clough 2022). In (a), which is bisection, the root is constrained within the interval prescribed by x_l and x_u. In contrast, for the open method depicted in (b) and (c), which is Newton-Raphson, a formula is used to project from x_i to x_{i+1} in an iterative fashion. Thus, the method can either (b) converge rapidly or (c) diverge, depending on the shape of the function and the value of the initial guess.

or move away from the true root as the computation progresses (Figure 7.12c). However, when the open methods converge (Figure 7.12b), they usually do so much more quickly than the bracketing methods.

Among the most popular and powerful (when it works) of these open methods is the *Newton-Raphson[3] method*. This approach requires only one initial estimate, and it would be best if that value were in the vicinity of the solution. That can be a good fit for the multiple solution scenario where the solution changes a bit from one time to the next. The reason for that is that we can use the solution from the last time as the initial estimate for the next time. Also, we will appreciate if the convergence is better than linear; for example, instead of reducing the error linearly with the number of iterations, reduction by the square of the number of iterations would be advantageous.

The concept behind the Newton-Raphson method is illustrated in Figure 7.13. An initial estimate, x_1, is used to evaluate $f(x_1)$. From the point $\{x_1, f(x_1)\}$, a tangent line is projected to the intersection with the $f(x)=0$ line, which determines the next estimate for the solution, x_2. Then, the method is repeated. The process is stopped when the relative error of x_1 to x_2 meets a convergence criterion, just as in the `falpos1` function (Figure 7.10) of the previous section.

Using the properties of the tangent line, we can write

$$\frac{0-f(x_1)}{x_2-x_1}=f'(x_1) \tag{7.14}$$

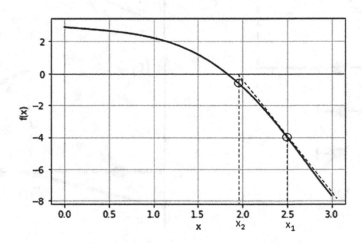

FIGURE 7.13   The Newton-Raphson method.

---

[3] We all know who Isaac Newton is, but who is Raphson? *Joseph Raphson* was a contemporary of Newton in England who lived from 1648 to 1715. He published a work in 1690 that contained the Newton-Raphson method. Frequently, this is called just Newton's method, but we are not alone in wanting to acknowledge Raphson's contribution.

and then solve this analytically for x_2,

$$x_2 = x_1 - \frac{f(x_1)}{f'(x_1)} \tag{7.15a}$$

or in general iterative form

$$x_{i+1} = x_i - \frac{f(x_i)}{f'(x_i)} \tag{7.15b}$$

This is the *Newton-Raphson formula*, which is the key relationship of the method. You can see that, to carry out the method, we need the derivative of $f(x)$. This may be difficult or impossible to derive analytically, but we will deal with that in the next section. Based on the `falpos1` function of Figure 7.10, we provide a Python function for the Newton-Raphson method in Figure 7.14. You will notice that there is only one `if` test in the `for` loop, that being for convergence. The maximum iteration condition is created if the `for` loop exceeds `maxit` and exits normally. Because of this, we have to assess the iteration value returned to see if maximum iterations were reached.

Notice how brief the code is—eight executable statements within the function. We can test the function with our previous example, Equation 7.1,

$$f(x) = \sin(x+2)\cosh(x) + 2 = 0 \tag{7.16}$$

```
"""
Uses the Newton-Raphson method to estimate a root of func(x).
The method is iterated a maximum of maxit (default = 30) times.
The method converges when the fraction relative error falls below
Ea (default value 1.e-7)
Input:
    f = name of the function
    fp = name of function providing the derivative of f
    x1 = initial guess
Output:
    x2 = root estimate
    iter = number of iterations required
    or
    error message if initial guesses do not bracket solution
"""
for i in range(maxit): # carry out maxit iterations
    x2 = x1 - f(x1)/fp(x1)  # calculate new x
    if abs((x2-x1)/x2) < Ea:  # check if converged
        iter = i+1
        return x2,iter  # if converged, return xnew and iterations
    x1 = x2   # if not converged, replace x1 with x2
iter = i+1
return x2,iter  # here if maxit reached
```

FIGURE 7.14 Python Newton-Raphson function.

but now we have the burden of deriving $f'(x)$ and supplying a separate function that evaluates it. For this case, that's not too difficult with the result obtained through knowledge of calculus

$$f'(x) = \cos(x+2)\cosh(x) + \sin(x+2)\sin(x) \qquad (7.17)$$

In the script below, we program the solution with an initial estimate of $x_1 = 2.5$. The results are also displayed.

```
import numpy as np

def f(x):
    return   np.sin(x+2)*np.cosh(x)+2.

def fp(x):
    return np.cosh(x)*np.cos(x+2)+np.sinh(x)*np.sin(x+2)

x1 = 2.5

xsoln,iter = newtraph(f,fp,x1)
print('x = {0:6.4f}'.format(xsoln))
print('number of iterations taken = {0:3d}'.format(iter))

x = 1.8229
number of iterations taken =    5
```

The same solution, to five significant figures, is determined as before, but you notice that only five iterations were required. You may recall that false position required 17 iterations.

Below, we attempt the solution for a different initial estimate, $x_1 = 0.5$, and the results are

```
x = 4.2246
number of iterations taken =    7
```

The Newton-Raphson method has found another solution, evidently outside the range of x we have been exploring. An expanded plot of the function is shown in Figure 7.15.

Ah, ha! We note immediately that our function has another solution at $x = 4.2246$, and that this is the one that the Newton-Raphson method found. Not only that, but our initial estimate was to the left of the solution at 1.8, and the method skipped right over that one and located the root to the far right.

Recalling that a graphical analysis can sometimes help us figure out what happened, we have replotted the function showing how the Newton-Raphson iterations evolved. Note that at our initial guess, the slope is very flat. That is, $f'(0.5)$ has a very small value of

$$f'(0.5) = \cos(0.5+2)\cosh(0.5) + \sin(0.5+2)\sin(0.5) = -0.59153 \qquad (7.18)$$

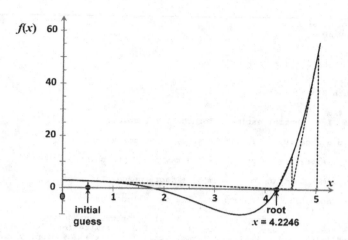

FIGURE 7.15 Expanded plot of function subject to the Newton-Raphson method.

Thus, the first iteration shoots the solution far to the right of the initial guess before it intercepts the abscissa at about $x=5$. Thereafter, Newton-Raphson rapidly converges on the root at $x=4.2246$.

For this particular example, the tendency to move away from the area of interest is because a near-zero slope was encountered. But beyond that, the example reveals a more general problem with the Newton-Raphson method, and with open methods in general. There is no guarantee that the method will converge upon the acceptable solution of the equation. In our example above, another solution has been found. In fact, the method may diverge and not find a solution at all. This is the reason why our Python code (Figure 7.14) specifies a maximum number of iterations. Further, although it does not necessarily ensure that the method will work, it would certainly be advantageous for our initial estimate to be in close proximity of the desired solution.

Example 7.2 Calibrating the Depth/Volume Relationship of Liquid in a Spherical Tank

Continuing our study from Example 7.1, we propose to create a calibration table of liquid volume in even increments versus the associated liquid depths for the example tank with radius of 5 m. The table will display volumes from zero to 520 m³ in increments of 10 m³. For each volume, the corresponding depth will be listed. A table like this will be used to calibrate a depth measuring instrument so that it reports directly in volume.

This means that we will have to solve the equation

$$f(h) = h^3 - 3Rh^2 + \frac{3V}{\pi} = 0 \qquad (7.19)$$

52 times in sequence. The Newton-Raphson method is attractive for this application because it is efficient, $f'(h)$ is readily available, and we can use

```
import numpy as np
import pylab

def f(h):
    return h**3 - 3*R*h**2 + 3*V/np.pi

def fp(h):
    return 3*h**2 - 6*R*h

R = 5.  # m
h1 = 0.5 # m  initial estimate for the first solution

Vcal = np.arange(10.,530.,10.)  # array of volume values
n = len(Vcal)
hcal = np.zeros((n))  # create zero array for depth solutions

print('Volume  Depth\n  m3      m')  # table header

for i in range(n):  # for loop to solve for all depths
    V = Vcal[i]  # current volume to be used in f(h)
    hcal[i],iter = newtraph(f,fp,h1)  # solve for current depth
    h1 = hcal[i]  # use current depth as initial estimate for next solution
    print('  {0:4.1f}    {1:6.3f}'.format(Vcal[i],hcal[i]))  # display line

# create plot of calibration table
pylab.plot(Vcal,hcal,c='k')
pylab.grid()
pylab.xlabel('Liquid Volume - m3')
pylab.ylabel('Liquid Depth - m')
pylab.title('Calibration Plot for Spherical Tank of Radius 5 meters')
```

FIGURE 7.16 Python script to produce a calibration table and plot for a spherical tank.

the solution from the previous volume increment as the starting estimate. The formula for the derivative is evaluated with calculus as

$$f'(h) = 3h^2 - 6Rh \qquad (7.20)$$

Using our newtraph function, a Python script to accomplish this task is displayed in Figure 7.16. The function definitions for f(h) and fp(h) are taken directly from the equations above. The tank radius is specified and a reasonable initial estimate for the depth is assigned to h1. The NumPy arange function is used to create an array of volumes, Vcal, for the Newton-Raphson solutions. Then, an array of zeros of corresponding size, hcal, is created for the depth solutions.

After displaying appropriately formatted column headings, a for loop is set up to solve for all the depths corresponding to the volumes in the Vcal array. Each time, the V variable is assigned the current value from the Vcal array so that it is available to the f(h) function. After invoking the newtraph function to solve for the current depth, hcal[i], that value is assigned to h1 as the initial estimate for the next solution. This is a key element of the solution because the next solution will be close to the current solution, and the Newton-Raphson method should converge in few iterations. The last statement in the loop displays a line of the table for the current volume and depth solution. The last few statements in the script produce a plot of the results. See Figure 7.17.

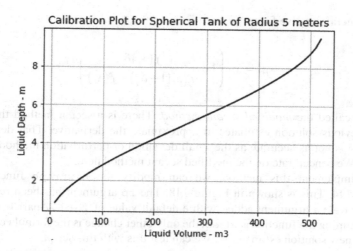

FIGURE 7.17   Calibration curve for spherical tank.

7.5 OPEN METHODS—MODIFIED SECANT

In introducing the Newton-Raphson method in the previous section, we pointed out that there could be difficulty in obtaining an analytical expression for the derivative, $f'(x)$, of the equation being solved. There are many examples of this, but a general circumstance that would cause the problem is that $f(x)$ may be a more involved calculation than one single formula. It might involve the solution of other equations or reading data from tables. Also, to be truthful, many would prefer to avoid a detailed analytical derivation of a derivative, although that challenge can be overcome frequently by using symbolic mathematics software, such as *Wolfram Alpha*.[4] In any case, such software is useful in checking your own derivation of the derivative. The purpose of this section is to provide an alternative method to use when do you do not want to derive $f'(x)$ or when an analytical derivative is not feasible.

The simple answer is to provide an approximation to $f'(x)$ using a local finite difference,

$$f'(x) \cong \frac{f\big(x_1(1+\delta)\big) - f(x_1)}{\delta \cdot x_1} \tag{7.21}$$

Here, we provide a small deviation in x_1, given by a fraction, δ, and compute the change in $f(x)$ divided by that deviation. The fraction is typically small, for example, 10^{-6}. If we substitute this into the Newton-Raphson formula, we get

$$x_2 = x_1 - \frac{f(x_1)\delta x_1}{f\big(x_1(1+\delta)\big) - f(x_1)} = x_1 \cdot \left(1 - \frac{f(x_1)\delta}{f\big(x_1(1+\delta)\big) - f(x_1)}\right) \tag{7.22a}$$

---

[4] www.wolframalpha.com

or in general iterative form

$$x_{i+1} = x_i \cdot \left(1 - \frac{f(x_i)\delta}{f(x_i(1+\delta)) - f(x_i)} \right) \qquad (7.22b)$$

This is called the *modified secant method*. There is a secant method that uses two previous solution estimates to approximate the derivative. That derivative estimate is not as accurate as the small deviation or perturbation method shown above. We concentrate on the modified secant method here.

To implement this method, we can modify the `newtraph` function of Figure 7.14. This is shown in Figure 7.18. The `fp` argument has been removed, and the `delta` argument added with a default value of `1.e-6`. Apart from that, and renaming the function `modsec`, the only other change is the formula calculating the new solution estimate, x_2. We can test this with this script:

```
import numpy as np

def f(x):
    return  np.sin(x+2)*np.cosh(x)+2.

x1 = 2.5

xsoln,iter = modsec(f,x1)
print('x = {0:6.4f}'.format(xsoln))
print('number of iterations taken = {0:3d}'.format(iter))
```

with the results

```
def modsec(f,x1,delta=1.e-6,Ea=1.e-7,maxit=30):
    """
    Uses the modified secant method to estimate a root of func(x).
    The method is iterated a maximum of maxit (default = 30) times.
    The method converges when the fraction relative error falls below
    Ea (default value 1.e-7). A fractional value, delta,
    (default = 1.e-6) is used to approximate the derivative of f(x).
    Input:
        f = name of the function
        x1 = initial guess
    Output:
        x2 = root estimate
        iter = number of iterations required
    """
    for i in range(maxit): # carry out maxit iterations
        x2 = x1*(1-f(x1)*delta/(f(x1*(1+delta))-f(x1)))   # calculate new x
        if abs((x2-x1)/x2) < Ea:  # check if converged
            iter = i+1
            return x2,iter  # if converged, return xnew and iterations
        x1 = x2   # if not converged, replace x1 with x2
    iter = i+1
    return x2,iter  # here if maxit reached
```

FIGURE 7.18   Python function for the modified secant method.

```
x = 1.8229
number of iterations taken =   5
```

These are the same results we obtained using the `newtraph` function.

We have shown here that the modified secant method appears to perform well, even almost as well as the Newton-Raphson method for our simple example problem. So, why not use it all the time? Good question. We did replace the need to derive $f'(x)$ with the use of the `delta` factor. The latter could be considered a "tuning" parameter. If we choose a value that is too small, Python's calculations may not yield a measurable change in $f(x)$, and the modified secant method will fail. If we choose `delta` too large, the approximation to the derivative may be too crude, and the method may be unstable and not converge. So, in using the modified secant method, we may have to find a `delta` value that works well. Although the default value in our function, `1.e-6`, works well for most cases, it may need to be adjusted for some problems.

7.6 CIRCULAR METHODS—FIXED-POINT ITERATION

As engineers and scientists confront problems that require numerical solutions, their analysis results in one or more equations that need to be solved. Generally, it is sound practice to deal with these equations in their natural format, that is, in the way that they arise via derivation. This is as opposed to carrying out analytical manipulations of the equations into different formats.

Consider this example. From your background, you are aware of the ideal gas law,

$$P = \frac{RT}{\hat{V}} \tag{7.23}$$

where P = pressure, $\hat{V}$ = specific volume, R = the gas law constant, and T = the absolute temperature. Typical units might be

P[=]kilopascals(kPa) $\hat{V}$[=]liters/mole of gas (L/mol)   T [=]kelvins(K)

for which $R \cong 8.3145$ L·kPa/(mol·K).

Note: You should always take care to use the correct value of R for the units being used in the problem you are solving. Values for different unit sets are conveniently available on the Internet; for example, Wikipedia under "gas constant."

When the conditions are extreme, particularly at high pressures, the ideal gas law becomes inaccurate, and modifications are required. One of the classic modified gas laws is the *van der Waals equation*,

$$P = \frac{RT}{\hat{V} - b} - \frac{a}{\hat{V}^2} \tag{7.24}$$

where a and b are parameters whose values depend on the gas under study.

We now wish to solve a problem where P and T are specified for a particular gas, and we need to solve for $\hat{V}$. Rearranging the equation of state, we obtain

$$\hat{V} = \frac{RT}{P + \dfrac{a}{\hat{V}^2}} + b \tag{7.25}$$

and immediately an issue appears. To calculate a value for $\hat{V}$, we need the same value on the right-hand side of the equation. One approach would be, rather than rearranging the van der Waals equation as first stated, to move all terms to one side of the equal sign and express the problem in the form

$$f(\hat{V}) = P - \frac{RT}{\hat{V} - b} + \frac{a}{\hat{V}^2} = 0 \tag{7.26}$$

and apply one of the methods from the previous sections to solve for $\hat{V}$.

An alternate approach, suggested by Figure 7.19, is to use the second form of the equation (Equation 7.25), and carry out a *successive substitution* method as follows:

1. Provide an initial estimate for $\hat{V}$.
2. Compute a new value for $\hat{V}$, using the formula.
3. Check whether the new value is equal to, or very close to, the initial estimate.
4. If not, let the new value replace the initial estimate and return to Step 2.
5. If so, accept the new value as a valid solution estimate.

Such schemes are called *circular* because of the loop depicted by the dashed lines in Figure 7.19 where $\hat{V}$ is recalculated as a function of $\hat{V}$ with the rearranged version of the original equation.

Let's try this scheme in Python with a set of parameter values: $P = 950\,\text{kPa}$, $T = 300\,\text{K}$, $a = 365.4\,\text{L}^2\cdot\text{kPa/mol}^2$, $b = 0.04280\,\text{L/mol}$. Here, the values for a and b are for carbon dioxide, CO_2.

$$P = 950\text{kPa}, \quad T = 300\text{K}, \quad a = 365.4\text{L}^2\cdot\text{kPa/mol}^2, \quad b = 0.04280\text{L/mol}$$

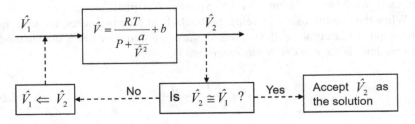

FIGURE 7.19 Circular calculation scheme.

```
R = 8.3145   # kPa*L/(mol*K)

a = 365.4   # L2*kPa/mol2
b = 0.04280   # L/mol

P = 950   # kPa
T = 300   # K

V1 = 2.0   # L/mol

V2 = R*T/(P+a/V1**2)+b

print(V1,V2)
```

and the display in the Console is

```
2 2.438104172468431
```

If we repeat the circular scheme by assigning 2.4381 to V1, the result is

```
2.4381 2.5088634490981945
```

Continuing this scheme yields the following table:

2.0000	2.4381
2.4381	2.5089
2.5089	2.5172
2.5172	2.5182
2.5182	2.5183

It is clear that the process is converging. At the point when V2 is virtually equal to V1, the equation is satisfied, and we have a valid solution estimate.

Another way of illustrating this is with a plot of V2 versus V1, shown in Figure 7.20. The solid line shows the progression of the values from left to right, and the dashed line is the line where V2=V1, the 45°-line. You can see that the method converges directly to the solution at the dashed line.

To show the speed of convergence, we can plot the absolute change in solution estimate from one iteration to the next. This is depicted in Figure 7.21 and uses a logarithmic y-axis scale. The linear nature of the curve suggests an exponential convergence.

Now that we have introduced the technique through an example, it is useful to discuss a few general concepts. The method is formally called *fixed-point itera-tion* or *successive substitution*. The scenario presents itself when the equation you are trying to solve is expressed as $x=g(x)$; that is, you need the solution for x to

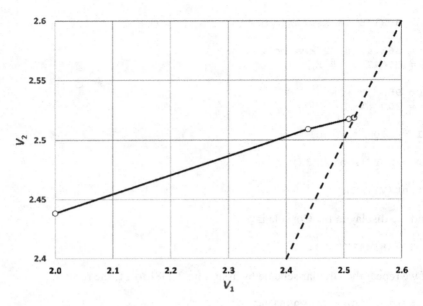

FIGURE 7.20 Approach to the solution by successive substitution.

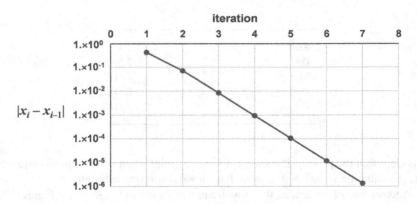

FIGURE 7.21 Convergence of successive substitution scheme.

compute the right-hand side of the equation. Evidently, the method worked with our example. Are there cases where it doesn't work?

To investigate that, we're going to manipulate van der Waals equation to solve analytically for the $\hat{V}$ that is located in the squared term,

$$\hat{V} = \sqrt{\dfrac{a}{\dfrac{RT}{\hat{V} - b} - P}} \tag{7.27}$$

and we will repeat the procedure, starting with V1 = 2.0.

2.0000	1.0612
1.0612	0.4937
0.4937	0.2824
0.2824	0.1965
0.1965	0.1546

Clearly, this process is taking us away from the valid solution we determined earlier. Apparently, the method is not working in this case.

This reveals a major disadvantage of the fixed-point iteration method. We are not assured that it will be stable and convergent. By plotting the right-hand sides versus $\hat{V}$ along with the progress of our solutions, we can see the problem. This is shown in Figure 7.22. The root is located at the intersection of the solid and the dashed line. The top plot, which corresponds to Equation 7.25, is convergent, whereas the bottom plot, which corresponds to Equation 7.27, is divergent. These plots are often called "cobweb" plots. See Chapra and Clough (2022) for more detail.

What we find in the top graph is that, with a starting estimate of 2.0, successive estimates move directly toward the solution at the intersection with the dashed line. In the lower graph, again starting at 2.0, the successive estimates move to the left and will approach a value less than b, yielding a negative square root and failure of the method.

You may have noticed already the difference in the two graphs. For the stable solution, the slope of $g(x)$ in the vicinity of the solution is less than one (the slope of the dashed line is one), and the opposite is true for the non-convergent case on the right. The condition for a stable solution can be expressed, in general, as (Chapra and Canale 2019)

$$\left| g'(x_{soln}) \right| < 1 \tag{7.28}$$

In practice, if we are confronted with such a non-convergent scheme, a way around this is to solve for another x and formulate a new $x = g(x)$ equation. One will usually work.

In Figure 7.23, a Python fixed-point iteration solving function, fixpt, is presented. This is similar to previous functions; however, the new estimate is simply the function g evaluated for the current estimate. Convergence is attained when the relative error meets the Ea criterion with a default value of 1.e-7.

If we apply this function to the van der Waals problem with the first, stable formulation, the Python script is

```
def V2(V1):
    return  R*T/(P+a/V1**2)+b
```

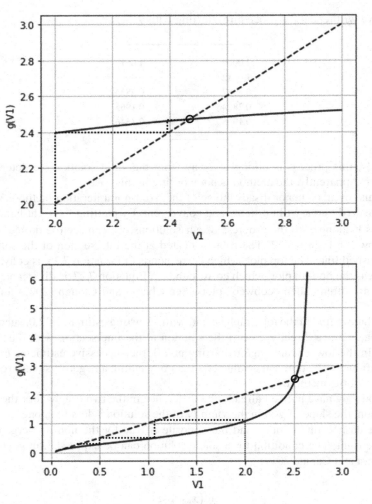

FIGURE 7.22 Comparison of cobweb plots for two formulas for fixed-point iteration. Top plot is convergent, whereas the bottom plot diverges.

```
R = 8.3145   # kPa*L/(mol*K)

a = 365.4   # L2*kPa/mol2
b = 0.04280   # L/mol

P = 950   # kPa
T = 300   # K

V1 = 2.0   # L/mol

Vsoln,iter = fixpt(V2,V1)
```

```
def fixpt(g,x1,Ea=1.e-7,maxit=30):
    """
    Uses the fixed-point iteration method to estimate a root of x = g(x).
    The method is iterated a maximum of maxit (default = 30) times.
    The method converges when the fraction relative error falls below
    Ea (default value 1.e-7)
    Input:
        g = name of the function, for x = g(x)
        x1 = initial estimate
    Output:
        x2 = root estimate
        iter = number of iterations required
    """
    for i in range(maxit):  # carry out maxit iterations
        x2 = g(x1)   # calculate new x
        if abs((x2-x1)/x2) < Ea:  # check if converged
            iter = i+1
            return x2,iter   # if converged, return xnew and iterations
        x1 = x2   # if not converged, replace x1 with x2
    iter = i+1
    return x2,iter   # here if maxit reached
```

FIGURE 7.23 Python function for fixed-point iteration.

```
print('V = {0:6.4f}'.format(Vsoln))
print('number of iterations taken = {0:3d}'.format(iter))
```

and the displayed results are

```
V = 2.5183
number of iterations taken =    8
```

7.7 CIRCULAR METHODS—THE WEGSTEIN METHOD

After studying the bisection method in Section 7.1, we considered an enhanced method based on a linear interpolation in Section 7.2, the false position method. Now, we're going to extend the fixed-point iteration method in a similar way.

Figure 7.24 illustrates the concept. Instead of one initial estimate, the *Wegstein method* requires two, but, unlike the bisection and false position methods, the two estimates, x_1 and x_2, do not have to bracket the solution.

As we have noted in the previous section, for an $x=g(x)$ formulation, the solution is where the $g(x)$ curve crosses the 45° line. The Wegstein method projects a straight line through the points $\{x_1, g(x_1)\}$ and $\{x_2, g(x_2)\}$ to the 45° diagonal to establish the next estimate, x_3. At this point, x_2 becomes the new x_1, and x_3 becomes the new x_2. The method is then repeated until x_3 and x_2 are sufficiently close, as measured against a relative error criterion.

To derive the update formula for x_3, we write the straight-line relationship as illustrated in the figure:

$$\frac{g(x_2) - g(x_1)}{x_2 - x_1} = \frac{x_3 - g(x_2)}{x_3 - x_2} \tag{7.29}$$

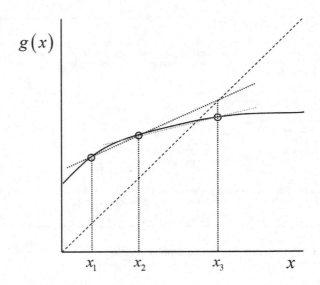

FIGURE 7.24   Wegstein method concept.

This equation is then rearranged to solve for x_3:

$$x_3 = \frac{x_1 \cdot g(x_2) - x_2 \cdot g(x_1)}{x_1 - x_2 + g(x_2) - g(x_1)} \qquad (7.30)$$

The Python `fixpt` function (Figure 7.23) is then modified to the `wegstein` function as shown in Figure 7.25.

```
def wegstein(g,x1,x2,Ea=1.e-7,maxit=30):
    """
    Uses the Wegstein method to estimate a root of x = g(x).
    The method is iterated a maximum of maxit (default = 30) times.
    The method converges when the fraction relative error falls below
    Ea (default value 1.e-7)
    Input:
        g = name of the function, for x = g(x)
        x1, x2 = initial estimates, do not have to bracket root
    Output:
        x3 = root estimate
        iter = number of iterations required
    """
    for i in range(maxit): # carry out maxit iterations
        x3 = (x1*g(x2)-x2*g(x1))/(x1-x2+g(x2)-g(x1))   # calculate new x
        if abs((x3-x2)/x3) < Ea:  # check if converged
            iter = i+1
            return x3,iter  # if converged, return xnew and iterations
        x1 = x2   # if not converged, replace x1 with x2
        x2 = x3   # and replace x2 with x3
    iter = i+1
    return x3,iter  # here if maxit reached
```

FIGURE 7.25   Python function to implement the Wegstein method.

First, we can test the `wegstein` function with the stable, convergent form of the van der Waals equation (Equation 7.25). Here is the Python script and the results:

```python
def g(V):
    return  R*T/(P+a/V**2)+b

R = 8.3145  # kPa*L/(mol*K)

a = 365.4  # L2*kPa/mol2
b = 0.04280  # L/mol

P = 950  # kPa
T = 300  # K

V1 = 2.0  # L/mol
V2 = 2.5

Vsoln,iter = wegstein(g,V1,V2)
print('V = {0:6.4f}'.format(Vsoln))
print('number of iterations taken = {0:3d}'.format(iter))

V = 2.5183
number of iterations taken =   4
```

Notice that the function converges to the solution quickly. To be fair, we should then test the method for the version of the van der Waals equation that was divergent under fixed-point iteration (Equation 7.27). Here is the modified script and results for that case:

```python
import numpy as np

def g(V):
    return  np.sqrt(a/(R*T/(V-b)-P))

R = 8.3145  # kPa*L/(mol*K)

a = 365.4  # L2*kPa/mol2
b = 0.04280  # L/mol

P = 950  # kPa
T = 300  # K

V1 = 2.0  # L/mol
V2 = 2.5

Vsoln,iter = wegstein(g,V1,V2)
print('V = {0:6.4f}'.format(Vsoln))
print('number of iterations taken = {0:3d}'.format(iter))
```

```
V = 2.5183
number of iterations taken =    7
```

What is interesting here is that the Wegstein method has produced a stable solution for a version of our $x = g(x)$ equation that failed using fixed-point iteration. The disadvantage, perhaps not significant, is that two initial estimates are required. This suggests that for many, perhaps most, applications, the Wegstein method should be chosen over fixed-point iteration.

Can the Wegstein method ever get into trouble? The answer is yes. For our last example, if initial estimates of 1.0 and 2.0 are used, this is the output from the script:

```
V =     nan
number of iterations taken =   30
   C:\Users\cloughd\Documents\IntroPythonText\Chapter7\
wegstein2.py:27: RuntimeWarning: invalid value encountered
in sqrt
   return  np.sqrt(a/(R*T/(V-b)-P))
```

Evidently, the function encountered a value for V that caused the argument in the square root function to be negative. So, we still must proceed with caution, and, as a lesson, it would always be preferable to use a convergent form of $x = g(x)$.

7.8   A HYBRID APPROACH—BRENT'S METHOD

Reviewing the methods presented so far in this chapter for solving single nonlinear equations, we have seen advantages and disadvantages for each technique. A hybrid method, introduced by Richard Brent,[5] attempts to capitalize on the advantages and mitigate the disadvantages. The strategy developed is to use open methods, like Newton-Raphson or modified secant, when possible for fast (quadratic) convergence to the root, and, if these methods wander outside a bracketing set of values, resort to a less efficient bracketing technique, like bisection, until it is possible to switch back to the open method and continue with accelerated convergence.

We will not take the time and space here to derive and code a function for Brent's method (see Chapra and Clough 2022 for this.) Rather, we will take advantage of a built-in brentq function in the SciPy optimize module. The syntax for using the brentq function is simple,

```
xsoln = brentq(func, x1,x2)
```

where func is the name of the function that evaluates $f(x)$, and x1, x2 are initial estimates which must bracket the solution. There are additional, optional arguments available:

---

[5] Richard Peirce Brent is an Australian mathematician and computer scientist.

maxiter: maximum number of iterations allowed, otherwise error message
xtol: absolute error tolerance limit, default=2.e-12
rtol: relative error tolerance limit, default=8.8e-16
args: additional arguments required by func, specified as args=(tuple)
full_output: if True, returns both xsoln and additional details on the
    solution,
default False returns just xsoln
If we apply the brentq function to solve for the root of our earlier example,

$$f(x) = \sin(x+2)\cosh(x) + 2 = 0 \qquad (7.4)$$

with initial estimates x1=1.0 and x2=3.0, here is the Python script followed by
the display in the IPython Console:

```
import numpy as np
from scipy.optimize import brentq

def f(x):
    return np.sin(x+2)*np.cosh(x)+2.

x1 = 1.0
x2 = 3.0

xsoln = brentq(f,x1,x2)

print('solution is {0:6.4f}'.format(xsoln))

solution is 1.8229
```

If we include full _ output=True, the code becomes

```
import numpy as np
from scipy.optimize import brentq

def f(x):
    return np.sin(x+2)*np.cosh(x)+2.

x1 = 1.0
x2 = 3.0

xsoln,results = brentq(f,x1,x2,full_output=True)

print('solution is {0:6.4f}'.format(xsoln))
print(results)

solution is 1.8229
      converged: True
           flag: 'converged'
```

```
function_calls: 10
     iterations: 9
           root: 1.8228849971054475
```

and we get more information about the performance of the algorithm. Often, we use this option at the start, and, once we are convinced that the brentq function is performing well, we remove the full_ output specification.

Example 7.3 Solving the van der Waals Equation for Volume with Brent's Method

In this example, we are going to formulate van der Waals equation as an $f(x)=0$ problem and employ the brentq function to solve for the specific volume, $\hat{V}$. In doing so, we are going to take advantage of the args option to provide additional arguments for pressure, P, temperature, T, and the a, b parameters. Writing van der Waals equation in $f(x)=0$ format, we have

$$f\left(\hat{V},P,T,a,b\right)= P - \frac{R \cdot T}{\hat{V} - b} + \frac{a}{\hat{V}^2} = 0 \qquad (7.31)$$

The Python function will then be

```
def f(V, P, T, a, b):
    return P - R*T/(V-b) + a/V**2
```

The rest of the script is

```
from scipy.optimize import brentq

R = 8.3145   # kPa*L/(mol*K)

a = 365.4   # L2*kPa/mol2
b = 0.04280   # L/mol

P = 950   # kPa
T = 300   # K

V1 = 1.0
V2 = 4.0

Vsoln,res = \
brentq(f,V1,V2,full_output=True,args=(P,T,a,b))
print('specific volume is {0:6.4f} L/mol'.format(Vsoln))
print(res
```

and the results displayed in the Console are

```
specific volume is 2.5183 L/mol
         converged: True
```

```
         flag: 'converged'
function_calls: 10
    iterations: 9
         root: 2.5182923306354965
```

Notice that the additional arguments (P, T, a, b) are passed through the `brentq` function to the `f` function which includes those arguments in its definition. The gas law constant is not included, since it is a standard value for the units set used. Because it is defined in the main script, it is available to the `f` function.

We can experiment with error tolerances that are not as tight as the defaults. The `brentq` statement would then look like

```
Vsoln,res = brentq(f,V1,V2,full_output=True,args=(P,T,a,b) \
                  ,xtol=1.e-5,rtol=1.e-5)
```

with the results displaying now as

```
specific volume is 2.5183 L/mol
     converged: True
          flag: 'converged'
function_calls: 8
    iterations: 7
         root: 2.5182924505143265
```

By comparison, because of the more relaxed tolerances, only seven iterations are now required instead of the original nine.

We fully expect that you will want to employ the `brentq` function in your work; however, there are times when you would prefer one of the simpler methods/ functions we have presented in this chapter. The advantage of the latter is that they are not "black boxes" like the `brentq` function where you cannot see inside to understand exactly how they work. Also, for problems that naturally present themselves in $x = g(x)$ format, you may want to consider using fixed-point iteration or the Wegstein method.

7.9　SOLVING FOR THE ROOTS OF POLYNOMIALS

In Example 7.1, we analyzed the relationship between liquid volume and depth in a spherical tank and determined the relationship

$$f(h) = h^3 - 3Rh^2 + \frac{3V}{\pi} = 0 \tag{7.9}$$

Given values for R and V, this is a cubic polynomial in h, and we briefly illustrated solving this polynomial for its three roots with the Python script

```
import numpy as np
V = 200  # m3
```

```
R = 5   # m
coef = np.array([1., -3.*R, 0., 3.*V/np.pi])
r = np.roots(coef)
print(r)
```

and results

```
[14.02970369  4.20648373 -3.23618742]
```

Since polynomials occur frequently in problem solving in engineering and science, it is worthwhile to spend some time addressing them and their solution. A general form for an nth-order polynomial equation is

$$a_n \cdot x^n + a_{n-1} \cdot x^{n-1} + \cdots + a_1 \cdot x + a_0 = 0 \qquad (7.32)$$

This equation will have n roots. They will either be real numbers or complex numbers. If there are complex roots, they must appear as complex conjugate pairs, that is,

$$\alpha + \beta j \quad \text{and} \quad \alpha - \beta j$$

The reason for this is that we are assuming that the coefficients of the polynomial, a_i, are real quantities. Since the polynomial can be represented as a product of its factors, i.e.

$$(x - r_1) \cdot (x - r_2) \cdots (x - r_n) = 0 \qquad (7.33)$$

where r_i are the roots, when multiplying out the factors, real coefficients must result. Note that the product of the conjugate pair is

$$\left(x - (\alpha + \beta j)\right)\left(x - (\alpha - \beta j)\right) = x^2 - 2\alpha x + \left(\alpha^2 + \beta^2\right) \qquad (7.34)$$

so that pair contributes real coefficients as the factors are multiplied out. Any complex root that does not have a conjugate root would result in complex coefficients.

We have introduced methods in the earlier sections of this chapter that provide for finding a root of a nonlinear, algebraic equation, $f(x)=0$, and these could certainly be applied to a polynomial, but they would determine only one root. How could we go about finding the rest of the roots?

Let's explore this with an example:

$$x^4 - 8x^3 - 3x^2 + 62x + 56 = 0 \qquad (7.35)$$

We will apply the modified secant method with initial estimate x1=1 to determine a root.

```
def f(x):
    return  x**4 - 8*x**3 - 3*x**2 + 62*x + 56

x1 = 1.

xsoln,iter = modsec(f,x1)
print('x = {0:6.4f}'.format(xsoln))
print('number of iterations taken = {0:3d}'.format(iter))
```

Here are the results:

```
x = -2.0000
number of iterations taken =   3
```

So, now we know one root. The next step will be to divide the factor associated with that root, $(x+2)$, into the original polynomial. We show long division in Figure 7.26, but, if we were going to develop a program for this, we would have to translate this into an algorithm.

Since we divided by a root factor, we expect the remainder to be zero. We can now proceed to find a root of the quotient polynomial (the original polynomial with the first root removed).

```
def f(x):
    return  x**3 - 10*x**2 + 17*x + 28

x1 = 5.

xsoln,iter = modsec(f,x1)
print('x = {0:6.4f}'.format(xsoln))
print('number of iterations taken = {0:3d}'.format(iter))
```

$$
\begin{array}{r}
x^3 - 10x^2 + 17x + 28 \\
x+2\,\overline{)\,x^4 - 8x^3 - 3x^2 + 62x + 56} \\
(-)x^4 + 2x^3 \\
\hline
-10x^3 - 3x^2 + 62x + 56 \\
(-)-10x^3 - 20x^2 \\
\hline
17x^2 + 62x + 56 \\
(-)17x^2 + 34x \\
\hline
28x + 56 \\
(-)28x + 56 \\
\hline
0
\end{array}
$$

FIGURE 7.26 Long division to determine quotient polynomial.

```
x = 4.0000
number of iterations taken =    5
```

We have the next root and its factor, $(x-4)$, and we can proceed with the next long division, which yields

$$x^2 - 6x - 7 \tag{7.36}$$

This second-order polynomial can be solved for its roots using the quadratic formula to determine the remaining roots, $x=7$ and $x=-1$.

Although this looks (and feels!) laborious, it is possible to code this method efficiently. It is also possible to determine complex roots. The process of factoring out a root and finding a root in the remaining polynomial is called *deflation*. It is the basis for a classic method for determining the roots of polynomials, *Muller's method* (Chapra and Canale 2019).

There is another popular method for determining polynomial roots based on linear algebra and the determination of factors called eigenvalues of a matrix containing the polynomial coefficients. We choose not to discuss the details of this method here because it is beyond the scope of preparation we expect from students. It is notable that this is the current method of choice because it is more efficient than Muller's method.

Python's NumPy module provides several functions that are useful in computations with polynomials. You have already had a peek at one of them, roots, which uses the aforementioned eigenvalue method. Here, we apply it to our example polynomial.

```
import numpy as np

coeff = [1., -8., -3., 62., 56.]
r = np.roots(coeff)
print('roots are\n',r)

roots are
 [ 7.   4.  -2.  -1.]
```

You will note here that the coefficients are provided in a list in order of highest power of x to lowest last, the constant. The coefficients can also be defined as a tuple or a NumPy array.

There are two companion functions in the NumPy module that complement the roots function. The first, poly, is essentially the inverse of roots. It composes the polynomial from its roots and provides the polynomial coefficients. Here, it is applied to our example.

```
coeff1 = np.poly([7., 4., -2., -1.])
print('coefficients are\n',coeff1)

coefficients are
 [ 1. -8. -3. 62. 56.]
```

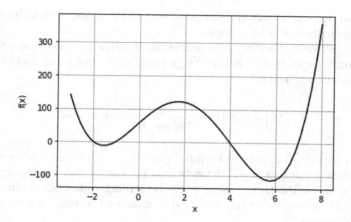

FIGURE 7.27 Polynomial plot showing roots at zero crossovers.

The second is `polyval`, which evaluates a polynomial, given its coefficients, for a specific value of x. Here, we use this function to generate a plot of our polynomial from $x=-5$ to $x=10$.

```
import pylab
xplot = np.linspace(-3., 8.)
yplot = np.polyval(coeff, xplot)
pylab.plot(xplot, yplot, c='k')
pylab.grid()
pylab.xlabel('x')
pylab.ylabel('f(x)')
```

The resulting plot is shown in Figure 7.27, where we can see the four real roots.

7.10 CASE STUDY: TRAJECTORIES OF PROJECTILES IN AIR

The study of the trajectory of a projectile is wide ranging, from sports to missiles to weapons ordnance. The horizontal distance of the trajectory is usually one important objective along with the horizontal, side-to-side position or windage. A typical trajectory is illustrated in Figure 7.28, not considering the horizontal position. If air resistance is neglected, such a trajectory can be described based on physics by the following equation:

$$y = \tan(\theta)x - \frac{g}{2 v_0^2 \cos^2(\theta)} x^2 + y_0 \tag{7.25}$$

where $y=$elevation, $x=$horizontal displacement or range, $\theta=$launch angle, $g=$gravitational acceleration, $v_0=$launch velocity, and $y_0=$initial elevation. Of course, air resistance and other factors like wind are important, but they complicate the mathematical description beyond the scope of this chapter. We will return to those in a later chapter.

The objective of this study is to determine, for given values of v_0 and y_0, what is the launch angle, θ, for a desired range (value of x when $y=0$). To obtain this objective, we need to solve

$$f(\theta) = \tan(\theta)x - \frac{g}{2v_0^2 \cos^2(\theta)}x^2 + y_0 = 0 \qquad (7.36)$$

This is a meaningful scenario because, given a desired range, a launch velocity which is set due to physical limits, and geography that establishes elevation differences, the launch angle is the remaining adjustable parameter. As Figure 7.28 shows, the initial elevation is measured in reference to the final elevation at zero.

In designing a Python script to solve this problem, it would be desirable to have a function that returns the launch angle for input values of range, r, launch velocity, v0, and launch elevation, y0:

```
def launch_angle(r, v0,y0):
.
.
return theta
```

Of course, consistent units must be used for these quantities. Since g is given as 9.807 m/s², the velocity's time units must be seconds. After that, the distance units must be the same, e.g. meters, kilometers, and miles.

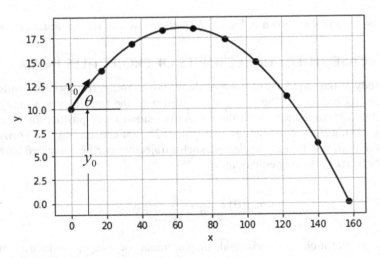

FIGURE 7.28 Projectile trajectory with no air resistance.

Within this function, we will want to invoke one of our solving methods. As we know, these will require either one or two initial estimates for the angle. For the bisection, false position, and Brent's methods, the pair of initial estimates must bracket the solution. As we look at the figure, it would seem that bracketing estimates of 0° and 90° would always contain the solution, but given the equation being solved, there is a problem. The tangent function, as $\theta \to 90°$, approaches infinity. To address this, we would have to assume a reasonable maximum value for the launch angle that is less than 90°, perhaps 80°. For the Newton-Raphson method or the modified secant method, only one initial estimate is required. A mid-range value like 45° or perhaps a value typical of the situation being studied, e.g. 15°, might be used. In the bracketing or single initial estimate cases, testing should be carried out to determine their reliability.

Here is a test script using the `modsec` function from Figure 7.18:

```python
import numpy as np

def y(th0):
    return np.tan(th0)*x - g/2/v0**2/np.cos(th0)**2*x**2 + y0

g = 9.807 # m/s2
th0d = 45.  # degrees
th0 = np.radians(th0d)

y0 = 10.  # m
v0 = 50.  # m/s
x = 160.

theta,iter = modsec(y,th0)
thetad = np.degrees(theta)
print('launch angle = {0:5.1f} degrees'.format(thetad))
print('iterations required =',iter)
```

with the results displayed in the Console:

```
launch angle =  15.4 degrees
iterations required = 5
```

This launch angle seems reasonable. If the launch angles for our application are typically below 20°, an initial estimate of 10° might be appropriate.

Alternately, we might try a bracketing method like the `brentq` function from the SciPy `optimize` module. This would then be the script:

```python
import numpy as np
from scipy.optimize import brentq

def y(th0):
    return np.tan(th0)*x - g/2/v0**2/np.cos(th0)**2*x**2 + y0

g = 9.807 # m/s2
th1d = 0.  # degrees
```

```
th1 = np.radians(th1d)
th2d = 25.   # degrees
th2 = np.radians(th2d)

y0 = 10.   # m
v0 = 50.   # m/s
x = 160.

theta = brentq(y,th1,th2)
thetad = np.degrees(theta)
print('launch angle = {0:5.1f} degrees'.format(thetad))
```

and the successful result is displayed:

```
launch angle = 15.4 degrees
```

You will note that the bracketing initial estimates are 0° and 25°.

There is a choice to be made as to the method to solve for the launch angle. Arbitrarily, we will choose the brentq function to continue. Now, we embed the launch angle solving script into the launch_angle function and test it below. You will note that we have passed the launch_angle arguments through to the y function by using the args=(r,v0,y0) argument in the call to brentq.

```
import numpy as np
from scipy.optimize import brentq

def y(th0,r,v0,y0):
    return np.tan(th0)*r - g/2/v0**2/np.cos(th0)**2*r**2 + y0

def launch_angle(r,v0,y0):
    th1d = 0.   # degrees
    th1 = np.radians(th1d)
    th2d = 25.   # degrees
    th2 = np.radians(th2d)
    return brentq(y,th1,th2,args=(r,v0,y0))

g = 9.807 # m/s2

y0 = 10.   # m
v0 = 50.   # m/s
r = 160.

theta = launch_angle(r,v0,y0)
thetad = np.degrees(theta)
print('launch angle = {0:5.1f} degrees'.format(thetad))
```

and it is successful:

```
launch angle = 15.4 degrees
```

A case study of range versus required launch angle can now be carried out. The script is shown in Figure 7.29.

The plot created is shown in Figure 7.30. A first observation is that the relationship is not quite linear, but approximately linear. Of course, this is for specific

```python
import numpy as np
from scipy.optimize import brentq
import pylab

def y(th0,r,v0,y0):
    return np.tan(th0)*r - g/2/v0**2/np.cos(th0)**2*r**2 + y0

def launch_angle(r,v0,y0):
    th1d = 0.   # degrees
    th1 = np.radians(th1d)
    th2d = 25.  # degrees
    th2 = np.radians(th2d)
    return brentq(y,th1,th2,args=(r,v0,y0))  # solve for launch angle

g = 9.807 # m/s2

y0 = 10.  # initial elevation - m
v0 = 50.  # initial velocity - m/s
r = np.linspace(100.,200.,25)  # array of angles
n = len(r)
thetad = np.zeros((n))  # empty angle array
for i in range(n):
    thetad[i] = np.degrees(launch_angle(r[i],v0,y0))  # solve for angle
#create plot
pylab.plot(r,thetad,c='k')
pylab.grid()
pylab.xlabel('range - meters')
pylab.ylabel('launch angle - degrees')
pylab.title('range vs. angle for v0 = 50 m/s, y0 = 10 m')
```

FIGURE 7.29   Python script for case study of launch angle versus range.

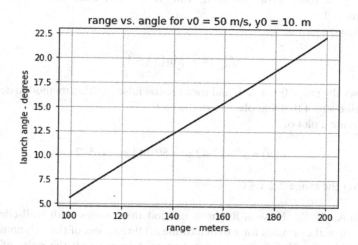

FIGURE 7.30   Plot of required launch angle to achieve a desired range.

values of launch velocity and initial elevation. We could certainly carry out additional case studies where we varied one of these parameters and explored how it affects launch angle.

This case study illustrates how functions can be developed and tested as building blocks for a larger project. We have seen how it is convenient to pass arguments through functions to subordinate functions using the `args` technique. It was also necessary to consider, and perhaps test, different solving methods before making a choice to proceed. The judicious selection of initial estimates is required. It is not difficult to get our solving techniques into trouble by picking arbitrary values. They need to be tailored to the situation being studied. A general piece of advice is the more complicated the subject under study, the more care in planning and building the solution step-by-step is required for success.

PROBLEMS

7.1   Use the bisection method to find a root of the following equation between $x=0$ and $x=2$.

$$f(x)=e^{-\frac{x}{4}}(2-x)-1=0$$

7.2   For the equation from Problem 1, devise and carry out a fixed-point iteration scheme to solve for x.

7.3   Determine

$$\sqrt[3]{5}$$

using a root-solving method. Hint: If $x=\sqrt[3]{5}$, cube both sides and proceed.

7.4   Create a plot of

$$f(x)=x^2|\sin(x)|-4$$

over the range $0 \le x \le 4$, and then use the false position method to determine a root that you observe in the plot.

7.5   Create a plot of

$$f(x)=x^3-12.42x^2+50.444x-66.552$$

over the range $2 \le x \le 6$.

(a) Apply the Newton-Raphson method three times with well-chosen initial estimates for x to determine all three roots of the polynomial.
(b) Use the NumPy `roots` function to determine all the roots of the polynomial and compare these with your results from part (a).

7.6 Determine the root of

$$f(x) = \tan(x) - 2x = 0$$

between $x=0$ and $x=\pi/2$ using the Newton-Raphson method.

7.7 A common shape for an underground tank to store liquids in a horizontal cylinder with hemispherical ends. This is illustrated in Figure P7.7. The volume of liquid, V, is related to the liquid depth, h, by considering two parts. Conceptually, the hemispherical ends can be put together to form a sphere of radius R. The volume in that part is then

$$V_{sph} = \pi h^2 \left(\frac{3R - h}{3} \right)$$

The volume in the cylindrical part is given by a more complicated formula:

$$V_{cyl} = \left(R^2 \cos^{-1}\left(\frac{R - h}{R} \right) - (R - h)\sqrt{2Rh - h^2} \right) L$$

Then, the total volume of liquid is

$$V = V_{sph} + V_{cyl}$$

For a tank with the dimensions, $L=5\,\text{m}$ and $R=0.75\,\text{m}$, write a Python script that finds the depth, h, for a given volume, V. Then, extend the script to provide a calibration table in even increments of volume in liters giving the corresponding depth for each volume value. Finally, produce a plot of depth in meters versus volume in liters.

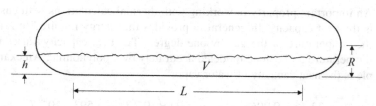

FIGURE P7.7 Horizontal tank with hemispherical ends.

7.8 From Example 3.1, we have the formula for computing the Great Circle distance between two points on the Earth as

$$d = 2\sin^{-1}\left(\sqrt{\left(\sin\left(\frac{lt_1 - lt_2}{2} \right) \right)^2 + \cos(lt_1)\cos(lt_2)\left(\sin\left(\frac{ln_1 - ln_2}{2} \right) \right)^2} \right) r$$

where $\{lt_1, \ln_1\}$ is the location of the first point by latitude and longitude. If we pick the Meridian at the Equator the location is $\{0,0\}$. For a longitude of 105°W, determine the latitude S that is 10,000 km from the Meridian/Equator. Describe approximately where on the globe this is located.

7.9   An alternate, and more recent equation of state than the van der Waals equation, which accounts for behavior of gases at nonideal conditions, is that due to *Soave, Redlich, and Kwong (SRK)*. The SRK equation is

$$P = \frac{RT}{\hat{V} - b} - \frac{\alpha a}{\hat{V}\left(\hat{V} + b\right)}$$

where, including example units, P=pressure in kPa, R=gas law constant, 8.3145 L·kPa/(mol·K), T=temperature in K, $\hat{V}$=specific volume in L/mol. The additional parameters, b in L/mol, a in (L/mol)^2, and α (dimensionless), are dependent on the gas under consideration. For propane, C_3H_8, their values are

$$a=9.3775 (L/mol)^2, \ b=0.06262 L/mol, \ and \ \alpha=0.903$$

For a temperature of 423 K and a pressure of 7,000 kPa, determine the specific volume using the SRK equation of state. Set this up as a circular calculation and use the Wegstein method. Compare the result to the specific volume determined by the ideal gas law,

$$P = \frac{RT}{\hat{V}}$$

7.10 An important property in working with thermal calculations with gases is the heat capacity. In general, it provides the energy required to raise the temperature of the gas by one degree. The heat capacity varies by temperature and can be modeled accurately by a polynomial. An example is the heat capacity of water vapor:

$$C_P = 33.46 + 0.006880\,T + 0.7604 \times 10^{-5}\,T^2 - 3.593 \times 10^{-9}\,T^3$$

where C_P is the heat capacity in J/(mol·°C) and T is the temperature in °C. This formula is valid for a wide range of temperatures, 0–1,500°C.

(a) Create a plot of heat capacity versus temperature for the entire valid range of temperatures.

(b) Create a Python script using the Newton-Raphson method to compute and display the temperature at which the heat capacity is 40 J/(mol·°C).

7.11 The upward velocity of a rocket can be computed with the following formula:

$$v = u \ln\left(\frac{m_0}{m_0 - qt}\right) - gt$$

where v is the upward velocity, u=the downward exit velocity of fuel relative to the rocket, m_0=mass of the rocket at $t = 0$, q=the fuel consumption rate, g=gravitational acceleration, 9.81 m/s². If $u=1,800$ m/s, $m_0=160,000$ kg, $q=2,600$ kg/s, compute the time at which $v=750$ m/s. Use the brentq function to solve this problem.

7.12 You plan to buy a Tesla Model S vehicle for $79,990 by paying 10% down and financing the balance over a 7-year term. You have budgeted a monthly payment of $1,000. So, now you need to shop for a loan at the required interest rate (or lower, if you can find it!). The formula that governs this is

$$A = P \frac{i(1+i)^n}{(1+i)^n - 1}$$

where A = the monthly payment, P = the loan amount, i = the monthly interest rate expressed as a fraction, not a percentage.

Note: Loan interest rates are typically quoted on an annual basis as "APR." To obtain the monthly interest rate, i, you divide the APR by 12. The actual annual interest rate you pay is greater than the quoted APR. It is $(1+i)^{12} - 1$ ($\times$ 100 for %). As an example, for an APR of 6%, with monthly payments, the actual annual interest rate is 6.17%.

Determine the APR you will need to obtain to meet your goal.

7.13 As depicted schematically in Figure P7.13, for any two massive bodies there are five points where the net force on a third smaller-mass body is zero. That is, the gravitational forces of the massive bodies and the centrifugal force are in balance. This feature makes them excellent locations for satellites, as minimal orbit corrections are needed to maintain a desired orbit. For our solar system, this is the case for the Sun and any planet, or for a planet and one of its moons. These points are commonly referred to as the *Lagrange points*.[6] Noteworthy spacecraft designed to operate near the Earth–Sun L_2 are the *Gaia Space Observatory* and the *James Webb Space Telescope*. The force balance equation for L_2 can be written as

---

[6] Joseph-Louis Lagrange (born Giuseppe Luigi Lagrangia) (1736–1813) was an Italian mathematician and astronomer, later naturalized French. He made significant contributions to the fields of analysis, number theory, and both classical and celestial mechanics. Together with Euclid, Euler, Gauss, Newton, and a few others, he is one of the giants of mathematics.

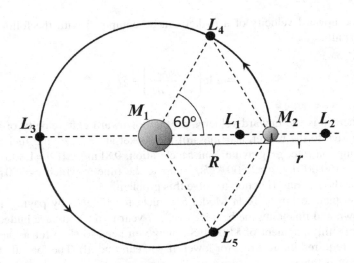

FIGURE P7.13   The Lagrange points for two massive bodies.

$$\frac{M_1}{(R+r)^2} + \frac{M_2}{r^2} = \left(\frac{M_1 R}{M_1 + M_2} + r \right) \frac{M_1 + M_2}{R^3}$$

where r is the distance of the L_2 point from the smaller of the two massive objects, M_1 and M_2 are the masses of the larger and smaller massive objects, respectively, and R is the distance between them. A summary of the parameters for the Sun, Earth, and our Moon are listed in the table below. Determine r for an L_2 satellite orbiting around **(a)** the Earth and **(b)** the moon.

System	Sun-Earth	Earth-Moon	Units
M_1	1.991×10^{30}	5.98×10^{24}	kg
M_2	5.98×10^{24}	7.35×10^{22}	kg
R	149,600,000	384,401	km

If the mass of the smaller object is much smaller than the mass of the larger object, a good initial estimate of r can be computed with

$$r \approx R \sqrt[3]{\frac{M_2}{3M_1}}$$

7.14 A four-bar linkage is illustrated in Figure P7.14. Such linkages are designed by mechanical engineers to transmit mechanical movement in various ways.

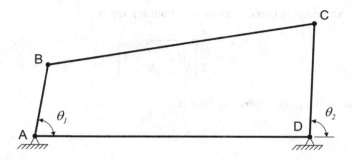

FIGURE P7.14 Four-bar linkage.

Member AD is anchored to a supporting base and does not move. Member AB rotates about point A, resulting in a reciprocating movement of members BC and CD. All motion is in the plane of the page. Therefore, angle θ_2 changes in response to a change in angle θ_1. This motion is constrained by the equation

$$\overline{AD} = \overline{AB}\cos\theta_1 - \overline{CD}\cos\theta_2 + \sqrt{\overline{BC}^2 - \left(\overline{CD}\sin\theta_2 - \overline{AB}\sin\theta_1\right)^2}$$

Suppose $\overline{AB} = 1.5\,\text{m}$, $\overline{BC} = 6\,\text{m}$, $\overline{CD} = 3.5\,\text{m}$, and $\overline{AD} = 5\,\text{m}$.

Determine angle θ_2, given a value of angle θ_1, for example, 45°. Use the false position technique.

Create a data table of θ_2 values for a range of θ_1 values. Present a plot of this relationship.

7.15 When water is flowing down a sloped, open channel, a phenomenon called a hydraulic jump can occur where the water with a depth, h_1, and a flowing velocity, v_1, suddenly jumps up to a depth, h_2, with a slower velocity, v_2. This is depicted in Figure P7.15.

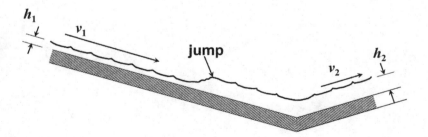

FIGURE P7.15 Hydraulic jump.

An equation that describes a hydraulic jump is

$$h_2 = \frac{h_1}{2}\left[\sqrt{1 + \frac{8v_1^2}{gh_1}} - 1\right]$$

and such a jump is possible only if

$$v_1 > \sqrt{gh_1}$$

If values of v_1 and h_2 are known, create a Python script to determine h_1 and whether the jump is possible. Typical velocities (v_1) would be 1-to-2 m/s and after-jump depths would be 2-to-3 cm.

8 Solving Sets of Algebraic Equations

CHAPTER OBJECTIVES

- Review the scenario for sets of n linear equations in n unknowns.
- Know how to solve a 2 × 2 system of linear algebraic equations graphically and understand how this provides insight into singular and ill-conditioned systems.
- Understand the determinant of a square matrix and how it can be used to detect singular and ill-conditioned systems.
- Know how Cramer's Rule uses determinants to solve a set of linear equations.
- Learn how to implement the Gaussian elimination method, and, from a vector/matrix perspective, how it achieves the solution of a set of linear algebraic equations.
- Understand the limitations of Gaussian elimination and how they can be overcome by partial pivoting.
- Be able to solve sets of linear equations with the NumPy `linalg` module.
- Learn how to solve small sets of nonlinear equations with an extension of the successive substitution method.
- For sets of nonlinear algebraic equations, see how the Newton-Raphson method can be extended, including the introduction of the Jacobian matrix of partial derivatives.
- Be able to solve sets of nonlinear algebraic equations with the `root` function from the SciPy `optimize` module.

Systems of linear algebraic equations occur repeatedly in problems across all disciplines of engineering and science. Common examples include structures in civil engineering, circuits in electrical engineering, material balances in chemical engineering, thermal balances in mechanical engineering, and analytical measurements in chemistry. Consequently, it is important to understand the nature of linear algebraic equations and their solution. In this chapter, we focus on a classical method for solution of linear equations, Gaussian elimination, which persists today as the most widely used technique.

Beyond linear systems, systems of nonlinear algebraic equations also arise frequently when modeling physical, chemical, and biological phenomena. Solution of these equations is significantly more challenging than for linear equations. Here, we introduce an extension of the Newton-Raphson method from single to multiple nonlinear algebraic equations.

DOI: 10.1201/9781003256861-8

$$a_{11}x_1 + a_{12}x_2 + \cdots a_{1n}x_n = b_1$$
$$a_{21}x_1 + a_{22}x_2 + \cdots a_{2n}x_n = b_2$$
$$\vdots \qquad \vdots$$
$$a_{n1}x_1 + a_{n2}x_2 + \cdots a_{nn}x_n = b_n$$

$$\Longrightarrow \quad \begin{bmatrix} a_{11} & a_{12} & \cdots & a_{1n} \\ a_{21} & a_{22} & \cdots & a_{2n} \\ \vdots & \vdots & \ddots & \vdots \\ a_{n1} & a_{n2} & \cdots & a_{nn} \end{bmatrix} \cdot \begin{bmatrix} x_1 \\ x_2 \\ \vdots \\ x_n \end{bmatrix} = \begin{bmatrix} b_1 \\ b_2 \\ \vdots \\ b_n \end{bmatrix}$$

$$\mathbf{Ax = b}$$

FIGURE 8.1 Vector-matrix description of linear algebraic equations.

Finally, it is important to know how to use the tools available in Python's NumPy `linalg` module and SciPy `optimize` module to solve systems of algebraic equations, both linear and nonlinear.

8.1 SYSTEMS OF LINEAR ALGEBRAIC EQUATIONS

In Chapter 6, we introduced the vector/matrix description of a set of linear algebraic equations. A general representation is illustrated in Figure 8.1. Here, we use subscripts typical to mathematical descriptions with origin of one. We must pay attention to this as we transition the scenario to Python with its array origin of zero.

Before describing methods for solving systems of equations, it's useful to understand why they so commonly occur in engineering and science problem solving.

Example 8.1 Linear Equations and Engineering/Science Problem Solving

Figure 8.2 depicts a factory discharging a biodegradable dissolved substance into a treatment plant which eventually discharges into a river. The plant consists of three completely mixed reactors where the pollutant's concentration is reduced before it is discharged to a river. The reactors are coupled by flows (Q) that move the pollutant from one reactor to another and biochemical reactions (k) that convert the pollutant to a nonharmful form.

If there were only one reactor, a balance based on conservation of mass can be written to determine its concentration as

$$Q_{in}c_{in} \quad - \quad Q_{out}c_i \quad - \quad kV_ic_i \quad = 0$$

$$\text{(inflow)} - \text{(outflow)} - \text{(biodegradation)} = 0$$

(8.1)

where V_i = volume (m^3), c_i = pollutant concentration (mg/m^3), t = time (d), Q_{in} and Q_{out} = inflow and outflow (m^3/d), respectively, c_{in} = pollutant concentration of the inflow (mg/m^3), and k = a first-order rate constant representing biodegradation (/d).

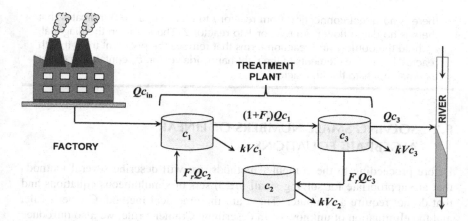

FIGURE 8.2 A factory that generates a waste stream of a toxic, but biodegradable, dissolved pollutant. A treatment plant, consisting of three reactors has been built to reduce the pollutant concentration discharge to an adjacent river. The flow and reaction paths are indicated by arrows.

Equation 8.1 is a linear algebraic equation that can be solved algebraically for the unknown, c. Although this is the case for this single equation, for the system in Figure 8.2, each reactor is linked by flows to the others. Hence, the concentration of each reactor cannot be determined independently. Because of their interdependence, the three reactors must be modeled as a system rather than as individual elements. By writing mass balances for each reactor following Figure 8.2, we have

$$Qc_{in} + F_r Qc_3 - (1 + F_r)Qc_1 - kVc_1 = 0 \qquad (8.2)$$

$$(1 + F_r)Qc_1 - (1 + F_r)Qc_2 - kVc_2 = 0 \qquad (8.3)$$

$$(1 + F_r)Qc_2 - (1 + F_r)Qc_3 - kVc_3 = 0 \qquad (8.4)$$

where F_r = the fraction of inflow that is recycled from reactor 3 back to reactors 2 and then 1. By collecting terms, the equations can be expressed in the general vector-matrix format of Figure 8.1:

$$\begin{bmatrix} (1+F_r)Q+kV & 0 & -F_rQ \\ -(1+F_r)Q & (1+F_r)Q+kV & 0 \\ 0 & -(1+F_r)Q & ((1+F_r)Q+kV) \end{bmatrix} \begin{pmatrix} c_1 \\ c_2 \\ c_3 \end{pmatrix} = \begin{pmatrix} Qc_{in} \\ 0 \\ 0 \end{pmatrix} \qquad (8.5)$$

Thus, our steady-state model of the three coupled reactors naturally yields a system of three linear algebraic equations with three unknowns.

Notice how each of the elements, a_{ij}, holds the parameters that cause reactor i to be directly influenced by reactor j. For example, a_{21} contains the parameters that quantify the flow to reactor 2 from reactor 1. The zeros indicate that there is no direct connection from reactor j to i. Hence, $a_{12} = 0$ indicates that there is no direct flow from reactor 1 to reactor 2. The terms on the diagonal, a_{ii}, hold the outflow and reaction terms that remove the pollutant from the ith reactor. Lastly, the elements of the right-hand-side vector, b_i, contain the direct external inputs to the ith reactor.

8.2 SOLVING SMALL NUMBERS OF LINEAR ALGEBRAIC EQUATIONS

Before proceeding to the computer methods, we will describe several methods that are appropriate for solving small ($n \leq 3$) sets of simultaneous equations and that do not require a computer. These are the graphical method, Cramer's rule, and the elimination of unknowns. In describing Cramer's rule, we also introduce the determinant, which provides a metric for detecting problematic linear systems.

8.2.1 GRAPHICAL METHOD

A graphical solution is obtainable for two equations by plotting them on Cartesian coordinates with one axis corresponding to x_1 and the other to x_2 (Figure 8.3). Because we are dealing with linear algebraic equations, each equation plots as a straight line. This can be easily illustrated for the following set of equations,

$$1.5x_1 + 2x_2 = 6$$
$$-0.5x_1 + 2x_2 = 2$$

$$(8.6)$$

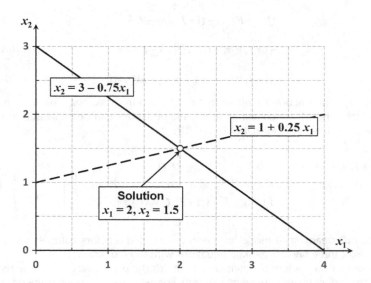

FIGURE 8.3 Graphical solution of a set of two simultaneous linear algebraic equations. The intersection of the lines represents the solution.

which can each be solved for x_2:

$$x_2 = 3 - 0.75x_1$$
$$x_2 = 1 + 0.25x_1 \qquad (8.7)$$

As plotted on Figure 8.3, these are two straight lines that intersect at the solution, $x_1 = 2$ and $x_2 = 1.5$. These values can be checked by substituting them into the original equations,

$$1.5(2) + 2(1.5) = 6$$
$$-0.5(2) + 2(1.5) = 2 \qquad (8.8)$$

For three simultaneous equations, each equation would be represented by a plane in a three-dimensional coordinate system. The point where the three planes intersect would be the solution. Beyond three equations, graphical methods break down and, consequently, have little practical value for solving simultaneous equations. However, they are useful for visualizing properties of the solutions for two or three equations.

For example, Figure 8.4 depicts three cases that can pose problems when solving sets of linear equations. Figure 8.4a shows the case where the two equations

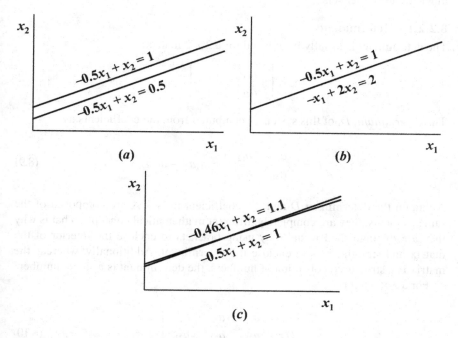

FIGURE 8.4 Graphical depiction of singular and ill-conditioned systems: (a) no solution, (b) infinite solutions, and (c) an ill-conditioned system where the slopes are so close that the point of intersection is difficult to detect visually.

represent parallel lines. For such situations, there is no solution because the lines never cross. Figure 8.4b depicts the case where the two lines are coincident. For such situations, there is an infinite number of solutions. Both types of systems are said to be *singular*. In addition, systems that are very close to being singular (Figure 8.4c) can also cause problems. These systems are said to be *ill-condi-tioned*. Graphically, this corresponds to the fact that it is difficult to identify the exact point at which the lines intersect. Ill-conditioned systems will also pose problems when they are encountered during the numerical solution of linear equations. This is because they will be extremely sensitive to round-off error.

The takeaway from this section is that not all sets of linear equations have a unique solution. The equations must be *independent*. That means that any equation cannot be duplicated by another equation (probably obvious to you!), and any equation cannot by obtained by a linear combination of other equations in the set (maybe not that obvious).

8.2.2 Determinants and Cramer's Rule

In your previous mathematics courses, you may have encountered Cramer's Rule to solve a set of linear equations. This method involves the calculation of the *determinant* of a square matrix. The method is usually illustrated with small equation sets ($n \leq 3$) because calculating the determinant manually becomes unwieldy for larger sets.

8.2.2.1 Determinants

The determinant is usually introduced for a 2×2 matrix:

$$\begin{bmatrix} a_{11} & a_{12} \\ a_{21} & a_{22} \end{bmatrix}$$

The *determinant*, D, of this system is computed from the coefficients as

$$D = \begin{vmatrix} a_{11} & a_{12} \\ a_{21} & a_{22} \end{vmatrix} = a_{11}a_{22} - a_{12}a_{21} \tag{8.9}$$

Although the determinant D and the coefficient matrix $\mathbf{A}$ are composed of the same elements, they are completely different mathematical concepts. That is why they are distinguished visually by using brackets to enclose the interior of the matrix and straight lines to enclose the determinant. Additionally, whereas the matrix is a structured collection of numbers, the determinant is a single number.

For a 3×3 matrix,

$$D = \begin{vmatrix} a_{11} & a_{12} & a_{13} \\ a_{21} & a_{22} & a_{23} \\ a_{31} & a_{32} & a_{33} \end{vmatrix} \tag{8.10}$$

the determinant can be computed as

$$D = a_{11} \begin{vmatrix} a_{22} & a_{23} \\ a_{32} & a_{33} \end{vmatrix} - a_{12} \begin{vmatrix} a_{21} & a_{23} \\ a_{31} & a_{33} \end{vmatrix} + a_{13} \begin{vmatrix} a_{21} & a_{22} \\ a_{31} & a_{32} \end{vmatrix} \qquad (8.11)$$

where the 2 × 2 determinants are called *minors*. There is a heuristic (in common parlance, "a rule of thumb") that many have learned that provides a shortcut for computing the determinants of these smaller matrices. This is shown in Figure 8.5. Note the patterns in the figure. Solid arrows indicate positive contributions and dashed arrows negative.

Observe that each minor is the submatrix left if you remove the row and column of the multiplying factor. For the first minor, the coefficient is a_{11} and the minor has row and column 1 of the 3×3 matrix removed. What about that minus sign on the second minor term? Well, the rule is that, if the sum of the indices on the coefficient is odd, the sign is negative. One could describe that mathematically for coefficient a_{ij} as

$$(-1)^{i+j}$$

It should be noted that the selection of the three factors, a_{11}, a_{12}, and a_{13}, is arbitrary. The method of minors can be applied with the selection of any three matrix elements. Also, the method of minors applies to the 2×2 matrix, except the minors are now individual elements.

Example 8.2 Determinants

Compute values for the determinants of the systems represented in Figures 8.3 and 8.4.

For Figure 8.3:

$$D = \begin{vmatrix} 3 & 2 \\ -1 & 2 \end{vmatrix} = 3(2) - 2(-1) = 8$$

For Figure 8.4a:

$$D = \begin{vmatrix} -0.5 & 1 \\ -0.5 & 1 \end{vmatrix} = -0.5(1) - 1(-0.5) = 0$$

For Figure 8.4b:

$$D = \begin{vmatrix} -0.5 & 1 \\ -1 & 2 \end{vmatrix} = -0.5(2) - 1(-1) = 0$$

For Figure 8.4c:

$$D = \begin{vmatrix} -0.5 & 1 \\ -0.46 & 1 \end{vmatrix} = -0.5(1) - 1(-46) = -0.04$$

The singular systems have zero determinants. Additionally, the results suggest that the system that is almost singular (Figure 8.4c) has a determinant that is close to zero. These ideas will be pursued further in our subsequent discussion of ill-conditioning and roundoff errors.

The takeaway from this example is that just as the graphical approach provided a visual indication, the determinant offers a means to detect whether a system of linear equations is singular ($D = 0$) or ill-conditioned (D near zero). But, in comparison with the graphical approach, it has the advantages that it (1) consists of a single number and (2) is not limited to 2×2 systems. Thus, as described later in this chapter, it will prove useful in detecting singular and near-singular (or ill-conditioned) linear systems.

8.2.2.2   Cramer's Rule

Cramer's rule states that each unknown in a system of linear algebraic equations may be expressed as a fraction of two determinants with denominator D and with the numerator obtained as the determinant of the matrix formed by replacing the column of coefficients of the unknown in question by the constants $b_1, b_2, \ldots, b_n$. For example, x_1 would be computed as

$$x_1 = \frac{\begin{vmatrix} b_1 & a_{12} & a_{13} \\ b_2 & a_{22} & a_{23} \\ b_3 & a_{32} & a_{33} \end{vmatrix}}{D} \tag{8.12}$$

Example 8.3 Cramer's Rule

We will use Cramer's rule to solve

$$0.3x_1 + 0.52x_2 + \quad x_3 = -0.01$$

$$0.5x_1 + \quad x_2 + 1.9x_3 = \quad 0.67 \tag{8.13}$$

$$0.1x_1 + 0.3x_2 + 0.5x_3 = -0.44$$

The determinant can be calculated following Equation 8.7:

$$D = 0.3 \begin{vmatrix} 1 & 1.9 \\ 0.3 & 0.5 \end{vmatrix} - 0.52 \begin{vmatrix} 0.5 & 1.9 \\ 0.1 & 0.5 \end{vmatrix} + 0.3 \begin{vmatrix} 0.5 & 1 \\ 0.1 & 0.3 \end{vmatrix} = -0.0022$$

Alternately, we can use the shortcut scheme illustrated in Figure 8.5:

$$D = 0.3 \cdot 1 \cdot 0.5 + 0.52 \cdot 1.9 \cdot 0.1 + 0.5 \cdot 0.3 \cdot 1$$
$$- 1 \cdot 1 \cdot 0.1 - 0.52 \cdot 0.5 \cdot 0.5 - 1.9 \cdot 0.3 \cdot 0.3 \cong -0.0022$$

Applying Equation 8.8, the solution is

$$x_1 = \frac{\begin{vmatrix} -0.01 & 0.52 & 1 \\ 0.67 & 1 & 1.9 \\ -0.44 & 0.3 & 0.5 \end{vmatrix}}{-0.0022} = \frac{0.03278}{-0.0022} \cong -14.9$$

$$x_2 = \frac{\begin{vmatrix} 0.3 & -0.01 & 1 \\ 0.5 & 0.67 & 1.9 \\ 0.1 & -0.44 & 0.5 \end{vmatrix}}{-0.0022} = \frac{0.0646}{-0.0022} \cong -29.5$$

$$x_3 = \frac{\begin{vmatrix} 0.3 & 0.52 & -0.01 \\ 0.5 & 1 & 0.67 \\ 0.1 & 0.3 & -0.44 \end{vmatrix}}{-0.0022} = \frac{-0.04356}{-0.0022} \cong 19.8$$

For more than three equations, Cramer's rule becomes impractical because, as the number of equations increases, the determinants are time-consuming to evaluate by hand (or by computer). Consequently, more efficient alternatives are used. Some of these alternatives are based on the last noncomputer solution technique—the elimination of unknowns.

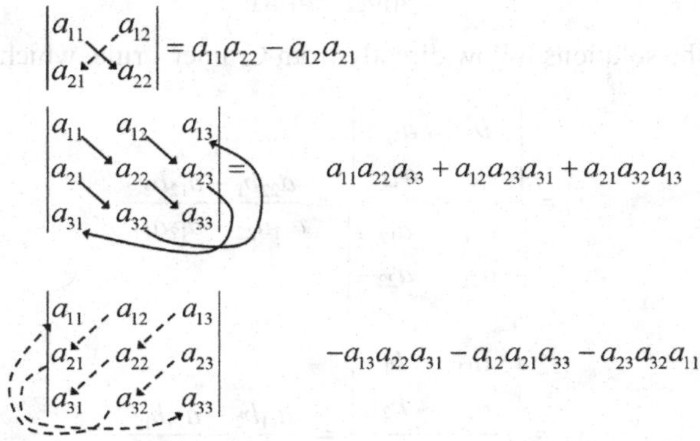

$$\begin{vmatrix} a_{11} & a_{12} \\ a_{21} & a_{22} \end{vmatrix} = a_{11}a_{22} - a_{12}a_{21}$$

$$\begin{vmatrix} a_{11} & a_{12} & a_{13} \\ a_{21} & a_{22} & a_{23} \\ a_{31} & a_{32} & a_{33} \end{vmatrix} = a_{11}a_{22}a_{33} + a_{12}a_{23}a_{31} + a_{21}a_{32}a_{13}$$

$$\begin{vmatrix} a_{11} & a_{12} & a_{13} \\ a_{21} & a_{22} & a_{23} \\ a_{31} & a_{32} & a_{33} \end{vmatrix} \quad -a_{13}a_{22}a_{31} - a_{12}a_{21}a_{33} - a_{23}a_{32}a_{11}$$

FIGURE 8.5 Shortcut patterns for determinants of small systems of linear algebraic equations.

8.2.3 ELIMINATION OF UNKNOWNS

The *elimination of unknowns*, which is probably familiar to you from your early algebra courses, can be illustrated for a set of two equations with two unknowns:

$$a_{11}x_1 + a_{12}x_2 = b_1$$
$$a_{21}x_1 + a_{22}x_2 = b_2$$

(8.14)

One solution strategy is to multiply the equations by a constant so that one of the unknowns will be eliminated when the two equations are combined. The result is a single equation that can be solved for the remaining unknown. This value can then be substituted into either of the original equations to compute the other variable.

For example, the first equation can be multiplied by a_{21} and the second by a_{11} to give

$$a_{21}a_{11}x_1 + a_{21}a_{12}x_2 = a_{21}b_1$$
$$a_{11}a_{21}x_1 + a_{11}a_{22}x_2 = a_{11}b_2$$

(8.15)

Subtracting the two equations will, therefore, eliminate the x_1 term from the equations to yield

$$a_{11}a_{22}x_2 - a_{12}a_{21}x_2 = a_{11}b_2 - a_{21}b_1$$

(8.16)

which can be solved for

$$x_2 = \frac{a_{11}b_2 - a_{21}b_1}{a_{11}a_{22} - a_{12}a_{21}}$$

(8.17)

This equation can then be substituted into either of the equations and the result solved for

$$x_1 = \frac{a_{22}b_1 - a_{12}b_2}{a_{11}a_{22} - a_{12}a_{21}}$$

(8.18)

Observe that the solutions follow directly from Cramer's rule, which states

$$x_1 = \frac{\begin{vmatrix} b_1 & a_{12} \\ b_2 & a_{22} \end{vmatrix}}{\begin{vmatrix} a_{11} & a_{12} \\ a_{21} & a_{22} \end{vmatrix}} = \frac{a_{22}b_1 - a_{12}b_2}{a_{11}a_{22} - a_{12}a_{21}}$$

(8.19)

$$x_2 = \frac{\begin{vmatrix} a_{11} & b_1 \\ a_{21} & b_2 \end{vmatrix}}{\begin{vmatrix} a_{11} & a_{12} \\ a_{21} & a_{22} \end{vmatrix}} = \frac{a_{11}b_2 - a_{21}b_1}{a_{11}a_{22} - a_{12}a_{21}}$$

(8.20)

Example 8.4 Elimination of Unknowns

Use the elimination of unknowns to solve the system we solved previously with the graphical method (Figure 8.3),

$$1.5x_1 + 2x_2 = 6$$
$$-0.5x_1 + 2x_2 = 2$$
(8.21)

Of course, we could use the same approach as above. But let's try a different strategy for this example by solving the first equation for x_2,

$$x_2 = \frac{6 - 1.5x_1}{2} = 3 - 0.75x_1$$
(8.22)

Substituting this result into the second equation

$$-0.5x_1 + 2(3 - 0.75x_1) = 2$$
(8.23)

and collecting terms gives

$$-2x_1 + 4 = 0$$
(8.24)

which can be solved for $x_1 = 2$. This result can then be substituted into either of the original equations to solve for the other unknown. For example, substituting $x_1 = 2$ into the second equation gives

$$-0.5(2) + 2x_2 = 2$$
(8.25)

which can be solved for

$$x_2 = \frac{2 + 0.5(2)}{2} = 1.5$$
(8.26)

The result, $x_1 = 2$ and $x_2 = 1.5$, is consistent with our graphical solution (Figure 8.3).

Now, you might be asking yourself: Why did we implement the elimination of unknowns with two different strategies in the preceding text and example? We did it to make the point that even for the simplest two equation system there would be alternative ways that different individuals would employ to generate a solution.

For two or three equations, that would not be a big deal. But what about when the elimination of unknowns is implemented on a computer for large systems of equations? For such applications the question arises: What is the **best** general-purpose elimination algorithm for solving large systems of simultaneous linear algebraic equations? As described in the next section, such a technique can be formalized and readily programmed with a language like Python.

8.3 GAUSSIAN ELIMINATION[1]

Gaussian elimination is the standard computer method for solving a system of linear algebraic equations,

$$\mathbf{A}\,\mathbf{x} = \mathbf{b} \tag{8.27}$$

In its simplest form, it is implemented as a two-step process consisting of forward elimination and back substitution (Figure 8.6).

To maintain the identity of a set of linear equations so that they have the same, valid solution, any manipulations have to satisfy the requirements of *elementary row operations*. These include

- shuffling or swapping the equations (or rows),
- multiplying any equation (or row) by a constant and
- replacing any equation (or row) by a linear combination of equations.

$$\begin{bmatrix} a_{11} & a_{12} & a_{13} \\ a_{21} & a_{22} & a_{23} \\ a_{31} & a_{32} & a_{33} \end{bmatrix} \cdot \begin{bmatrix} x_1 \\ x_2 \\ x_3 \end{bmatrix} = \begin{bmatrix} b_1 \\ b_2 \\ b_3 \end{bmatrix}$$

Forward elimination

$$\begin{bmatrix} 1 & a'_{12} & a'_{13} \\ 0 & 1 & a'_{23} \\ 0 & 0 & 1 \end{bmatrix} \cdot \begin{bmatrix} x_1 \\ x_2 \\ x_3 \end{bmatrix} = \begin{bmatrix} b'_1 \\ b'_2 \\ b'_3 \end{bmatrix}$$

Back substitution

$$x_3 = b'_3$$
$$x_2 = b'_2 - a'_{23}x_3$$
$$x_1 = b'_1 - a'_{12}x_2 - a'_{13}x_3$$

FIGURE 8.6 Depiction of Gaussian elimination consisting of forward elimination and back substitution steps. The primes that appear after the elimination pass indicate that the elements have been changed from their original values.

---

[1] The method is named after Carl Friedrich Gauss (1777–1855). Gauss is considered one of the giants of mathematics. He also made significant contributions in astronomy and physics, notably magnetism.

In the forward elimination step, the second and third of these are employed to transform the matrix of coefficients into *upper triangular* form. We will use the first of the three in an enhancement to Gaussian elimination later. To maintain the identity of the original system so that it has the same valid solution, all these operations are applied to both the **A** matrix and the **b** vector.

After the forward elimination step has been implemented, the last equation will have a single unknown and the solution can be obtained by *back substitution*. The algorithm is a relatively simple, elegant method that can be coded in Python in only a few statements.

We will first illustrate it in a step-by-step fashion. Subsequently, a more compact version will be developed. Finally, we will consider including the method of partial pivoting to avoid pitfalls that the original method can encounter. The implications of dealing with singular and almost singular coefficient matrices will also be addressed.

8.3.1 NAIVE GAUSSIAN ELIMINATION

This section includes the systematic techniques for forward elimination and back substitution that comprise Gaussian elimination. We first implement the method in a step-by-step fashion for a simple 3×3 system. We then generalize the method to n equations with n unknowns.

Although these techniques are ideally suited for computer implementation, some modifications will be required to obtain a reliable algorithm. In particular, the computer program must avoid divisions by zero. Because it does not avoid this problem, the method described in the following example is called *naive Gaussian elimination*. A subsequent section will add features like pivoting and determinant evaluation that are required for a reliable and effective computer program.

Example 8.5 Naive Gaussian Elimination

Solve the following system of equations with naive Gauss elimination,

$$\begin{bmatrix} 3 & -2 & 7 \\ -2 & 4 & -3 \\ -1 & 9 & 4 \end{bmatrix} \cdot \begin{bmatrix} x_1 \\ x_2 \\ x_3 \end{bmatrix} = \begin{bmatrix} 15 \\ 12 \\ 27 \end{bmatrix} \tag{8.28}$$

We introduce first the *forward elimination step* of the method (or algorithm). This starts by creating a 1 in the (1,1) diagonal position, also called the *pivot element*.[2] This is accomplished by the elementary operation of dividing the first row (including the right-hand-side constant) by the row's pivot element, in this case $a_{11} = 3$.

---

[2] Note that the individual coefficients of a vector or matrix are called *elements*.

$$\begin{bmatrix} 1 & -\dfrac{2}{3} & \dfrac{7}{3} \\ -2 & 4 & -3 \\ -1 & 9 & 4 \end{bmatrix} \cdot \begin{bmatrix} x_1 \\ x_2 \\ x_3 \end{bmatrix} = \begin{bmatrix} 5 \\ 12 \\ 27 \end{bmatrix} \qquad (8.29)$$

This operation is called *normalization*.

Next, we subtract −2 times the normalized first row from the second row, placing the result in the second row. The factor, −2, comes from the (2,1) element so that when the subtraction is implemented, the a_{21} element is converted to a zero

$$\begin{bmatrix} -2 & 4 & -3 & 12 \end{bmatrix} - \begin{bmatrix} -2 & \dfrac{4}{3} & -\dfrac{14}{3} & -10 \end{bmatrix}$$

$$= \begin{bmatrix} 0 & \dfrac{8}{3} & \dfrac{5}{3} & 22 \end{bmatrix}$$

with the system now

$$\begin{bmatrix} 1 & -\dfrac{2}{3} & \dfrac{7}{3} \\ 0 & \dfrac{8}{3} & \dfrac{5}{3} \\ -1 & 9 & 4 \end{bmatrix} \cdot \begin{bmatrix} x_1 \\ x_2 \\ x_3 \end{bmatrix} = \begin{bmatrix} 5 \\ 22 \\ 27 \end{bmatrix}$$

We repeat this operation by subtracting the product of −1 times the first row from the third row and placing the result in the third row.

$$\begin{bmatrix} -1 & 9 & 4 & 27 \end{bmatrix} - \begin{bmatrix} -1 & \dfrac{2}{3} & -\dfrac{7}{3} & -5 \end{bmatrix}$$

$$= \begin{bmatrix} 0 & \dfrac{25}{3} & \dfrac{19}{3} & 32 \end{bmatrix}$$

Note that because a_{31} already happens to be −1 and would cancel when added to a_{11}, we could have written to just "add the first row to the third row." But because we are trying to establish a general algorithm here that is designed for computer implementation, we repeat the identical operations we used to eliminate a_{21}. Now, the system looks like this

$$\begin{bmatrix} 1 & -\dfrac{2}{3} & \dfrac{7}{3} \\ 0 & \dfrac{8}{3} & \dfrac{5}{3} \\ 0 & \dfrac{25}{3} & \dfrac{19}{3} \end{bmatrix} \cdot \begin{bmatrix} x_1 \\ x_2 \\ x_3 \end{bmatrix} = \begin{bmatrix} 5 \\ 22 \\ 32 \end{bmatrix}$$

We have normalized the (1,1) pivot element and reduced the elements below it to zero and we are on our way to creating the upper triangular coefficient matrix.

For the next step in the forward pass, we move to the second row and normalize the (2,2) pivot element by dividing that row by 8/3.

$$
\begin{bmatrix}
1 & -\dfrac{2}{3} & \dfrac{7}{3} \\[2mm]
0 & 1 & \dfrac{23}{8} \\[2mm]
0 & \dfrac{25}{3} & \dfrac{19}{3}
\end{bmatrix}
\cdot
\begin{bmatrix}
x_1 \\ x_2 \\ x_3
\end{bmatrix}
=
\begin{bmatrix}
5 \\[2mm] \dfrac{27}{2} \\[2mm] 32
\end{bmatrix}
$$

This is followed by a reduction step to create a zero below the (2,2) pivot element. We subtract 25/3 times the second row from the third row and place the result in the third row.

$$
\begin{bmatrix}
0 & \dfrac{25}{3} & \dfrac{19}{3} & 32
\end{bmatrix}
-
\begin{bmatrix}
0 & \dfrac{25}{3} & \dfrac{125}{24} & \dfrac{825}{12}
\end{bmatrix}
$$

$$
=
\begin{bmatrix}
0 & 0 & \dfrac{9}{8} & -\dfrac{147}{4}
\end{bmatrix}
$$

Now, the system looks like

$$
\begin{bmatrix}
1 & -\dfrac{2}{3} & \dfrac{7}{3} \\[2mm]
0 & 1 & \dfrac{5}{8} \\[2mm]
0 & 0 & \dfrac{9}{8}
\end{bmatrix}
\cdot
\begin{bmatrix}
x_1 \\ x_2 \\ x_3
\end{bmatrix}
=
\begin{bmatrix}
5 \\[2mm] \dfrac{33}{4} \\[2mm] -\dfrac{147}{4}
\end{bmatrix}
$$

The final step of the forward pass is to normalize the (3,3) pivot element by dividing the third row by 9/8 with the result:

$$
\begin{bmatrix}
1 & -\dfrac{2}{3} & \dfrac{7}{3} \\[2mm]
0 & 1 & \dfrac{5}{8} \\[2mm]
0 & 0 & 1
\end{bmatrix}
\cdot
\begin{bmatrix}
x_1 \\ x_2 \\ x_3
\end{bmatrix}
=
\begin{bmatrix}
5 \\[2mm] \dfrac{33}{4} \\[2mm] -\dfrac{98}{3}
\end{bmatrix}
$$

We see that we have accomplished the objective of the forward elimination step to transform the coefficient matrix into upper triangular form.

Next, we begin the *back-substitution* step by recognizing that we have already determined the solution for $x_3 = -98/3$. We can also see that the second row involves only x_2 and x_3,

$$x_2 + \frac{5}{8}x_3 = \frac{33}{4}$$

Since we already know x_3, we can "back-substitute" that value and solve algebraically for x_2,

$$x_2 = (33/4) - (5/8)(-98/3) = 86/3$$

Another way of accomplishing this via row operations is to create a zero in the second row above the (3,3) pivot element by subtracting 5/8 times the third row from the second row and place the result in the second row.

$$\begin{bmatrix} 0 & 1 & \dfrac{5}{8} & \dfrac{33}{4} \end{bmatrix} - \begin{bmatrix} 0 & 0 & \dfrac{5}{8} & \dfrac{2205}{108} \end{bmatrix} = \begin{bmatrix} 0 & 1 & 0 & \dfrac{86}{3} \end{bmatrix}$$

$$\begin{bmatrix} 1 & -\dfrac{2}{3} & \dfrac{7}{3} \\ 0 & 1 & 0 \\ 0 & 0 & 1 \end{bmatrix} \cdot \begin{bmatrix} x_1 \\ x_2 \\ x_3 \end{bmatrix} = \begin{bmatrix} 5 \\ \dfrac{86}{3} \\ -\dfrac{98}{3} \end{bmatrix}$$

So, we know that $x_2 = 86/3$. Since we have values for x_2 and x_3, we could back-substitute these into the first row to obtain the solution for x_1. However, we can again achieve the same objective with a pair of row operations: use row 3 to create a zero in the (1,3) position then use row 2 to create a zero in the (1,2) position. We first multiply the third row by 7/3 and subtract it from the first row to yield

$$\begin{bmatrix} 1 & -\dfrac{2}{3} & \dfrac{7}{3} & 5 \end{bmatrix} - \begin{bmatrix} 0 & 0 & \dfrac{7}{3} & -\dfrac{6174}{81} \end{bmatrix}$$

$$= \begin{bmatrix} 1 & -\dfrac{2}{3} & 0 & \dfrac{731}{9} \end{bmatrix}$$

Then, the second row can be multiplied by $-2/3$ and subtracted from the latest first row,

$$\begin{bmatrix} 1 & -\dfrac{2}{3} & 0 & \dfrac{731}{9} \end{bmatrix} - \begin{bmatrix} 0 & -\dfrac{2}{3} & 0 & -\dfrac{1548}{81} \end{bmatrix}$$

$$= \begin{bmatrix} 1 & 0 & 0 & \dfrac{301}{3} \end{bmatrix}$$

This yields our final equivalent system of equations, now solved with the coefficient matrix as an identity matrix. The values in the right vector are the solutions.

$$
\begin{bmatrix} 1 & 0 & 0 \\ 0 & 1 & 0 \\ 0 & 0 & 1 \end{bmatrix} \cdot \begin{bmatrix} x_1 \\ x_2 \\ x_3 \end{bmatrix} = \begin{bmatrix} \dfrac{301}{3} \\[4pt] \dfrac{86}{3} \\[4pt] -\dfrac{98}{3} \end{bmatrix} \cong \begin{bmatrix} 100.33 \\ 28.667 \\ -32.667 \end{bmatrix} \tag{8.30}
$$

We have carried fractions, somewhat laboriously, throughout this example to illustrate the solution in a rational, precise form. The solutions are also shown as approximate numbers with decimal fractions to five significant figures. The latter can be substituted to check whether they yield the **b** vector. Note the slight roundoff error due to our use of five significant digits. We could have used the fractional forms for this, and they would produce an exact check.

$$3(100.33) - 2(28.667) + 7(-32.667) \cong 14.996 \cong 15$$

$$-2(100.33) + 4(28.667) - 3(-32.667) \cong 12.003 \cong 12$$

$$-(100.33) + 9(28.667) + 4(-32.667) \cong 27.002 \cong 27$$

Of course, when solving such a well-conditioned system in Python on a 64-bit computer, we would obtain results with about 15-digits of precision. In the following section we show how this is done.

8.3.2 GAUSSIAN ELIMINATION COMPUTER ALGORITHM

Now that we have seen how the method works with a step-by-step example, we will translate this into a computer algorithm that can be applied to a general $n \times n$ system of equations. We will do this in two steps. First, we'll replicate the method shown above. Then, we will see how to combine operations to make the method more efficient.

8.3.2.1 Naive Gaussian Elimination Algorithm

Here is a general description of the algorithm that precedes coding it in Python:

1. Forward pass:
    1.1 Step down through pivot elements (1, 1) through (n, n)
        1.1.1 Normalize the row of the current pivot element including the constant by dividing by its value.
        1.2.1 Step down through the rows below the current pivot element.
            1.2.1.1 Reduce below the pivot element by multiplying the pivot row by the element in the row below and subtracting from that row. Skip this for the last pivot element (n, n) since there are no elements below it.

2. Back-substitution pass
   2.1 Step back up from pivot elements ($n-1$, $n-1$) through pivot (2,2).
      2.1.1 Reduce above the pivot element by multiplying the pivot row
          by the elements in the row above and subtracting from those.

A Python function that implements this version of Gaussian elimination is shown in Figure 8.7. The coding is tricky because we must deal with the zero-based indexing of arrays. The first for loop uses range(n) which creates a list of integers from 0 to n-1. This provides the correct range of zero-based subscripts for the pivot elements as the forward pass proceeds. At each pivot level, the next for loop, with a j index from i+1 to n-1, ranges across these columns to normalize row i by dividing by the pivot element. Note that it doesn't divide A[i, i] by itself to produce a 1 because that is a trivial calculation, and the pivot element of A is never used again. After normalizing the ith row of A, the ith element of b is divided by A[i, i] so the linear equation relationship is preserved.

After normalizing the pivot row i and the corresponding element of b, there is a for loop with an index k that takes on values from i+1 to n-1, representing the rows below the pivot row. If the pivot row is already n-1, this for loop is skipped automatically since its start index is greater than n-1. This loop reduces each element below the pivot element to zero from row i+1 to n-1. The indented for loop ranging j from column i+1 to n-1 subtracts the element in the reduction row times the corresponding j column element in the pivot row from the element in the reduction row. It does not carry out the subtraction to create the zero (starts in column i+1) because we no longer use that element in the algorithm. It then makes the appropriate subtraction for the b vector element to maintain the integrity of the linear equation. This completes the forward pass of the algorithm.

The back-substitution pass of the algorithm is then implemented. Here, there is a for loop with index i that ranges the pivot index in descending order from row n-1 to 1. For each pivot i, there is a for loop with index j that carries out the back-substitution calculation which would create a zero above the pivot and

```
def gausselim(A,b):
    n = len(b)
    # begin forward pass
    for i in range(n): # step down from row 0 through row n-1
        # normalize row i
        for j in range(i+1,n): # step across from column i+1 through n-1
            A[i,j]=A[i,j]/A[i,i]
        b[i]=b[i]/A[i,i]
        # reduce below the i,i pivot element
        for k in range(i+1,n): # step down from row i+1 through n-1
        # note: this will be skipped when i = n-1
            for j in range(i+1,n):
                A[k,j]=A[k,j]-A[k,i]*A[i,j]
            b[k]=b[k]-A[k,i]*b[i]
    # begin back-substitution pass
    for i in range(n-1,0,-1): # step back up from row n-1 to row 1
        for j in range(i-1,-1,-1):  # back-substitute from row i-1 to 0
            b[j]=b[j]-A[j,i]*b[i]
    return b
```

FIGURE 8.7 Python function gausselim that implements naive Gaussian elimination.

make the corresponding b vector calculation. It doesn't actually calculate the zero because that is trivial and not needed later. When this pass of the algorithm is complete, the b vector holds the solution of the set of equations.

You will note that the gausselim function is very compact, only 12 executable statements. If we add code to test it with our previous example, this is the result, replicating our manual solution,

```python
import numpy as np

A = np.array([[3., -2., 7.],[-2., 4., -3.],[-1., 9., 4.]])
b = np.array([15., 12., 27.])

x = gausselim(A,b)
print(x)
```

```
[100.33333333  28.66666667 -32.66666667]
```

After completing and testing a prototype algorithm such as the gausselim function, it is good practice to see how it might be made more efficient. By examining the code in Figure 8.7, we recognize that, in the forward pass, we first divide the pivot row i by its pivot value, A[i,i], and then, for the row k reduction step, we multiply the pivot row by the element in row k below the pivot, A[k,i], and then subtract it from row k. If we combine those two factors into one, A[k,i]/A[i,i], we can carry out the reduction step without the need for the normalization step. This reduces the number of computations. Then, during the back-substitution pass, we must recall that the pivot rows were not normalized. We must incorporate the updated A[i,i] values then.

8.3.2.2 Adding Determinant Evaluation

In this section, we introduce the matter of the *determinant* of a square matrix and its relationship to Gaussian elimination. If we refer to an earlier example of linear equations,

$$\begin{bmatrix} 3 & -2 & 7 \\ -2 & 4 & -3 \\ -1 & 9 & 4 \end{bmatrix} \cdot \begin{bmatrix} x_1 \\ x_2 \\ x_3 \end{bmatrix} = \begin{bmatrix} 15 \\ 12 \\ 27 \end{bmatrix}$$

we can use the scheme presented in Figure 8.5 to calculate the determinant of the coefficient matrix.

$$\det(\mathbf{A}) = \begin{vmatrix} 3 & -2 & 7 \\ -2 & 4 & -3 \\ -1 & 9 & 4 \end{vmatrix} = 3 \cdot 4 \cdot 4 + (-2) \cdot (-3) \cdot (-1) + (-2) \cdot 9 \cdot 7$$

$$-(7 \cdot 4 \cdot (-1) + (-2) \cdot (-2) \cdot 4 + (-3) \cdot 9 \cdot 3) = -84 - (-93) = 9$$

If we go back to our manual application of Gaussian elimination and tabulate the pivot values that were used to normalize the three rows, these were 3, 8/3, and 9/8. Then, if we calculate the product of these three values, the result is 9, which matches the determinant. By example, this points out that we can compute the determinant of a square matrix via the forward pass of the Gaussian elimination algorithm by accumulating the normalizing factors and computing their product. We incorporate this scheme in our Python functions below.

Figure 8.8 provides a modified gausselim1 function that includes these changes. Testing this function, the script and results are

```
import numpy as np

A = np.array([[3., -2., 7.], [-2., 4., -3.], [-1., 9., 4.]])
b = np.array([15., 12., 27.])

x, D = gausselim1(A, b)
print(x)
print(D)

[100.33333333 28.66666667-32.66666667]
9.000000000000014
```

8.3.2.3 Partial Pivoting

As mentioned previously in this chapter, the gausselim1 function implements *naive Gaussian elimination*. The method has an important flaw. It will fail to solve the following system of equations.

$$
\begin{bmatrix} 0 & -2 & 7 \\ -2 & 4 & -3 \\ -1 & 9 & 4 \end{bmatrix} \cdot \begin{bmatrix} x_1 \\ x_2 \\ x_3 \end{bmatrix} = \begin{bmatrix} 15 \\ 12 \\ 27 \end{bmatrix} \tag{8.31}
$$

```
def gausselim1(A,b):
    n = len(b)
    # begin forward pass
    for i in range(n):  # step down from row 0 through row n-1
        # reduce below the i,i pivot element
        for k in range(i+1,n): #step down from row i+1 through n-1
            factor = A[k,i]/A[i,i]
            # note: this will be skipped when i = n-1
            for j in range(i+1,n):
                A[k,j] = A[k,j] - factor*A[i,j]
            b[k] = b[k] - factor*b[i]
    # begin back-substitution pass
    D = 1
    for i in range(n-1,-1,-1): # step back up from row n-1 to row 1
        D = D * A[i,i]
        b[i] = b[i]/A[i,i]
        for j in range(i-1,-1,-1): # back-substitute from row i-1 to 0
            b[j] = b[j] - A[j,i]*b[i]
    return b,D
```

FIGURE 8.8   Gaussian elimination function gausselim1 with improvements.

The first step of the method will be to compute the factor ratio. This will cause an immediate "divide by zero" error. But the equations do have a solution, so we need a way around this. Practically, we could see that just swapping the first two rows would avoid the zero pivot element. Yes, that would work, and it introduces an important enhancement to our method which is called *pivoting*. The strategy is, at each pivot level, swap the pivot row with the row below it that has the largest absolute value below in that column. If the pivot element is already the largest, no swap occurs.

The pivot strategy can be implemented in modular fashion by creating its own function with arguments of the current A and b arrays and the current pivot index. That function returns the A and b arrays with appropriate swapping of rows. The Python code for the modified gausselimpivot function and the pivotswap function is provided in Figure 8.9. This modification to the naive gausselim1 function is simple; just before the normalization, the pivotswap function is invoked to rearrange the A and b arrays, if necessary.

The pivotswap function first sets a maximum value as the absolute value of the current pivot element, Amax, and a locator index, imax, as the current pivot index. Then, through a for loop that ranges from the row below the current

```
import numpy as np

def pivotswap(A,b,ipivot):
    n = len(b)
    Amax = abs(A[ipivot,ipivot]) # set maximum to pivot location
    imax = ipivot
    for i in range(ipivot+1,n):  # look for greater value below
        if abs(A[i,ipivot]) > Amax:
            Amax = abs(A[i,ipivot])  # reset maximum if found
            imax = i
    if imax != ipivot:  # swap rows of A and b if needed
        for j in range(ipivot,n):
            Atemp = A[ipivot,j]
            A[ipivot,j] = A[imax,j]
            A[imax,j] = Atemp
        btemp = b[ipivot]
        b[ipivot] = b[imax]
        b[imax] = btemp
    return A,b

def gausselimpivot(A,b):
    n = len(b)
    # begin forward pass
    for i in range(n):  # step down from row 0 through row n-1
        # reduce below the i,i pivot element
        A,b = pivotswap(A,b,i)
        for k in range(i+1,n): # step down from row i+1 through row n-1
            factor = A[k,i]/A[i,i]
            # note: this will be skipped when i = n-1
            for j in range(i+1,n):
                A[k,j] = A[k,j] - factor*A[i,j]
            b[k] = b[k] - factor*b[i]
    # begin back-substitution pass
    D = 1
    for i in range(n-1,-1,-1): # step back up from row n-1 to row 1
        D = D * A[i,i]
        b[i] = b[i]/A[i,i]
        for j in range(i-1,-1,-1):  # back-substitute from row i-1 to 0
            b[j] = b[j] - A[j,i]*b[i]
    return b,D
```

FIGURE 8.9 Gaussian elimination function with pivotswap function added.

pivot row, ipivot+1 to n-1, the maximum absolute value and location, imax, are updated if warranted. Finally, with the imax locator in hand, a swap of the ipivot and imax rows of A and b is carried out with a for loop. If the maximum value is the current pivot location, no swap is implemented.

We can test the gausselimpivot function with the previous set of equations with a zero value in the first pivot location.

```
import numpy as np

A = np.array([[0., -2., 7.], [-2., 4., -3.], [-1., 9., 4.]])
b = np.array([15., 12., 27.])

x, D = gausselimpivot(A, b)
print('Solution is\n', x)
print('Determinant = ', D)

Solution is
 [-7.525  1.075 2.45 ]
Determinant = -120.0
```

The improved strategy solves the modified system of equations successfully.

8.3.2.4   Detecting Singular and Ill-Conditioned Systems

Adding the pivot swapping strategy to the naive Gaussian elimination algorithm protects against division by zero when a normalization of the pivot row is carried out. However, there is one lingering problem. What will happen if the set of linear equations has no solution? That is, the $n \times n$ A matrix is singular indicating that there are not n independent linear equations. If this is the situation, the algorithm will get to a point where the pivot element is zero and any elements below it are also zero. It is then unable to normalize the pivot row, and the method fails.

We need to protect against this by providing for an error exit from the gausselimpivot function. Also, it is possible that, rather than encountering a zero pivot that can't be swapped, there is an Amax value that is so tiny that the set of equations is "almost" singular, or singular, except for numerical roundoff error. This is called an *ill-conditioning*. We can protect against this by testing the absolute value of the pivot element value, after the pivot swap takes place, against a small value, e.g. 10^{-15}, instead of testing if it is identically zero. This code is added to the gausselimpivot function in Figure 8.10.

If the gausselimpivot1 function is evaluated with a singular system of equations,

$$\begin{bmatrix} 1 & 2 & 3 \\ 4 & 5 & 6 \\ 7 & 8 & 9 \end{bmatrix} \cdot \begin{bmatrix} x_1 \\ x_2 \\ x_3 \end{bmatrix} = \begin{bmatrix} 15 \\ 12 \\ 27 \end{bmatrix} \tag{8.32}$$

```
def gausselimpivot1(A,b,tol=1.e-15):
    n = len(b)
    # begin forward pass
    for i in range(n):   # step down from row 0 through row n-1
        # reduce below the i,i pivot element
        A,b = pivotswap(A,b,i)
        if abs(A[i,i]) < tol:
            return 'system of equations singular or ill-conditioned'
        for k in range(i+1,n):  # step down from row i+1 through n-1
            factor = A[k,i]/A[i,i]
            # note: this will be skipped when i = n-1
            for j in range(i+1,n):
                A[k,j] = A[k,j] - factor*A[i,j]
            b[k] = b[k] - factor*b[i]
    # begin back-substitution pass
    d = 1
    for i in range(n-1,-1,-1): # step back up from row n-1 to 1
        D = D * A[i,i]
        b[i] = b[i]/A[i,i]
        for j in range(i-1,-1,-1):  # back-substitute from row i-1 to 0
            b[j] = b[j] - A[j,i]*b[i]
    return b,D
```

FIGURE 8.10 Gaussian elimination with pivot strategy and protection against singular and ill-conditioned sets of equations.

this is the code and the result.

```
import numpy as np

A = np.array([[1., 2., 3.], [4., 5., 6.], [7., 8., 9.]])
b = np.array([15., 12., 27.])

result = gausselimpivot1(A, b)
if type(result) == str:
    print(result)
else:
    (x, D) = result
    print('Solution is\n', x)
    print('Determinant = ', D)
```

The result is

```
system of equations singular or ill-conditioned
```

Since the return from the gausselimpivot1 function can be either an error message or two variables, the script evaluates the result to see whether it is a string or not using Python's type function and str constant and prints out the corresponding information.

The coefficient array **A** for this example is called a *circular matrix*. Notice the pattern of the elements. Even though it may not be apparent from its elements, a circular matrix of any dimension $n \times n$ is singular.

Example 8.6 Construction Materials: A Blending Problem with Linear Equations

At a construction site, there are three piles of granular material that are blended to provide a specified composition of particulates for foundation backfill. The required solid blend contains 4,800 m³ of sand, 5,800 m³ of fine gravel, and 5,700 m³ of sand. The composition of each pile is given in the table below. Determine the amount to be used from each pile to provide the specified solid blend for the construction project.

Pile	Sand	Percent Composition	
		Fine Gravel	Coarse Gravel
A	55	30	15
B	25	45	30
C	25	20	55

To solve this problem, we write equations for each material where the unknowns are the amounts to be used from each pile

$$0.55x_A + 0.25x_B + 0.25x_C = 4800$$

$$0.30x_A + 0.45x_B + 0.20x_C = 5800 \tag{8.33}$$

$$0.15x_A + 0.30x_B + 0.55x_C = 5700$$

In vector/matrix format, this system of equations is

$$\begin{bmatrix} 0.55 & 0.25 & 0.25 \\ 0.30 & 0.45 & 0.20 \\ 0.15 & 0.30 & 0.55 \end{bmatrix} \cdot \begin{bmatrix} x_A \\ x_B \\ x_C \end{bmatrix} = \begin{bmatrix} 4800 \\ 5800 \\ 5700 \end{bmatrix} \tag{8.34}$$

We can modify our script that uses gausselimpivot1 function to solve this problem.

```
A = np.array([[0.55, 0.25, 0.25], [0.30, 0.45, 0.20], [0.15, 0.30, 0.55]])
b = np.array([4800., 5800., 5700.])

x = gausselimpivot1(A, b)
print('Amount from Pile A: {0:6.1f} m3'.format(x[0]))
print('Amount from Pile B: {0:6.1f} m3'.format(x[1]))
print('Amount from Pile C: {0:6.1f} m3'.format(x[2]))
```

The solution is displayed in the Console as

```
Amount from Pile A: 2416.7 m3
Amount from Pile B: 9193.3 m3
Amount from Pile C: 4690.0 m3
```

Of course, now it's important to check the feasibility of this solution with the inventories of the three piles. Is there enough material in each to satisfy the blend requirements? We need more information to address this question.

8.4 SOLVING SETS OF LINEAR EQUATIONS WITH THE NUMPY linalg MODULE

Now that we have learned the basics of solving sets of linear equations with Gaussian elimination, we can proceed to employ built-in functions in the NumPy linalg module to accomplish the same. Even though we often use built-in functions for numerical tasks, it is always important to underlay these with fundamental knowledge, here provided by our introduction of Gaussian elimination.

In Chapter 6, the solution of a set of linear algebraic equations was expressed as

$$\mathbf{x} = \mathbf{A}^{-1} \cdot \mathbf{b} \tag{8.35}$$

Since the linalg module has a function inv that computes the inverse of a square matrix, we can use this along with the dot method or the matmul function to compute the solution. Here is a Python code script that accomplishes this. You can observe that the two methods yield the same result.

```
import numpy as np

A = np.array([[3., -2., 7.], [-2., 4., -3.], [-1., 9., 4.]])
b = np.array([15., 12., 27.])

Ainv = np.linalg.inv(A)
x = Ainv.dot(b)
print(x)
x = np.matmul(Ainv, b)
print(x)
```

The result is

```
[100.33333333  28.66666667-32.66666667]
[100.33333333  28.66666667-32.66666667]
```

If the number of individual calculations required to solve a set of equations using the matrix inverse is tabulated, it is much greater than for methods like Gaussian elimination. The linalg module provides a solve function that implements a more sophisticated, efficient algorithm adapted from a software package called LAPACK,[3] where the routines are written in the Fortran 90 programming language. Here is the solution of our example set using the solve function.

---

[3] LAPACK is the successor to the MINPACK and EISPACK libraries for linear algebra and eigenvalue numerical methods. It is based on the Fortran 90 language and was released in 1992.

```
x = np.linalg.solve(A, b)
print(x)
```

```
[100.33333333  28.66666667-32.66666667]
```

There is a family of functions in the `linalg` module, most of which are beyond the scope of this text. One that we will illustrate is the `det` function that computes the determinant of a square matrix.

```
import numpy as np

A = np.array([[3., -2., 7.], [-2., 4., -3.], [-1., 9., 4.]])
DA = np.linalg.det(A)
print(A)
```

```
9.000000000000005
```

We note there is a tiny roundoff error associated with the determinant computation.

8.5   SOLVING SETS OF NONLINEAR ALGEBRAIC EQUATIONS

In Sections 8.3 and 8.4, methods to solve sets of linear algebraic equations were introduced. A characteristic of their solution is that it is a once-through calculation. Given modern computer technology, the solution is rapid. If the equation set is *well-conditioned* (not singular or nearly so, described as ill-conditioned in Section 8.3), the methods can solve hundreds of simultaneous equations with relative ease. As we now consider sets of nonlinear algebraic equations, the scenario changes dramatically. First, iterative methods are necessary which require an initial estimate of the solution. Second, a solution may be difficult-to-impossible for sets of more than just a few equations. The first is a characteristic we encountered in Chapter 7 for single equations, and the second compounds the difficulty of the task.

Let's start with a simple example of two nonlinear equations with two unknowns. Later we will generalize it to n equations in n unknowns.

$$x_1^2 + x_2^2 - 4 = 0$$
$$x_1 x_2 - 1 = 0$$

(8.36)

For this example, we have the luxury of being able to plot the two equation curves on the x_2–x_1 phase plane. This is shown in Figure 8.11. It is immediately evident that there are four possible solutions to the equations indicated where the lines cross. So, we have a first characteristic of nonlinear equation sets: multiple solutions. If our equations model a physical or chemical phenomenon, it may be possible to restrict the domains of the unknowns so that only one practical solution is found. But our example raises an important question. Which of the four solutions will be obtained for a given set of initial guesses for x_1 and x_2? For this

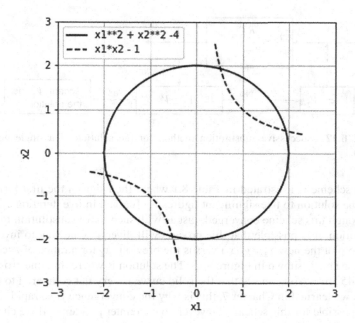

FIGURE 8.11 Plot of two nonlinear functions on the x_1–x_2 plane.

example, we will focus on the two solutions in the upper-right quadrant, assuming that negative solutions make no practical sense.

There are many approaches to the solution of nonlinear algebraic equation sets, and many of those are more complex and sophisticated than we want to introduce here. We will begin by introducing an extension of successive substitution (or fixed-point iteration).

8.5.1 SOLUTION OF NONLINEAR ALGEBRAIC EQUATIONS BY SUCCESSIVE SUBSTITUTION

Recall the successive substitution method introduced in Chapter 7 for the solution of one nonlinear algebraic equation, $x = g(x)$. This is illustrated in Figure 8.12.

Using the two equations introduced above, we can solve the first equation analytically for x_1 and the second equation for x_2.

$$x_1 = \pm\sqrt{4 - x_2^2} = g_1(x_2)$$

$$x_2 = 1/x_1 = g_2(x_1)$$

(8.37)

In this form, we can start with an estimated value for x_2 and compute the formulas in sequence with new values for x_1 and x_2 as a result. Then, we can repeat the calculation with the new x_2 and, hopefully, after numerous iterations, the process will converge to a solution.

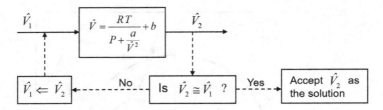

FIGURE 8.12 Successive substitution method for the solution of a single nonlinear equation.

This scheme is illustrated in Table 8.1 where the + sign in the first formula is used. The solution to five significant figures is obtained in five iterations.

Although this scheme converged, just as with successive substitution for a single equation, it is possible that this process will diverge. One way to investigate this is to plot the new $x_2 = g_2(x_1)$ versus the previous x_2 for a range of acceptable x_2 values. This is shown in Figure 8.13. The solution is where that line crosses the dashed 45° line. You can see that the solid curve is very flat compared to the 45° line. As we learned in Chapter 7, this is why the convergence is so rapid.

It is possible for this scheme, however, to encounter problems. If we choose an initial x_2 greater than 2, the square root will be of a negative number yielding a complex result. Even if we choose an initial x_2 equal to 2, this will cause a divide by zero in the second formula. Also, we know from Figure 8.11 that there are four solutions to the equations. Our substitution scheme has only "discovered" one of those solutions. By reversing the formulation of the $g(x)$ equations to

$$x_2 = \pm\sqrt{4 - x_1^2} = g_1(x_1)$$

$$x_1 = 1/x_2 = g_2(x_2)$$

(8.38)

the solution flips to equivalent but opposite values for x_1 and x_2. If we use the minus sign with the square root, and with appropriate initial estimates, we can determine the solutions in the other quadrant in Figure 8.11.

TABLE 8.1

Successive Substitution Process

Iteration	x_2	$x_1 = g_1(x_2)$	$x_2 = g_2(x_1)$
1	0.5	1.93649	0.51640
2	0.51640	1.93218	0.51755
3	0.51755	1.93188	0.51763
4	0.51763	1.93185	0.51764
5	0.51764	1.93185	0.51764

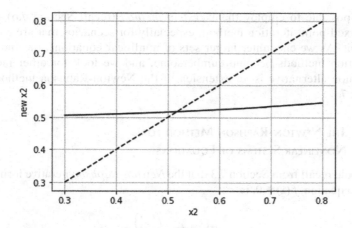

FIGURE 8.13   Plot of the new $x_2 = g_2(x_1)$ versus x_2.

The implementation of the successive substitution method in Python is to use our `fixpt` function from Chapter 7 directly and formulate the g function argument as $g_2(g_1(x_2))$. The code is shown in Figure 8.14, and the results displayed in the Console are

```
x1 = 1.9319
x2 = 0.5176
number of iterations taken =   6
```

These confirm the solution from Table 8.1.

```
import numpy as np

def fixpt(g,x1,ea=1.e-7,maxit=30):
    for i in range(maxit): # carry out maxit iterations
        x2 = g(x1)   # calculate new x
        if abs((x2-x1)/x2) < ea:   # check if converged
            iter = i+1
            return x2,iter   # if converged, return xnew and iterations
        x1 = x2   # if not converged, replace x1 with x2
    iter = i+1
    return x2,iter   # here if maxit reached

def g1(x2):
    return  np.sqrt(4.-x2**2)

def g2(x2):
    return 1/g1(x2)

x2 = 0.5
x2soln,iter = fixpt(g2,x2)
print('x1 = {0:6.4f}'.format(g1(x2soln)))
print('x2 = {0:6.4f}'.format(x2soln))
print('number of iterations taken = {0:3d}'.format(iter))
```

FIGURE 8.14   Adaptation of the `fixpt` function to solve two nonlinear equations.

It is possible to employ the *Wegstein method* (recall Section 7.6) instead of the fixed-point iteration method, especially for scenarios that are naturally divergent. As we encounter larger sets of nonlinear equations, the successive substitution methods become cumbersome, and we look for other methods. A common alternative is an extension of the Newton-Raphson method from Chapter 7.

8.5.2   THE NEWTON-RAPHSON METHOD FOR NONLINEAR SYSTEMS OF EQUATIONS

You should recall from Section 7.3 that the *Newton-Raphson* iterative formula for a single equation, $f(x) = 0$, is

$$x^{i+1} = x^i - \frac{f(x^i)}{f'(x^i)} \tag{8.39}$$

where $f'(x)$ is the derivative of $f(x)$ with respect to x, and the formula describes how the $(i+1)$th estimate of x is obtained from the ith estimate.

To see how we can extend this method to the solution of multiple equations, let's start with our example from Figure 8.11:

$$x_1^2 + x_2^2 - 4 = 0$$
$$x_1 x_2 - 1 = 0 \tag{8.40}$$

We can express these equations in more general form as

$$f_1(x_1, x_2) = 0$$
$$f_2(x_1, x_2) = 0 \tag{8.41}$$

By defining the vector quantities,

$$\begin{bmatrix} x_1 \\ x_2 \end{bmatrix} = \mathbf{x} \qquad \begin{bmatrix} f_1 \\ f_2 \end{bmatrix} = \mathbf{f} \qquad \text{where the latter represent the two equations,}$$

we can express the nonlinear equations in the form

$$\mathbf{f}(\mathbf{x}) = \mathbf{0} \tag{8.42}$$

So, we would be tempted to rewrite the Newton-Raphson formula as

$$\mathbf{x}^{i+1} = \mathbf{x}^i - \frac{\mathbf{f}(\mathbf{x}^i)}{\mathbf{f}'(\mathbf{x}^i)} \tag{8.43}$$

but there are two problems with the $f'(x^i)$ term in the formula. First, what is the meaning of the derivative of a vector function, f, with respect to a vector variable, x? And then, how do we go about dividing that into the vector function, f? This just doesn't work; so we must reinterpret it.

First, since we have in our example two functions and two variables, which indicates we have four possible derivatives:

$$
\begin{bmatrix} \dfrac{\partial f_1}{\partial x_1} & \dfrac{\partial f_1}{\partial x_2} \\[2mm] \dfrac{\partial f_2}{\partial x_1} & \dfrac{\partial f_2}{\partial x_2} \end{bmatrix} = \begin{bmatrix} \dfrac{\partial}{\partial x_1}\left(x_1^2 + x_2^2 - 4\right) & \dfrac{\partial}{\partial x_2}\left(x_1^2 + x_2^2 - 4\right) \\[2mm] \dfrac{\partial}{\partial x_1}(x_1 x_2 - 1) & \dfrac{\partial}{\partial x_2}(x_1 x_2 - 1) \end{bmatrix}
$$

$$
= \begin{bmatrix} 2x_1 & 2x_2 \\ x_2 & x_1 \end{bmatrix}
$$

(8.44)

You will note that we have arranged these in matrix form with the first row being the two derivatives of the first function with respect to the two variables and the second row being the two similar derivatives, but of the second function.

In the case that you are not that familiar with *partial derivatives*, we point out that

$$
\frac{\partial}{\partial x_1}(\bullet)
$$

is the derivative with respect to x_1 with x_2 treated like a constant, and vice versa for

$$
\frac{\partial}{\partial x_2}(\bullet).
$$

Using this scheme, we have shown above how those partial derivatives are derived for our two example equations. This matrix of partial derivatives is called the *Jacobian matrix*, J.[4]

So now we have a representation of $f'(x)$ in the form of a matrix, but the second issue, dividing by a matrix, still doesn't make any sense. The answer here is instead to multiply by the inverse of the matrix, J^{-1}. This gives us the formula for the Newton-Raphson method for multiple nonlinear equations:

$$
x^{i+1} = x^i - J^{-1}\left(x^i\right) \cdot f\left(x^i\right)
$$

(8.45)

If we write this out in detail for our example equations, we get

---

[4] The name of this matrix is due to the German mathematician, Carl Gustav Jacob Jacobi (1804–1851), who made fundamental contributions in several areas of mathematics. In 1832, he was the first Jewish mathematician to be appointed to a German university at Königsberg. Other notable alumni and faculty of Königsberg were Immanuel Kant, David Hilbert, Gustav Kirchhoff, and Hermann von Helmholtz.

$$\begin{bmatrix} x_1^{i+1} \\ x_2^{i+1} \end{bmatrix} = \begin{bmatrix} x_1^i \\ x_2^i \end{bmatrix} - \begin{bmatrix} 2x_1^i & 2x_2^i \\ x_2^i & x_1^i \end{bmatrix}^{-1} \cdot \begin{bmatrix} x_1^{2i} + x_2^{2i} - 4 \\ x_1^i x_2^i - 1 \end{bmatrix} \qquad (8.46)$$

and you can see that to move from iteration i to $i+1$, we have to compute the inverse of the Jacobian matrix evaluated for the x values at iteration i.

This formula can be illustrated with our example system of equations, with starting estimates of {0.5, 1.4}. This is shown in Figure 8.15. After four iterations, the method converges to the solution {0.5176, 1.9319}, and you will recognize this as the intersection in the upper right on Figure 8.10. If we start with initial estimates reversed, {1.4, 0.5}, the method converges to the solution {1.9319, 0.5176}, the intersection below and to the right of the previous solution. By selecting initial estimates with some forethought, the method will also converge to the solutions in quadrant III in the lower left.

Now that we have seen how to extend the Newton-Raphson method to two nonlinear equations, we can consider the more general case of a set of n equations in n unknowns. These can be described as follows.

$$\begin{matrix} f_1(x_1, x_2, \ldots, x_n) = 0 \\ f_2(x_1, x_2, \ldots, x_n) = 0 \\ \vdots \\ f_n(x_1, x_2, \ldots, x_n) = 0 \end{matrix} \qquad \Rightarrow \qquad \mathbf{f(x) = 0} \qquad (8.47)$$

As before, you can see that it is convenient to represent the n functions as a vector of functions, $\mathbf{f}$, in a vector of n unknowns, $\mathbf{x}$. We can generalize our description of the Jacobian matrix to

$$\begin{bmatrix} \dfrac{\partial f_1}{\partial x_1} & \dfrac{\partial f_1}{\partial x_2} & \cdots & \dfrac{\partial f_1}{\partial x_n} \\ \dfrac{\partial f_2}{\partial x_1} & \dfrac{\partial f_2}{\partial x_2} & \cdots & \dfrac{\partial f_2}{\partial x_n} \\ \vdots & \vdots & \ddots & \vdots \\ \dfrac{\partial f_n}{\partial x_1} & \dfrac{\partial f_n}{\partial x_1} & \cdots & \dfrac{\partial f_n}{\partial x_n} \end{bmatrix} = \mathbf{J(x)} \qquad (8.48)$$

$$\mathbf{x}^0 = \begin{bmatrix} 0.5 \\ 1.4 \end{bmatrix} \quad \mathbf{f(x^0)} = \begin{bmatrix} -1.79 \\ -0.3 \end{bmatrix} \quad \mathbf{J(x^0)} = \begin{bmatrix} 1.0 & 2.8 \\ 1.4 & 0.5 \end{bmatrix} \quad \mathbf{J^{-1}(x^0)} \cong \begin{bmatrix} -0.1462 & 0.8187 \\ 0.4094 & -0.2924 \end{bmatrix} \quad \mathbf{x}^1 = \begin{bmatrix} 0.4839 \\ 2.045 \end{bmatrix}$$

$$\mathbf{x}^1 = \begin{bmatrix} 0.4839 \\ 2.045 \end{bmatrix} \quad \mathbf{f(x^1)} \cong \begin{bmatrix} 0.4163 \\ -0.0104 \end{bmatrix} \quad \mathbf{J(x^1)} \cong \begin{bmatrix} 0.9678 & 4.090 \\ 2.045 & 0.4839 \end{bmatrix} \quad \mathbf{J^{-1}(x^1)} \cong \begin{bmatrix} -0.06129 & 0.5180 \\ 0.02590 & -0.1226 \end{bmatrix} \quad \mathbf{x}^2 \cong \begin{bmatrix} 0.5148 \\ 1.9359 \end{bmatrix}$$

FIGURE 8.15   Two iterations of the Newton-Raphson method.

The same general formula can then be utilized to attempt to find a solution.

This raises a couple of important points. First, just as in the single-equation Newton-Raphson method, the solution obtained is sensitive to the initial estimates. Second, it is often the case that the method doesn't converge.

There are two variations of the Newton-Raphson method that merit our consideration. First, when the method diverges and is unsuccessful, a modification of the method's formula may remedy the situation. This problem may occur because the adjustment made by the term

$$\mathbf{J}^{-1}\left(\mathbf{x}^i\right) \cdot \mathbf{f}\left(\mathbf{x}^i\right)$$

is too ambitious and causes instability and divergence. The modification is to include a "decelerator" factor,[5] d, a constant between zero and one, in the formula as follows:

$$\mathbf{x}^{i+1} = \mathbf{x}^i - d \cdot \mathbf{J}^{-1}\left(\mathbf{x}^i\right) \cdot \mathbf{f}\left(\mathbf{x}^i\right) \tag{8.49}$$

The value of d usually has to be adjusted by trial-and-error. This modification often obtains success where the original formula is unstable and fails.

Next, there are occasions where the partial derivatives in the Jacobian matrix are difficult, or even impossible, to derive analytically. The strategy here is like the modified secant method described in Section 7.4. In this case, we replace the elements of the Jacobian matrix with numerical approximations. For each element of the Jacobian matrix, we introduce an approximation based on a small variation in the differentiating variable. For example, with our two-equation set, the approximation of the first element of the Jacobian matrix would be

$$\frac{\partial f_1}{\partial x_1} \cong \frac{f_1\left(x_1 \cdot (1+\delta), x_2\right) - f_1(x_1, x_2)}{x_1 \cdot \delta} = \frac{\left(\left(x_1 \cdot (1+\delta)\right)^2 + x_2^2 - 4\right) - \left(x_1^2 + x_2^2 - 4\right)}{x_1 \cdot \delta}$$

$$\tag{8.50}$$

where δ is a small number, e.g., 1×10^{-6}. If we apply this approximation using our initial estimates from above, $\{0.5, 1.4\}$, the result is

$$\frac{\partial f_1}{\partial x_1} \cong \frac{\left(\left(0.5 \cdot (1+10^{-6})\right)^2 + 1.4^2 - 4\right) - \left(0.5^2 + 1.4^2 - 4\right)}{0.5 \cdot 10^{-6}} \cong 1.0000005$$

Note that our approximation is very close to the true value of the partial derivative: $2x_1 = 2 \cdot 0.5 = 1.0$. We can use similar approximations for the other elements of the Jacobian matrix. Of course, it's not necessary to use the approximation in this case because the derivatives are readily derived.

---

[5] Sometime called an *under-relaxation* factor.

A Python function, `multinewt`, that implements the multivariable Newton-Raphson method is presented in Figure 8.16. The following Python script solves our example equation set using this function.

```python
import numpy as np

def f(x):
    fn = np.zeros(2)
    fn[0] = x[0]**2 + x[1]**2 - 4
    fn[1] = x[0]*x[1] -1
    return fn

def J(x):
    Jac = np.zeros((2,2))
    Jac[0,0] = 2*x[0]
    Jac[0,1] = 2*x[1]
    Jac[1,0] = x[1]
    Jac[1,1] = x[0]
    return Jac

x0 = np.array([0.5, 1.4])
xsoln,niter = multinewt(f,J,x0)
print(xsoln)
print(niter)
```

and the results displayed in the Console are

```
[0.51763809 1.93185165]
4
```

Observe that the code for the `multinewt` function is compact, only 12 statements. It relies on the user supplying two functions, `f` and `J`, that compute and return the equation residuals, the f's, and the Jacobian matrix, `J`, for a given set of x's. The function has an `x0` argument for the initial estimates and then keyword arguments for the relative error, `ea`, the maximum iterations allowed, `maxiter`, and the deceleration factor, `decel`. The latter is assigned a default value of one – meaning no deceleration.

```python
def multinewt(f,J,x0,ea=1.e-7,maxiter=30,decel=1.0):
    xold = x0
    for iter in range(maxiter):
        Jinv = np.linalg.inv(J(xold))
        xnew = xold - decel*Jinv.dot(f(xold))
        xdev = xnew - xold
        xerr = xdev.dot(xdev)
        if xerr < ea:
            break
        xold = xnew
    return xnew,iter+1
```

FIGURE 8.16 Python function `multinewt` to solve sets of nonlinear algebraic equations.

The error criterion is compared to the sum of the squares of the differences between the x's this iteration and those from the previous iteration. This is computed as the dot product of the xdev array with itself. The keyword arguments can be respecified when the function is invoked; otherwise, the default values are used. The function returns the latest solution estimates and the number of iterations taken. If the latter is equal to maxiter, that means the method did not converge.

Example 8.7 Equilibrium between Water Liquid and Vapor in a Boiler Vessel

Consider a boiler vessel where the steam that is generated and the remaining liquid are in equilibrium with each other. This is illustrated in Figure 8.17. There are two equations for the vapor phase that govern the equilibrium conditions of the boiler. These are an equation of state, here the ideal gas law, and the Antoine equation for the vapor pressure of water at a given temperature.

$$PV = \frac{m_V}{MW}RT \quad \text{and} \quad \log_{10}(P) = A - \frac{B}{C+T} \tag{8.51}$$

where P: pressure in the vessel, kPa
  V: volume of the vapor space, m³
  m_V: mass of vapor, kg
  MW: molecular weight of water, 18.02 kg/kmol
  R: gas law constant, 8.314m³·kPa/(kmol·K)
  T: temperature, K
  A, B, C: Antoine parameters for water: $A = 8.21$ $B = 2354.7$ $C = 7.56$

Given values for m_V and V, we want to determine the equilibrium temperature, T, and pressure, P. This scenario then is described by two equations in two unknowns,

$$f_1(P,V) = PV - \frac{m_V}{MW}RT = 0$$

$$f_2(P,V) = \log_{10}(P) - A + \frac{B}{C+T} = 0 \tag{8.52}$$

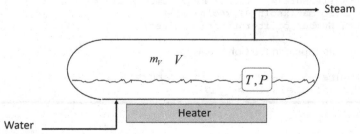

FIGURE 8.17 Steam boiler vessel with water in equilibrium with vapor.

In order to use the Newton-Raphson method, we need to derive the Jacobian matrix of partial derivatives. These are

$$\mathbf{J} = \begin{bmatrix} \dfrac{\partial f_1}{\partial P} = V & \dfrac{\partial f_1}{\partial T} = -\dfrac{m_V}{MW}R \\ \dfrac{\partial f_2}{\partial P} = \dfrac{1}{P \cdot \ln(10)} & \dfrac{\partial f_2}{\partial T} = -\dfrac{B}{(C+T)^2} \end{bmatrix} \tag{8.53}$$

Next, we need values for m_V and V and initial guesses for P and T.

$m_V = 3.755\,\text{kg} \quad V = 3.142\,\text{m}^3 \quad P^0 = 200\,\text{kPa} \quad T^0 = 380\,\text{K}$

This information provides what we need to set up a Python script, using the `multinewt` function, to solve the equations. Here is the script:

```
R = 8.314  # m3-kPa/[kmol-K]
MW = 18.02  # kg/kmol
A = 8.21; B = 2354.7; C = 7.56

mV = 3.755  # kg
V = 3.142  # m3

P0 = 200.  # kPa
T0 = 380.  # K

def f(x):
    P = x[0]; T = x[1]
    fn = np.zeros(2)
    fn[0] = P*V - mV/MW*R*T
    fn[1] = np.log10(P) - A + B/(C+T)
    return fn

def J(x):
    P = x[0]; T = x[1]
    Jac = np.zeros((2,2))
    Jac[0,0] = V
    Jac[0,1] = -mV/MW*R
    Jac[1,0] = 1/P/np.log(10)
    Jac[1,1] = -B/(C+T)**2
    return Jac

x0 = np.array([P0, T0])
xsoln,niter = multinewt(f,J,x0)
print('Pressure = {0:6.1f} kPa, Temperature = {1:6.1f} K' \
      .format(xsoln[0],xsoln[1]))
print('Number of iterations: ',niter)
```

The results appear in the Console as

```
Pressure =  216.9 kPa, Temperature = 393.3 K
Number of iterations:   17
```

8.6   USE OF THE root FUNCTION FROM THE SCIPY optimize MODULE TO SOLVE NONLINEAR EQUATIONS

There is a built-in function in the SciPy optimize submodule, root, which provides a more sophisticated approach to solving sets of nonlinear equations. The user can select from seven different methods with a method argument. The default is a modified Powell hybrid method adapted from a library of routines called MINPACK (Moré, Garbow, and Hillstrom, 1980). We do not go into the details of this method here. The simplest syntax for using the root function is

```
xsoln = root(f, x0)
```

where f is a function that computes the equation functions for a given set of x values, and x0 is a set of initial estimates for the x's.

It is also possible to pass additional arguments through to the f function using an args(...) argument. The root function doesn't require us to supply a function for the Jacobian, although it is possible to do so.

The Python script below uses the root function to solve the example system illustrated in Figure 8.11.

```
import numpy as np
from scipy.optimize import root

def f(x):
    fn = np.zeros(2)
    fn[0] = x[0]**2 + x[1]**2 - 4
    fn[1] = x[0]*x[1] -1
    return fn

x0 = np.array([0.5, 1.4])
result = root(f,x0)
print(result)
print('\nSolution is: \n',result.x)
```

The root function returns a result object with various attributes. One is x, which provides the solution. In the code above, both the complete object result and the solution only as result.x are displayed separately in the Console.

```
    fjac: array([[-0.47905266, -0.87778616],
       [ 0.87778616, -0.47905266]])
     fun: array([4.85922413e-12, 1.98183692e-11])
 message: 'The solution converged.'
    nfev: 11
     qtf: array([2.56353178e-09, 6.57163450e-10])
       r: array([-2.12867493, -1.97061865,  3.23224566])
  status: 1
 success: True
       x: array([0.51763809, 1.93185165])
```

The solution is:

```
[0.51763809 1.93185165]
```

In the output above, you will note an `fjac` array displayed. This is the numerical approximation to the Jacobian that the `root` function produced at the solution. It also displays the final function evaluations as `fun`, very close to zero. The number of iterations (or f evaluations), `nfev`, is 11. The output indicates that the method was successful. The solution matches that which we obtained with our `multinewt` function but requires 11 iterations instead of 4. To be fair, the error tolerance for `root` is tighter than that for `multinewt`, and we provided the Jacobian matrix for the latter.

Although the `root` function is convenient to use, it is very much a "black box" when it comes to its internal operations. Since Python is an open-source language, you can obtain the source code for `root`, but that is over 600 lines and likely would require too much time to fathom for most typical Python users. The `multinewt` function works well for many applications and has the advantage of simplicity. Also, its method is out in the open and can by well understood by the user. You will often have to make a choice between a home-grown function and one that is built-in with Python. You can even use both to confirm your results. It is a choice that engineers and scientists must make frequently in problem solving.

PROBLEMS

8.1   Given the system of equations

$$-3x_2 + 7x_3 = 4$$

$$x_1 + 2x_2 - x_3 = 0$$

$$5x_1 - 2x_2 = 3$$

Compute the following manually. For parts **(b)** and **(c)**, check your solutions in the equations.
(a) Compute the determinant of the coefficient matrix.
(b) Solve the system of equations using Cramer's rule.
(c) Solve the system of equations using Gaussian elimination with pivoting.

8.2   Solve the following system of equations by hand using naive Gaussian elimination. Check that your answers satisfy the equations.

$$8x_1 + 2x_2 + 3x_3 = 30$$

$$x_1 - 9x_2 + 2x_3 = 1$$

$$2x_1 + 3x_2 + 6x_3 = 31$$

8.3　Solve the following system of equations, shown in vector/matrix form, by hand using Gaussian elimination with pivoting. Check your answers by substituting them in the equations. Using information from your solution steps, compute the determinant.

$$\begin{bmatrix} 4 & 3 & -1 \\ 7 & -2 & 3 \\ 5 & -18 & 13 \end{bmatrix} \mathbf{x} = \begin{bmatrix} 6 \\ 9 \\ 3 \end{bmatrix}$$

8.4　Use the `gausselimpivot1` function to solve the following system of equations. Report your solutions to four significant figures. Write Python code to test your solutions in the equations and comment on any roundoff errors.

$$-0.083x_1 - 0.875x_2 + 0.645x_3 + 0.675x_4 = 62.1$$

$$-0.258x_1 - 0.730x_2 + 0.898x_3 - 0.797x_4 = 91.8$$

$$0.262x_1 - 0.467x_2 + 0.251x_3 - 0.127x_4 = 74.9$$

$$0.582x_1 + 0.025x_2 - 0.907x_3 + 0.362x_4 = 130.9$$

8.5　A special matrix called the *Hilbert matrix* is famous for being ill-conditioned. Its form used in the following four equations in four unknowns is

$$\begin{bmatrix} 1 & 1/2 & 1/3 & 1/4 \\ 1/2 & 1/3 & 1/4 & 1/5 \\ 1/3 & 1/4 & 1/5 & 1/6 \\ 1/4 & 1/5 & 1/6 & 1/7 \end{bmatrix} \mathbf{x} = \begin{bmatrix} 2 \\ 9/7 \\ 1 \\ 3/4 \end{bmatrix}$$

(a) Write Python code to compute the determinant of the coefficient matrix. What do you observe?

(b) Write Python code to solve the system of equations using the `inv` function from the NumPy `linalg` module.

(c) Write Python code to solve the system of equations using the `solve` function from the NumPy `linalg` module and compare your results to those from part (b). What do you conclude are the true solutions to these equations?

8.6   A production process for three different electronic components uses three materials: copper, polystyrene, and neoprene. The amounts of these materials required to produce each component are presented in the table below.

Component	Amount Required per Component		
	Copper (g)	Polystyrene (g)	Neoprene (g)
A	15	3	1.2
B	17	4	1.5
C	19	5.5	1.9

If 98.5 kg of copper, 23.6 kg of polystyrene, and 8.77 kg of neoprene are available, how many of each component can be produced? Solve this problem using a Python script. Round your results down to the nearest integer since we are dealing with discrete components.

8.7   Figure P8.7 described a bridge support or truss structure. The equations that determine the truss are horizontal and vertical force balances at the seven nodes. For example, at node 2,

$$h_2 + f_4 + \overline{s}f_3 - \overline{s}f_1 = 0$$

$$v_2 + \overline{c}f_1 + \overline{c}f_3 = 0$$

where h_i: horizontal load applied at node i, positive to the right
v_i: vertical load applied at node i, positive downward
f_j: force in member j, negative for compression, positive for tension
$\overline{s}$: sin 30°
$\overline{c}$: cos 30°

   The unknowns in the above equations are the member forces and the knowns are the loads. Write a Python script that determines the member forces in this truss.

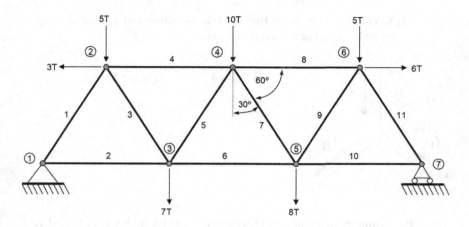

Statically determinate, simply supported, eleven-member, plane truss

FIGURE P8.7   Bridge support truss structure.

8.8   The diagram presented in Figure P8.8 describes an electrical circuit comprised of resistors. You are to develop a Python script that solves for the voltages at nodes 2, 3, 6, and 7, and solves for the currents in all branches of the circuit. The values of the resistances in ohms are given in the table below:

R_{12}	60	R_{13}	60	R_{15}	10
R_{56}	50	R_{57}	50	R_{67}	10
R_{23}	10	R_{24}	50	R_{34}	50
R_{36}	75	R_{68}	60	R_{78}	60
R_{48}	20				

There are two electrical laws that give rise to the equations necessary to solve this circuit.

(1) *Ohm's Law* states that the current through a resistive branch is proportional to the voltage across the branch and inversely proportional to the resistance of the branch. For the diagram below,

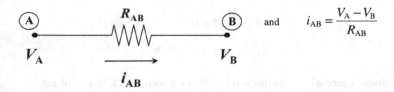

$$i_{AB} = \frac{V_A - V_B}{R_{AB}}$$

(2) *Kirchhoff's Law* states that the sum of currents at a node must be equal to zero. For the diagram below,

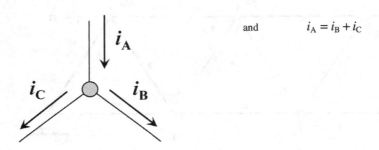

and $i_A = i_B + i_C$

By writing node equations (Kirchhoff's law) for nodes 2, 3, 6, and 7, and substituting Ohm's Law relationships for the currents in the equations, one can develop a set of four linear equations in four unknowns, the voltages at the nodes. These equations are solved; then, with the voltages known, Ohm's Law can be used to compute currents for all 16 branches in the circuit.

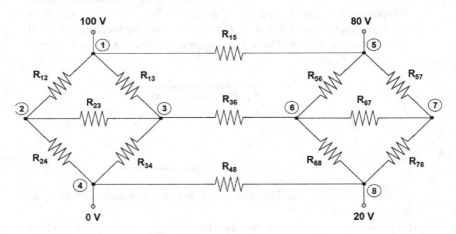

FIGURE P8.8   Electrical circuit comprised of resistors.

8.9   For the following system of nonlinear equations,

$$x_1^2 + 3x_2^2 - 5 = 0$$

$$x_1^2 - x_2 - 1 = 0$$

(a) Employ successive substitution to obtain a solution. Use initial estimates $x_1 = x_2 = 1.5$.

(b) Solve the equations using the multivariable Newton-Raphson method with the same initial estimates.

Use Python scripts to solve this problem.

8.10 Solve the following set of nonlinear equations,

$$x_1^2 - x_1 + x_2 - 0.75 = 0$$

$$x_1^2 - 5x_1x_2 - x_2 = 0$$

(a) using the multivariable Newton-Raphson method, and
(b) using the `root` function from the SciPy `optimize` submodule.
Use a phase plot (x_2 vs. x_1) of the two equations to determine suitable initial estimates.

8.11 Solve the following set of nonlinear equations to determine positive roots.

$$x_1^2 - x_2 + 1 = 0$$

$$2\cos(x_1) - x_2 = 0$$

(a) using successive substitution,
(b) using the multivariable Newton-Raphson method and
(c) using the `root` function from Python's SciPy `optimize` submodule.
Use a phase plot (x_2 vs. x_1) of the two equations to determine suitable initial estimates.

8.12 The following chemical reactions take place in equilibrium at a fixed temperature and pressure.

$$2A + B \rightleftarrows C$$

$$A + D \rightleftarrows C$$

The equilibrium of each reaction is described in terms of concentrations of the reactants and two equilibrium constants, K_1 and K_2.

$$K_1 = \frac{c_c}{c_a^2 c_b} \qquad K_2 = \frac{c_c}{c_a c_d}$$

If x_1 and x_2 represent the number of moles of C that are produced by the first and second reactions, respectively, reformulate the equilibrium relationships based on the initial concentrations of the constituents before equilibrium is established. For example,

$$c_c = c_{c,0} + x_1 \text{ and } c_a = c_{a,0} - 2x_1 - x_2$$

Solve the resulting nonlinear algebraic equations for the following parameter values:

$$K_1 = 4 \times 10^{-4}, K_2 = 3.7 \times 10^{-2}, c_{a,0} = 50, c_{b,0} = 5, c_{c,0} = 0, \text{ and } c_{d,0} = 10.$$

(a) Use the multivariable Newton-Raphson method to solve for x_1 and x_2.
(b) Use the `root` function from the Python SciPy `optimize` submodule to solve the equations and compare to your results from (a).

9 Solving Differential Equations

CHAPTER OBJECTIVES

- Become familiar with the different forms of differential equations encountered by engineers and scientists.
- Be able to recognize differential equations that can be solved numerically by the methods of quadrature (finding the area under the curve).
- Introduce the trapezoidal rule method for solving quadrature problems and the quad function from the SciPy integrate module.
- Understand how to solve a differential equation with the Euler method.
- Appreciate the limitations of the Euler method when it comes to the accuracy of the solution.
- See how the Heun method is an improvement in accuracy over the Euler method.
- Understand how to extend the methods to the solution of multiple differential equations.
- Be able to transform a second-order differential equation into two first-order equations and solve the resulting system.
- See how to use the solve_ivp function from the SciPy integrate module to solve one or several differential equations.

The ability of scientists and engineers to model rates of change is critically important. Equations that describe rates of change are also called differential equations because they involve derivatives. Most engineering and science students take a course in differential equations, typically in their second year, and this course emphasizes analytical solution of these equations. Whereas this is important, many, and perhaps most, differential equations that arise from modeling physical and chemical phenomena cannot be solved by analytical methods, and a numerical approach is required.

As you will learn in this chapter, it is possible to employ elementary numerical methods to solve equations that describe rates of change prior to understanding the analytical aspect of these equations. Eventually, it will be important to learn and appreciate the latter, but that doesn't prevent us from moving forward now.

First, we need to recognize the different forms that differential equations take and how the form will dictate the method we use to solve them. Next, the methods that compute the "area under the curve," called quadrature, will be introduced. We will also see how to solve these problems using the quad function from the SciPy integrate module. When the rate of change of a variable depends on the variable itself, another class of methods is required, and we will introduce the

DOI: 10.1201/9781003256861-9

most elementary of these, the Euler method. By studying the limitations of this method, we will see that improvements are possible and introduce an enhancement, called Heun's method.

The numerical methods we study first are designed for a single differential equation with one first-order derivative. We will extend these methods to systems of multiple differential equations. Also, equations arise in modeling physical and chemical phenomena that have second-order and even higher-order derivatives. Decomposing these equations into a system of first-order equations will be illustrated with a second-order differential equation as the example. Finally, we will demonstrate how to use a built-in Python function, `solve_ivp`, to solve single or multiple differential equations.

9.1 DESCRIBING DIFFERENTIAL EQUATIONS

Differential equations model rates of change; in fact, in some circles they have been called *rate equations*. A simple form of a differential equation is

$$\frac{dy}{dt} = f(y,t) \qquad\qquad y(0) = y_0 \qquad\qquad (9.1)$$

Here, y is a dependent variable, such as position, temperature, pressure, and t is an independent variable, such as time, t, here, or location, x. In the case of time, an initial value of y is required at $t = 0$. In this case, we want to develop a solution in the form of y versus t up to a final $t = t_f$.

When the rate of change of y only depends on time, a simpler version of the above equation is

$$\frac{dy}{dt} = f(t) \qquad\qquad y(0) = y_0 \qquad\qquad (9.2)$$

where $y_0 =$ is the initial value of y. We are interested in the result of the integral form

$$\int_{y_0}^{y} dy = y - y_0 = \int_{0}^{t_f} f(t)\,dt \qquad\qquad (9.3)$$

The integral result corresponds to finding the area under the $f(t)$ curve, a procedure called *quadrature*. A variation of this scenario is given by

$$\frac{dy}{dt} = y f(t) \qquad\qquad y(0) = y_0 \qquad\qquad (9.4)$$

This equation, called *separable*, can be reformulated as

$$\int_{y_0}^{y} \frac{dy}{y} = \ln\left(\frac{y}{y_0}\right) = \int_{0}^{t_f} f(t)\,dt \tag{9.5}$$

The right side of this equation still conforms to finding the area under the $f(t)$ curve from 0 to t_f.

Another common scenario is where the rate of change is influenced by another variable, called an input or *forcing variable*, w. This would be described as

$$\frac{dy}{dt} = f(y,w,t) \qquad\qquad y(0) = y_0 \qquad\qquad w = g(t) \tag{9.6}$$

The two differential equation forms in Equations 9.1 and 9.6 can be pictured in *block diagrams*. See Figure 9.1. The diagrams introduce the concept of solving the differential equations using an integration method. Since the solution requires y_0 to "get off the ground," these scenarios are called *initial value problems* (IVPs). We will see in this chapter how the solver takes the derivative at a given time, t, and computes an approximate value of y at $t + \Delta t$. This process is repeated until a desired final time, t_f.

Through developing mathematical models of many physical and chemical systems, we also encounter *second derivatives*. A common example is Newton's Second Law: $F = ma$, which describes the acceleration, a, of an object of mass, m, when subjected to a force, F. For one dimensional motion, acceleration can

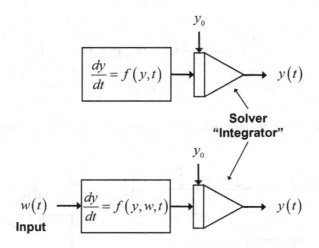

FIGURE 9.1 Initial value differential equations without and with an input variable.[1]

---

[1] The triangular "integrator" symbol is one that has been used for decades in analog electronics based on operational amplifiers.

be represented as the second derivative of position ($a = d^2x/dt^2$). Therefore, the Second Law can be expressed as a differential equation:

$$m\frac{d^2x}{dt^2} = F \tag{9.7}$$

This relationship can be combined with models for spring force (Hooke's Law) and friction to produce the differential equation for the shock absorber system shown in Figure 9.2. The motion of the mass, m, is governed by its own inertia, the second derivative term, a frictional force proportional to the velocity ($v = dx/dt$) described by the coefficient, b, and the forces provided by the two springs proportional to their displacement from their rest positions (*Hooke's Law*).

A block diagram for this system (Figure 9.3) illustrates that it is necessary to integrate twice, once to get the velocity from the acceleration, and a second time to obtain the position from the velocity. It also shows that two initial conditions are required and denotes the constant parameter values that must be supplied. This is called an *information flow diagram*, and it is helpful in organizing and visualizing differential equation models, especially those that are more complex.

A common misconception that arises from studying the diagram is that the velocity and position are required to obtain the acceleration, but the acceleration

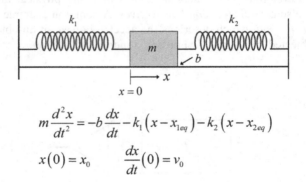

$$m\frac{d^2x}{dt^2} = -b\frac{dx}{dt} - k_1\left(x - x_{1eq}\right) - k_2\left(x - x_{2eq}\right)$$

$$x(0) = x_0 \qquad \frac{dx}{dt}(0) = v_0$$

FIGURE 9.2   Shock absorber system with second-order differential equation model.

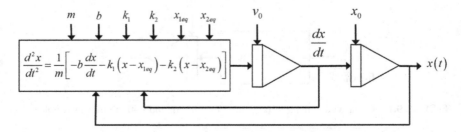

FIGURE 9.3   Block diagram of differential equation model for a shock absorber.

is required to obtain the velocity and then the position. However, this is *not* the case here. This is because the nature of solving the differential equation is to approximate the solution at time $t + \Delta t$ from values of x and dx/dt at time t. Described in a different way, the system is not implicit as long as the information flow passes through an integrator.

You will also note that, in effect, we have broken down the second-order differential equation into two first-order integrations with an intermediate variable, the velocity (dx/dt). We will discuss this further in Section 9.3.3. Also, because our original equation includes a second derivative, we require two initial conditions.

Many problem contexts evolve mathematical models with more than one differential equation. An example would be the following two equations:

$$\frac{dx_1}{dt} = -2x_1^2 + 2x_1 + x_2 - 1 \quad x_1(0) = 2$$

$$\frac{dx_2}{dt} = -x_1 - 3x_2^2 + 2x_2 + 2 \quad x_2(0) = 0 \qquad 0 \le t \le 2 \qquad (9.8)$$

As before, these equations can be depicted in a block diagram. See Figure 9.4. It is easy to see that the two equations are interdependent. In other words, they are coupled – we must solve them simultaneously.

Equations that involve only one independent variable are called *ordinary differential equations* (ODEs). Although we do not consider them here, it is worth mentioning differential equations that involve more than one independent variable, which are called *partial differential equations* (PDEs). You will likely encounter these later in your engineering or science education, and should you take a course in numerical methods, their solution will be a topic covered. In the coming sections of this chapter, we will consider numerical solutions of the ordinary differential equations discussed to this point.

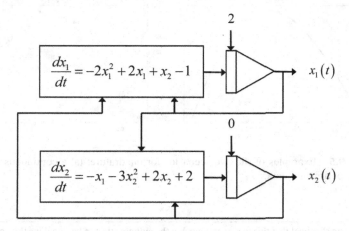

FIGURE 9.4 Information flow diagram for two coupled differential equations.

9.2 QUADRATURE – FINDING THE AREA UNDER THE CURVE

There are two common scenarios that present the situation described by Equations 9.2 and 9.3. The first is when $f(t)$ is an analytical expression. In this case, values of $f(t)$ are available at any value of t. The second is where $f(t)$ is represented by experimental data taken at n discrete values of t; that is, $\{f(t_i), i = 1, \ldots, n\}$. Figure 9.5 illustrates examples of these two scenarios. When experimental data are involved, they may contain random error, which is evident in the (b) plot. The fact that the experimental data are only available at given values of the independent variable makes the quadrature task more difficult. We will consider both in this section.

9.2.1 PRE-COMPUTER METHODS

Historically, before the advent of computer methods, calculating the areas under curves or within closed boundaries was a common activity. There were several curious methods used.

1. *Counting the squares method.* Here, we count the squares that are completely below the curve (Figure 9.5a). Then, we count the squares that are below and at least partially above the curve. Finally, we take the average of the two and apply the dimensions of the squares to produce an estimate of the area. For Figure 9.5a, the result is $(21 + 34)/2 \times (0.2 \times 0.1) = 0.55$.
2. *Weighing the curve method.* In this method, with the curve plotted on paper, we carefully cut out the area under the curve in Figure 9.5a. Then, we cut out a known rectangular area. Both are weighed on an analytical balance, and, using the rectangle's weight as a calibration standard, the area under the curve is computed.[2]

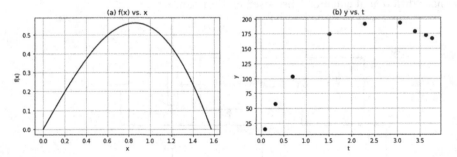

FIGURE 9.5 Examples of the two scenarios for quadrature: (a) a continuous function and (b) experimental data.

---

[2] You may be skeptical that this was ever done, but the authors attest to having done this to compute areas under the peaks produced by a gas chromatograph in the 1960s!

3. *Cartographer's planimeter method.* This curious device is shown in Figure 9.6. One traces carefully around a closed curve in a clockwise direction, and the dial on the planimeter arm shows the area. Then, the procedure is repeated but in the counterclockwise direction. The two results are then averaged. Since the planimeter returns the result as a dimensional area (e.g. cm²), a calibration rectangle is required here too. The planimeter has been in use since 1854 and is still employed today. Its common application is finding irregular areas on maps (also becoming obsolete because of geographical information systems and supporting software), but it can be used to find areas under curves as well.

The first computer-based method we introduce is akin to the "counting the squares" method above. Figure 9.7 illustrates two versions of this method. For the continuous, $f(t)$, scenario, it is based on discretizing the function. This is usually done by choosing a single Δt value for the entire t domain; however, it is possible to choose different Δt's based on the extent of the curvature. This method is called *rectangular integration* or rectangular quadrature.

As the figure illustrates, the two methods either underestimate or overestimate the area depending on whether the curve is ascending or descending. Hence, the two estimates could be implemented and averaged to obtain a superior estimate.

You can also see that, as we decrease Δt, the error of the area estimate will decrease. Since we have an analytical function, it is feasible to adjust the interval in this fashion. With experimental data (Figure 9.5b), we do not have that luxury.

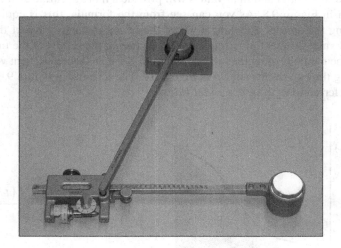

FIGURE 9.6 Polar planimeter.[3] (From Polar planimeter 01—Planimeter. https://en.wikipedia.org/wiki/Planimeter. (Last edited date June 18, 2022).)

---

[3] The authors also used this device in the past. The geometry associated with the design of this device is interesting, worth some extra reading if you're interested. Also, you may be able to find a planimeter among the surveying equipment in your civil engineering program.

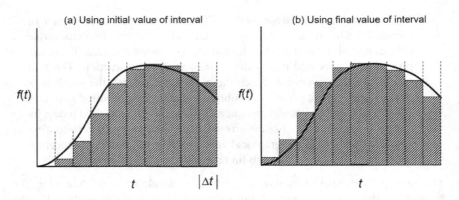

FIGURE 9.7 Rectangular quadrature using (a) the initial value or (b) the final value of the interval.

A logical step would be to take the average of the two area estimates shown in Figure 9.7. That leads us to the most common, elementary quadrature method, *trapezoidal rule*.

9.2.2 QUADRATURE FOR CONTINUOUS FUNCTIONS

Rather than choosing the initial or final value of the interval and computing the area of the rectangle below that point, computing the area of a trapezoid with vertices at the initial and final values will provide a more accurate estimate. This is shown in Figure 9.8. As you can see from the formula, this is equivalent to computing the area of a rectangle where the height is the average of the initial and final values. In fact, it is equivalent to averaging the results of the initial and final value methods of rectangular quadrature! So, it is a more efficient version of averaging the two results shown in Figure 9.7. The formula in Figure 9.8 is commonly referred to as the *trapezoidal rule*.

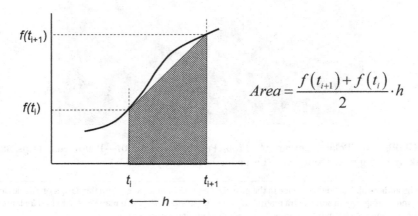

$$Area = \frac{f\left(t_{i+1}\right)+f\left(t_{i}\right)}{2}\cdot h$$

FIGURE 9.8 Computing the trapezoidal area for two points on the curve.

Given the scheme and formula in Figure 9.8, we can develop a simple Python function, `trap1`, to implement the method across a domain, $a \le t \le b$, divided into n equal intervals. This function is shown in Figure 9.9. We can apply this function to compute the integral

$$y = \int_0^{\pi/2} t\cos(t)\,dt \tag{9.9}$$

This is the area under the curve shown in Figure 9.5a. Here is the outcome of applying `trap1` to this equation,

```
import numpy as np
def f(t):
return t*np.cos(t)
y = trap1(f, 0., np.pi/2)
print(y)
0.5705516230802059
```

In one sense, this isn't a particularly good example because the integral can be derived analytically using integration by parts to be

$$\int_a^b t\cos(t) = \cos(b) + b\sin(b) - \cos(a) - a\sin(a) \tag{9.10}$$

For $a = 0$ and $b = \pi/2$, this evaluates to 0.5707963267948966. An advantage here is that we can use the analytically based result to verify and evaluate the trapezoidal rule result. The percentage error is 0.04%. If we used a higher value for n, the error would be less; however, we cannot do that without a limitation on how small we can make the size of h as the precision of calculations and round-off error would intervene. We will explore this thought in the end-of-chapter Problem 9.14.

The `trap1` function is very compact, only nine statements. However, it is not the most efficient way to code trapezoidal rule. If we consider the repeated use of the formula in Figure 9.8, this can be represented as

```
def trap1(f,a,b,n=100):
    x = a  # set x = to left side
    h = (b-a)/n  # compute interval
    sm = 0  # set integral sum to zero
    for i in range(n-1):  # for loop to sum the areas
        ar = (f(x)+f(x+h))/2*h  # area of the current interval
        sm = sm + ar  # add to the sum of areas
        x = x + h  # advance x to the next interval
    return sm  # return the total area
```

FIGURE 9.9 Python function `trap1` for trapezoidal rule quadrature.

$$\frac{f(a)+f(a+h)}{2}h+\frac{f(a+h)+f(a+2h)}{2}h+\cdots$$

$$+\frac{f(b-2h)+f(b-h)}{2}h+\frac{f(b-h)+f(b)}{2}h$$

(9.11)

where h is the interval width.

There are two features of Equation 9.11 that bear mention. First, each term is multiplied by h and divided by 2, and we can factor these out and apply them only once. Second, all the f terms enter twice, except the first and last term. This allows us to simplify the repeated application of trapezoidal rule to the formula

$$\left(f(a)+2f(a+\Delta t)+2f(a+2\Delta t)+\cdots+2f(b-2\Delta t)+2f(b-\Delta t)+f(b)\right)\frac{h}{2}$$ (9.12)

perhaps a better representation consistent with the code would be:

$$\left(f(a)+2f(a+\Delta t)+2f(a+2\Delta t)+\cdots+2f(a+(n-1)\Delta t)+f(b)\right)\frac{h}{2}$$

and we can modify our trap1 function to make it more efficient. See the new trap function in Figure 9.10.

If we evaluate this new function with similar code to that for the trap1 test, the result is

```
0.5707434665276926
```

and the error when compared to the analytical result is 0.009%, somewhat better than the previous result.

There is an important general lesson here. We often develop Python scripts and functions to accomplish given numerical tasks. The first time through, we should consider these as prototypes, and later, seek ways to improve them in their efficiency, compactness, and clarity.

```
def trap(f,a,b,n=100):
    x = a  # set x to left side a
    h = (b-a)/n  # compute interval width
    sm = f(a)  # first term of sum
    for i in range(n-1):
        x = x + h  # advance x
        sm = sm + 2*f(x)  # add 2 * f(x) to sum
    sm = sm + f(b)  # add last term to sum
    ar = sm*h/2  # complete integral formula
    return ar
```

FIGURE 9.10 Modified trapezoidal rule function trap.

Example 9.1 Computing Probability for the Gaussian Distribution

In the previous section of this chapter, we numerically integrated a function that could also be integrated analytically. This raises the obvious question whether the numerical quadrature methods should even be considered. Well, for one thing, there are many scenarios where the function, $f(t)$, doesn't have an analytical form for its integral. And, in other cases, the integral may be very difficult to derive analytically. These are where quadrature methods are of great value.

The density function for the *normal, Gaussian distribution* defines the well-known bell-shaped curve. This function takes two common forms:

$$f(x) = \frac{1}{\sigma\sqrt{2\pi}} e^{-\frac{1}{2}\left(\frac{x-\mu}{\sigma}\right)^2} \tag{9.13}$$

where x is a random variable, μ is the mean value of x, and σ is the standard deviation of x. We will discuss these variables in more detail in the next chapter.

The second form, called the *standard normal density*, is

$$f(z) = \frac{1}{\sqrt{2\pi}} e^{-\frac{1}{2}z^2} \tag{9.14a}$$

where

$$z \triangleq \frac{x - \mu}{\sigma} \tag{9.14b}$$

The standard normal variable, z, has a mean of zero and a standard deviation of one. Figure 9.11 depicts the standard density function and its relation to the

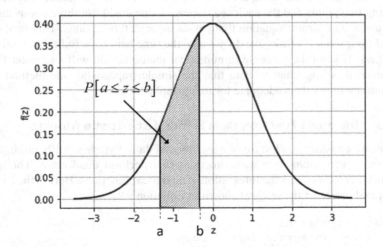

FIGURE 9.11   Standard normal density function with probability of $a \leq z \leq b$ shown.

probability of z falling between two limits, a and b. This can be represented with the following equations:

$$\frac{dP}{dz} = f(z) \qquad P[a \le z \le b] = \int_a^b f(z)dz \qquad (9.15)$$

Consequently, to compute the probability of the random variable z falling between a and b, an integral is required. In this case, there is no analytical solution to the integral, and quadrature is required.

We can employ our `trap` function to compute the probability for the standard normal distribution for the case displayed in Figure 9.11. Here is the Python script and the result displayed in the Console:

```
import numpy as np
stdnormdens = lambda z: 1/np.sqrt(2*np.pi)*np.exp(-1/2*z**2)
a = -1.3
b = -0.3
P = trap(stdnormdens, a, b)
print('probability = {0:6.1f}%'.format(P*100))
probability = 28.5%
```

With minor modifications, we could perform the same computation for the normal distribution shown in Equation 9.13. Given the use of the default 100 intervals, we can be assured of an accurate result.

Historically, values for the quadrature of the standard normal density have appeared in tables in common references and statistics textbooks. Today, many computer software packages, especially those dedicated to applied statistics, compute these values with built-in functions. Python has built-in functions for statistical distributions in the SciPy `stats` submodule.

It is worth mention that there are other methods available for quadrature. Instead of using two points and the enclosed trapezoid, one could use three points and an area under a quadratic equation that passes through those points. That method is called Simpson's 1/3 Rule. We do not take the time here to introduce that method or others. If you take a course in numerical methods, you will encounter these. However, it is important to note that the simple trapezoidal rule method with appropriate intervals is adequate for many applications.

9.2.3   THE quad FUNCTION FROM SciPy's integrate MODULE

Before we consider quadrature of experimental data, Python's SciPy module has an `integrate` submodule with functions that perform quadrature. The `quad` function accommodates the integration of analytical functions. Here is the Python script and result for the integral shown in Equation 9.9.

```
import numpy as np
from scipy.integrate import quad
f = lambda t: t*np.cos(t)
```

```
a = 0
b = np.pi/2
y, ey = quad(f, a, b)
print(y)
0.5707963267948966
```

The result here is indistinguishable from the analytical solution result. An advanced method is used by the quad function. You can read more about the function in the SciPy User Guide (https://docs.scipy.org/doc/scipy/tutorial/index.html) as well as numerical methods texts such as Chapra and Clough (2022).

9.2.4 QUADRATURE FOR DISCRETE DATA

The second scenario for quadrature is when, rather than an analytical function, $f(t)$, we have a set of experimental data, $\{y_i, x_i, i = 1, n\}$, as illustrated in Figure 9.5b. As in the figure, it is common that the data are not measured at a constant interval. This requires a modification of the formula in Figure 9.8:

$$Area = \frac{f(t_{i+1}) + f(t_i)}{2}(t_{i+1} - t_i) \qquad (9.16)$$

Following this change, we can modify the trap function to create a trapdata function as shown in Figure 9.12. We can write a Python script to estimate the quadrature of the data that produced Figure 9.5b.

```
import numpy as np
t = np.array([0.09,0.32,0.69,1.51,2.29,3.06,3.39,3.63,3.77])
y = np.array([15.1,57.3,103.3,174.6,191.5,193.2,178.7,172.3,
167.5])
A = trapdata(t, y)
print(A)
570.134
```

There is also a function, trapz, in the SciPy integrate submodule that performs the same task as our trapdata function. Here is a Python script to duplicate the above calculations and result.

```
import numpy as np
```

```
def trapdata(t,y):
    n = len(t)
    sm = 0
    for i in range(n-1):
        ar = (y[i]+y[i+1])/2*(t[i+1]-t[i])
        sm = sm + ar
    return sm
```

FIGURE 9.12 Function for trapezoidal rule method with experimental data.

```
from scipy.integrate import trapz
t = np.array([0.09,0.32,0.69,1.51,2.29,3.06,3.39,3.63,3.77])
y = np.array([15.1,57.3,103.3,174.6,191.5,193.2,178.7,172.3,
167.5])
A = trapz(y, t)
print(A)
570.134
```

You can see that the result is the same.

An alternate approach for quadrature of data is to estimate or "fit" an analytical model to the data. Although we won't go into the process for doing that in this chapter, assume that the following model has been proposed to fit the data above.

$$y = 4.351t^3 - 53.88t^2 + 185.6t + 0.559$$

If we add this curve to the plot from Figure 9.5b, the result is shown in Figure 9.13.

Given the model and observing that it fits the data well, we can use our trap function to implement the quadrature. Here is the Python script and the result.

```
import numpy as np
A = trap(f, 0.09,3.77)
print(A)
def f(t):
return 4.351*t**3-53.88*t**2 + 185.6*t + 0.559
577.640263867974
```

The result is close to the previous one, differing by 1.3%.

We will now leave the topic of quadrature and proceed to differential equations that are not separable.

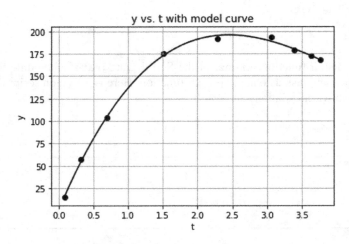

FIGURE 9.13   Experimental data with model curve.

9.3 SOLVING DIFFERENTIAL EQUATIONS WITH INITIAL CONDITIONS

The general form of the differential equation, as represented in Equation 9.1, repeated here, is

$$\frac{dy}{dt} = f(y,t) \qquad\qquad y(0) = y_0 \qquad\qquad (9.1)$$

This formulation includes terms in the dependent variable, y, on the right side of the equation in $f(y, t)$. The quadrature methods of the previous section no longer apply. This opens the door to a wide variety of methods that have been developed. Although many are sophisticated, simpler methods can suffice for a considerable number of problems in engineering and science. We will focus on two of those methods here.

9.3.1 EULER'S METHOD[4]

Equation 9.1 describes an initial value problem. We know the conditions at an initial value of the independent variable, here denoted as zero. We would like to develop the solution for the dependent variable, y, out to a given independent variable value, t_f.

To motivate our first method, we consider what we know at $t = 0$. This is depicted in Figure 9.14. We see that we can locate the solution at $t = 0$, and, by applying the differential equation, we know the initial direction of the solution given by $f(0, y_0)$. We would assume that, as the solution departs from the initial condition, the derivative value (and slope of the solution) is likely to change. However, if that departure is a small interval, Δt, the projection of the straight line

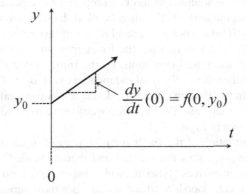

FIGURE 9.14 Information on solution at $t = 0$.

---

[4] The method is named after Leonhard Euler (1707–1783), a Swiss mathematician, physicist, astronomer, geographer, logician, and engineer. He founded graph theory and topology as well as making seminal discoveries in analytic number theory, complex analysis, and infinitesimal calculus. He is considered one of the greatest mathematicians in history and the greatest of the 18th century.

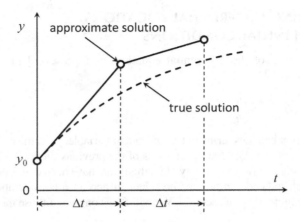

FIGURE 9.15 First two steps of the Euler method.

from $t = 0$ to Δt will be close to the true solution. This is the basis for the *Euler method*. That first solution step is represented as

$$y(t_0 + \Delta t) \cong y(t_0) + \frac{dy}{dt}(t_0, y_0)\Delta t \tag{9.17}$$

After the first step to approximate the solution, it is natural to consider extending the method with a second step and beyond. This is illustrated in Figure 9.15. What we notice is that the approximate solution departs from the true solution after the first step, and this departure continues after the second step. Imagine taking smaller steps; say, 10 steps for each single step shown in the figure. You can recognize that the true solution would be computed more accurately. That is the essence of the Euler method. On the other hand, if the step size taken is too small, the computation will take much longer and round-off errors could come into play.

To develop a Python function for the Euler method, we will need to supply the function $f(t, y)$, the initial condition, y_0, the initial value of the independent variable value, t_0 (often zero), the final independent variable value, t_f, and the step size, Δt, called h in the Python code. One detail is that the final step to take us to t_f may not be h, in which case, the final step would have to be adjusted. This function, `euler`, is shown in Figure 9.16.

In this implementation of the Euler method, instead of creating arrays for the $\{t, y\}$ solutions, empty arrays are created and then expanded using the `append` method as the solution evolves.[5] Also, instead of using a `for` loop with a given number of iterations, a `while` loop is used and exited when the computation is complete.

To evaluate the `euler` function, we will use a differential equation that has an analytical solution, as we did previously with the trapezoidal rule method. This is the equation:

---

[5] The use of the *append method* is shown here as an illustration, an alternative to creating arrays of given dimensions using the `zeros` function. Either approach is acceptable, and we illustrate both.

```
def euler(f,y0,t0,tf,h):
    t = []    # start with empty arrays for t and y
    t.append(t0)    # assign initial conditions to
    y = []          # the first elements of t and y
    y.append(y0)
    i = 0
    while True:
        i = i + 1
        t.append(t[i-1]+h)    # step t ahead by h
        if t[i] > tf:    # check whether tf is exceeded
            t[i] = tf    # if so, set t[i] equal to tf
            h = t[i]-t[i-1]    # and adjust h
        y.append(y[i-1] + f(t[i-1],y[i-1])*h)    # Euler step
        if t[i] >= tf: break    # out of while loop when done
    return t,y
```

FIGURE 9.16 Function `euler` to implement the Euler method for one differential equation.

$$\frac{dy}{dt} = -0.05y + 2 \quad y(0) = 0 \tag{9.18}$$

and the analytical solution is

$$y = 40\left(1 - e^{-0.05t}\right) \tag{9.19}$$

For parameter values, $t_f = 80$ and $h = 10$, the Python script below computes the approximate solution using the `euler` function and compares it to the analytical solution. A plot is generated and presented in Figure 9.17 that shows both results.

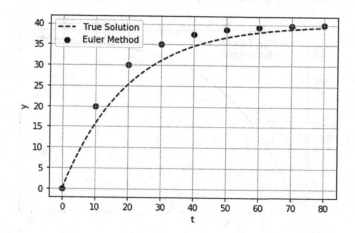

FIGURE 9.17 Euler method solution of differential equation compared to analytical solution for $h = 10$.

```
import numpy as np
import matplotlib.pyplot as plt
def f(t, y):
dy = -0.05 * y + 2.
return dy
t0 = 0
tf = 80.
y0 = 0.
h = 10.
t, y = euler(f, y0,t0,tf, h)
def fa(t):
return 40*(1-np.exp(-0.05*t))
ta = np.linspace(t0,tf)
plt.scatter(t, y, c='k', marker='o', label='Euler Method')
plt.plot(ta, fa(ta), c='k', ls='--', label='True Solution')
plt.grid()
plt.xlabel('t')
plt.ylabel('y')
plt.legend()
```

It is clear that the Euler method approximate solution overshoots the true solution. If we change the *h* value to 0.1, the result is shown in Figure 9.18. As far as we can detect on the plot, the Euler method solution and the analytical solution are identical (at least visually).

A question that arises is, when we have a differential equation that has no analytical solution, how do we determine a step size, *h* value, which provides an accurate solution. A common technique is to solve the equation several times with reducing values of *h* until the solution doesn't change significantly. And as will be discussed in Section 9.4, advanced differential equation solvers employ clever adaptive techniques to determine step size.

FIGURE 9.18   Euler method with $h = 0.1$ provides an accurate solution.

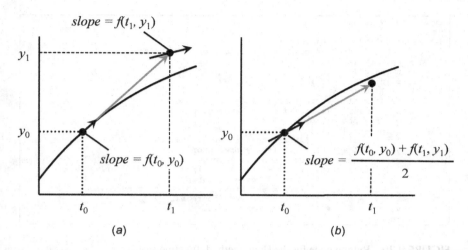

FIGURE 9.19   Basis for the Heun method. The solid black curve is the analytical solution to provide context for assessing the accuracy of the Heun method. (a) Predictor step. (b) Iterative corrector step

9.3.2   Heun's Method

As you might suspect, improvements to the Euler method address the error of the method, noting that the error tends to increase as the solution proceeds. We will introduce one of these improved methods, called the *Heun method,* here. You will likely encounter additional methods later in your studies, such as the Runge-Kutta methods.

The Heun method is based on the insight that a fundamental source of error in Euler's method is that the derivative at the beginning of the interval is assumed to apply across the entire interval. The Heun method addresses this shortcoming as illustrated in Figure 9.19. The standard Euler method is used to predict to estimate the solution at the end of the first step, y_1^1. Then, the derivative (or slope) at t_1 is computed as $f(t_1,y_1^1)$. The derivative for the original step is then corrected by averaging the two slopes, $f(0,y_0)$ and $f(t_1,y_1^1)$. This average slope is then used to predict y_1^2. The second step can be iterated until the prediction converges. This type of approach is generally called a *predictor-corrector method.*

The first step is represented by the following formulas:

$$\text{prediction step: } y_1^1 = y_0 + f\left(t_0,y_0\right)\Delta t$$

$$\overline{f}^1 = \frac{f\left(t_0,y_0\right)+f\left(t_1,y_1^1\right)}{2} \tag{9.20}$$

$$\text{corrector step: } y_1^2 = y_0 + \overline{f}^1\,\Delta t$$

```
import numpy as np

def heun(f,y0,t0,tf,h,ea=1.e-7):
    n = int((tf-t0)/h) # compute the number of intervals
    t = np.zeros(n)    # create empty arrays for t and y
    y = np.zeros(n)
    for i in range(n):  # fill the t array
        t[i] = i*h
    if t[n-1] < tf:  # check if an interval left over
        t = np.append(t,tf)  # if so, augment t and y
        y = np.append(y,0)
    for i in range(n):
        h = t[i+1]-t[i]  # h for this interval (may change at end)
        y1 = y[i] + f(t[i],y[i])*h  # predictor step
        while True:  # enter iterative loop
            fbar = (f(t[i],y[i])+f(t[i+1],y1))/2  # average deriv
            y2 = y[i] + fbar*h  # corrector step
            if abs((y1-y2)/y2) < ea: break  # check for convergence
            y1 = y2  # not converged yet, so repeat
        y[i+1] = y2  # converged, set y value
    return t,y
```

FIGURE 9.20 Python code for the Heun method, function heun.

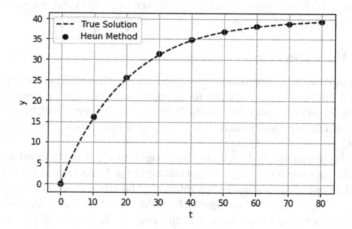

FIGURE 9.21 Heun method solution of differential equation compared to analytical solution for $h = 10$.

Steps repeated until $\left| \dfrac{y_1^i - y_1^{i-1}}{y_1^i} \right| < \varepsilon_a$

After convergence, the method moves on to the next step, from t_1 to t_2.

We can modify the euler function to incorporate the Heun method. The Python code for the heun function is shown in Figure 9.20. In this case, we incorporate a while loop to provide convergence of the scheme shown in Equations 9.20.

We can evaluate the Heun method with the same example as shown in Figure 9.17. The results are surprising and are illustrated in Figure 9.21. The numerical Heun solution for a step size, $h = 10$, follows the analytical solution closely and performs much better than the Euler method. In fact, the Heun method performs similarly to the Euler method with a step size 100 times smaller.

9.3.3 SYSTEMS OF DIFFERENTIAL EQUATIONS

Next, we consider the related scenario where there are multiple differential equations that must be solved simultaneously. Equations 9.8 with Figure 9.4, introduced earlier, provide an example.

$$\frac{dx_1}{dt} = -2x_1^2 + 2x_1 + x_2 - 1 \quad x_1(0) = 2$$

$$\frac{dx_2}{dt} = -x_1 - 3x_2^2 + 2x_2 + 2 \quad x_2(0) = 0$$

(9.8)

We can extend the previous Euler and Heun methods, as Python functions `euler` and `heun`, to accommodate multiple equations. The function `eulerm def` statement for the Euler method would be

```
def eulerm(f,y0,t0,tf,h):
```

This appears to be the same as for the `euler` function, but the difference is that the `f` function argument now returns an array of more than one derivative, and the `y0` initial condition is also an array of initial values for the y dependent variables. The modified function is shown in Figure 9.22. The solution arrays, `t` and `y`, are created with the `zeros` function, and the initial values, `y0`, are assigned to the first row of the `y` array. The `for` loop carries out the solution in the same way as the `euler` function. Note the use of the `:` index to include the dependent variable values, `y`, of all the equations.

The following Python script solves the differential equations (Equation 9.8) with `tf = 2` and creates the plot depicted in Figure 9.23. You will note that the step size, $h = 0.01$, is fairly small, yielding 200 intervals to obtain a smooth, accurate solution. The accuracy of the result could be checked by solving the equations with a smaller `h` and comparing the solutions.

```
def eulerm(f,y0,t0,tf,h):
    n = len(y0)  # number of equations
    m = int((tf-t0)/h)+1  # number of intervals
    t = np.zeros(m)  # empty t array
    y = np.zeros((m,n))  # empty two-dimensional y array
    y[0,:] = y0  # initial conditions assigned to y array
    for i in range(1,m):  # loop to step through solution
        t[i] = t0 + i*h  # t at end of current interval
        if t[i] > tf:  # check whether tf is exceeded
            t[i] = tf  # if so, set t[i] equal to tf
            h = t[i]-t[i-1]  # and adjust h
        y[i] = y[i-1,:] + f(t[i-1],y[i-1,:])*h  # Euler step
        if t[i] >= tf: break  # out of while loop when done
    return t,y
```

FIGURE 9.22 Euler method for multiple equations: `eulerm`

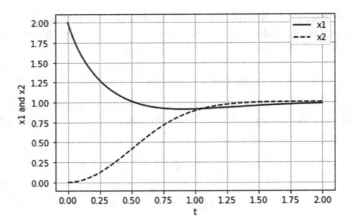

FIGURE 9.23   Solution of two coupled differential equations.

```
import numpy as np
import matplotlib.pyplot as plt
def f(t, y):
dy = np.zeros(2)
dy[0] = -2*y[0]**2 + 2*y[0] + y[1] -1
dy[1] = -y[0] -3*y[1]**2 +2*y[1] + 2
return dy
t0 = 0
tf = 2.
y0 = np.array([2., 0.])
h = 0.01
t, y = eulerm(f, y0,t0,tf, h)
plt.plot(t, y[:, 0], c='k', label='x1')
plt.plot(t, y[:, 1], c='k', ls='--', label='x2')
plt.grid()
plt.xlabel('t')
plt.ylabel('x1 and x2')
plt.legend()
```

Similar modifications could be made to the heun function. In general, it would be advantageous to have functions for any other, more advanced methods be designed to manage multiple differential equations.

Consider now the shock absorber model described in Figure 9.2. Here, we have a single differential equation, called second order because it includes a second derivative. The information flow diagram suggests how we might solve this equation with two "integrators," or, if you prefer, as two first-order equations:

$$\frac{dv}{dt} = \frac{1}{m}\left[-b\frac{dx}{dt} - k_1\left(x - x_{1eq}\right) - k_2\left(x - x_{2eq}\right)\right] \qquad v(0) = v_0$$

$$\frac{dx}{dt} = v \qquad\qquad\qquad\qquad\qquad\qquad x(0) = x_0$$

(9.9)

In general, we can always decompose an equation with derivatives up to nth order into n first-order differential equations. Now that we have two first-order equations, we can solve these with an extension of the Euler or Heun methods, such as our `eulerm` function. A Python script to accomplish this is shown below. The equilibrium values, `x1eq` and `x2eq`, are set to zero, indicating that the two springs would be relaxed at $x = 0$. The initial value of x is set equal to 1, indicating that the mass is pushed one meter to the right at $t = 0$.

```
g = 9.801 # m/s2
m = 10. # kg
b = 5. # N/[m s] or kg/s
k1 = 1. # N/m or kg/s2
k2 = 1.
x1eq = 0.
x2eq = 0.
v0 = 0. # m/s
x0 = 1. # m
def f(t, y):
v = y[0]
x = y[1]
dy = np.zeros(2)
dy[0] = 1/m * (-b*v - k1*(x-x1eq)) - k2*(x-x2eq)
dy[1] = v
return dy
t0 = 0
tf = 20. # seconds
y0 = np.array([v0, x0])
h = 0.01 # seconds
t, y = eulerm(f, y0,t0,tf, h)
plt.plot(t, y[:, 1], c='k', label='displacement - m')
plt.plot(t, y[:, 0], c='k', ls='--', label='velocity - m/s')
plt.grid()
plt.xlabel('time - s')
```

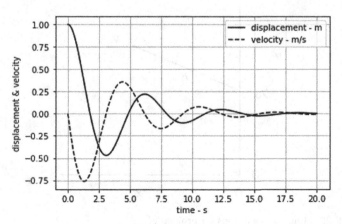

FIGURE 9.24 Simulation of shock absorber.

```
plt.ylabel('displacement & velocity')
plt.legend()
```

The plot produced by the script is shown in Figure 9.24. You can see that the shock absorber system oscillates, the oscillations dampen out in 20 seconds. By paying attention to more realistic parameter values, we could evaluate and make design changes to a given shock absorber to obtain the desired performance. We would also want the model to include an external force that causes the shock absorber to deflect, and this force might change with time, such as one would find driving a vehicle over an uneven surface, like a dirt road with washboard ripples.

Example 9.2 Trajectory of a Projectile with Air Resistance

In the case study in Section 7.9, we modeled the trajectory of a projectile with the equation

$$y = \tan(\theta)x - \frac{g}{2 v_0^2 \cos^2(\theta)} x^2 + y_0 \qquad (7.25)$$

where y = elevation, x = horizontal displacement or range, θ = launch angle, g = gravitational acceleration, v_0 = launch velocity, and y_0 = initial elevation. We mentioned that this model is compromised because it leaves out important features, such as air resistance.

If we modify the model to include air resistance, it results in four differential equations for the range, x, and elevation, y, and their components of the velocity, v_x and v_y. The terms involving the parameter c_d, a *dimensional drag coefficient* (kg/m), model the frictional drag force that retards the motion. That drag force is in the opposite direction of the velocity, v, and proportional to the velocity squared. The terms in the equations correspond to the components

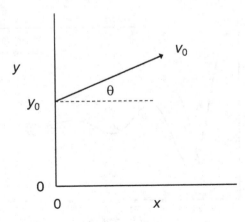

FIGURE 9.25 Launch conditions for projectile.

of that force in the x and y directions. Figure 9.25 depicts the initial launch of the projectile.

$$\frac{dx}{dt} = v_x \qquad\qquad x(0) = x_0$$

$$\frac{dy}{dt} = v_y \qquad\qquad y(0) = y_0 \qquad\qquad (9.10)$$

$$m\frac{dv_x}{dt} = -c_d \frac{v_x}{2}\sqrt{v_x^2 + v_y^2} \qquad\qquad v_x(0) = v_{x0} = v_0 \cos(\theta)$$

$$m\frac{dv_y}{dt} = -mg - c_d \frac{v_y}{2}\sqrt{v_x^2 + v_y^2} \qquad\qquad v_y(0) = v_{y0} = v_0 \sin(\theta)$$

We propose to study the trajectory of a golf ball, $m = 46\,g$. The launch velocity, v_0, is 240 km/hour (or 67 m/s) and the launch angle, θ, is 9°.[6] The location of the launch is an elevated tee box at 10 m above ground level, $y = 0$.

The dimensional drag coefficient, c_d, is related to a *dimensionless drag coefficient*, C_d, by the formula

$$c_d = \rho A C_d \qquad\qquad (9.10)$$

where ρ: the fluid density, here for air at 30°C, 60% relative humidity, and sea-level atmospheric pressure $\cong 1.2\,kg/m^3$,
A: the cross-sectional area of the golf ball, $\cong 1.43 \times 10^{-3}\,m^2$, and
C_d: in the range of 0.3–0.7 for golf balls, $\cong 0.5$, a mid-range value.
For these values, $c_d \cong 4.3 \times 10^{-4}\,kg/m$.

We can use the `eulerm` function, the above equations, and parameter values to create a Python script to simulate the flight of the golf ball with and without air drag. Here is the script:

```
g = 9.801   # m/s2
m = 46/1000 # kg
cd = 4.3e-4   # kg/m

def f(t,yy):
    vx = yy[2]
    vy = yy[3]
    dy = np.zeros(4)
    dy[0] = vx
    dy[1] = vy
    dy[2] = - cd*vx*np.sqrt(vx**2 + vy**2)/2/m
    dy[3] = - g - cd*vy*np.sqrt(vx**2 + vy**2)/2/m
    return dy
```

---

[6] These are typical figures for a driver club wielded by a professional golfer.

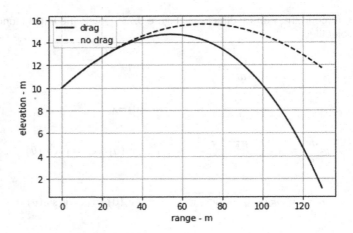

FIGURE 9.26 Simulation of golf ball trajectory with and without air resistance.

```
t0 = 0
tf = 2.7  # seconds
v0 = 67.  # m/s
theta = 9.*np.pi/180.  # radians
y0 = 10.
yy0 = np.array([0., y0, v0*np.cos(theta), v0*np.sin(theta)])
h = 0.01
t,y = eulerm(f,yy0,t0,tf,h)

xp = y[:,0]
yp = np.tan(theta)*xp - g/2/v0**2/np.cos(theta)**2*xp**2 + y0

plt.plot(y[:,0],y[:,1],c='k',label='drag')
plt.plot(xp,yp,c='k',ls='--',label='no drag')
plt.grid()
plt.xlabel('range - m')
plt.ylabel('elevation - m')
plt.legend()
```

The resulting trajectory is depicted in Figure 9.26. Including air drag has a pronounced effect of the trajectory of the ball.

This model of golf ball flight is still lacking key features. Perhaps the most important is the spin of the ball and a related phenomenon called the *Magnus effect*.[7] Also, important (and often tragic) to any golfer is the lateral movement of

---

[7] If you are familiar with golf, you may find our range result, about 130 m or 143 yd, suspicious. The range should be at least 100 m longer. That shows you what accounting for spin brings to the simulation. Our simulation is like a "knuckle ball" or "float serve" in baseball, association football (soccer), or volleyball. These float in toward the opponent at a relatively slow speed and will move, dip, or wobble in the air unpredictably. In baseball, the fast ball may be 50% faster than the knuckle ball, but it involves spin.

the ball (slice, draw). This model predicts only a linear trajectory. Understanding the fundamentals behind these extensions of our model requires more knowledge of fluid mechanics that many students will gain during their later engineering and science studies. If you would like to peek at a more sophisticated modeling approach, we refer you to Burglund and Street (2011).

9.4   SOLVING DIFFERENTIAL EQUATIONS WITH THE `solve_ivp` FUNCTION FROM SCIPY'S `integrate` MODULE

Just as with quadrature, Python provides functions to solve differential equations via its SciPy `integrate` submodule. One that is frequently the function of choice is `solve_ivp`. The syntax for this function is

```
from scipy.integrate import solve_ivp
result = solve_ivp(f,t_span,y0,t_eval=[•])
```

The `f` argument is the same as for our `eulerm` function, a function that evaluates the derivatives for given values of `t` and `y`. The `t_span` argument is an array of the initial and final values of `t`. The `y0` argument is an array specifying the initial values of the dependent variables. If there is only one dependent variable, it is a single variable or value; whereas for two or more dependent variables, it is an array. The `t_eval` argument contains an array of `t` values at which the solution is desired. If it is left out, the `solve_ivp` function will determine the output intervals.

The return from `solve_ivp`, `result`, is an object that contains various attributes. Most important to us are

```
result.t
result.y
```

that contain the independent and dependent variable values at the `t` values specified in the `t_eval` array or, in the case that only `t0` and `tf` are specified in `t_span`, the `t` values will be chosen by the `solve_ivp` function.

The `solve_ivp` provides six different methods of integration. The details of these are beyond the scope of this text. The default is RK45, a *Runge-Kutta method* with automatic step-size adjustment. An alternate method commonly used when the RK45 method encounters difficulty is the *LSODA method*. You can read more about these in SciPy help. The method is specified as a named argument, e.g. `method = 'RK45'` or `= 'LSODA'`.

We will illustrate the use of `solve_ivp` with two examples. The first is that described in Equation 9.8 and Figure 9.23. Here is the Python script we will use:

```
import numpy as np
from scipy.integrate import solve_ivp
import matplotlib.pyplot as plt

def f(t,y):
    dy = np.zeros(2)
    dy[0] = -2*y[0]**2 + 2*y[0] + y[1] -1
```

```
    dy[1] = -y[0] -3*y[1]**2 +2*y[1] + 2
    return dy

tf = 2.
tspan = [0., tf]
teval = np.linspace(0., tf)
y0 = np.array([2., 0.])
result = solve_ivp(f,tspan,y0,t_eval=teval)
tm = result.t
x1 = result.y[0,:]
x2 = result.y[1,:]

plt.plot(tm,x1,c='k',label='x1')
plt.plot(tm,x2,c='k',ls='--',label='x2')
plt.grid()
plt.xlabel('t')
plt.ylabel('x1 and x2')
plt.legend()
```

The function f is identical to what we used with eulerm. The tspan variable is set with initial value 0 and final value tf. With the linspace function, we request 50 evenly spaced values across the domain of the solution. The y0 argument is as before.

The result from the solve_ivp function is unpacked into independent and dependent variable arrays, tm, x1, and x2, and then a plot is generated. The plot is shown in Figure 9.27, and it looks identical to that in Figure 9.23.

For the second example, we will solve a notorious, single differential equation (Hornbeck, 1975):

$$\frac{dy}{dt} = 5\left(y - t^2\right) \qquad\qquad y(0) = 0.08 \qquad\qquad 0 \le t \le 5 \qquad (9.12)$$

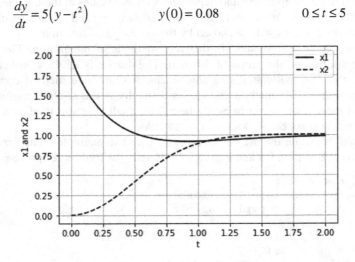

FIGURE 9.27   Solution of two, coupled differential equations with solve_ivp.

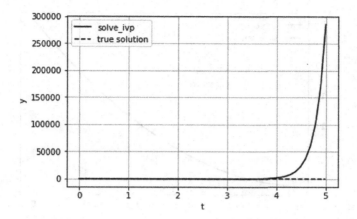

FIGURE 9.28 Comparison of numerical and analytical solutions with numerical solution blowing up.

We can compare our numerical solution to the analytical solution available here:

$$y = t^2 + 0.4t + 0.08 \qquad (9.13)$$

Note that at $t = 5$, $y = 27.08$.

This Python script attempts the numerical solution using `solve_ivp` and compares it with the analytical solution in a plot. The plot is shown in Figure 9.28. There is obviously a problem with the numerical solution.

```python
import numpy as np
from scipy.integrate import solve_ivp
import matplotlib.pyplot as plt

def f(t,y):
    return 5.*(y-t**2)

tf = 5.
tspan = [0., tf]
teval = np.linspace(0., tf)
y0 = [0.08]
result = solve_ivp(f,tspan,y0,t_eval=teval)
tm = result.t
ym = result.y[0,:]

ya = tm**2 + 0.4*tm + 0.08

plt.plot(tm,ym,c='k',label='solve_ivp')
plt.plot(tm,ya,c='k',ls='--',label='true solution')
plt.grid()
```

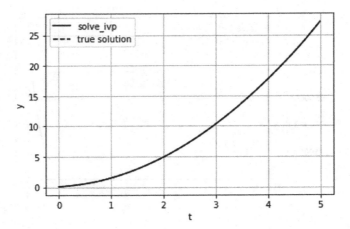

FIGURE 9.29 Comparison of `solve_ivp` and analytical solutions with tight error tolerances.

```
plt.xlabel('t')
plt.ylabel('y')
plt.legend()
```

What is going on here? The general analytical solution to this equation is

$$y = t^2 + 0.4t + 0.08 + c\,e^{5t} \tag{9.14}$$

where the constant c is determined with the initial condition. Since y_0 is chosen as 0.08, $c = 0$, and the exploding exponential term drops out analytically. But, if the numerical solution ever deviates measurably from the analytical solution (e.g. due to roundoff error), that exponential term rears its ugly head and causes the numerical solution to blow up. This is called a *parasitic solution*.

There are different approaches to remedying the numerical problem. One is to experiment with different solver methods. Another is to require the `solve_ivp` to meet more stringent error criteria. The two criteria, with their default values, are

absolute error tolerance, `atol = 1.e-6`
relative error tolerance, `rtol = 1.e-3`

If we make these much more stringent via a modification of the `solve_ivp` statement,

```
result = solve_ivp(f,tspan,y0,t_eval=teval \
              , atol = 1.e-12,  rtol = 1.e-12)
```

the plot that is produced is shown in Figure 9.29. The two solutions are indistinguishable.

The lesson here is that solving differential equations numerically can present challenges that require different approaches to be successful. Also, eventually for you, it will be important to study differential equations, their theory and structure, and their application in the modeling of different phenomena in engineering and science. The purpose of this chapter has been to give you a start in this important endeavor.

PROBLEMS

9.1 Indicate which solution strategy would be appropriate for the following differential equations.

(a) $\dfrac{dy}{dt} = \dfrac{e^t}{1+e^t}$ $y(0) = 0.5$ $0 \le t \le 1$

(b) $\dfrac{dy}{dx} = x\,y\,e^{-x^2}$ $y(0) = 0$ $0 \le x \le 1$

(c) $\dfrac{d^2y}{dt^2} = -9y$ $y(0) = 1 \quad \dfrac{dy}{dt}(0) = 0$ $0 \le t \le 4$

(d) $\dfrac{d^2y}{dx^2} + 2x\dfrac{dy}{dx} = 0 \quad y(0) = 1$ $y(10) = 0.1$

9.2 Draw information flow diagrams for the equations in parts (c) and (d) in Problem 9.1.

9.3 Hand draw a plot on graph paper of the function

$$f(t) = \ln(5 - 4\cos(x))$$

over the domain $0 \le x \le \pi$. Using an interval of $\Delta x = 0.2$, employ the counting the squares method to produce low and high estimates of

$$\int_0^\pi f(x)\,dx$$

and then average the two results to obtain your final estimate.

9.4 Employ trapezoidal rule to compute the integral in Problem 9.3. Use Python to compare the results from this chapter's trap function and Python's built-in quad function.

9.5 Many vessels (tanks) that store liquids have a circular cross-section, but the radius (or diameter) and cross-sectional area vary with height. This is illustrated in Figure P9.5. A practical way to calculate the volume of the vessel is to know the radius, r, as a function of height, h, and then use the integral and associated formula for area, A.

$$V = \int_0^H A(h)\,dh \quad A(h) = \pi r^2(h)$$

The relationship, $r(h)$, might be obtained from measurements or an analytical formula used to design the vessel. Consider a vessel with

$$r(h) = 8 + 0.34h - 0.002h^2 \text{ cm} \quad \text{and} \quad H = 50 \text{ cm}$$

Use Python and the method of your choice to compute the volume of this vessel.

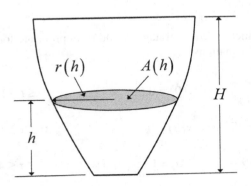

FIGURE P9.5   Vessel with circular cross-section.

9.6   An important task in public utilities and industry is the totalization of flow of materials, whether gases, liquids, or solids. Measurements are often made of the flow rate of a material, but monetary charges are calculated for the total volume of material that flows over a given time interval. The relationship is given by an integral,

$$V = \int_{t_0}^{t_f} q(t) dt$$

where $q(t)$ is the flow rate, for a liquid in units like liters/min or m³/s, and V is the volume that flowed over the interval from t_0 to t_f.

Flow rate data are typically samples collected at equal intervals of time. The data in the table below were collected for a liquid chemical that is transferred from one company to another through a pipeline. Use the built-in Python function `trapz` to totalize the flow for these data.

Time (min)	Flow Rate (L/min)	Time (min)	Flow Rate (L/min)	Time (min)	Flow Rate (L/min)
0	17.0	55	17.4	105	17.4
5	16.6	60	17.2	110	17.4
10	16.3	65	17.4	115	17.5
15	16.1	70	17.4	120	17.4
20	17.1	75	17.0	125	17.6
25	16.9	80	17.3	130	17.4
30	16.8	85	17.2	135	17.3
35	17.4	90	17.4	140	17.0
40	17.1	95	16.8	145	17.8
45	17.0	100	17.1	150	17.5
50	16.7				

9.7 For the differential equation,

$$\frac{dy}{dt} = -0.2y^2 \qquad y(0) = 3$$

(a) Compute by hand one step of the Euler method for $\Delta t = 1$.

(b) Compute by hand one step of the Heun method for $\Delta t = 1$, including five iterations of the predictor-corrector procedure. Does the method appear to be converging?

9.8 A famous second-order differential equation, called the *van der Pol* equation, is

$$\frac{d^2y}{dt^2} = (1 - y^2)\frac{dy}{dt} - y$$

For the initial conditions, $y(0) = 1$ and $dy/dt(0) = 0$, use the Euler method to solve the equation over the domain $0 \le t \le 10$. Find a step size, Δt, which yields an accurate solution. Produce a plot of your results.

9.9 Solve this differential equation using the Python built-in `solve_ivp` function.

$$\frac{dy}{dt} = -750y - 1100e^{-2t} \qquad y(0) = 5 \qquad 0 \le t \le 5$$

Compare the performance of the default RK45 method and the LSODA method. Adjust the error tolerances if needed. Produce a plot of your results.

9.10 Figure P9.10 is a schematic diagram of a simple electrical circuit with five components, a battery source, on-off switch, coil or inductor, resistor, and capacitor.

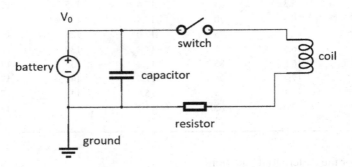

FIGURE P9.10 Electrical circuit.

When the switch is closed, the voltage shown initially as V_0 changes. A differential equation describes this:

$$LC\frac{d^2V}{dt^2} + RC\frac{dV}{dt} + V = 0 \qquad V(0) = V_0 \qquad \frac{dV}{dt}(0) = 0$$

Solve this equation for $0 \le t \le 0.2$ seconds, $V_0 = 100$ volts, and the parameter values[8]

$$C = 2 \times 10^{-6} \text{ farads} \quad L = 0.5 \text{ henries} \quad R = 100 \text{ ohms}$$

Compare the solution using the `eulerm` function with a step size, $\Delta t = 0.0001$ seconds, and the `solve_ivp` built-in function. Show the comparison on a plot.

9.11 In this chapter, we extended the `euler` function to its `eulerm` counterpart with the ability to solve multiple differential equations. In a similar fashion, extend the `heun` function to a new function called `heunm` that will solve multiple differential equations. Solve the Equations 9.8 using your `heunm` function and confirm the solution by comparison to Figure 9.23.

Hint: The criterion to determine the convergence of the corrector step has to change from the `heun` function because there are multiple equations and thus multiple errors. One way to manage this is to use the maximum absolute error as the criterion. Another is to use the sum of squares of the errors of the equations.

---

[8] One ohm (Ω) is the resistance that provides a current of one ampere (A) if the voltage difference across the resistor is one volt (V). The henry is a unit of inductance that corresponds to the inductance in a circuit producing one volt (V) of potential caused by a current variation of one ampere (A) per second. One farad is the capacitance unit which, when charged with one coulomb, provides a potential difference of one volt (V).

9.12 For the second-order differential equation,

$$\frac{d^2y}{dt^2} = \frac{1}{4}\frac{dy}{dt} + y \quad y(0) = 5 \quad y(10) = 8 \quad 0 \le t \le 10$$

you will note that there is no initial condition for dy/dt, but there is a final condition for y. To solve this problem, we suggest that you guess an initial condition for dy/dt. Then solve the equation with `solve_ivp`. Check your solution's value of $y(10)$ versus the requirement of 8. Then, adjust $dy/dt(0)$, and, by trial-and-error, find a solution that matches closely the $y(10) = 8$ requirement. This is a manual strategy to solve a two-point boundary value problem. There are more sophisticated, automatic techniques, but these are not requested here.

9.13 Differential equations are important in structural engineering. Figure P9.13 illustrates a cantilever beam (beam fixed at one end) subject to a load (force) at its end. The profile of deflection of the beam is described by a second-order differential equation,

$$\frac{d^2y}{dx^2} = -\frac{F}{EI}(L - x) \quad y(0) = 0 \quad \frac{dy}{dx}(0) = 0 \quad 0 \le x \le L$$

where y: vertical displacement of the beam at a given value of x, m,
x: location on the beam from 0 to L, m,
F: downward load placed at the beam end, N,
E: modulus of elasticity (stiffness) of the beam material, Pa,
I: moment of inertia of the beam cross-section, m⁴, and
L: length of the beam, m.
For the following parameter values and conditions,
$L = 4$ m, $F = 5{,}000$ N, $E = 5 \times 10^{11}$ Pa, $I = 4 \times 10^{-4}$ m⁴,
solve the differential equation using a numerical method of your choice. It turns out that there is an analytical solution to this differential equation,

$$y = -\frac{FL}{2EI}x^2 + \frac{F}{6EI}x^3$$

Plot and compare the analytical result along with your numerical solution.

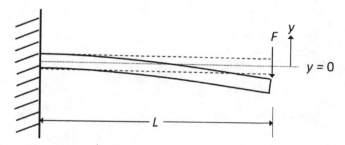

FIGURE P9.13 Deflection of cantilever beam under a load placed at the end.

9.14 Use a modified version of the Python code from Figure 9.10 to evaluate the integral (Equation 9.9),

$$y = \int_0^{\pi/2} t\cos(t)\,dt$$

Starting with $n = 4$, progressively double the number of intervals 20 times. For each function call, return the integral estimate, the step size, and the error, where

$$error = |true\ value - estimated\ value|$$

where the *true value* is computed with Equation 9.10. Generate log-log plots of the step sizes and the errors versus n.

10 Working with Data

CHAPTER OBJECTIVES

- Learn how to make initial observations on data sets with the help of graphical depictions.
- Be able to compute typical sample statistics to characterize a data set.
- Understand how data relate to populations, and how distributions describe the latter.
- Learn how to simulate numbers drawn from different distributions using random number generators from the Python NumPy `random` module.
- Be able to make claims with data – an introduction to hypothesis testing.
- Learn how to fit mathematical models to data and evaluate their adequacy.

Scientists and engineers make discoveries and decisions based on information obtained through experiments and observations. Experiments are planned and carried out. Observations are made of phenomena, most often in nature, the laboratory, or existing processes. All yield data, and the field of *applied statistics* is dedicated to reaching conclusions from the examination of data.

The topic of statistics is very large. Many, perhaps most, engineers and scientists take a course in applied statistics as undergraduate students. Many universities offer entire degree programs in statistics, and these may be housed in their own academic unit or department. So, what can we do here to introduce this topic in the context of Python?

One of the common problems in the treatment and interpretation of data is the misapplication of statistics. There are countless examples of practitioners and researchers reaching erroneous conclusions, sometimes with disastrous results, because they applied statistical methods incorrectly.[1] A problem associated with this is the availability of statistical software packages that produce an avalanche of results which are difficult for engineers or scientists to understand unless they have a sound background in applied statistics.

What we will attempt to do here is introduce you to sound fundamentals and practices in the treatment of data. By doing this, we want to inspire you to further your education in this important topic. Along the way, we also warn you against using statistical results that you do not understand well to make conclusions. That is a typical trap that investigators fall into.

---

[1] And besides errors due to misunderstanding, some inaccuracies are intentional as nicely outlined in Darrell Huff's popular 1954 book: *How to Lie with Statistics* (Norton, New York, ISBN 0-393-31072-8). In both cases, the antidote is to have a sound background in applied statistics. This chapter is designed to get you started on this journey.

DOI: 10.1201/9781003256861-10

329

This chapter starts out with the typical initial steps taken to characterize a set of data. These include recognizing the data type and the constraints on the data. You will learn how to extract sample statistics from the data which help in their description. Since data contain random error, it is important to understand its nature and how the random error relates to the concept of a population from which the data are sampled. We will also introduce the process of simulating random numbers that are drawn from different populations.

With this background, this chapter continues to two important topics in applied statistics. The first, called *hypothesis testing*, has to do with making claims based on a set of data and assessing the uncertainty of the claims and decisions that might be made. The second introduces the important field of *regression* — fitting models to data. Mathematical models can be used in various ways to increase the understanding of phenomena and make predictions.

10.1   CHARACTERIZING DATA SETS: INITIAL OBSERVATIONS AND SAMPLE STATISTICS

Data take different forms.[2] A first distinction is whether the information is categorical or not. Categorical data take on only certain values which may or may not be numerical. Qualitative judgment of product quality is one example. Results might be classified as excellent, good, average, sub-par, or unacceptable. An even simpler scale for the quality of discrete products might be pass/fail. Once the scale of measurement is established, there are no values between the categories. We focus in this chapter on data which are measurements of continuous quantities and have numerical values.

10.1.1   GENERAL DATA CONCEPTS

The concept of *resolution* is a key aspect of making numerical measurements. This is illustrated in Figure 10.1 showing weather station pressure data acquired at 5-minute intervals. Observing closely, you can see that the measurements jump up and down in intervals of 0.01 inHg. There are no intermediate values. Of course, the true relative pressure is a continuous quantity, but, through the lens of the weather station's pressure measurement, we only see it to the nearest 0.1 inHg. As we look at the figure, we judge that the resolution is fine enough so that our measurements provide a good profile and estimate of the variations in pressure.

However, if we observe the relative humidity measurements from the same weather station, we can look at Figure 10.2. Here, the matter of resolution is of concern because it is only to the nearest 1%. If these measurements do not provide enough detail, we will have to invest in a humidistat with higher

---

[2] You will note that the authors consider the word *data* to be plural. Perhaps we are old-fashioned, educated thoroughly in the English language decades ago (Dave by Canadian educators and Steve by nuns), but that's the way it is. Along with yelling at kids to "get off our lawn," we have a long list of pet peeves having to do with current practices in the English language.

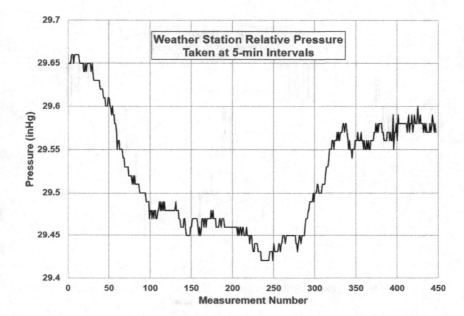

FIGURE 10.1   Weather station atmospheric pressure measurements relative to sea level.[3]

resolution (and higher cost). As we can see here, over the range measured, there are only five possible values. This gives us the impression that these measurements are discrete and not a good representation of a continuous quantity, the true relative humidity.

The next term we introduce is *stationarity*. This has to do with whether a set of measurements appear to have a trend in the order they are presented. The weather station data presented in Figures 10.1 and 10.2 are taken chronologically. They reveal trends in time, so we conclude that the data do not represent a stationary series. If the data set is not stationary, it is difficult for us to estimate statistical quantities such as a central tendency or mean and dispersion or variance.

Terms that cause confusion and are frequently mis-applied are accuracy and precision. In brief, *accuracy* is how close a given set of measurements are to their true value, whereas *precision* is how close the measurements are to each other. Although these provide a simple description of the concepts, there are nuances that must be recognized to understand them fully.

---

[3] You will note that the units here, inHg, are not SI (metric), such as pascals (Pa or kPa). Across the world, and in different application areas, there are more than a dozen pressure units in common usage. Here, one might find mmHg, also known as torr – not an SI unit. In the U.S., one finds psi, and, in Europe, kg/m^2 — not SI units. You will also find the bar (100 kPa) in common use in the laboratory – not an SI unit. We apologize for the use of inHg here, as these are the units of this particular weather station, but we also welcome you to the confusing world of pressure measurement.

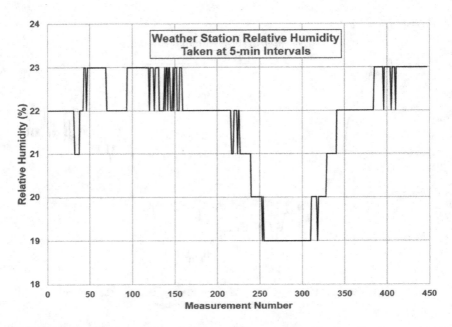

FIGURE 10.2   Weather station relative humidity measurements.

Imagine we measure temperature with an instrument that provides a digital display with high resolution, 0.01°C. There is a natural temptation to presume that the measurements are "accurate" to the same extent. That is a mistake. *Accuracy* has to do with comparison to a standard of measurement. Standards of measurement are maintained by organizations such as the National Institute of Standards and Technology (NIST) in the U.S. and the Système International d'Unités (SI) in France. Secondary standards are calibrated against the primary NIST standards. Temperature instruments are generally accompanied with an accuracy specification. For our example above, that might be ± 0.1°C − ten times greater than the resolution. Many consider the term *precision* as a poor descriptor of data because it often refers to resolution, but it is easily confused with accuracy. Also, it may be confused with repeatability and dispersion. Figure 10.3 illustrates these concepts.

Repeatability corresponds to taking repeated measurements of the same quantity and obtaining consistent results. *Dispersion* describes this in the opposite way, as it refers to the scatter in the data set.

With a relatively small set of data, we can estimate a *central tendency*, most commonly by computing their average. If we were to increase the number of measurements to a very large number, our average would approach a constant value; yet this value might yet be displaced from the accurate value because of inaccuracy of our measurement system. So, there are two concepts here: first, as we increase our sample size, our average values (or mean estimates) approach a constant value with greater and greater certainty. Second, that constant value is

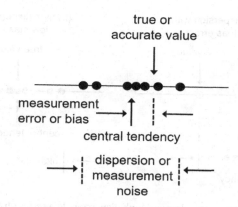

FIGURE 10.3   Dot diagram of repeated measurements.

still limited by the lack of accuracy or *bias error* of our measurement system. These two sources of error are combined in the measurements we take.

The *dispersion* of the data has to do with the noisiness of the measurements. Measurements may by noisy (or have random error) because of the nature of the quantity we are measuring or noise may be induced by our measurement instrumentation alone. The latter may be minimized through careful attention to the instrumentation. The former tends to be "the nature of the beast" that we must live with. The more the data are dispersed, the harder it is to estimate the central value with certainty. Where these concepts become very meaningful is when, from a set of data, we want to make a claim, and we must deal with the accuracy (or lack thereof) and the uncertainty.

To be clear, a set of data may have little dispersion and yet have a significant error when compared to a true or accurate value. And conversely, a set of measurements may be centered well on the true value, but, with a large amount of dispersion, may be difficult to make claims because of the associated uncertainty. This is illustrated in Figure 10.4.

To complete this discussion, we return to the concept of stationarity. The concept of a central value is a moving target for a data series that is non-stationary. For Figures 10.1 and 10.2, we can certainly calculate the average temperature and relative humidity over the time period presented; however, calling that a central tendency will be overstating the case.

10.1.2   SAMPLE STATISTICS: CENTRAL TENDENCY AND DISPERSION

When we collect a set of data, we introduce the concept that these data come from a *population*. There are occasions when populations are finite. For example, the entire student body of a university. If we select 100 students at random and measure their heights, this would be a *sample* with $n = 100$. If we select another sample, we will have a different set of data. But both sets were obtained from the

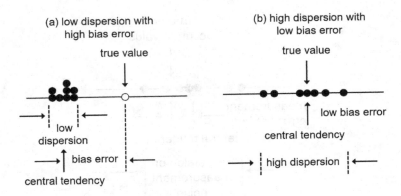

FIGURE 10.4   Comparison of low and high dispersion data sets with different bias errors.

same population. With a finite population, the concept of measuring all members is feasible.

For most data samples in engineering and science, the population is infinite. In Figure 10.1, we can imagine that there are an infinite number of pressures possible in nature. Subsequently, our measurement system, with finite resolution, reduces this to a finite population of possible measured pressures. If the measurement resolution is fine, the measurement population approaches the population in nature.

10.1.2.1   Central Tendency

In characterizing a data set, a first concept is that of *central tendency*. The most common measure of this is the *arithmetic average* of the sample $\{x_i, i=1,\ldots, n\}$,

$$\bar{x} = \frac{\sum_{i=1}^{n} x_i}{n} \tag{10.1}$$

Notice the notation, x with an overscore bar, $\bar{x}$. This is alternately called the *sample average* or the *sample mean*. Occasionally, it is referred to as the mean, but that is not appropriate.

Generally, the term *mean* corresponds to the central tendency of the entire population, and the symbol used is the Greek letter "mu," μ. Figure 10.5 illustrates two data sets, their *dot diagrams*, and their corresponding sample average calculations. These data are measured or extracted from the same population. We note that the samples are different and yield average calculations that differ by about 3%.

The *dot diagrams* in Figure 10.5 raise another issue. Each data set contains one value that is significantly high and separated from the rest of the measurements. Such values are commonly called *outliers*. There is a temptation, and it is a trap

10.1	
11.5	$\bar{x} = \dfrac{\sum\limits_{i=1}^{n} x_i}{n} = \dfrac{99.6}{10} = 9.96$
9.6	
9.6	
10.4	
9.4	
10.2	
9.9	
9.1	
9.8	

11.4	
10.5	$\bar{x} = \dfrac{\sum\limits_{i=1}^{n} x_i}{n} = \dfrac{96.4}{10} = 9.64$
9.3	
14.6	
8.4	
7.9	
7.3	
9.7	
8.6	
8.7	

FIGURE 10.5 Average calculations and dot diagrams for two data sets from the same population.

fallen into by many investigators, to remove outliers from the data set without cause. This is absolutely a bad practice. The well-founded reason to remove an outlier is the discovery of a *blunder* in the experiments or data collection; otherwise, outliers should not be removed. After all, they could be telling you something exceedingly important about the phenomenon you are measuring. And one should always document removals.

When outliers exist, especially in smaller data sets, there is a concern that they may influence the average calculation inordinately. One answer to this is to use an alternate measure of central tendency. The most common of these is the *median*, designated $\tilde{x}$. The definition of the median is simple: sort the data and pick the one in the middle — if the number of the data is even, pick the two in the middle and compute their average. The calculation of the median for our two data sets in Figure 10.5 is shown in Figure 10.6. You will note that the median values are less than the average values, especially for the second data set. This is because the high values, possibly outliers, in the two data sets influence the average calculation more than the median calculation. The high value in the second data set is more extreme than that of the first data set. We will address diagnosing outliers a bit later.

There are other measures of central tendency, such as the *mode* (most frequently occurring value) and the *m-estimator* (gradually discounts values far from the central result), but we will not spend time on those here. They are used less frequently, but if you are curious about them see Chapra and Clough (2022) or a good statistics texts like Montgomery and Runger (2018) or Mason, Gunst, and Hess (1989).

It is useful to know how to compute the average and the median with Python. Here is a script that illustrates this for the second data set.

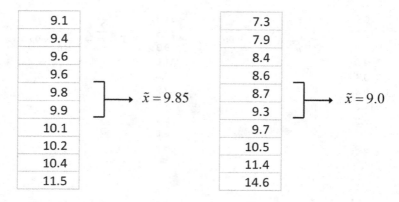

FIGURE 10.6   Computation of the median for two data sets.

```
import numpy as np

x = np.array([11.4,10.5,9.3,14.6,8.4,7.9,7.3,9.7,8.6,8.7])

xbar = np.mean(x)
xmed = np.median(x)
print('average = {0:5.2f}'.format(xbar))
print('median =  {0:5.2f}'.format(xmed))
```

The results displayed in the Console are

```
average =  9.64
median =   9.00
```

Note that the function for average (or sample mean) in the NumPy module is mean.

10.1.2.2   Spread or Dispersion

The next quantity of interest for a data sample and its population is a measure of spread or *dispersion*. Perhaps the easiest-to-compute measure of spread is the *range*. This is simply the difference between and maximum and minimum values in the data set. This is not a particularly good measure because it is too sensitive to extreme values and ignores the data interior to the minimum and maximum values. Further, it is not a stable estimator in that the range gets wider as the number of data points increases.

Just as the sample average is an estimate of the true central value or population mean, we commonly use a similar measure for dispersion. This is the *sample standard deviation* (or its square, the *sample variance*) as an estimate of the population standard deviation (or its square, the population variance). The formula for the sample standard deviation is

$$s = \sqrt{\frac{\sum_{i=1}^{n}(x_i - \bar{x})^2}{n-1}}$$ (10.2)

In words, this measure sums the squares of the deviations between the individual data and the sample average, divides the result by $n-1$, and takes the square root. Without the square root, this is called the sample variance, s^2. Because of the square, you can see that larger deviations weigh more heavily into the result than small ones. As with the mean, the sample standard deviation is an estimate of the standard deviation of the population, which is designated by the Greek letter "sigma," σ.

A question that arises frequently is why $n-1$ is used in the denominator of Equation 10.2 and not just n. We explain this here in two ways:

- The number of *degrees of freedom* in the data set is n. When we calculate and use the sample average, that removes one degree of freedom, leaving $n-1$. Another way to think of this is that if we know the mean and are given $n-1$ of the values, the nth value can be computed.
- If we use n, instead of $n-1$, and increase the sample size gradually to high values of n, the result does not approach σ, but has an offset or *bias error*.

There is a way to demonstrate this second point with a mathematical derivation, but we choose not to include this since it involves the use of concepts beyond our scope here. It is worth mentioning that a common error in calculating the sample standard deviation is to use n when $n-1$ should be used. Conversely, in the case where the sample is the entire population, n should be used.

Figure 10.7 illustrates the calculation of the sample standard deviation for our two data sets. Note that the two results are quite different — the second is over three times the first. This reveals two issues with estimating the standard deviation. First, compared to the mean, it is more difficult to get a reliable estimate with smaller sample sizes, and second, potential outliers, such as that in the second data set, have a strong influence on the estimate.

This last observation leads us to consider another method for estimating the standard deviation, just as we did with the median as an estimator for the mean. An answer here is provided by the *median absolute deviation*, or *MAD*. This is a description of the steps in calculating the MAD:

1. Find the median of the data.
2. Compute the absolute values of the deviations of the data from the median.
3. Find the median of those absolute values.
4. Divide the result by 0.6745.

Figure 10.8 describes the calculation of the MAD for the two data sets. Notice that the MAD values are lower than the sample standard deviation values. This is

10.1			11.4	
11.5	$\bar{x} = 9.96$		10.5	$\bar{x} = 9.64$
9.6			9.3	
9.6	$\sum_{i=1}^{n}(x_i - \bar{x})^2 \cong 3.98$		14.6	$\sum_{i=1}^{n}(x_i - \bar{x})^2 \cong 40.6$
10.4			8.4	
9.4	$s \cong 0.665$		7.9	$s \cong 2.12$
10.2			7.3	
9.9			9.7	
9.1			8.6	
9.8			8.7	

FIGURE 10.7 Sample standard deviation calculations.

because the MAD is less sensitive to outliers than the s value. Also, we observe that the two MAD values are different. This emphasizes the difficulty of getting a tight estimate of σ with small samples.

A natural question is about the use of the 0.6745 factor. This value comes from theory and is necessary so that the MAD approaches σ as the sample size becomes large.

Now we consider how to compute these estimates of dispersion with Python. See the script below.

```python
import numpy as np

x = np.array([10.1,11.5,9.6,9.6,10.4,9.4,10.2,9.9,9.1,9.8])

s = np.std(x,ddof=1)
```

10.1	0.25		11.4	2.4	
11.5	1.65	$\tilde{d} = 0.30$	10.5	1.5	$\tilde{d} = 0.90$
9.6	0.25		9.3	0.3	
9.6	0.25	$MAD \cong 0.44$	14.6	5.6	$MAD \cong 1.33$
10.4	0.55		8.4	0.6	
9.4	0.45		7.9	1.1	
10.2	0.35		7.3	1.7	
9.9	0.05		9.7	0.7	
9.1	0.75		8.6	0.4	
9.8	0.05		8.7	0.3	
$\tilde{x} = 9.85$	$d = |x_i - \tilde{x}|$		$\tilde{x} = 9.85$	$d = |x_i - \tilde{x}|$	

FIGURE 10.8 Calculation of the median absolute deviation (MAD).

```
def MAD(x):
    xmed = np.median(x)
    xdev = abs(x-xmed)
    dmed = np.median(xdev)
    return dmed/0.6745

MADx = MAD(x)

print('sample standard deviation = {0:5.3f}'.format(s))
print('median absolute deviation (MAD) = {0:5.3f}'.
format(MADx))
```

The results are

```
sample standard deviation = 0.665
median absolute deviation (MAD) =  0.445
```

which duplicate those in Figures 10.7 and 10.8. You will note that, in the std function, we use an optional argument, ddof = 1. This is required for the sample standard deviation with its $n-1$ denominator. The default, ddof = 0, uses a denominator n as appropriate for the population standard deviation. It is also worth mentioning that, from the stats submodule in SciPy, there is a median_ abs_deviation function that performs the calculations of our MAD function in the script above. You will notice the argument, scale='normal'. This incorporates a precise value of the 0.6745 constant.

```
from scipy.stats import median_abs_deviation
MADx2 = median_abs_deviation(x, scale='normal')
```

As we leave this topic, we will mention that, for very small sample sizes, $n \leq 5$, an adequate estimate of the standard deviation can be computed using the range, as

$$\frac{range}{\sqrt{n}} \tag{10.3}$$

Although this value is not particularly applicable for our sample size of 10, the results for our two data sets are 0.76 and 2.31, respectively.

10.1.3 USING BOXPLOTS TO DIAGNOSE OUTLIERS

The *boxplot* is a useful graphical device to accompany the sample statistics calculations.[4] It is especially effective in judging whether extreme results should be classified as outliers. Boxplots are also useful in comparing different data sets, and we will see their use for this later. These are the steps necessary in constructing a boxplot:

---

[4] The *box and whisker plot* was first introduced in 1970 by John Tukey, an American mathematician and statistician. He later published on the subject in his book *Exploratory Data Analysis* (Addison-Wesley. ISBN 9780201076165) in 1977.

1. Find the median of the data set.
2. Compute the 25th percentile and 75th percentile of the data set.
3. Draw a box on a vertical scale appropriate to the data with these two limits.
4. Calculate the interquartile range (*iqr*) as the difference of these two percentiles.
5. Draw lines, called *whiskers*, above and below the box that extend a maximum length of 1.5·*iqr*, but only to the largest (or smallest) data point still within 1.5·*iqr*.
6. Identify any data beyond the whiskers as outliers by plotting them as points.

In Chapter 4, we developed a function pctile that computes a given percentile value of an array of values. We can include this in our previous script that computes the median for our second data set as follows:

```python
import numpy as np

def pctile(x,pct):
    y = np.sort(x)
    n = len(y)
    mp = pct/100*(n-1)
    mp1 = int(mp)
    xp = (mp-mp1)*y[mp1]+(1-(mp-mp1))*y[mp1+1]
    return xp

x = np.array([11.4,10.5,9.3,14.6,8.4,7.9,7.3,9.7,8.6,8.7])
n = len(x)

xmed = np.median(x)
x25 = pctile(x,25.)
x75 = pctile(x,75.)
iqr = x75 - x25
xwhiskhimax = x75 + 1.5*iqr
xwhisklomin = x25 - 1.5*iqr

xs = np.sort(x)
for i in range(n):
    if xs[i] > xwhisklomin:
        xwhisklo = xs[i]
        break
for i in range(n-1,-1,-1):
    if xs[i] < xwhiskhimax:
        xwhiskhi = xs[i]
        break

print('median =  {0:5.2f}'.format(xmed))
print('25th %-ile =  {0:5.2f}'.format(x25))
print('75th %-ile =  {0:5.2f}'.format(x75))
print('iqr = {0:5.2f}'.format(iqr))
print('low whisker =  {0:5.2f}'.format(xwhisklo))
print('high whisker =  {0:5.2f}'.format(xwhiskhi))
```

These then are the parameters for the boxplot:

```
median =    9.00
25th %-ile =   8.55
75th %-ile =   9.90
iqr =   1.35
low whisker =   7.30
high whisker =  11.40
```

Using these parameters, we can draw the boxplot and note any values that are outside the whiskers. Examining the array, we see one high value, 14.6. The boxplot is shown in Figure 10.9. We note that the 14.6 value is an outlier; in fact, it appears to be an *extreme outlier*. This might not have been obvious just through an examination of the numbers in the set. Also, you will note that we draw a dashed line for the median location, and that line is not centered vertically in the box. When the median line is displaced from the 50th percentile, the middle of the box, that indicates that the distribution of the data, as would be shown in a *histogram* plot (recall Section 5.4), is asymmetric. The histogram would show a tail in the direction of the greater box space, above or below the median.

Python's Matplotlib `pyplot` module provides a function that generates boxplots. Here is a very compact script that produces a similar plot to that in Figure 10.9. This is displayed in Figure 10.10. There is a red line across the box at $x=9$, like our dashed line in Figure 10.9.

```
import matplotlib.pyplot as plt
plt.boxplot(x)
```

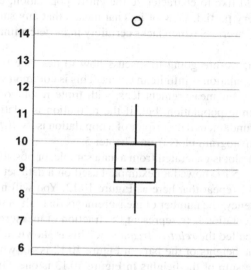

FIGURE 10.9 Boxplot of the second data set.

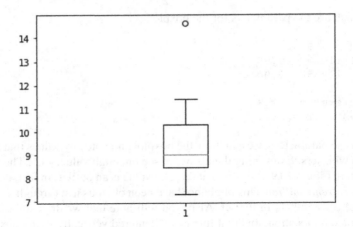

FIGURE 10.10   Boxplot produced by the Matplotlib pyplot function boxplot.

For now, consider the use of boxplots to explore the characteristics of a data set. If outliers are identified, that should initiate an investigation to determine causes. If a cause associated with a blunder or other significant error can be identified, the outlier should be removed from the data set. This should be documented. Otherwise, the outlier should not be excluded.

10.2   DISTRIBUTIONS

We have discussed the relationship between a data sample and its related population. Figure 10.11 describes this concept. We do not know the true nature of the population. Our data set represents sampled observations of the population. From the data, we would like to characterize the entire population, but we only have a partial, often very partial, view of it. That means that any sample statistics or estimates, like the average, which lacks certainty in its determination of the mean of the population.

In this section, we are going to discuss how to describe the population. In most cases, the population is infinite in extent. This is common when the contents are real numbers. Our measurement lens, with finite resolution, may not allow us to see the infinite population, but, if the resolution is relatively fine, it may come close. The fundamental descriptor of a population is its *distribution*. We can relate this to the histogram plots from Chapter 5.

The histogram plot is generated from a data sample, or possibly an entire finite population. Figure 5.19 showed an example based on a data set of 40 piston ring measurements. We repeat that here as Figure 10.12. You will note that the ordinate here is frequency, the number of measurements that fall in the given interval. An alternate presentation is to represent the fraction of measurements that occur in each interval, called the *relative frequency*. This is shown in Figure 10.13.

The sum of the heights of the bars in Figure 10.12 is 40, which is the sample size; whereas, the sum of the heights in Figure 10.13 is one. Given our data set,

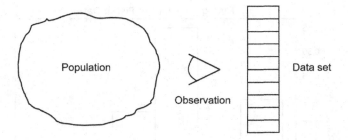

FIGURE 10.11   Relationship of data set to population through observation.

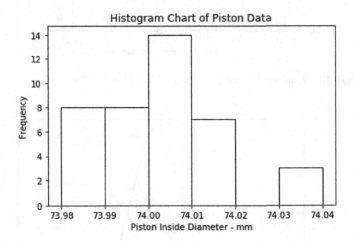

FIGURE 10.12   Histogram chart of piston data.

we can estimate that the probability of measuring a value in each interval is the height of its bar. Now, imagine that we increase the sample size greatly and narrow the bin widths to a tiny value. Concurrently, we divide the relative frequency by the interval width. If we just plot the peaks of the bars versus the piston diameter, the picture emerging might be that illustrated in Figure 10.14.

Instead of dealing with individual bar heights, in Figure 10.14 we have a continuous curve. The area under the curve is one, just as the sum of the heights in Figure 10.13 is one. To be clear, the area under one point on the curve is zero. This curve is called a *density function, f(x)*. If we want to determine the probability of obtaining a measurement in a finite interval, that corresponds to the area under the curve for that interval, or

$$P[a \le x \le b] = \int_a^b f(x)\,dx \tag{10.4}$$

You will note that the density function must have the units of $1/x$. We solved a problem like this in the previous chapter; see Example 9.1 and Figure 9.11.

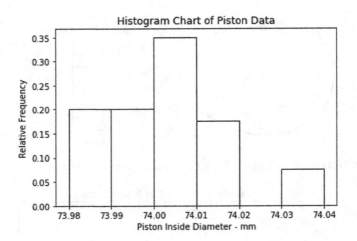

FIGURE 10.13 Relative frequency histogram chart of piston data.

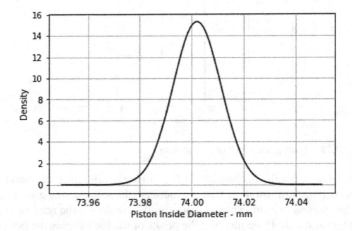

FIGURE 10.14 Possible density function for distribution of piston diameters.

Given a density function for a population, we want to introduce the definitions of population mean and variance (square of the standard deviation). The formulas for these are[5]

$$\mu = \int_{-\infty}^{\infty} x f(x) \, dx \qquad \sigma^2 = \int_{-\infty}^{\infty} (x-\mu)^2 f(x) \, dx \tag{10.5}$$

---

[5] Even if you have not learned integration yet, recall from Chapter 9, the analogy between integration and summation.

Taking a close look at the first formula, we see that the mean, μ, is a weighted average of the variable, x, over the entire domain, where the weighting is the density function, $f(x)$. For the second formula, the variance is the weighted average of the squared deviation from the mean. These are the population parameters, and, in general, we do not have direct knowledge of them. However, if we have a mathematical model for the density, we can determine them.

10.2.1 Several Important Distributions

There are many different theoretical *density functions*. We will highlight three here because they are commonplace in reference or use.

10.2.1.1 Uniform Distribution

The *uniform distribution* is illustrated in Figure 10.15. Evaluating the formulas in Equations 10.4 and 10.5, we get

$$P[\alpha \le x \le \beta] = \frac{\beta - \alpha}{b - a} \qquad \mu = \frac{b + a}{2} \qquad \sigma = \frac{b - a}{2\sqrt{3}} \qquad (10.6)$$

For example, if $a = -1$ and $b = +1$,

$$P[\alpha \le x \le \beta] = \frac{\beta - \alpha}{2} \qquad \mu = 0 \qquad \sigma = \frac{1}{\sqrt{3}} \qquad (10.7)$$

In practice, we don't run into the uniform distribution that often. With discrete variables, it's common in situations like coin tosses or the toss of a six-sided die. Each result is equally probable. With data acquired from measurements of physical and chemical phenomena, there is usually a central tendency that is more probable than values far from the mean. However, if the range is reasonably defined, but there is no evidence supporting a particular distribution, the uniform distribution is sometimes used to reflect our lack of knowledge.

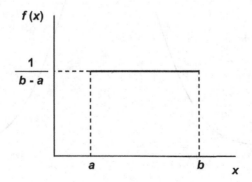

FIGURE 10.15   Density function for the uniform distribution.

10.2.1.2 Normal Distribution

The most common and frequently encountered distribution is the *normal distribution* (also called *Gaussian distribution*). As we illustrated in Example 9.1, its density function is

$$f(x) = \frac{1}{\sigma\sqrt{2\pi}} e^{-\frac{1}{2}\left(\frac{x-\mu}{\sigma}\right)^2} \tag{10.8}$$

As implied by the symbols used, its mean is μ, and standard deviation is σ. The density is a bell-shaped curve centered on μ. This is shown in Figure 10.16. We know how the curve is related to μ, but how is it related to σ? In the figure, since $\sigma = 10$, we can judge that most of the area under the curve is accounted for between $\mu \pm 3\sigma$. There is a useful interpretation called the *normal probability rule* relating the area (or probability) to multiples of σ.

$\pm \sigma$	probability
1	68%
2	95%
3	99.7%

As we mentioned in Chapter 9, there is a simplified version of this distribution called the *standard normal distribution* where $\mu = 0$ and $\sigma = 1$. Typically, the

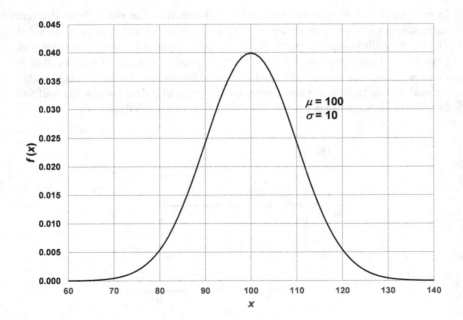

FIGURE 10.16 Normal distribution density function for $\mu = 100$ and $\sigma = 10$.

random variable name used with this distribution is z, and its relationship to x in the normal distribution is

$$z = \frac{x - \mu}{\sigma} \tag{10.9}$$

10.2.1.3 Weibull Distribution

As we observe histogram charts of data sets, we find many well-suited to modeling with the normal distribution. However, there is one characteristic we observe that is counter to that distribution. That is lack of symmetry, or *asymmetry*. There are several distributions that allow for the modeling of asymmetry. One which is commonly used in the manufacturing industry to model product reliability is the *Weibull distribution*. Its density function is

$$f(x) = \frac{\alpha}{\beta^{\alpha}} x^{\alpha-1} e^{-(x/\beta)^{\alpha}} \quad x \geq 0 \tag{10.10}$$

where α: scale parameter > 0, and
β: shape parameter > 0.

It is depicted in Figure 10.17. You can see how this example of the density function allows for asymmetry with a longer "tail" to the right. There are other distributions, such as the log-normal and gamma, that also provide asymmetric density functions.

10.2.2 PYTHON AND DISTRIBUTIONS

The SciPy `stats` submodule provides functions to compute probabilities for various distributions. For example, the brief Python script below computes a value of the normal density and a probability for two values of x. The normal density is computed using the `norm.pdf` function. The `pdf` notation stands for "probability density function." To compute the area between a and b values of x, the `norm.cdf` function is used twice. The `cdf` notation is for "cumulative probability function." It calculates the area from the extreme left up to the first argument. First, the area up to b is computed; then the area up to a is computed. The area or probability between a and b is then the difference of the two cumulative probabilities.

```
from scipy import stats

mu = 100
sigma = 10
a = 75
b = 95

f = stats.norm.pdf(b,mu,sigma)
print('normal density = {0:6.4f}'.format(f))
```

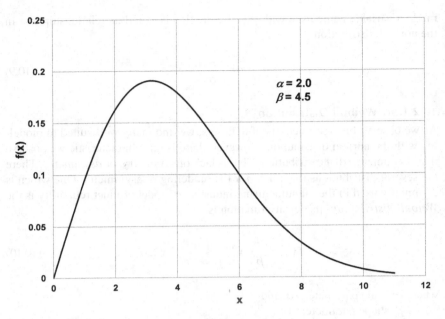

FIGURE 10.17   Density function for the Weibull distribution, $\alpha = 2.0$ and $\beta = 4.5$.

```
cp1 = stats.norm.cdf(b,mu,sigma)
cp2 = stats.norm.cdf(a,loc=mu,scale=sigma)
p = cp1-cp2
print('probability = {0:5.1f}%'.format(p*100))

normal density = 0.0352
probability =   30.2%
```

It is worth noting that, following Example 9.1, we can compute probabilities using quadrature of the density function. Similar functions are available in the stats module for different distributions, e.g. uniform, Weibull, log-normal, and gamma.

A natural question to ask at this point is how we determine from our data set which distribution appears to be appropriate to represent the population. And, once a distribution is identified, how do we estimate the parameters of the distribution. We will get to that in the next main section.

10.2.3   RANDOM NUMBERS

There are occasions in numerical calculations where we want to simulate values that are drawn at random from specific distributions. This is called *random number generation*. The methods used to generate random numbers are interesting, but they are beyond the scope of this text. Here, we will use Python's built-in functions that provide these. Such random numbers are formally called *pseudorandom* since they are not ideally sampled from a population but are close to that.

An effective way to test random number generation is to create a histogram chart of the results and see how they relate to the corresponding density function. Here is an example Python script for the uniform distribution with 10,000 random samples.

```
import numpy as np
import matplotlib.pyplot as plt

x = np.random.uniform(0,1,10000)

histvals,bin_edges = np.histogram(x)

bin_width = bin_edges[1]-bin_edges[0]
n = len(histvals)
bin_centers = np.zeros((n))
for i in range(n):
    bin_centers[i] = (bin_edges[i]+bin_edges[i+1])/2

plt.bar(bin_centers,histvals,width=bin_width,color='w',
edgecolor='k')
plt.title('uniform random numbers')
```

The histogram chart created is shown in Figure 10.18. We recognize the pattern as being relatively flat. That is what we would expect from the uniform distribution population.

As a second example, we will create an array representing a sinusoidal signal with random noise added where the random number generator is for the normal distribution.

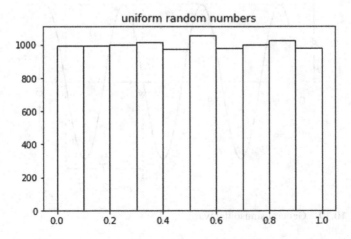

FIGURE 10.18 Uniform random number generation. Sample size = 10,000.

Example 10.1 Simulating a Noisy Signal with Random Number Generation

A general sinusoidal signal can be generated with the formula

$$y = A\sin(\omega t + \phi) + B \tag{10.10}$$

where A: amplitude or peak height of the sine wave
   ω: frequency in radians/time, related to the period by $\omega = 2\pi/T$
   T: period (the time of one complete cycle of the sine)
   t: time
   ϕ: phase shift in radians
   B: offset or bias

The general wave along with the parameters is illustrated in Figure 10.19. Note that the sine function alone is centered at zero, but the wave is shifted up by B. Also, the sine wave would normally be zero at $t=0$, but it is shifted backward or delayed by ϕ radians. The period of the wave is T, and that is related to the angular frequency, ω, by $2\pi/T$. You may be familiar with the cyclical frequency, f in cycles/time.[6] That frequency is related to ω by $2\pi f$.

With the smooth, analytical sinusoid in hand, we now want to create a "noisy" version of that to simulate a more realistic measured signal. We will do that by adding random noise that is generated from the normal distribution. The mean of this noise will be zero, and its strength will be specified by the standard deviation. This causes us to modify Equation 10.10 as follows:

$$y = A\sin(\omega t + \phi) + B + N(0,\sigma) \tag{10.11}$$

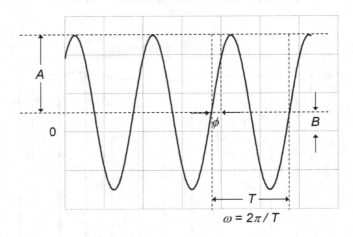

FIGURE 10.19   General sinusoidal wave.

---

[6] When the time units are seconds, the hertz unit (Hz) is used.

where N: normally distributed random signal with zero mean and σ standard deviation.

The specific example illustrated is based on the following parameter values:
$A=1$, $T=1$, $\phi=\pi/4$, $B=0.25$, $\sigma=0.1$

The following Python script produces the plot in Figure 10.20, where the added noise is evident. A random value is added for each of the 100 points plotted. We could adjust this by increasing the number of points or the σ value.

```python
import numpy as np
import matplotlib.pyplot as plt

A = 1.   # amplitude
T = 1.   # period
w = 2*np.pi/T  # angular frequency
phi = np.pi/4  # phase shift
B = 0.25  # offset or bias
sigma = 0.1  # noise standard deviation

tf = np.pi  # final t value

t = np.linspace(0,tf,100)

y1 = lambda t: A*np.sin(w*t+phi) + B

yn = np.random.normal(0,sigma,100)

y = y1(t) + yn

plt.plot(t,y,c='k')
plt.grid()
plt.xlabel('t')
plt.ylabel('y')
```

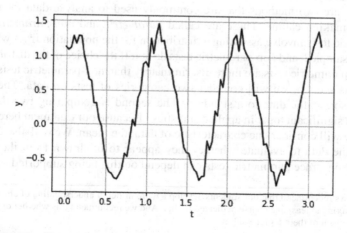

FIGURE 10.20   Sinusoidal wave with noise added.

Creating simulated data sets that are patterned after real measurements is useful because the simulations can then be used in subsequent calculations to allow a preview of what will happen when real data are acquired. They also provide information that can yield understanding of the nature of the real data as well as quantitative inferences regarding the underlying phenomenon generating the data. Python's random number generators are useful for this work.

10.3   MAKING CLAIMS BASED ON DATA

The real world provides us with data that are variable and uncertain. This uncertainty must be assessed when data are used to make important decisions and claims. Here are several practical scenarios:

1. A product must meet a certain specification. Data are collected and used to support a claim that the specification is met or not met.
2. Environmental measurements were made decades ago. A new set of measurements is acquired, and a claim is made that there has been a significant change.
3. A customer has noted that the variability in the quality of a product is too high. Measures are considered to reduce variability and need to be judged whether they would be successful.
4. To proceed with an analysis, we must support a claim that the variability in a data set is adequately modeled by the normal distribution.

Although it may appear as an academic exercise to you now, sooner or later you will be required to make claims based on data. For example, most engineering and science curricula will require you to take one or more laboratory courses where conclusions must be made regarding measurements. Further, you should realize that, at some point in the coming years, your job and future may depend on doing this with care and taking uncertainty into account. This section is designed to introduce you to the methods and issues associated with doing this correctly.

There are two methods that are commonly used to analyze data for the purpose of making claims. These are called *parametric* and *non-parametric* tests. Parametric tests involve assuming a distribution for the population from which the data are sampled, and non-parametric tests do not. If the choice of the distribution is correct, parametric tests are more discriminatory than non-parametric tests.

In this section, we will consider two categories of tests on data. The first is comparison of the data to a standard. The second is comparing two data sets. This is a significant topic in applied statistics.[7] Because our treatment here will be brief, we will consider one characteristic of data: the mean. We will also consider testing the data to evaluate whether they appear to be drawn from the normal distribution, since parametric tests can depend on this being supported.

---

[7] We always recommend that our students develop a more in-depth understanding of applied statistics by taking at least one course dedicated to this. And we recommend this whether or not this is a requirement of their degree studies.

10.3.1 COMPARISON OF DATA WITH A STANDARD

As a precaution, it is worth mentioning that statistical methods and arguments should not be used where they are not needed. Figure 10.21 illustrates one such situation with a boxplot. The data represent the weights in grams of 200 product packets. The specification is that the packets must weigh at least 40 g. We can see that all 200 weights are well above 40 g, despite four outliers. We can make a strong claim that the specification is met. We might be concerned about the variability and the outliers, but that is a separate issue. So, a first consideration before diving into statistical methods and analysis is whether they are needed at all. No need to do work that is not required.

First, we will consider how to use a data set to make a claim about the mean (or median) value of the population. It may be obvious, but is worth stating anyway, that the larger your sample size, the easier it will be to make a claim. The problem with this is that often collecting data is time-consuming and possibly expensive. So, you must find a middle ground where you have enough data to evaluate a claim without exceeding your time and budgetary constraints.

Since uncertainty is associated with any statistical analysis, there is the possibility that a claim may be false. One could describe this as "the risk of being wrong." Formally, this is called a *Type I error*[8] and is represented by a probability, α. Of course, we would like for this value to be small. Typical desired values are 5% and 1% (one chance in 20, and 1 in 100, respectively).

One of the simplest non-parametric tests is called the *sign test*. It applies to claims about the median value, not the mean value. If a histogram chart of the data looks symmetric, these two values will be close. The procedure for the sign test is as follows for a data set with a sample size, n, where the claim is $\tilde{\mu} > \tilde{\mu}_0$.

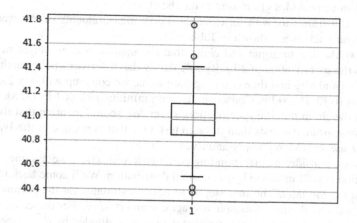

FIGURE 10.21 Boxplot of 200 product measurements.

---

[8] You might wonder whether there is another Type error. There is. It is called a *Type 2 error* with associated probability β. It corresponds to the risk that your claim is actually true, but you miss it.

1. Specify a standard value of the median, $\tilde{\mu}_0$, for comparison.
2. Compute the differences between the data and the standard.
3. Count the numbers of + signs, r^+, from the differences.

If $r^+ > n/2$, calculate this probability[9]

$$P = \sum_{r=r^+}^{n} \begin{pmatrix} n \\ r \end{pmatrix} 0.5^r 0.5^{n-r} \tag{10.12}$$

where

$$\begin{pmatrix} n \\ r \end{pmatrix} = \frac{n!}{r!(n-r)!} \Rightarrow \text{the number of combinations of } n \text{ items taken } r \text{ at a time}$$

$n! \Rightarrow n$ factorial, $n \cdot (n-1) \cdot (n-2) \cdots 2$

The *P-value* is the probability that you could have counted r^+ or greater if $\tilde{\mu} = \tilde{\mu}_0$. The *P*-value represents the risk of being wrong if we make the claim, $\tilde{\mu} > \tilde{\mu}_0$. If it is small, we have grounds to make the claim.

Alternately, we can formulate the test for the claim, $\tilde{\mu} < \tilde{\mu}_0$. Repeating steps 1 and 2 above, we replace step 3 with counting the − signs, r^-, from the differences. If $r^- < n/2$, this probability is calculated

$$P = \sum_{r=0}^{r^-} \begin{pmatrix} n \\ r \end{pmatrix} 0.5^r 0.5^{n-r} \tag{10.13}$$

This *P*-value is the probability that you could have counted r^- or less if $\tilde{\mu} = \tilde{\mu}_0$. A small *P*-value provides grounds to make the claim.

Let's illustrate this with an example. Forty measurements of the weight of small sugar packets are shown in Table 10.1.

We would like to argue and claim that the median packet weight meets or exceeds the specification of 40 g. By calculating the differences between the measurements and 40 g and then counting the + signs, we come up with $r^+ = 29$. Using Equation 10.12, $P \cong 0.1\%$. Consequently, with minimal risk of 1 in 1,000, we can support the claim that the specification is met. We should mention that there are other non-parametric tests than the sign test. One that is popular is the *Wilcoxon signed-rank test* (Montgomery and Runger, 2018).

Now we consider a corresponding parametric test where we assume that the population is well-modeled by the normal distribution. We'll come back to check this assumption later. The first step is to obtain estimates for the parameters of the normal distribution of sample averages, μ and $\sigma/\sqrt{n}$.[10] For these, we use the sample average, $\bar{x}$, and sample standard deviation, s, divided by $\sqrt{n}$, respectively.

---

[9] This calculation is made with the *cumulative binomial distribution*. The 0.5 corresponds to an equal probability of a + sign and − sign. The summation provides the probability of an r+ result and all results greater than r+, given the 0.5 probability.

[10] For a random variable, x, with a standard deviation, σ, the standard deviation of averages of samples of x is $\sigma/\sqrt{n}$.

TABLE 10.1

Weights of 40 Sugar Packets (g)

40.31	41.05	39.85	40.27
40.75	40.80	39.67	40.34
39.71	40.31	40.70	40.00
40.34	40.69	40.44	40.42
40.06	40.30	40.23	40.17
40.34	40.50	40.46	40.10
40.11	40.45	40.58	39.79
40.32	39.55	39.54	39.69
40.42	40.04	40.73	40.39
39.78	40.17	39.66	39.90

Next, using the normal distribution with a mean of the standard, μ_0, and standard deviation, s, we calculate what the probability of computing a sample mean $\geq \mu$. If that probability is small, it supports our claim.[11]

For our packet data, $\bar{x} \cong 40.22$, $s \cong 0.37$, $n=40$. The probability that the average of such a sample would be ≥ 40.22, if μ is actually 40, can be computed in a Python script as

```
import numpy as np
from scipy import stats

mu0 = 40   # mean standard
n = 40   # sample size
xbar = 40.22   # sample average
s = 0.37   # sample standard deviation

# probability to the right of xbar
P = 1 - stats.norm.cdf(xbar,mu0,s/np.sqrt(n))

print('probability = {0:6.3f}%'.format(P*100))
```

and the result is

```
probability = 0.008%
```

This small probability provides a strong basis to support our claim that $\mu > 40$ g. Notice that the probability here is even smaller than that for the sign test. This is because the parametric test is more discriminatory, but it comes with the assumption of a normal distribution.

---

[11] If sample sizes are relatively large, $n \geq 25$ or so, this is a valid approach. For smaller sample sizes, we cannot use the normal distribution for this because we also estimated the standard deviation from the data. In this latter case, we use a distribution called *Student's t*, or just the *t* distribution. In essence, the Student's t distribution is similar to the normal distribution but designed to account for the impact of uncertainty due to small sample size on the result. If you want to pursue additional information on this distribution, you should consult a good statistics book.

10.3.2   COMPARISON BETWEEN TWO SAMPLES

Next, we will consider a comparison test between two samples, denoted A and B. First, we would like to claim that the means of the two samples are significantly different, for example, $\mu_B > \mu_A$. This is an important test that engineers and scientists encounter frequently. A common non-parametric test for this is the *Wilcoxon rank-sum test*. As above, we will illustrate this with two example data sets.

A	B
11.29	11.67
9.65	9.58
8.17	10.23
9.86	9.00
10.76	10.25
9.10	11.55
7.75	12.19
9.05	11.94
10.95	8.71
8.34	12.38

It is useful to examine a side-by-side boxplot of these data. Here is the Python script that produces that comparison in Figure 10.22.

```
import numpy as np
import matplotlib.pyplot as plt

xA = np.array([11.29,9.65,8.17,9.86,10.76,9.1,7.75 \
               ,9.05,10.95,8.34])
xB = np.array([11.67,9.58,10.23,9.,10.25,11.55\
               ,12.19,11.94,8.71,12.38])

x = np.array([xA, xB]).transpose()

plt.boxplot(x, labels=('A', 'B'))
plt.grid()
```

This is interesting because the box of sample B is above that of sample A, but the difference isn't clear, as they overlap. The message here is that statistics are needed.

With the Wilcoxon test, we sift the two samples together, keeping track of their sample designation, and sort the result in ascending order. We assign the ranks (sequence of numbers 1, 2, 3,...) to the resulting array. Then, we sum the A and B ranks separately. If the means of the two samples are the same, we would expect these sums to be roughly equal. If the sums are different, we can judge if this difference is significant enough to support our claim.

The table below shows the combined samples with A and B designations and ranks. The sum of the ranks for A is 80 and for B is 130. For these sample sizes, available tables for the Wilcoxon test[12] provide threshold values of 82 and 128 for

---

[12] http://plantsys.elte.hu/oktatas/Biometria/tablazatok/Wilcoxon_table_ketmintas_probahoz.pdf

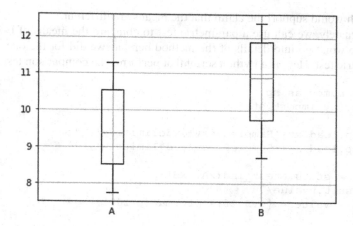

FIGURE 10.22 Side-by-side boxplot of samples A and B.

an α risk value of 5% (i.e. a 1 in 20 chance that the conclusion is wrong). To support our claim for this level of risk, the sum of ranks for A must be ≤ 82 and for B must be ≥ 128. That is the case here, so the claim would be supported. We would be taking a risk lower than 5% to support the claim that the two samples are different.

7.75	A	1	10.23	B	11
8.17	A	2	10.25	B	12
8.34	A	3	10.76	A	13
8.71	B	4	10.95	A	14
9.00	B	5	11.29	A	15
9.05	A	6	11.55	B	16
9.10	A	7	11.67	B	17
9.58	B	8	11.94	B	18
9.65	A	9	12.19	B	19
9.86	A	10	12.38	B	20

Python's SciPy module has a `ranksums` function that performs the Wilcoxon test. Here is a script that shows you how to use it.

```
import numpy as np
from scipy import stats

xA = np.loadtxt('SampleA.csv', delimiter=', ')
xB = np.loadtxt('SampleB.csv', delimiter=', ')

result = stats.ranksums(xA, xB, alternative='less')
print('P-value = {0:5.2f}%'.format(result.pvalue*100))
```

The *P*-value displayed is

```
P-value =   2.94%
```

which would support the claim that the means are different.

Alternately, we can use a parametric test to compare the means of two samples. We won't go into details of the method here, as we did for the one-sample parametric test. Here is a Python script that performs the comparison test.

```python
import numpy as np
from scipy import stats

xA = np.loadtxt('SampleA.csv', delimiter=', ')
xB = np.loadtxt('SampleB.csv', delimiter=', ')

result = stats.ttest_ind(xA, xB)
p = result.pvalue/2
print('P-value = {0:5.2f}%'.format(p*100))
```

The *P*-value displayed in the Console is

```
P-value = 2.20%
```

If our criterion for acceptable risk were 5%, the lower *P*-value meets that and supports our claim that the mean of sample A is less than the mean of sample B. You will note again that the *P*-value for the parametric test is lower than that for the Wilcoxon test, the parametric test being more discriminatory.

Tests on the variance, and related standard deviation, are important in the modeling and management of product variability. High variability impacts product quality and customer satisfaction negatively. Also, the lower the variability, the closer we can control the mean to meet a specification. These tests are important, but we don't take the time to detail them here.

10.3.3 DETERMINING WHETHER DATA ARE NORMALLY DISTRIBUTED

In the previous sections, we have seen that the more discriminatory parametric tests are only appropriate when we have confidence that the data adequately follow a particular distribution; in our examples, the normal distribution. Therefore, the final topic we address in this section is determining whether the population from which data are extracted is adequately modeled by the normal distribution. A useful tool in assessing this is the *cumulative distribution*, which is given by the following integral,

$$F(x) = \int_{-\infty}^{x} f(x')dx' \tag{10.13}$$

where $f(x)$: the normal density function and x' is a dummy variable.

In words, this is the area to the left of x on the plot of the density function. This is illustrated in Figure 10.23. Since the normal density cannot be integrated analytically, we must find the cumulative distribution numerically using quadrature, as we introduced in the previous chapter in Example 9.1[13].

---

[13] Traditionally, the values of the cumulative standard normal distribution have been presented in table form. Such tables are still included in most applied statistics texts.

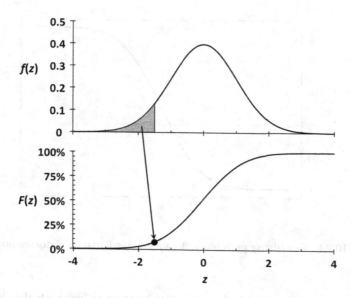

FIGURE 10.23 Relationship between the density function and cumulative probability function.

Plotting the cumulative distribution, we get an S-shaped or *sigmoidal curve* instead of the bell-shaped curve of the density function. To illustrate this, we will use the standard normal density ($\mu = 0$ and $\sigma = 1$),

$$f(z) = \frac{1}{\sqrt{2\pi}} e^{-\frac{z^2}{2}}$$

(10.14)

Based on Example 9.1, we create a Python script to produce a plot of the cumulative distribution. The result is shown in Figure 10.24. Here, we have displayed the cumulative probability in per cent.

```
import numpy as np
from scipy.integrate import quad
import matplotlib.pyplot as plt

stdnormdens = lambda z: 1/np.sqrt(2*np.pi)*np.exp(-1/2*z**2)

z = np.linspace(-4,4,200)
n = len(z)
F = np.zeros(n)
for i in range(n):
F[i], eF = quad(stdnormdens, -4,z[i])

plt.plot(z, 100*F, c='k')
plt.grid()
plt.xlabel('z')
plt.ylabel('F(z) %')
```

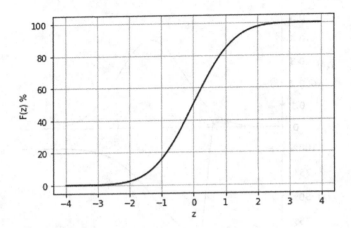

FIGURE 10.24   Cumulative probability plot for the standard normal distribution.

A data set can be displayed on this plot in order to judge whether the data follow a normal distribution. To do this, we first must "standardize" the data using the formula

$$z = \frac{x - \mu}{\sigma} \cong \frac{x - \bar{x}}{s} \qquad (10.15)$$

Next, we sort the z array and compute the percentile for each data point using

$$pct = \frac{i - 0.5}{n} \cdot 100 \quad i = 1, \ldots, n \qquad (10.16)$$

The pct array can then be added to the plot in Figure 10.24 as data markers.

Using the sugar packet data from Table 10.1, we can add to the above script to place the standardized data on the plot. This is shown in Figure 10.25. You can see that the data follow the standard normal curve closely. This leads us to conclude, at least qualitatively, that the data are representative of a normally distributed population.

```python
x = np.loadtxt('PacketData.csv', delimiter=', ')
xs = np.sort(x)
xbar = np.mean(xs)
s = np.std(xs)
z = (xs-xbar)/s
n = len(xs)
p = np.zeros(n)
for i in range(n):
    p[i] = (i+0.5)/n

plt.scatter(z, p*100,c = 'k', marker='.')
```

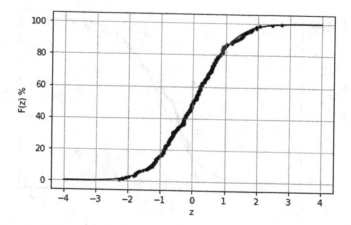

FIGURE 10.25   Cumulative probability plot with standardized data added.

This raises a question: How would it look if the data were not drawn from a normal population? Here is an alternate script line which uses data simulated from the Weibull distribution.

```
x = np.random.weibull(1.2,100)
```

The plot is shown in Figure 10.26, and it is obvious that the data are not representative of samples from a normal distribution.

It is also possible to create a nonlinear vertical scale that transforms the cumulative probability curve into a straight line. Then, judging the alignment of data is easier. This has been done manually for decades using *probability graph paper*.[14]

It is also possible to "linearize" the cumulative probability curve using *z-scores* instead of cumulative probabilities. For example, for a cumulative probability of 5%, the point on the z axis that corresponds is called the *z-score*. It is found by using the inverse of the cumulative probability function. In Python, via the SciPy `stats` module, you can compute this with the `norm.ppf` function. For the 5% z-score,

```
from scipy import stats

cumP = 0.05
zscore = stats.norm.ppf(cumP)
print('z-score = {0:5.2f}'.format(zscore))

z-score = -1.64
```

If we modify the script that produces Figure 10.25 to replace percentiles with z-scores, here is the resulting script. The probability plot is then shown in Figure 10.27, where you can easily recognize the linearization.

---

[14] You can download a sample at www.weibull.com/GPaper/. There are graph papers for different distributions, not only the normal. When plotting on these graphs, one doesn't need to transform the data into a z array.

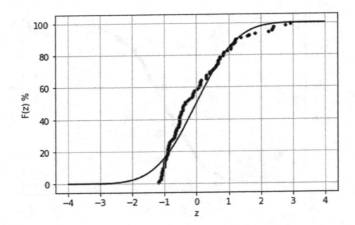

FIGURE 10.26 Simulated data from the Weibull distribution on the standard normal cumulative probability plot.

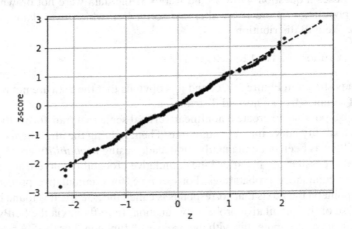

FIGURE 10.27 Probability plot with z-scores.

```python
import numpy as np
import matplotlib.pyplot as plt
from scipy import stats

x = np.loadtxt('PacketData.csv', delimiter=', ')
xs = np.sort(x)
xbar = np.mean(xs)
s = np.std(xs)
z = (xs-xbar)/s
n = len(xs)
p = np.zeros(n)
zsc = np.zeros(n)
for i in range(n):
```

```
p[i] = (i+0.5)/n
zsc[i] = stats.norm.ppf(p[i])

plt.scatter(z, zsc, c = 'k', marker='.')
plt.plot(z, z, c='k', ls='--')
plt.grid()
plt.xlabel('z')
plt.ylabel('z-score')
```

Note that Python SciPy's `stats` module has a `probplot` function that produces a similar plot based on z-scores. The plot produced by `probplot` reverses the axes and doesn't transform the data into a z array. We will illustrate the use of `probplot` in Section 10.4.3.

Earlier, we introduced the idea of a statistical test and a P-value to assess the Type I error (α) risk. There are similar tests for probability distributions. We will illustrate one here, called the *Anderson-Darling test*, with an addition to our Python script. This test seeks to prove that the distribution is not normal.

```
result = stats.anderson(x, dist='norm')
print(result)
```

The display is

```
AndersonResult(statistic=3.088203603370033, critical_
values=array([0.555, 0.632, 0.759, 0.885, 1.053]),
significance_level=array([15. , 10. ,  5. ,  2.5,  1. ]))
```

We interpret this in the following way. For a significance level of 5., the critical value of the statistic is 0.759. Since the statistic, 3.088..., is greater than the critical value, it leads to the claim that the data do not follow a normal distribution. If we apply the same test to the sugar packet data, the results are

```
AndersonResult(statistic=0.25340941601047007, critical_
values=array([0.565, 0.644, 0.772, 0.901, 1.071]),
significance_level=array([15. , 10. ,  5. ,  2.5,  1. ]))
```

and, since $0.253... < 0.772$, the claim that the distribution is not normal is rejected.

As we have stated before, this section is, in fact, a brief introduction to statistical tests, often called *hypothesis tests*. In a course on applied statistics, you will acquire a broader knowledge of this topic. We recommend that you take such a course.

10.4   FITTING MATHEMATICAL MODELS TO DATA

Scientists and engineers frequently develop methods to interpret data to gain understanding and predict behavior and values not in the data set. This is most often done by developing mathematical models based on the data. We've seen an example of this in Figure 9.13. Although we show a proposed polynomial model there that appears to follow the data well, we deferred explaining how we came up with that model. We then utilized the model to accomplish a quadrature. We will show how we developed that model in this section.

10.4.1 Straight-Line Linear Regression

The mathematical procedure to fit a model to data is called *regression*. We start here with the simple scenario of fitting a straight line to a data set. Then we move on to models which allow curvature, mainly polynomials. Finally, we review models for which we cannot use the linear regression methods developed for straight lines and polynomials.

Consider the scenario presented in Figure 10.28. Here we have plotted a set of 11 data from $\{x_i, y_i, i = 1, \ldots, 11\}$. A straight-line model, $y = a x + b$, is proposed and plotted. For each value of x, we can use the model to compute a model prediction,

$$\hat{y}_i = a x_i + b \tag{10.17}$$

For each prediction, there is a *residual error*,

$$e_i = \hat{y}_i - y_i \tag{10.18}$$

A general sense of fitting the model to the data is that we would like the residual errors to be small. To do this, we need a single criterion or objective to use in judging the residual errors. We could use the sum of absolute values of the

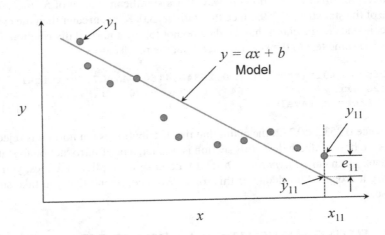

FIGURE 10.28   Scenario for straight-line regression.

residuals, but it is preferred to use the sum of the squares of the residual errors because this is more sensitive to the influence of one or more large errors. We then want to adjust our straight line, the a and b parameters, to minimize this "least squares" criterion,

$$V = \sum_{i=1}^{n} e_i^2 = \sum_{i=1}^{n} (\hat{y}_i - y_i)^2 = \sum_{i=1}^{n} (a x_i + b - y_i)^2 \tag{10.19}$$

The question then is how do we minimize V by the selection of a and b? It turns out that we can use calculus to determine this by finding the partial derivatives of V with respect to those two parameters, setting those two expressions equal to zero, and solving for a and b. Here are the derivative expressions:

$$\frac{\partial V}{\partial a} = 2 \sum_{i=1}^{n} x_i (a x_i + b - y_i) = 2a \sum_{i=1}^{n} x_i^2 + 2b \sum_{i=1}^{n} x_i - 2 \sum_{i=1}^{n} x_i y_i \tag{10.20}$$

$$\frac{\partial V}{\partial b} = 2 \sum_{i=1}^{n} (a x_i + b - y_i) = 2a \sum_{i=1}^{n} x_i + 2nb - 2 \sum_{i=1}^{n} y_i \tag{10.21}$$

Setting both derivative expressions equal to zero to find the minimum,

$$a \sum_{i=1}^{n} x_i^2 + b \sum_{i=1}^{n} x_i - \sum_{i=1}^{n} x_i y_i = 0 \tag{10.22}$$

$$a \sum_{i=1}^{n} x_i + nb - \sum_{i=1}^{n} y_i = 0 \tag{10.23}$$

Solving Equation 10.23 for b, we get

$$b = \frac{\sum_{i=1}^{n} y_i}{n} - a \frac{\sum_{i=1}^{n} x_i}{n} = \bar{y} - a\bar{x} \tag{10.24}$$

Substituting Equation 10.24 into Equation 10.23 and solving for a, the steps are

$$a\sum_{i=1}^{n}x_i^2 + \left(\frac{\sum_{i=1}^{n}y_i}{n} - a\frac{\sum_{i=1}^{n}x_i}{n}\right)\sum_{i=1}^{n}x_i - \sum_{i=1}^{n}x_iy_i = 0$$

$$an\sum_{i=1}^{n}x_i^2 - a\left(\sum_{i=1}^{n}x_i\right)^2 + \sum_{i=1}^{n}x_i\sum_{i=1}^{n}y_i - n\sum_{i=1}^{n}x_iy_i = 0 \qquad (10.25)$$

$$a = \frac{n\sum_{i=1}^{n}x_iy_i - \sum_{i=1}^{n}x_i\sum_{i=1}^{n}y_i}{n\sum_{i=1}^{n}x_i^2 - \left(\sum_{i=1}^{n}x_i\right)^2}$$

By solving for a using the final form of Equation 10.25, we can substitute that in Equation 10.24 to determine b.

Example 10.2 Fitting a Straight Line to U.S. CO_2 Emissions from Fossil Fuels

The data in Table 10.2 represent the annual emissions of carbon dioxide in the U.S. from fossil fuel sources from 2007 to 2020. Before we consider fitting a straight line to the data, or any data, we should plot the data and judge whether a linear model is appropriate. A plot of the data is shown in Figure 10.29.

Examining the plot, there is a steadily decreasing trend. With the exception of 2020,[15] a straight-line fit might be appropriate. Here is a Python script that computes the slope and intercept of the line using Equations 10.25 and 10.24 and adds the line to the plot as depicted in Figure 10.30.

```
import numpy as np
import matplotlib.pyplot as plt

yr, amt = np.loadtxt('CO2_Emissions.csv', delimiter=', ',
unpack=True)

plt.scatter(yr, amt, c='k', marker='o')
plt.grid()
plt.xlabel('Year')
plt.ylabel('CO2 Emissions - MMT/yr')

n = len(yr)
x = yr
```

---

[15] The large drop in 2020 is likely an effect of the COVID-19 pandemic and corresponding reductions in transportation.

TABLE 10.2
Annual Emissions of CO_2 in the U.S. in Million Metric Tons

Year	Amount
2007	6,016
2008	5,823
2009	5,404
2010	5,594
2011	5,455
2012	5,236
2013	5,359
2014	5,414
2015	5,262
2016	5,169
2017	5,131
2018	5,277
2019	5,144
2020	4,575

Source: https://www.eia.gov/environment/emissions/carbon/.

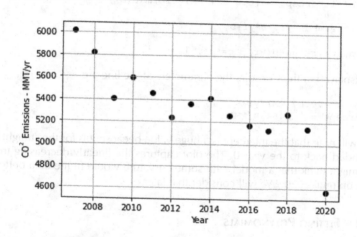

FIGURE 10.29 Annual emissions of CO_2 in the U.S. from fossil fuels.

```
y = amt
Sx = np.sum(x)
Sy = np.sum(y)
Sx2 = 0
Sxy = 0
ybar = np.mean(y)
xbar = np.mean(x)
for i in range(n):
    Sx2 = Sx2 + x[i]**2
    Sxy = Sxy + x[i]*y[i]
```

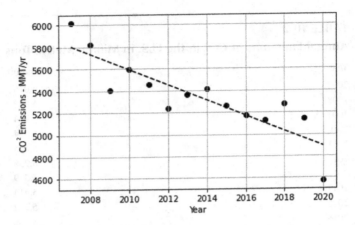

FIGURE 10.30 Annual CO_2 emissions with fitted straight line added.

```
a = (n*Sxy-Sx*Sy)/(n*Sx2-Sx**2)
b = ybar - a*xbar
print('slope = {0:6.2f} MMT/yr'.format(a))

print('intercept = {0:8.0f} MMT'.format(b))

amtp = lambda yr: a*yr+b

plt.plot(yr, amtp(yr), c='k', ls='--')
```

As displayed in the Console, the parameters of the line are

```
slope = -70.07 MMT/yr
intercept =   146438 MMT
```

You will note that the intercept is a huge value because it is for the straight line extended back to the year 0. The plot captures the linearly decreasing trend. We might think that a model with some curvature would fit the data better, at least up until 2020. We will consider that later.

10.4.2 FITTING POLYNOMIALS

Next, we will consider fitting models that are more complicated than just a straight line. For example, we might want to fit a second-order polynomial model,

$$y = b_0 + b_1 x + b_2 x^2 \tag{10.26}$$

and we can generalize this to a polynomial of order m,

$$y = b_0 + b_1 x + \ldots + b_{m-1} x^{m-1} + b_m x^m \tag{10.27}$$

If we attempt to derive the formulas for the least squares fit of the model parameters in the same manner as we did for the straight line, these become very cumbersome. There is a more compact, efficient way to approach the problem using a vector/matrix description, but we do not introduce that here (see Chapra & Clough 2022 for more information on the vector/matrix description). It would be more appropriate for a course in applied statistics or numerical methods. Instead, we will rely on a function available from the NumPy module, `polyfit`.

The syntax for the `polyfit` function is

```
coeff = polyfit(x,y,order)
```

where x is the independent variable array, y is the response array, and `order` is an integer for the order of the polynomial being fit. The `coeff` result is an array of the polynomial coefficients from highest order to the intercept. As a simple example, we can replicate our straight-line fit of the CO_2 data as follows:

```
import numpy as np

yr, amt = np.loadtxt('CO2_Emissions.csv', delimiter=', ',
unpack=True)

b = np.polyfit(yr, amt, 1)
print(b)

[-7.00725275e+01  1.46438105e+05]
```

The coefficients displayed are the same as those we computed previously.

With the `polyfit` function in hand, we have a general method for polynomial models of any order. We can apply this to the data from Chapter 9, Figure 9.13.

t	y
0.09	15.1
0.32	57.3
0.69	103.3
1.51	174.6
2.29	191.5
3.06	193.2
3.39	178.7
3.63	172.3
3.77	167.5

We proposed a third-order polynomial to fit these data. Here is a Python script that carries that out.

```
import numpy as np

t = np.array([0.09,0.32,0.69,1.51,2.29,3.06,3.39,3.63,3.77])
y = np.array([15.1,57.3,103.3,174.6,191.5,193.2,178.7,/
172.3, 167.5])
```

```
b = np.polyfit(t, y, 3)

print('cubic polynomial parameters:\n', b)
```

The results displayed in the Console are

```
cubic polynomial parameters:
 [   4.3507208   -53.87521322  185.62642213    0.55854906]
```

which yield the polynomial model we proposed in Chapter 9,

$$y = 0.559 + 185.6t - 53.88t^2 + 4.351t^3$$

Figure 9.13 shows the model line and the data.

10.4.3   GENERAL ISSUES AND PRECAUTIONS

To complete our discussion of polynomial regression, we will discuss some general issues and precautions. First, the concept of *parsimony* is important. By parsimony, we mean that we should seek the simplest model that fits the data well.[16] This leads us to the concept of *model adequacy*.

A way to quantify these concepts is to define the overall variability of the data, also called *the total corrected sum of squares, SS_T*.

$$SS_T = \sum_{i=1}^{n} (y_i - \overline{y})^2 \tag{10.28}$$

You can see that this is the sum of squares of the differences between the data and their average value. When we are considering a model that involves an independent variable, also called a *regressor variable*, we expect that our model will account for some of that total variability. By our regression calculations, what is left over is the set of residual values, $\{e_i, i=1,\ldots, n\}$. These are computed by

$$e_i = y_i - \hat{y}_i \qquad i = 1,\ldots,n \tag{10.29}$$

where $\hat{y}_i$: the model prediction for the regressor variable x_i.

The residuals represent the remaining variability that the model couldn't explain, and we can quantify that by

$$SS_E = \sum_{i=1}^{n} e_i^2 \tag{10.30}$$

---

[16] The sentiment expressed here is commonly referred to as Occam's (or Ockham's) Razor. This is a philosophical heuristic attributed to the 14th-century English friar and logician, William of Ockham (ca. 1285–1349). Although it has been paraphrased in many forms, a nice concise expression is "When you have two competing hypotheses that make exactly the same predictions, the simpler one is best."

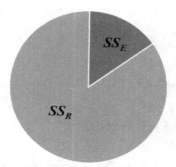

Total Variability
SST

FIGURE 10.31 Partition of total variability.

A useful way to picture this is with a pie chart showing the partition of the total variability into that accounted for by the model, SS_R, and the residual error, SS_E. See Figure 10.31. We can observe from the figure that the regression sum of squares, SS_R, can be obtained from $SS_T - SS_E$. An obvious goal then is to find a model that provides a small value of SS_E.

A common statistic used to quantify the performance of a model in fitting the data is *the coefficient of determination* or "*R-squared*." This is the fraction of the total variability accounted for by the model or

$$R^2 = \frac{SS_R}{SS_T} = 1 - \frac{SS_E}{SS_T} \qquad (10.31)$$

The R^2 value is often reported as a percentage.

With reference to polynomial models, there is a significant problem in using R^2 as a measure of performance of the model. As we increase the order of the polynomial, the number of fitted parameters obviously increases. As we do this, R^2 always increases up to the point where the number of parameters, $m+1$, equals the number of data, n. At that point, the model will pass exactly through every data point, and R^2 will equal one. Generally, this latter model will be a poor one because it will have unusual behavior between the data points and so will not be suitable for predictions and understanding.

The Python script below computes and displays R^2 for the straight-line fit of the CO_2 emissions data.

```
import numpy as np

yr,amt = np.loadtxt('CO2_Emissions.csv',delimiter=',',
unpack=True)

b = np.polyfit(yr,amt,1)
print(b)
```

```
amtp = np.polyval(b,yr)

e = amt - amtp
SSE = e.dot(e)
n = len(yr)
amtbar = np.mean(amt)
SST = 0
for i in range(n):
    SST = SST + (amt[i]-amtbar)**2
SSR = SST - SSE
R2 = SSR/SST
print('R-squared = {0:6.1f}%'.format(R2*100))
```

You will note that we used the `polyval` function above. It gives us the ability to compute a polynomial with coefficients b for one or more values of the independent variable, `yr`. The R^2 value displayed is

```
R-squared = 74.7%
```

Is a value of 74.7% good or bad? That is unclear. If the residual errors are mainly random noise, this R^2 value may be adequate. The residuals then represent random behavior that we can't explain with a model. Along with many statisticians, we recommend against using R^2 as a measure of regression performance. A reasonable alternative is the *standard error of the estimate*, given by

$$s_e = \sqrt{\frac{SS_E}{n-(m+1)}} \tag{10.32}$$

This value for our straight-line fit is 177.4. You can think of the standard error as the "standard deviation" relative to the fit. Thus, the lower the s_e, the better the fit.

An objective of regression is to determine the model that accounts for all the systematic behavior in the dependent or response, y, leaving a residual series that contains no systematic behavior. We also expect that the residuals will be random values that can be modeled adequately by the normal distribution with mean of zero and standard deviation, σ_e. This is the concept of *adequacy*, and we often assess it with plots.

For our straight-line example, Figure 10.32 depicts a plot of the residual errors versus year. We connect the data markers with lines to help recognize any patterns or systematic behavior. Perhaps we judge that the residuals start high, drop down, and then return high. If this is the case, we might seek to fit the data with a second-order polynomial instead of a straight line. The model that results is

$$am\,t = 1.081yr^2 - 4423yr + 4.529 \times 10^6 \tag{10.33}$$

and the corresponding residuals plot is shown in Figure 10.33. There is very little change in the pattern, so we haven't gained much by using the higher-order model. We note here that the R^2 and s_e values for this fit are $R^2 = 75\%$ and $s_e = 184.4$. As

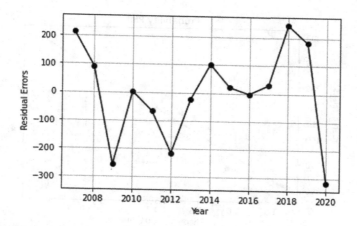

FIGURE 10.32   Residual errors versus year for straight-line model.

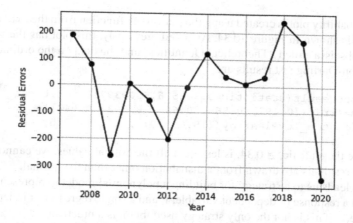

FIGURE 10.33   Residual errors versus year for second-order model.

expected, by adding a term to the model, the R^2 value increased, but only slightly, from 74.7%; however, the s_e value also increased, indicating that the second-order fit doesn't perform as well as the straight-line.

We can also test whether the residual errors appear to belong to a normally distributed population. Here is the addition to the straight-line script to do that.

```
import matplotlib.pyplot as plt
from scipy import stats
stats.probplot(e, plot=plt)
plt.grid()
result = stats.anderson(e, dist='norm')
print(result)
```

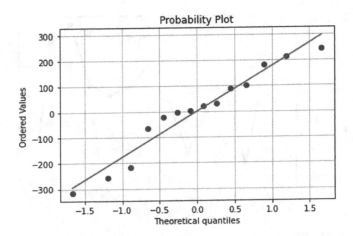

FIGURE 10.34   Probability plot of residuals from straight-line fit of CO_2 emissions data.

The probability plot is created using the probplot function from the stats module and is shown in Figure 10.34. As noted previously, this plot has the z-scores on the abscissa called "Theoretical Quantities" and the data on the ordinate. The Anderson-Darling test results are

```
AndersonResult(statistic=0.3425761550939743, critical_
values=array([0.497, 0.566, 0.68 , 0.793, 0.943]),
significance_level=array([15. , 10. ,   5. ,  2.5,  1. ]))
```

Since the statistic, $\cong 0.34$, is less than all the critical values, we cannot claim that the residuals are drawn from a distribution other than the normal.

This leads us to a strategy for building a polynomial model to represent a data set with a response or dependent variable, y, and a single regressor or independent variable, x. This is not the only strategy used, but it is a practical one.

1. Start with a simple polynomial model based on observation of a plot of the data.
2. Fit the model, compute R^2 and s_e, and make residual plots to judge adequacy.
3. Increase the polynomial order and repeat step 2.
4. Stop when the s_e value no longer decreases.
5. Select the simplest model that shows adequacy in the residual plots.

Example 10.3 Fitting a Polynomial to Data on the Density of Water versus Temperature

Many data sets that we acquire are relatively noisy, that is have a fair amount of random error. However, data for properties of materials that represent careful

TABLE 10.3
Density of Water versus Temperature at One Atmosphere Pressure

Temperature (°C)	Density (kg/m³)	Temperature (°C)	Density (kg/m³)
0	999.87	50	988.07
2	999.97	55	985.73
4	1,000	60	983.24
6	999.97	65	980.59
10	999.73	70	977.81
15	999.13	75	974.89
20	998.23	80	971.83
25	997.08	85	968.65
30	995.68	90	965.34
35	994.06	95	961.92
40	992.25	100	958.38
45	990.25		

measurements made in a laboratory setting are generally noise-free. Table 10.3 presents data on the density of water from 0°C to 100°C. This is the same table as in Chapter 4, Problem 4.4. We wish to develop a polynomial model that can be used to predict density values at intermediate temperatures accurately.

Following our strategy, we first write a Python script to produce a plot of the data.

```
import numpy as np
import matplotlib.pyplot as plt

T,rho = np.loadtxt('H2ODensityVsTemperature.csv',delimiter=','
\
                    ,unpack=True)

plt.scatter(T,rho,c='k')
plt.grid()
plt.xlabel('Temperature - degC')
plt.ylabel('Density - kg/m3')
```

The plot is displayed in Figure 10.34. First, it is clear that we would not fit a straight line to the data. Therefore, we start with a second-order polynomial. Here are the results:

```
[-3.60517790e-03 -6.67273530e-02  1.00052105e+03]
se = 0.3646166867986853
R2 = 0.9993561813821505
```

You can see that the R^2 value is very close to 1.0. The s_e value is what it is – to be compared with other models. To check the model and adequacy, see Figures 10.36 and 10.37. Although the model in Figure 10.36 may look reasonable, it doesn't quite follow the data. This is evident with the residuals

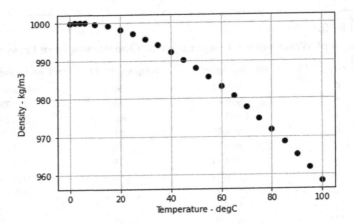

FIGURE 10.35   Data on the density of water versus temperature.

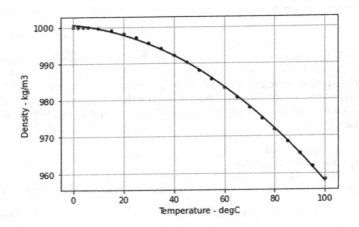

FIGURE 10.36   Second-order polynomial fit.

plot in Figure 10.37 where there is clear systematic behavior. This model is inadequate.

We summarize the s_e values in Table 10.4 for increasing orders of polynomials.

Notice that the minimum s_e value occurs for a seventh-order polynomial. However, by studying the residuals plots, we find the absence of any pattern first occurs for a fifth-order polynomial. This is shown in Figure 10.38. We are left with the decision to select any model from fifth-order through seventh-order polynomials. Based on parsimony, the simplest model that is adequate, we select the fifth-order model, which is

$$\rho = 9999 + 0.06279T - 0.00841T^2 + 6.678 \times 10^{-5}T^3$$

$$- 4.218 \times 10^{-7}T^4 + 1.173 \times 10^{-9}T^5 \qquad (10.34)$$

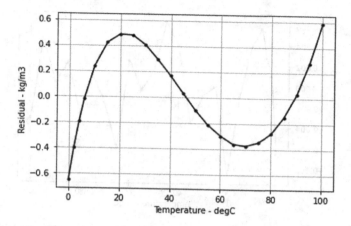

FIGURE 10.37 Residuals versus temperature for a second-order polynomial model.

TABLE 10.4
Standard Errors of the Estimate for Different Polynomials

Order	s_e
2	3.65E–01
3	7.98E–02
4	1.90E–02
5	4.45E–03
6	3.25E–03
7	2.97E–03
8	3.01E–03

The plot for this model with the data is shown in Figure 10.39. As far as we can tell, the fit is excellent. Also, in Figure 10.38, the residual errors are less than ± 0.01 kg/m³ for density values about 1,000.

The method we have illustrated with polynomial models is called *linear regression* because the parameters enter the model linearly. Obviously, the polynomial terms are nonlinear in the independent, regressor variable, but the method applies as long as it is linear in the parameters, the b's. There are many other model forms that work with linear regression. Here are several examples:

$$y = b_0 + b_1 \frac{1}{x} + b_2 \ln(x) \tag{10.40}$$

$$y = b_0 + b_1 \sin(x) + b_2 \cos(x) \tag{10.41}$$

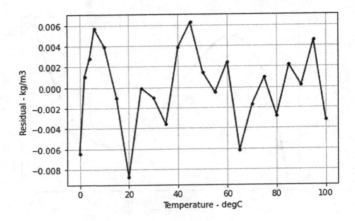

FIGURE 10.38 Residuals versus temperature plot for fifth-order polynomial fit.

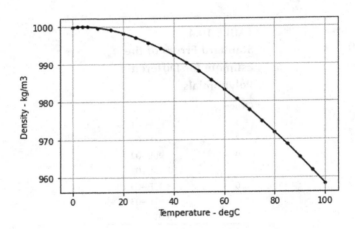

FIGURE 10.39 Fifth-order polynomial fit to H_2O density data versus temperature.

$$y = b_0 + b_1 x_1 + b_2 x_2 + b_{12} x_1 x_2 \qquad (10.42)$$

The model shown in Equation 10.42 is often called *multilinear* because it includes two regressor (independent) variables, x_1 and x_2. All three models can be regressed using a method similar to that we illustrated with polynomials.

There are models that appear as nonlinear but can be transformed into models suitable for linear regression. A common example is

$$y = b_0 \, e^{b_1 x} \qquad \Rightarrow \qquad \ln(y) = \ln(b_0) + b_1 x \qquad (10.43)$$

We would regress a straight-line model of ln(y) versus x. The estimated intercept would be ln(b_0), and we would calculate b_0 as the exponential of this.

And then there are models that are nonlinear in the parameters and cannot be transformed as above. Here are two examples:

$$y = 10^{b_0 + \frac{b_1}{b_2 + x}} \tag{10.44}$$

$$\frac{dy}{dt} = b_0 t + b_1 y + b_2 y t \tag{10.45}$$

In the case of Equation 10.45, with a data set $\{t_i, y_i, i = 1,\dots, n\}$, we would have to solve the differential equation numerically with the methods of Chapter 9 to obtain model predictions, $\hat{y}_i$, for a given set of parameters. For models like those in Equations 10.44 and 10.45, the fitting method is called *nonlinear regression*. One needs a procedure to search iteratively for the parameters that minimize the V criterion.

Fitting models to data is important for engineers and scientists. In this section, we have provided you with a good start into this topic. Polynomial models are the ones most frequently fit to data, so you're ready to go with that. We encourage that you learn more about this topic, especially extending the techniques for general linear and nonlinear regression.

PROBLEMS

10.1 Table 3.12 lists the number of Atlantic hurricanes from 1851 to 2020, and the data are presented in a plot in Figure 3.11.

(a) Using the concepts discussed in Section 10.1.1, describe this data set. Provide your observations from the plot.

(b) Write a Python script to divide the data set into two parts, 1851–1949 and 1950–2020. Compute the average of each subset and comment on the results.

10.2 The table below reports *biological oxygen demand* (BOD) measurements taken at 2-hour intervals from a small river. This measurement requires taking two samples at each site. One is tested immediately for dissolved oxygen, and the second is incubated in the dark at 20°C for 5 days and then evaluated for the amount of dissolved oxygen remaining. The difference in these two measurements is the BOD.

(a) Compute the average, median, sample standard deviation, and MAD for these data.

(b) Create a boxplot of the data and interpret the result.

(c) If there are one or more outliers, imagine that an investigation has justified its removal from the data set. Do so and repeat the calculations of part (a). Comment on the results.

Sample Number	BOD (mg/L)
1	6.5
2	5.8
3	13.1
4	6.4
5	7.0
6	6.3
7	7.0
8	9.2
9	6.7
10	6.7

10.3 Conduct a study of the piston diameter data in Table 5.6 as follows:
   (a) Apply the sign test to support the claim that the median diameter is less than 74.01 mm.
   (b) Evaluate and test whether the data appear to have been drawn from a normal distribution.
   (c) Assuming the data appear normally distributed, carry out a parametric test to support the same claim as in part **(a)**.

10.4 A product is produced in batches. The process operates in batches of 16 hours/day in two shifts. Data in the table below have been collected during the day and night shifts.
   (a) Create side-by-side boxplots of the data, and comment on your observations.
   (b) Apply the Wilcoxon rank sum test to the data to assess whether the mean quality is different between shifts.
   (c) Apply the test illustrated with the A and B samples in this chapter to test whether the mean quality is different between shifts. Comment on the differences between the conclusions in part **(b)** and **(c)**.

Shift	
Day	**Night**
40	47
27	42
39	41
46	34
32	45
46	52
40	49
44	35
48	43
41	44

10.5 Fit a straight-line model to the data of Problem 10.1 and interpret the results.

10.6 Table 5.1 presents freezing point data for antifreeze solutions. Fit an appropriate polynomial model to these data. Document how you arrive at your final selection and be sure to address the adequacy of your model.

10.7 Figure 5.3 presents a plot of the Wolf sunspot data.
(a) Based on observations from the plot, comment on the data set.
(b) Fit a straight-line model to the data and add it to the plot. Comment on the stationarity of the data set.
(c) Produce a histogram plot of the data. Analyze whether the data appear to be drawn from a normally distributed population.

10.8 Table 5.5 presents densities of NaCl and MgCl salt solutions at 0°C for different salt concentrations.
(a) Fit straight-line models for each salt and compare the results.
(b) Analyze the residuals of each fit and comment on model adequacy.

10.9 Write a Python script that generates 100 random numbers according to the uniform distribution in the range −1 to 1.
(a) Compute the average and sample standard deviation of the data set and compare that to the theoretical values for the uniform distribution.
(b) Modify your script to compute the 100-sample data set 100 times. Store the 100 sample averages in an array and create a histogram plot of the results. Comment on the plot.
(c) Create a probability plot based on the normal distribution of your 100 averages from part (b). Also, perform and interpret the Anderson-Darling test. Interpret your results. You may have illustrated a principle named the *Central Limit Theorem*. Look this up and document it as part of your solution.

10.10 Table 5.6 presents 40 measurements of the inside diameter of piston rings, and these data are used in the histogram plots of Figures 10.12 and 10.13. Analyze whether it is likely that these data are drawn from a normally distributed population. Utilize a probability plot and the Anderson-Darling test.

10.11 Compute and plot the cumulative probability distribution for the Weibull distribution with $\alpha=2.0$ and $\beta=4.5$ for $0 \leq x \leq 12$.

10.12 In the sugar industry, a concentrated sucrose solution is produced and then sent to a crystallizer. The sugar concentration in the solution is measured with the refractive index.[17] The table below reports careful laboratory measurements of per cent sucrose versus refractive index. Plot the data and fit an appropriate model. Add your model curve to the plot. Assess model adequacy and check whether the residuals appear to be normally distributed.

---

[17] Refractive index. https://en.wikipedia.org/wiki/Refractive_index. (Last edited date June 15, 2022.)

Per cent Sucrose	Refractive Index	Per cent Sucrose	Refractive Index	Per cent Sucrose	Refractive Index
0	1.3330	30	1.3811	60	1.4418
5	1.3403	35	1.3902	65	1.4532
10	1.3479	40	1.3997	70	1.4651
15	1.3557	45	1.4096	75	1.4774
20	1.3639	50	1.4200	80	1.4901
25	1.3723	55	1.4307	85	1.5033

10.13 The data in the table below show the depression in the freezing point of water (H_2O) that occurs with the addition of hydrochloric acid (HCl) to different concentrations.

(a) Create a plot of the data as shown in the table. Then create a plot of freezing point depression versus $\log_{10}$(HCl concentration).

(b) Fit an appropriate model based on the second plot of part (a). Assess the adequacy of the model.

HCl Concentration (mol/kgH$_2$O)	Freezing Pt Depression (°C)
0.001	3.690
0.005	3.635
0.01	3.601
0.02	3.568
0.05	3.532
0.1	3.523
0.2	3.540
0.5	3.680
1	3.950
2	4.430

10.14 Table 5.7 shows the wind capacity in GW for the ten countries that are the largest producers of wind power. Collect data on the population of each country and compute the wind power generation per capita. Study the results, apply any calculations you see as appropriate, and comment on your observations.

10.15 Global temperature data can be obtained from https://www.ncdc. noaa.gov/cag/global/time-series for the years 1880–2021. These data are reported as a *temperature anomaly*, the difference to the Jan 1951–Dec 1980 average temperature.

(a) Download these data in a text file. Using either a text editor, for example, Notepad, WordPad, or Excel, create a text file with only the data, no headings. Write a Python script that loads the text file and creates a plot of the data, just lines connecting the data points and no markers. Comment on your observations of the plot.

(b) Fit a straight-line model to the data. Report the R^2 and s_e values. Assess the model's adequacy by plotting the residuals versus year.
(c) Fit an appropriate higher-order polynomial model to the data and carry out the same steps as in part (b). You may need to evaluate several polynomial models.
(d) Use your chosen model to predict the temperature anomaly in 2030, 2040, and 2050.

References

Burglund, B. and Street, R., 2011. *Golf Ball Flight Dynamics*. Flathead Valley Community College. Available online: http://www.math.union.edu/~wangj/courses/previous/math238w13/Golf%20Ball%20Flight%20Dynamics2.pdf.

Chapra, S.C. and Canale, R.P., 2019. *Numerical Methods for Engineers with Software Applications and Programming*, 8th ed., WCB/McGraw-Hill, New York, NY.

Chapra, S.C. and Clough, D.E., 2022. *Applied Numerical Methods with Python for Engineers and Scientists*. WCB/McGraw-Hill, New York, NY.

Deitel, P. and Deitel, H., 2020. *Intro to Python for Computer Science and Data Science*. Pearson, New York, NY.

Gaddis, T., 2018. *Starting Out with Python*, 4th ed., Pearson, New York, NY.

Hill, C., 2015. *Learning Scientific Programming with Python*. Cambridge University Press, Cambridge, UK.

Hornbeck, R. W., 1975. *Numerical Methods*. Quantum, New York, NY.

Mason, R. L., Gunst, R. F., and Hess, J. L., 1989. *Statistical Design and Analysis of Experiments with Applications to Engineering and Science*. Wiley, New York, NY, p. 37.

Montgomery, D.C. and Runger, G.C., 2018. *Applied Statistics and Probability for Engineers*, 7th ed., Wiley, New York, NY.

Moré, J.J., Garbow, B. S., and Hillstrom, K. E., 1980. User Guide for MINPACK-1, Argonne National Laboratory Report ANL-80-74, Argonne, Ill.

Index

Note: Page numbers followed by "n" denote footnotes.

Index of Python Terminology

Printed in the United States
by Baker & Taylor Publisher Services